Beiträge zum
ausländischen öffentlichen Recht und Völkerrecht

Edited by

the Max Planck Society
for the Advancement of Science
represented by Prof. Dr. Armin von Bogdandy
and Prof. Dr. Anne Peters

Volume 317

Angelo Jr. Golia | Matthias C. Kettemann
Raffaela Kunz [Eds.]

Digital Transformations in Public International Law

Nomos

Open Access funding provided by Max Planck Society.

The Deutsche Nationalbibliothek lists this publication in the Deutsche Nationalbibliografie; detailed bibliographic data are available on the Internet at http://dnb.d-nb.de

ISBN 978-3-7560-0275-7 (Print)
978-3-7489-3163-8 (ePDF)

British Library Cataloguing-in-Publication Data
A catalogue record for this book is available from the British Library.

ISBN 978-3-7560-0275-7 (Print)
978-3-7489-3163-8 (ePDF)

Library of Congress Cataloging-in-Publication Data
Angelo Jr. Golia | Matthias C. Kettemann | Raffaela Kunz
Digital Transformations in Public International Law
Golia, Angelo Jr. | Kettemann, Matthias C. | Kunz, Raffaela (Eds.)
286 pp.
Includes bibliographic references.

ISBN 978-3-7560-0275-7 (Print)
978-3-7489-3163-8 (ePDF)

1st Edition 2022

Published by
Nomos Verlagsgesellschaft mbH & Co. KG
Waldseestraße 3–5 | 76530 Baden-Baden
www.nomos.de

Production of the printed version:
Nomos Verlagsgesellschaft mbH & Co. KG
Waldseestraße 3–5 | 76530 Baden-Baden

ISBN 978-3-7560-0275-7 (Print)
ISBN 978-3-7489-3163-8 (ePDF)
DOI https://doi.org/10.5771/9783748931638

Onlineversion
Nomos eLibrary

Acknowledgements

Developments in information and communication technologies have had a substantial impact on both individuals and society as a whole. Digitalization has transformed the way we act, and interact, alone and in societal contexts. New challenges to individual rights and societal cohesion have emerged; and new technologies to overcome them. The law, as a tool to ensure rights, distribute obligations, and provide for stable societies, has had to change in line with technology. This applies to national law, but even more so to international law. How digital developments have transformed public international law is the key topic of this book.

The project that has led to the publication of this volume – and the parallel special issue 3/2021 dedicated to 'International Law and the Internet' in the ZaöRV/Heidelberg Journal of International Law – has been conceived, developed, and implemented during a global pandemic that has brought great disruption into routines, research plans, and, most importantly, lives. We owe numerous debts of gratitude to those who have helped us sail through this challenging time and bring this ship into its port. Anna Sophia Tiedeke has provided early support. Elisabeth Alexander, Sarah Gebel, Carolin Eschenfelder, Thomas Lenfers, Leon Seidl, Marieke Simons, and Grace Ubaruta have provided valuable editing support over the months. Andrea Hug, Verena Schaller-Soltau, and Angelika Schmidt provided technical and editorial assistance.

The Max Planck Institute for Comparative Public Law and International Law (MPIL) in Heidelberg and particularly its directors, Prof. Dr. Anne Peters and Prof. Dr. Armin von Bogdandy, supported the realization of the project from its early stages until the publication of this volume.

Most importantly, we are indebted to all the people around us – too many to name them all – who have shared us, more or less willingly, with this project.

Angelo Jr Golia, Matthias C. Kettemann, Raffaela Kunz

Heidelberg and Hamburg, Germany

February 2022

Table of Contents

Part III Rights

Part IV Participation

Introduction

Digital Transformations in Public International Law: An Introduction

Angelo Jr Golia, Matthias C. Kettemann, and Raffaela Kunz[*]

In the digital age and in the midst of a global pandemic, in which digital technologies have played a greater role than ever in all aspects of human interaction, editing a volume about the regulatory challenges the internet poses to public international law is almost a non-starter. Of course, there already exists an extremely rich body of scholarship in all sub-fields of the legal discipline and writing about the interface between international law and the internet is by no means a novel endeavour.

What prompted us to, nonetheless, start this project was that even more than ten years after the popularization of the term 'Internetvölkerrecht' ('international internet law' or 'international law of the internet'),[1] the myth of the internet as an unregulated space persists. In this sense, although the field is abundantly researched and much discussed, many fundamental questions remain open – and much disputed – from both an analytical and normative perspective. In this context, our aim was not (only) to analyse the application of public international law to the new regulatory fields that have emerged with the internet. Rather, our purpose is to bring out, explore, and critically assess the *impact* of the internet and digital technologies – that is, what we understand as the *digital transformations* – on the structures of public international law itself.

Indeed, processes of digital transformation have had a profound impact on the actors and instruments of international relations. The mode and the tools of stabiliszing the international normative order have changed significantly. Private actors have emerged and created important communication spaces with flanking normative orders in which processes of social self-determination take place.[2] The role and power relations of states have also changed in the digital constellation. From the initially unipolar post-

---

* The indicated order of authors is alphabetic.

1 See Antonio Segura-Serrano, 'Internet Regulation and the Role of International Law,' Max Planck UNYB 10 (2006), 191–272 (192).

2 On the concept of normative order (of the internet), see Matthias C. Kettemann, *The Normative Order of the Internet. A Theory of Online Rule and Regulation* (Oxford:

Cold War world order, centred around the US hegemony, a system of global multi-polar power relations has emerged. Technological change is leading to structural reconfiguration in international political processes, which are particularly evident in global internet governance. From the cybersecurity challenges of the Internet of (Connected) Things to the algorithmic governance of opinion power for private profit maximization to the use of digital spying tools against journalists and civil rights activists, the protection of fundamental and human rights as a central benchmark of international politics, both internally and externally, is coming under pressure.

Democratic participation in these communication spaces requires access. The UN aimed to provide universal and affordable access to the internet in the least developed countries by 2020.[3] The German Government also committed itself to nationwide broadband expansion in the last coalition agreement.[4] Both goals were clearly missed. The pressure to act arising from human rights obligations continues unabated. In the light of increasing centrality – especially in times of COVID-19 – of online com-

---

Oxford University Press, 2020); and Matthias C. Kettemann (ed.), *Navigating Normative Orders. Interdisciplinary Perspectives* (Frankfurt/New York: Campus, 2020).

3 See UNGA Res 70/01 of 25 September 2015, Transforming our world: the 2030 Agenda for Sustainable Development, A/RES/70/1, Goal 9.c. Already in 2015, one of us (Kettemann) wrote a study on the international law of the web (Matthias C. Kettemann, *Völkerrecht in Zeiten des Netzes: Perspektiven auf den effektiven Schutz von Grund- und Menschenrechten in der Informationsgesellschaft zwischen Völkerrecht, Europarecht und Staatsrecht* (Bonn: Friedrich-Ebert-Stiftung, 2015)). Among other things, that study found that states have agreed that building a people-centered, development-oriented information society can only work if the goals and principles of the United Nations Charter and respect for international law and human rights are taken into account. Even then, the study found that an international law of the internet already existed (in the sense that international law is to be applied to the internet and significant obligations can already be found in existing international law that states have to observe when shaping their digital policy).

4 The fact that the new 2021–2025 coalition agreement once again contains the phrase 'We strive for an international law of the Internet' ('Coalition agreement 2021–2025 between SPD, Bündnis 90/Die Grünen and FPD,' available at: https://www.spd.de/fileadmin/Dokumente/Koalitionsvertrag/Koalitionsvertrag_2021-2025.pdf, 144) without specifying what is meant by this and how it is to be achieved is surprising, especially since the global process of negotiating cyber norms, which is also being pursued significantly by Germany, is well advanced – as shown by the contributions to this book. See also Matthias C. Kettemann and Alexandra Paulus, 'An Update for the Internet. Reforming Global Digital Cooperation in 2021,' Global Governance Spotlight 4/2020, available at: https://www.sef-bonn.org/publikationen/global-governance-spotlight/42020.

munication for processes of social self-determination, the description of the European Court of Human Rights (ECtHR) has to be agreed with: 'the Internet has now become one of the principal means by which individuals exercise their right to freedom to receive and impart information and ideas, providing as it does essential tools for participation in activities and discussions concerning political issues and issues of general interest.'[5]

A further example of the many ways in which digital technologies affect the structures of public international law concerns the standards of evidence. Do tweets count as state conduct for the purpose of attribution under State responsibility?[6] In 2020 a WTO panel gave a positive answer for 'the tweets [that] are in fact governmental tweets.'[7] Similarly, in a request for the indication of provisional measures, the International Court of Justice (ICJ) has recently been presented with tweets ultimately tied to the Government of Armenia to probe an alleged disinformation campaign to spread ethnic hatred.[8] While it did not address the evidentiary value of the tweets as such, in its subsequent order, the ICJ granted the sought measures, noting that acts prohibited under Article 4 of the International Convention on the Elimination of All Forms of Racial Discrimination (CERD) – such as propaganda promoting racial hatred and incitement to racial discrimination – can generate a pervasive racially charged environment within society, 'particularly (...) when rhetoric espousing racial discrimination is employed by high-ranking officials of the State.'[9]

But such transformations do not only concern disputes before international courts. In 2021, Germany and Italy were only the latest European countries issuing position papers on the application of international law

---

5 ECtHR, *Cengiz and Others v. Turkey*, judgment of 1 December 2015, nos. 48226/10 and 14027/11, para. 49.

6 For this issue, see Annalisa Ciampi, 'The Role of the Internet in International Law-Making, Implementation and Global Governance,' HJIL 81 (2021), 677–700 (690–694); as well as, in the specific field of international criminal law, the chapter by Rossella Pulvirenti in this volume.

7 WTO Panel, *Saudi Arabia – Measures Concerning the Protection of Intellectual Property Rights*, report of 16 June 2020, WT/DS567/R, para. 7.161.

8 *Interpretation and Application of the International Convention on the Elimination of All Forms of Racial Discrimination (Republic of Azerbaijan v. Republic of Armenia)*, Request for the Indication of Provisional Measures of Protection, 23 September 2021, paras 19–22, available at: https://www.icj-cij.org/public/files/case-related/181/181-20210923-REQ-01-00-EN.pdf.

9 ICJ, *Application of the International Convention on the Elimination of All Forms of Racial Discrimination (Republic of Azerbaijan v. Republic of Armenia)*, Provisional measures, Order of 7 December 2021, para. 83, available at: https://www.icj-cij.org/public/files/case-related/180/180-20211207-ORD-01-00-EN.pdf.

in cyberspace,[10] following the example of other states. The coming decade will most likely see further attempts by states to develop their own 'internets,' controlled to different degrees by national governments. It would mean that the states will prioritisze protecting their interest and their citizens to prevent real or supposed dangers emanating from the use of the internet through censorship, mass surveillance, geo-blocking, etc. One of the results is that the potential of the internet as a truly global and borderless space is being put into question. Chien-Huei Wu has recently used the phrase 'sovereignty fever' to describe this territorial turn in the global cyber order.[11]

What does this mean for the global internet, and can (or should) international law be used to stop its fragmentation? Another related question concerns how such ongoing and accelerating politicisization/territorialisization of the internet contributes to transforming (the self-perception of) the main subjects of international law: not anymore – or not only – the self-contained units of the Westphalian/Vattelian order – based on stark internal/external divides – but rather macro-geopolitical units which increasingly act 'imperially,' that is, in terms of center/periphery.

Further, it remains very much an open question how the public interest and the common good on the internet can be protected and defended in times of 'platform capitalism' and mass surveillance. Indeed, private actors seem to hold as much power as never before, pushing the public-private distinction to its boundaries. It is a well-known fact that today it is big tech companies such as Facebook, Twitter, and YouTube who control the respect of freedom of expression and the prohibition of hate crimes on their channels. The result is a de-facto delegation of the protection of human rights to these private bodies with little public oversight, participation, and accountability.

These few examples show how, even after many years into debates about the relationship between international law and the internet, it is still necessary to measure the commitments made by states in 2003 in

10 See the position paper of the German Government 'On the Application of International Law in Cyberspace,' 5 March 2021, available at: https://www.auswaertiges-amt.de/blob/2446304/32e7b2498e10b74fb17204c54665bdf0/on-the-application-of-international-law-in-cyberspace-data.pdf; and the position paper of the Italian Government 'International Law and Cyberspace,' 4 November 2021, available at: https://www.esteri.it/MAE/resource/doc/2021/11/italian_position_paper_on_international_law_and_cyberspace.pdf.

11 Chien-Huei Wu, 'Sovereignty Fever: The Territorial Turn of Global Cyber Order,' HJIL 81 (2021), 651–676.

the framework of the World Summit on the Information Society, to achieve 'people-centered, inclusive and development-oriented Information Society [...] premised on the purposes and principles of the Charter of the United Nations and respecting fully and upholding the Universal Declaration of Human Rights.'[12]

Indeed, one of the main questions is how the internet changes the ways in which human rights are mobiliszed and/or implemented globally. In this context, ensuring human rights is a key aspect of legitimiszing normative orders. At least since 2006, the protection of human rights on the internet has been closely studied,[13] with freedom of expression identified as the key 'enabling' right.[14] The importance of ensuring human rights on the internet globally has been recognized on the UN level, where states confirmed their obligation to respect rights offline just as online.[15] This is an important precedent for procedures to establish internet-related duties of states based on existing international law. Indeed, the international monitoring of human rights violations online, through filtering and blocking, gave rise to early analyses of the international legal duties of states regarding the internet.[16] Questions of internet access and the bridging of

---

12 World Summit on the Information Society, 'Declaration of Principles. Building the Information Society: a global challenge in the new Millennium,' WSIS-03/GENEVA/DOC/4-E, 12 December 2003, Principle A.1. See also Nula Frei, 'Equality as a Principle of the Networked World? An Exploratory Search for 'Cyber-Equality' in the Field of Internet Governance,' HJIL 81 (2021), 627–650 (640–643).

13 Rikke F. Jørgensen (ed.), *Human Rights in the Global Information Society* (Cambridge: MIT Press 2006).

14 Dragos Cuceranu, *Aspects of Regulating Freedom of Expression on the Internet* (Antwerp: Intersentia 2012); Wolfgang Benedek and Matthias C. Kettemann, *Freedom of Expression on the Internet* (Strasbourg: Council of Europe 2014). See also, Molly Land, 'Toward an International Law of the Internet,' HILJ 54 (2013), 393–458.

15 See the Human Rights Council Resolution 'The promotion, protection and enjoyment of human rights on the Internet,' UN Doc. A/HRC/RES/20/8 of 5 July 2012; and, more recently, the Human Rights Council Resolution 'The promotion, protection and enjoyment of human rights on the Internet,' A/HRC/RES/32/13 of 18 July 2016. For an introduction, see Rebecca MacKinnon, *Consent of the Networked: The Worldwide Struggle for Internet Freedom* (New York: Basic Books 2012) and Rikke F. Jørgensen, *Framing the Net. The Internet and Human Rights* (Cheltenham: Edward Elgar Publishing 2013).

16 Ronald Deibert, John Palfrey, Rafal Rohozinski and Jonathan Zittrain (eds), *Access Denied: The Practice and Policy of Global Internet Filtering* (Cambridge: MIT Press 2008); Ronald Deibert, John Palfrey, Rafal Rohozinski and Jonathan Zittrain (eds), *Access Controlled: The Shaping of Power, Rights, and Rule in Cyberspace* (Cambridge: MIT Press 2010); Ronald Deibert, John Palfrey, Rafal Rohozinski

the digital divide have also led to research on the international duties of states regarding infrastructure development.[17]

Against this backdrop, in spring 2020, we started a collective project at the Max Planck Institute for Comparative Public Law and International Law in Heidelberg and subsequently issued a call for papers in which we identified three macro-questions that in our opinion still warrant further research:

1) What influence does 'the internet' (information and communication technologies and the socio-legal changes they have brought) have on international law and international legal scholarship?
2) Conversely: What impact does international law – treaties, custom, principles, procedures, actors, legitimacy conceptions – have on the development (the fragmentation or integrity) of the internet? How does the geographical and geopolitical dimension of international law affect the unity and/or fragmentation of international internet law?
3) Finally: How does the interface between international law and the internet affect the relationships and the power balance between the Global South and Global North, in terms of positive law, participation in processes of norm development, hegemonic structures in scholarship, and participation in the epistemic communities of international internet law?

The response to the call was extremely generous, both in quantitative and qualitative terms, and we decided to organize the submissions addressing different aspects of these questions in two distinct publications. This book is the second scientific output of our project, after a special issue of the *Zeitschrift für ausländisches öffentliches Recht und Völkerrecht* (the Heidelberg Journal of International Law) published in Autumn 2021.[18] Importantly, we thought and shaped these two publications as complementing parts of a single, coherent research project which should be read accordingly, that

---

and Jonathan Zittrain (eds), *Access Contested: Security, Identity, and Resistance in Asian Cyberspace* (Cambridge: MIT Press 2011).

17 Nivien Saleh, *Third World Citizens and the Information Technology Revolution* (London: Palgrave Macmillan 2010); Gaëlle Krikorian and Amy Kapczynski (eds), *Access to Knowledge in the Age of Intellectual Property* (Cambridge: MIT Press 2010).

18 Angelo Jr Golia, Matthias C. Kettemann, and Raffaela Kunz (eds), 'Special Issue: International Law and the Internet,' HJIL 81 (2021), 597–866, available at: https://www.nomos-elibrary.de/10.17104/0044-2348-2021-3/zeitschrift-fuer-auslaendische s-oeffentliches-recht-und-voelkerrecht-heidelberg-journal-of-international-law-vol ume-81-2021-issue-3.

is, in dialogue with each other. This book, in particular, focuses on aspects that can be grouped under the four guiding ideas of sovereignty, security, rights, and participation.

Part I explores the impact of digital technologies on (the conceptualization of) sovereignty as one of the *topoi* of international legal thinking.[19] To be sure, even this topic can be addressed through many different lenses, for example (the preservation of) the open cyberspace as a global public good[20] or broader geopolitical analyses.[21] Here, *Pia Hüsch* discusses the application of state sovereignty in cyberspace and analyzes the usefulness – and limits – of analogies in this area. At a time when reflections on the real-world impacts of legal metaphors and fictions are becoming increasingly relevant,[22] she comes to the conclusion that analogies and metaphors often lead to more confusion rather than clarification and recommends that, at times, a straightforward analysis of sovereignty in cyberspace is preferable.

Yet another perspective focuses on the traditional link between sovereign entities and constitutions. How and to what extent does the digitalization of social relations contribute to putting further into question the genetic link between states and constitutionalization? What lessons can global constitutionalism scholarship give to the *digital* constitutionalism field? While other approaches focus on phenomena of self-organization and self-regulation in the digital sphere,[23] in the second chapter of this book *Edoardo Celeste* notes that international law theory already projected the notion of constitution beyond the state dimension, helping explain how the emergence of globalized problems in the digital ecosystem necessarily engenders the materialization of a plurality of constitutional responses. The sense of this Gordian knot – he argues – can be deciphered only if these emerging constitutional fragments are interpreted as complementary tesserae of a single mosaic.

---

19 See, in most recent literature, Neil Walker, 'The Sovereignty Surplus,' ICON 18 (2020), 370–428; and Fleur Johns, 'The Sovereignty Deficit: Afterword to the Foreword by Neil Walker,' ICON 19 (2021), 6–12.

20 Cf. Rolf H. Weber, 'Integrity in the 'Infinite Space'– New Frontiers for International Law,' HJIL 81 (2021), 601–626.

21 Cf. Wu (n. 11).

22 Cf. Alessandro Morelli and Oreste Pollicino, 'Metaphors, Judicial Frames and Fundamental Rights in Cyberspace,' AJCL 68 (2020), 616–646.

23 Căcilia Hermes, 'Cyberspace as an Example of Self-Organisation from a Network Perspective,' HJIL 81 (2021), 817–839. See also Michael A. Cusumano, Annabelle Gawer, David B. Yoffie, 'Can Self-Regulation Save Digital Platforms?,' Industrial & Corporate Change, Special Issue 'Regulating Platforms and Ecosystems' (2021).

Part II turns to security issues. Indeed, as use of force, sanctions, non-interference in domestic affairs lie at the very core of traditional public international law – as inter-*state* law – the internet and digital technologies have also radically changed the way international law deals – has to deal – with security, at both regional and global levels. Although the legal treatment of cybersecurity goes well beyond the traditional issues of collective security,[24] how international law conceptualizes and regulates sanctions in the digital sphere remains an open question, especially when it comes to regional regimes. In the third chapter, *Uchenna Jerome Orji* offers an original analysis of the 2005 African Union Non-Aggression and Common Defense Pact,[25] exploring the potential of this instrument to govern the behavior of Member States with respect to activities that can constitute aggression in cyberspace. In particular, he makes a case for the application of the Pact's principles to promote responsible State behavior in cyberspace, based especially on the need for legal certainty.

Moving to a more global perspective, in the fourth chapter *Alena Douhan* starts from the analysis of UN Security Council resolutions 2419(2018), 2462(2019), and 2490(2019) in order to develop her reflections on the legal qualification of cyber attacks and the application of cyber measures. In particular, she provides an overview of different scenarios where the application of sanctions is affected by the emergence of cyber technologies. She also focuses on the changes in and legal qualifications for the grounds, subjects, targets, means, and methods of introduction and implementation of sanctions regimes in the digital age.

Part III explores the implications of the internet for the protection of rights at the international level. Especially in the early years of the internet, there was great enthusiasm about the potential of the internet, which provided unseen global spaces for communication and exchange for the protection and improvement of human rights. However, the darker sides also accompanying this development soon came to light.[26] While the so-called Arab Spring was seen by many as witnessing the liberating potential of the internet, at the latest, the atrocities and possibly genocidal acts committed against the Rohingya in Myanmar showed that the development could

24 Cf. Antonio Segura-Serrano, 'Cybersecurity and Cybercrime: Dynamic Application versus Norm-Development,' HJIL 81 (2021), 701–731.

25 AU Non-Aggression and Common Defense Pact (Addis Ababa, 2005), opened for signature 31 January 2005 (entered into force 18 December 2009).

26 In most recent literature, see only Tiberiu Dragu and Yonatan Lupu, 'Digital Authoritarianism and the Future of Human Rights,' International Organization 75 (2021), 991–1017.

very well also go in the opposite direction. More recently, the dispute between Armenia and Azerbaijan before the ICJ recalled above[27] shows how digital technologies might offer governments new and more sophisticated possibilities for disseminating hatred and possibly pave the way to genocidal acts.

In the fifth chapter, *Stefanie Schmahl* examines from the general perspective the opportunities and challenges that digitaliszation offers to human rights law. In an impressive *tour de force*, she provides an overview of the main issues in this context, ranging from the question of whether there is a right to access the internet to new challenges arising for the protection against discrimination through the use of algorithms and discussions about cyborgs and robots as new rights holders or duty bearers. Her contribution, in particular, assesses to what extent the digital environment *critically* challenges the functioning of the international human rights regime.

In the sixth chapter, *Rossella Pulvirenti* examines these questions from the specific perspective of international criminal law. She argues that while the internet has changed international armed conflicts and thus brought new challenges, at the same time, it has become an invaluable tool in the fight against crimes committed. She concludes that, overall, the internet and digital tools have had a positive influence on International Criminal Law and the gathering of evidence before International Criminal Courts and Tribunals, as it gives individuals the power to gain control over the information and evidence that are then forwarded to the international criminal courts and tribunals; and strengthens the outreach programmes enhancing the quality and the quantity of data released via the internet by the tribunals to local communities.

In the seventh chapter, *Adam Krzywoń* addresses what has long become a classic in the field of 'international internet law,' that is, the (limits to the) freedom of expression online and the related obligations of states, an issue that unavoidably touches upon the role of private (business) actors.[28] At a time of ever-growing attempts to regulate (and exploit) the systemic position reached by private actors in the field of online content moderati-

27 ICJ, *Azerbaijan v. Armenia* (n. 9).

28 On the international law framework concerning online business actors, see Christine Kaufmann, 'Responsible Business in a Digital World – What's International Law Got to Do With It?,' HJIL 81 (2021), 781–815; as well as Hans-W. Micklitz and Aurelie Anne Villanueva, 'Responsibilities of Companies in the Algorithmic Society' in: Hans-W. Micklitz et al. (eds), *Constitutional Challenges in the Algorithmic Society* (Cambridge: Cambridge University Press 2022), 263–280.

on – especially at the European level –[29] his analysis focuses on states' obligations under the specific framework of the ECHR. In particular, he argues that a strict distinction between negative and positive obligations is anachronistic and that the negative understanding of the freedom of expression and protection of privacy does not provide the conceptual apparatus to deal with many current problems.

Finally, part IV sheds further light on questions of participation via digital tools. This is a central issue that goes well beyond debates on the right to access the internet and the dynamics of individual inclusion/exclusion triggered by the digital revolution; or the principle of equality within the digital sphere.[30] Again, the internet, in unprecedented ways, provides global spaces for communication, mobilization, conflict, and deliberation. The digital sphere radically changes the codes and dynamics, sustaining the generation of (political) consensus. Put differently, the digital revolution requires broader legal reflections – involving *also* public international law – on the conditions through which consensus to the purposes of collective decision-making in modern interconnected societies may be generated, especially when it comes to issues (e.g., climate) with an intrinsic global reach. There is, of course, the vast literature on the impact of digital technologies and algorithms on political processes and participation, with several and sometimes contrasting views on whether such new technologies contribute to positive or negative developments.[31] However, the present volume aims to contribute to the debate with a perspective that at least in part transcends well-established analyses on (de-)democratization processes at the national level. Indeed, we have decided to conclude the volume with two contributions that, in different ways, offer a more global perspective, linking issues related to participation/democratization, digital technologies, and climate.

In particular, the chapter by *Katharina Luckner* offers an analysis of how in certain cases, the internet may sustain bottom-up processes and

---

29 See the Proposal for a Regulation of the European Parliament and of the Council on a Single Market for Digital Services (Digital Services Act) and amending Directive 2000/31/EC, COM/2020/825 final, available at: https://eur-lex.europa.eu/legal-content/en/TXT/?uri=COM%3A2020%3A825%3AFIN.

30 See again Frei (n. 12).

31 For different perspectives, see among many Oren Perez, 'Electronic Democracy as a Multi-Dimensional Praxis,' North Carolina J. Law & Technology 4 (2003), 275–306; Dragu and Lupu (n. 26); Ngozi Okidegbe, 'The Democratizing Potential of Algorithms?,' Conn. L. Rev. 53 (2021), available at: https://papers.ssrn.com/sol3/papers.cfm?abstract_id=3835370.

their relevance to public international law. She starts from the observation that through the internet, most inhabited places in the world are a mere click away, which greatly facilitates the constitution of social movements with relevance way beyond their local context. She then uses the 'Fridays for Future' movement as a case study and, drawing from legal, political science, and media studies, shows how social media enables the impact of civil society movements on the development of international law.

Relatedly, in the same context of democratization and social mobilization, a field that has gained a particularly central standing is the so-called strategic human rights litigation. This has proved increasingly relevant to international legal scholarship, especially when it comes to climate legal activism. In the last chapter of this volume, *Vera Strobel* takes a closer look at a relatively underexplored issue, that is, the interplay between strategic litigation and the internet. She argues that the internet has played a multidimensional role in strategic litigation activities and their influences on society, international legal scholarship, and the development and interpretation of public international law itself.

This is not the end of the debate on how to apply international law to the internet and how the internet impacts international law. But perhaps it is the end of the beginning, as we progress to a more nuanced and mature picture of the challenges to the norms and normative actors, institutions, and institutional practices of international law in the digital age. The rules might be digitalized now, and their enforcement partially problematic, but the underlying questions remain similar: from the first four paragraphs of the Code Hammurabi onwards, the rules on how rules are developed and what may be said play a central role in the earliest codifications of the law; and in modern times, citizens' participation in these rules can be seen as a central demand and great achievement of many democratic revolutions. But what about our participation in communication-related decisions on digital platforms today, where significant parts of our public discourse have shifted? Well-established democratic principles do not easily translate to allow users' participation in shaping private selection algorithms and moderation practices. The platforms themselves have become rule-makers, rule-enforcers, and judges of their own decisions. The separation of powers looks different. Communication power or democratic power control (i.e., neither checks nor balances) leads to tensions in the inner fabric of public discourse. International law can alleviate some of this tension, as the contributions to this book show.

They have also shown that online, just as offline, (international) law applies. *Ubi societas, ibi ius* was true in ancient Greece, China, Africa, and South America. It is true today 'online.' Or as Malcolm N. Shaw put it in the first lines of his introduction into international law: 'in the long march of mankind from the cave to the computer a central role has always been played by the idea of law – the idea that order is necessary and chaos inimical to a just and stable existence.'[32] What we are seeing, and struggling with, therefore, is not the fact that international law applies to the internet and is changed by it, but rather the speed of change.

It took 200 years, Niklas Luhmann recalled, until the disruptive potential of the printing press started to influence all segments of society, eventually leading to a fundamental change in the structure of Western European societies.[33] With the internet having started some fifty years ago (and commercialized social media landscapes emerged in essence only twenty years ago), we will have to wait and see whether the internet has a disruptive potential similar to that of the printing press. We believe it will, and the contributions to this book set the tone and can help steer the debate on the relationship of this development with international law.

---

32 Malcolm N. Shaw, *International Law* (8th edn, Oxford: Oxford University Press 2017), 1.

33 Niklas Luhmann, *Die Wissenschaft der Gesellschaft* (Frankfurt am Main: Suhrkamp 1990), 600; See also Mireille Hildebrandt, *Smart Technologies and the End(s) of Law* (Cheltenham: Edward Elgar 2015) 159 ff. (distinct characteristics of modern law were triggered by the printing press).

Part I
Sovereignty

Error 404: No Sovereignty Analogy Found

Pia Hüsch

Abstract: The debate on the application of state sovereignty in cyberspace is complex and includes a range of issues, such as the governance of cyberspace, exercising jurisdiction in cyberspace, or the question of whether low-intensity cyber operations violate state sovereignty. Next to legal and political questions, technological details further complicate the analysis. Due to this complexity, authors often rely on the use of analogies to conceptualise their arguments. This chapter addresses the use of such analogies by examining two analogies made by legal scholars in the field, one referring to the law of the sea and the other to quantum physics. It argues that the two analogies are exemplary of a wider problem: either the referenced analogy remains superficial without contributing comparative insights to the debate, or the analogy is taken so far that it further complicates the assessment of the original subject matter. Given the difficulties of 'getting the analogy right,' this chapter concludes that the contribution of analogies in the sovereignty in cyberspace debate should not be over-estimated and that in light of the two examples studied, no adequate analogy clarifying the sovereignty in cyberspace debate could be found.

I. Introduction

Following the invention of the internet, more recent trends such as digitalisation, surveillance capitalism, and an increase in malicious cyber operations have all challenged the application of existing public international law to cyberspace. These challenges have not gone unnoticed, and international legal scholarship has covered a range of questions as to how existing rules and principles could be applied to cyberspace and, more generally, how the predominantly territorial understanding of existing international law finds application in cyberspace. To an unprecedented extent, cyberspace even challenges the understanding of what arguably constitutes 'a founding principle of the international legal order':[1] state sovereignty.[2]

The debate on the application of sovereignty in cyberspace is broad and complex and involves many aspects, such as the governance of cyberspace,

1 Samantha Besson, 'Sovereignty' in: Rüdiger Wolfrum (ed.), *MPEPIL* (online edn, Oxford: Oxford University Press 2011), para. 5.

2 Patrick Franceze, 'Sovereignty in Cyberspace: Can It Exist?,' A. F. L. Rev. 64 (2009), 1–42; Pallavi Khanna, 'State Sovereignty and Self-Defence in Cyberspace,' BRICS Law Journal 5 (2018), 139–154; Michael Schmitt and Liis Vihul, 'Respect for Sovereignty in Cyberspace,' Tex L. Rev. 95 (2017), 1639–1676.

exercising jurisdiction in cyberspace, or the question of whether low-intensity cyber operations violate state sovereignty. Next to legal questions, which are closely related to political considerations, quickly developing and complex technological details further complicate the analysis. For these reasons, it is at times difficult to keep up with the sovereignty in cyberspace debate and to analyse the application of sovereignty to cyberspace in terms that are easily understandable to readers. Regularly, authors thus rely on the use of analogies to illustrate their arguments, raising the question of whether the use of analogies actually contributes to the scholarly debate on the application of sovereignty in cyberspace.

The following chapter addresses this question and therefore takes a closer look at what constitutes sovereignty in cyberspace debate. Even though the understanding of state sovereignty continues to vary amongst the discussants, the debate has seen recent trends in the last few years that will be set out in the second part of this chapter. In a third section, this chapter will elaborate on how complex and broad the discussion is and identify a range of key issues in the debate. Such complexity has led many scholars in the cyberspace debate to rely on analogies and metaphors to conceptualise the characteristics of cyberspace. In a fourth section, this chapter will introduce two of such analogies. Firstly, Roguski's 'Layered Approach,' an analogy to the maritime zones in the law of the sea, will be analysed.[3] Secondly, this chapter will consider Cornish's analogy with quantum physics in which he looks at how multiple interpretations of state sovereignty can co-exist.[4] The analogies chosen are considered suitable examples as they illustrate what is often the problem with choosing these analogies: they either remain superficial and do not genuinely provide comparative insights or add more complexity by providing a very detailed analogy without adding clarity to the original subject matter. Given the difficulties of 'getting the analogy right,' this chapter concludes by arguing that the value of analogies in the cyber debate should not be over-estimated. What the sovereignty in cyberspace debates needs instead is clarity, straightforwardness, and precision as opposed to hiding arguments behind unclear metaphors and insufficiently explored analogies.

---

3 Przemyslaw Roguski, 'Layered Sovereignty: Adjusting Traditional Notions of Sovereignty to a Digital Environment,' 11th International Conference on Cyber Conflict, NATO CCD COE Publications (2019), https://ccdcoe.org.

4 Paul Cornish, 'Governing Cyberspace through Constructive Ambiguity,' Survival – Global Politics and Strategy 57 (2015), 153–176.

II. The Application of Sovereignty in Cyberspace

State sovereignty is a concept that is highly relevant to the cyberspace debate as it potentially plays a crucial role in the regulation of many aspects of cyberspace, such as the governance of cyberspace, matters of jurisdiction, or the regulation of low-intensity, inter-governmental cyber operations. Given the widely held consensus that international law applies to cyberspace[5] and the absence of a comprehensive international cyber treaty – and the unlikeliness that there will be one for the foreseeable future[6] – the application of existing public international legal norms has received widespread attention in legal scholarship.[7]

However, it remains far from clear how sovereignty applies in cyberspace exactly. One example of uncertainties with respect to the application of sovereignty in cyberspace is the question of whether disruptive cyber operations[8] falling below the use of force and non-intervention thresholds

---

5 Group of Governmental Experts on Developments in the Field of Information and Telecommunications in the Context of International Security (hereafter: UN GGE), 24 June 2013, UN Doc A/68/98, para. 19. This was reconfirmed in 2015, UN GGE, 22 July 2015, A/70/174, para. 28(b).

6 On the topic of a cyber treaty generally and its feasibility in particular see Stephen Moore, 'Cyber Attacks and the Beginning of an International Cyber Treaty,' N.C.J. Int'l L. & Com. Reg. 39 (2013), 223–257, (250 ff.), in reference to Russia and the US he argues that 'it is becoming increasingly less likely that the two states would have interest in negotiating a cyber treaty. […] Any viable cyber treaty will need agreement or at least mutual respect from the two states.,' (252–253). See also more recently, arguing 'that the collapse of the UN GGE process is likely to lead to a shift away from ambitious global initiatives and towards regional agreements between 'like-minded states'.' Anders Henriksen, 'The End of the Road for the UN GGE Process: The Future Regulation of Cyberspace,' Journal of Cybersecurity 5 (2019), 1–9 (1).

7 See e.g. Kriangsak Kittichaisaree, *Public International Law of Cyberspace* (Cham: Springer 2017); Harriet Moynihan, 'The Application of International Law to State Cyberattacks – Sovereignty and Non-intervention,' 2 December 2019, https://www.chathamhouse.org; Oona A. Hathaway and others, 'The Law of Cyber-Attack,' Cal. L. Rev. 100 (2012), 817–886 or Nicholas Tsagourias, 'Cyber attacks, self-defence and the problem of attribution,' Journal of Conflict & Security Law 17 (2012), 229–244.

8 Low-intensity cyber operations are operations that fall below the use of force and non-intervention threshold. Examples of operations that alter, disrupt or destroy computer systems are the Sony attack leading to the deletion of one hundred terabytes of Sony's data and furthermore the leak of confidential documents or the attack on the Sands Casino attributed to Iran which has caused significant financial damages and destroyed data as well as computer systems. See e.g. Beatrice A.

are regulated by state sovereignty as a primary rule of international law or whether sovereignty is merely a related principle yet not an alone standing rule.[9] Arguably, these difficulties in the application are rooted in a much older problem, namely that state sovereignty means everything and nothing at the same time, some calling it 'organised hypocrisy'[10], others naming it 'a funny thing' as '(i)t is allegedly the foundation of the Westphalian order, but its exact contours are frustratingly indeterminate.'[11] Indeed, there is no authoritative definition of sovereignty as there is also no common understanding of what constitutes state sovereignty.

Since Bodin first reshaped the idea of sovereignty to reflect no longer its medieval interpretation but a concept separated from a person who acts as the sovereign, the notion of sovereignty has been developed further over the centuries.[12] Nowadays, scholarly attempts to define state sovereignty are manifold, traditionally revolving around the idea of territoriality and exclusive authority. Besson refers to it as 'supreme authority within a territory,'[13] Schrijver notes that '(i)nternally it means that the government of a State is considered the ultimate authority within its borders and jurisdiction,' and adds an external component, i.e. 'that a State is not subject to the legal power of another State of any other higher authority.'[14] Similarly, Oppenheimer defines state sovereignty by stating that 'sovereignty is *independence*... As comprising the power of a state to exercise supreme authority over all persons and things within a territory, sovereignty involves *territorial* authority.'[15]

Many of such definitions could be added, yet all of them remain scholarly attempts to grasp what state sovereignty means as there is no

---

Walton, 'Duties Owed: Low-Intensity Cyber Attacks and Liability for Transboundary Torts in International Law,' Yale L.J. 126 (2017), 1460–1519.

9 Michael Schmitt and Liis Vihul, 'Sovereignty in Cyberspace: Lex Lata vel Non,' AJIL Unbound 11 (2017–2018), 213–218.

10 Stephen D. Krasner, *Sovereignty – Organized Hypocrisy* (Princeton: Princeton University Press 1999).

11 Jens David Ohlin, 'Did Russian Cyber Interference in the 2016 Election Violate International Law?,' Tex L. Rev. 95 (Forthcoming), Cornell Legal Studies Research Paper No. 17–15, (2017) https://papers.ssrn.com, 1.

12 Besson (n. 1), para. 16.

13 Besson (n. 1), para. 1.

14 Nico Schrijver, 'The Changing Nature of State Sovereignty,' BYIL 70 (1999), 65–98 (70–71).

15 Robert Jennings and Arthur Watts (eds), L Oppenheim, *Oppenheim's International Law, Vol 1: Peace* (9th ed, Oxford: Oxford University Press 2008), 382, quoted in Moynihan (n. 7), 11.

universal definition that states agree upon. Despite the fact that many of these definitions share a common core – that perhaps is even agreed upon by some states – the cyberspace debate challenges such definitions yet again, as it becomes evident that the terms territoriality, exclusive authority, and even independence have been challenged by the realities of complex interconnected cyberspace. As Schmitt and Vihul put it: 'On its face, the principle of sovereignty appears to be incompatible with cyberspace. Whereas sovereignty is an inherently territorial concept, cyberspace connects states in ways that seem to dilute territoriality. Nevertheless, the two phenomena have continued to exist in parallel since the emergence of cyber capabilities.'[16] In line with this observation, the following section thus takes a closer look at how the interplay of cyberspace and the principle of sovereignty have been approached so far and what issues have been identified by state practice as well as scholarship. For the purposes of this chapter, sovereignty is used as an umbrella term which, in line with Besson's definition, encompasses different rights and obligations.[17] Some of these rights and obligations are addressed in more detail, e.g., the right to exercise jurisdiction.

III. Different Approaches to the Application of State Sovereignty in Cyberspace

Against this backdrop of different definitions of state sovereignty and the challenge to apply these above-mentioned territorial concepts to cyberspace, it is evident that the issue of state sovereignty in cyberspace is part of an already extremely complex topic. The unique characteristics of cyberspace add yet another layer of difficulty to the challenge of understanding state sovereignty, leaving states in fundamental disagreement as to how to approach sovereignty in cyberspace. The following section will outline some of the approaches taken by key players in the cyber discussion, i.e., the US and like-minded states as well as China and Russia. This section does not aim to provide a comprehensive overview of all positions available but illustrates the broad range of approaches and priorities that can be taken with respect to sovereignty in cyberspace and how many areas and issues of international law and international relations can fall under the broad term of the 'sovereignty in cyberspace debate.'

16 Schmitt and Vihul (n. 9), 218.
17 Besson (n. 1), para. 118 f.

The first area where there are decisive differences is that of the regulation of the use of the internet and the regulation of free speech online. Often seen as a counter-position to the arguably more liberal US approach favouring strong protections of freedom of speech, China and Russia represent a view that strongly favours extending their territorial sovereignty to cyberspace. Despite the previously mentioned difficulties in understanding how territoriality plays out in cyberspace, China, Russia, and some other states push for an increasingly fragmented, territorial approach to the internet over which they can exercise exclusive authority. These positions are based on claims of state sovereignty, used in these instances to influence the interpretation of cyberspace in order to shape it in a way that is in line with the interests of authoritarian regimes. The reliance on state sovereignty has been used as a justification to impose strict regulations on the use of the internet and free speech online and to advance the fragmentation of cyberspace and is based on the idea of stressing the sovereign independence of each state and the principle of non-intervention, prohibiting outside interference in a state's internal affairs. Despite the fact that both China and Russia have at the time of writing not yet published a comprehensive analysis of how international law applies to cyberspace (as, for example, France,[18] Estonia,[19] and more recently, Germany[20] have), a practice already shows that their interpretations are restrictive, especially where the use of the internet is concerned.

In China, the use of the internet has been increasingly limited and controlled under President Xi Jing and is closely monitored by the Communist party. Those who advocated for reform behind what is now widely called 'The Great Firewall' and saw the internet as a tool to bring about political change in the communist state were soon silenced on the basis of what Xi calls 'China's sovereign right to determine what constitutes harmful content.'[21] Khanna notes that 'China's attempts to preserve its

18 French Ministry of Armies, 'International Law Applied to Operations in Cyberspace' (2019), https://www.justsecurity.org. For further analysis see Michael Schmitt, 'France's Major Statement on International Law and Cyber: An Assessment,' 16 September 2019, https://www.justsecurity.org.

19 Statement of the Estonian President at the International Conference on Cyber Conflict 2019 (2019), https://president.ee. For further analysis see Michael Schmitt, 'Estonia Speaks out on Key Rules for Cyberspace,' Just Security (2019), https://www.justsecurity.org.

20 Statement of the German Federal Government, 'On the Application of International Law in Cyberspace' (2021), https://www.auswaertiges-amt.de.

21 Elizabeth C. Economy, describing the Great Chinese Firewall as 'the largest and most sophisticated online censorship operation in the world,' in 'The Great Fire-

informational sovereignty by insulating its internet from Western websites are a clear example of how anxiety over sovereignty has been responsible for restrictions.'[22]

Russia has also tightened its regulation of the use of the internet. In May 2019, it passed a new 'Sovereign Internet Law,' a measure to 'protect Russia in the event of an emergency or foreign threat like a cyber attack.'[23] Behind what some consider the 'Online Iron Curtain,'[24] critics point out that Russia is increasingly aiming to disconnect its internet from global cyberspace, a step that it is allowed to take in case of a self-defined emergency.[25] To this end, Russia now routes its web traffic through state-controlled infrastructure and launched a national system of domain names. These measures might not be technically sufficient to completely isolate the Russian internet from the global internet, yet, allow the Kremlin to enforce online censorship[26] by blocking unwanted content according to 'usefully vague' criteria and without judicial consent.[27] This move has been heavily criticised by human rights advocates.[28]

The approaches followed by Russia and China exemplify practices to disconnect 'their' internet from global cyberspace. In addition to human rights concerns,[29] the fragmented approach advanced by several authoritarian states also fundamentally challenges the idea of global cyberspace. Although some have pointed to the technical difficulty to realise the fragmented approach to cyberspace,[30] Chinese internet policy shows how a large share of the world's population can effectively be put under severe

---

wall of China: Xi Jinping's internet shutdown,' 29 June 2018, https://www.theguardian.com.

22 Pallavi Khanna, 'State Sovereignty and Self-Defence in Cyberspace,' BRICS Law Journal 5 (2018), 139–154 (144).

23 Elizabeth Schulze, 'Russia just brought in a Law to Try to Disconnect its Internet from the Rest of the World,' 1 November 2019, https://www.cnbc.com.

24 Schulze (n. 23).

25 Sarah Rainsford, 'Russia Internet: Law Introducing New Controls Comes Into Force,' 1 November 2019, https://www.bbc.co.uk.

26 Schulze (n. 23).

27 Rainsford (n. 25).

28 Human Rights Watch, 'Russia: New Law Expands Government Control Online,' 31 October 2019, https://www.hrw.org.

29 Kenneth Roth describes China as 'an Orwellian high-tech surveillance state' with a 'sophisticated internet censorship system to monitor and suppress public criticism' in 'China's Global Threat to Human Rights,' Human Rights World Report 2020, https://www.hrw.org.

30 The comments were made in respect to Russia's new sovereign internet law, Schulze (n. 23).

restrictions – a practice that exemplifies how the internet is shaped from a global to a fragmented network – a development which is justified by claims of relying on state sovereignty.

A second related area where there is disagreement on how state sovereignty should play out in cyberspace relates to the question of governance of cyberspace. Whereas China and Russia support a state-centred approach in favour of negotiating a new international cyber treaty by traditional diplomatic means as they perceive them as a sovereign state's prerogative, many other states are of the opinion that existing international law is sufficient to regulate cyberspace and instead of negotiating a new treaty amongst states, they favour a multi-stakeholder approach for the regulation of cyberspace.[31]

These different approaches are also reflected within the UN, which set up two working groups that enjoy similar mandates to work on the regulation of cyberspace. On the one hand, there is the UN Open-Ended Working Group (OEWG), in which Russia enjoys support for its pro-sovereignty efforts, which have previously been backed by countries such as China, Brazil, India, Iran and Nigeria.[32] On the other hand, there is the US led UN Governmental Group of Experts (UN GGE),[33] which is backed by liberal democracies such as Australia, France and the UK.[34]

In these platforms, it becomes evident that the differences between states concern much broader aspects of cyberspace than the exact definition of state sovereignty, and that much depends on how sovereignty is to be applied and the different priorities states follow in their national interests. Some even argue that with the most recent developments in the UN mandates, i.e., the OEWG publishing its final substantive report on 12 March 2021[35] and the UN GGE's 2021 report,[36] the two working groups are, in fact, coming closer to finding similar conclusions.[37]

---

31 Cornish (n. 4), 161.

32 Justin Sherman and Mark Raymond, 'The U.N. Passed a Russian-backed Cybercrime Resolution. That's not Good News for Internet Freedom,' 4 December 2019, https://washingtonpost.com.

33 Samuele De Tomas Colatin, 'A Surprising Turn of Events: UN creates two working groups on cyberspace,' https://ccdcoe.org.

34 Sherman and Raymond (n. 32).

35 UN OEWG, 'Final Substantive Report,' (12 March 2021), UN DOC A/AC.290/2021/CRP.2.

36 Available here as an advanced copy, UN GGE, 'Report of the Group of Governmental Experts on Advancing responsible State behavior in cyberspace in the context of international security,' (28 May 2021).

The relationship between the two mandates certainly remains subject to further analysis. For the purposes of this chapter, it suffices to say that even where differences remain, the reality is that the differences in interpretation do not necessarily overlap with more traditional lines of geopolitics. Whereas it is true that Western states are generally following similar approaches supporting their interpretation of free speech and advocate for free flow of information online, even France and the UK do not agree when it comes to the third issue concerning sovereignty in cyberspace, i.e., the nature of sovereignty in cyberspace. When the UK put out their statement regarding the interpretation of international law in cyberspace in May 2018,[38] it became evident that its position is not necessarily shared by other Western countries. According to the British interpretation, sovereignty does not amount to a self-standing rule of international law. As sovereignty is merely a principle, an intrusive cyber operation that does not amount to a violation of the non-intervention principle (or the prohibition of the use of force) does not constitute an international wrong.[39] In contrast, the French interpretation of international law in cyberspace argues that 'any cyber attack against French digital systems or any effects produced on French territory by digital means [...] constitutes a breach of sovereignty,' implying that sovereignty constitutes a self-standing rule of international law and consequently, all violations thereof amount to a wrongful act.[40] These two statements represent the two positions at the ends of the sliding scale of the principle-vs-rule debate, one of the key discussions in legal scholarship on the topic of sovereignty in cyberspace.[41] In recent years, more and more states have published their interpretation on the matter, many agreeing on sovereignty as a rule assessment. However, differences remain with respect to the exact threshold needed to violate

---

37 This impression arises given that the UN OEWG confirmed in its final report that it is indeed based on the findings of the UN GGE's previous reports of 2010, 2013 and 2015. However, differences also remain: for example, the OEWG does not explicitly endorse the multistakeholder approach nor does it go into depth on the application of international law to cyberspace. For more, see e.g. Pavlina Ittelson and Vladimir Radunovic, 'What's new with cybersecurity negotiations? UN Cyber OEWG Final Report analysis,' 19 March 2021, https://www.diplomacy.edu.

38 UK Attorney General Jeremy Wright, 'Cyber and International Law in the 21st Century,' 23 May 2018, https://www.gov.uk.

39 Wright (n. 38).

40 French Ministry of Armies (n. 18), 6–7.

41 See e.g. Gary Corn and Robert Taylor, 'Symposium on Sovereignty, Cyberspace, And Tallinn Manual 2.0,' AJIL Unbound 111 (2017), 206–212 or Schmitt and Vihul (n. 9), 213–218.

state sovereignty – a matter that Schmitt calls 'the real task at hand,' which has been addressed more explicitly by the recent German statement.[42]

Finally, a fourth issue that determines the sovereignty in cyberspace debate is that of jurisdiction. Due to the general demand for international law to apply to cyberspace, the internet, to a certain extent, has to match the understanding of existing international law. With respect to the application of the principle of sovereignty and the exercise of jurisdiction, in particular, this means that the importance of territorial or physical aspects of cyberspace is often overstated.[43] Such over-reliance on physical aspects stresses that servers, computers, and other components of communication infrastructure are physically located in a country. On the one hand, such assertion makes a valid point, especially with respect to the establishment of the respective state's jurisdiction.[44] The UN GGE confirmed that states enjoyed jurisdiction with respect to such items of infrastructure in 2013.[45] It also reflects common practice according to which 'states regularly assert jurisdiction, both civil and criminal, over activities within their cyber infrastructure.'[46] On the other hand, overreliance on territorial aspects of activities in cyberspace does not solve the problem that cyber activities often function without a straight-forward territorial connection. This is especially true as offensive cyber operations can 'be mounted from a multitude of globally dispersed locations,'[47] but also affects cloud services and increasingly also applies to state functions conducted via cyberspace.[48] Thus, it has been noticed by Corn and Jensen that cyberspaces have 'at most a tenuous connection to geography.'[49] It follows that 'territorial con-

42 For further analysis see Michael Schmitt, 'Germany's Positions on International Law in Cyberspace Part I,' 9 March 2021, https://www.justsecurity.org.

43 See for example Roguski's criticism of Rule 4 of the Tallinn Manual 2.0, applying an effects-based analysis which 'overemphasizes physical effects on territory' and 'does not sufficiently take into account the technical side of most cyber operations,' Przemyslaw Roguski, 'Violations of Territorial Sovereignty in Cyberspace – an Intrusion-based Approach' in: Dennis Broeders and Bibi van den Berg (eds), *Governing Cyberspace – Behavior, Power, and Diplomacy* (London: Rowman & Littlefield 2020), 65–84 (74).

44 Khanna (n. 2), 143, referencing Catherine Lotrionte, 'State Sovereignty and Self-Defense in Cyberspace: A Normative Framework for Balancing Legal Rights,' Emory Int'. L. Rev. 26 (2012), 825–919 (829).

45 UN GGE A/68/98 (n. 5), para. 19–20.

46 Roguski, 'Violations of Territorial Sovereignty in Cyberspace' (n. 43), 72.

47 Roguski. (n. 43), 68–69, referencing Gary Corn and Eric Jensen, 'The Technicolor Zone of Cyberspace, Part 2,' 8 June 2018, https://www.justsecurity.org.

48 Roguski, 'Layered Sovereignty' (n. 3), 6–9.

49 Corn and Jensen (n. 47).

cepts are not readily transposable to an aterritorial medium by way of simple analogy.'[50]

The four different areas of priorities and the positions established by states, may it be by their practice or set out in statements, as well as scholarly debates show that the internet has clearly challenged the way state sovereignty is understood and that particularly the application of the ultimately territorial principle of sovereignty to largely a-territorial cyberspace remains a decisive challenge which is part of a broader, complex puzzle that plays out in many different ways.

IV. Using Analogies to Analyse the Application of State Sovereignty in Cyberspace

Against this backdrop of a broad and complex debate, scholarship has attempted to grasp the meaning of state sovereignty in cyberspace in a way that better reflects the plurality of interpretations of sovereignty but also one that explains the complexity of the topic by using analogies. In the remaining parts of the chapter, two examples of approaches using an analogy to conceptualise different issues of sovereignty in cyberspace will be examined.

Firstly, Roguski's 'layered approach', which borrows from the law of the sea by establishing several layers of nuancing degrees of state sovereignty in cyberspace, will be analysed.[51] Secondly, Cornish's analogy with quantum physics will be examined, which argues that 'allowing different understandings and expectations of sovereignty to co-exist rather than conflict' could be the solution to the problem of how to regulate state sovereignty in cyberspace.[52]

Whereas these are only two of the analogies used in legal scholarship addressing the sovereignty in cyberspace debate, they are chosen as examples in this chapter as they represent what in the opinion of the current author is a more common problem: the use of analogies does not often make a contribution to the discussion, especially where the analogy remains under-explored or further complicates an already complex analysis.

50 Roguski, 'Violations of Territorial Sovereignty in Cyberspace' (n. 43), 68.
51 Roguski, 'Layered Sovereignty' (n. 3).
52 Cornish (n. 4).

1. Roguski and a 'Layered Approach' to State Sovereignty in Cyberspace

In a paper for the 11th International Conference on Cyber Conflict, Roguski proposes a 'Layered Approach' to find a suitable interpretation to the question of how sovereignty can be applied in cyberspace. Roguski suggests a gradual model of three layers.

Firstly, the model envisages a 'Baseline Sovereignty' layer, which constitutes the 'physical layer of cyberspace' in which the 'proximity to the State is absolute through the criterion of territory.'[53] Such the first layer comprises information and communication technologies (ICT) infrastructure, which are widely accepted to fall under the state's sovereignty and jurisdiction in which they are located.[54]

Secondly, he proposes a 'Logical Layer' over which states have limited authority. This essentially a-territorial layer 'consists of the codes and standards that drive physical network components and make communication and exchange of information between possible.'[55] This applies, for example, to the allocation of IP addresses and domain names.[56] As has been seen in reference to Chinese and Russian approaches to cyber sovereignty, the degree of authority states have over these functions depends on whether they are taking an approach similar to the Russian and Chinese model or whether they are following a multi-stakeholder approach – in the first case 'sovereignty over […] the logical layer […] would be restored.'[57]

The third layer of 'Concurrent Sovereignty over Data located on ICT Infrastructure in Another State' foresees that next to the hosting state, concurrent sovereignty would be established 'if the data stored within the ICT infrastructure is sufficiently proximate to the State asserting sovereignty.'[58] It applies a criterion of proximity, a flexible test that 'describes the degree of the link between the data or service stored abroad and the State.'[59]

Roguski's proposal deserves credit as he finds a way to apply existing terms such as the authority to the realities of cyberspace. It is also a practical approach in the sense that it proposes ways to establish jurisdiction

53 Roguski, 'Layered Sovereignty' (n. 3), 10.
54 Ibid. (n. 3), 10–11; UN GGE A/68/98 (n. 5), para. 20; UN GGE A/70/174 (n. 5), para. 27.
55 Roguski, 'Layered Sovereignty' (n. 3), 11, referencing Joint Chiefs of Staff, 'Cyberspace Operations, Joint Publication 3–12,' 8 June 2018.
56 Roguski, 'Layered Sovereignty' (n. 3), 11.
57 Ibid. (n. 3), 12.
58 Ibid. (n. 3),12.
59 Ibid. (n. 3), 10.

and finds compelling examples of application. Roguski further rightly draws attention to the widely used function of cloud services and their potential impact on questions of sovereignty and jurisdiction. He also successfully moves away from territoriality where necessary by replacing it with the proximity criterion, a flexible approach that allows for the degree of connection between state and data to be established. The model applies existing terms and concepts such as authority, the layered approach borrowed from the law of the sea and the proximity criterion, which bears similarities to the 'genuine connection' test to establish extraterritorial jurisdiction.[60] As such, the proposed approach seems plausible, especially as it conveys a sense of familiarity with established terms and approaches.

The analogy layered approach is, therefore, indeed a laudable starting point; however, a deeper analysis of the analogy seems necessary. Roguski's model borrows from the maritime zones established in the Law of the Sea Convention, but there is little engagement with the question of why this analogy was chosen and what the law of the sea approach implies for the sovereignty debate. The value of the United Nations Convention on the Law of the Sea (UNCLOS) arguably lies in the regulation of corresponding rights and obligations and how these are applied in each zone. It seems that Roguski's model only refers to the law of the sea in a superficial manner yet misses the decisive aspect of how and why the layered approach works on the sea and what insights for the application and understanding of sovereignty in cyberspace can be gained from drawing such an analogy to sovereignty at sea. He does not provide a deeper insight or more nuanced analysis on how rights and obligations would be applied in the different zones of cyberspace. The question of jurisdiction is, after all, only one of the aspects of sovereignty and the analogy to 'layered *sovereignty*' leaves room for exploring more rights and obligations that can be regulated by the application of layers.

This relates to a more general point. The fact that Roguski continues to use terms such as authority creates a sense of familiarity and places the proposal within the established lines of the discussion, yet also precludes a deeper discussion of these notions and the conceptual difficulties surrounding them. This is especially true for the term sovereignty, in which respect Roguski's analysis does not provide a conceptual understanding – one that could be compared to the understanding of sovereignty at sea given the use of the analogy in the first place.

---

60 Ibid. (n. 3), 10. For the genuine connection test, see ICJ, *Nottebohm* (Liechtenstein v. Guatemala), judgement of 6 April 1955, ICJ Reports 1955, 4 (para. 4 ff.).

This is reflected in the fact that Roguski's analysis leaves open some questions: despite the fact that his proposal addresses *who* and *when* a state can act when its data stored abroad is targeted (e.g., when a state has 'an overwhelming interest in asserting authority over the data in question'[61]), Roguski does not dig deeper on the question *why* exactly they can act. As he does not explicitly weigh in on the principle-vs-rule debate here, the question of whether the violation of sovereignty in these instances constitutes a wrongful act remains open. Roguski suggests that where a state storing data abroad is affected, 'an attack *might* be qualified as a violation of the sovereignty of the attacked State irrespective of the fact that the territory of the State has not been affected,' adding that it can resort to 'countermeasures or the plea of necessity.'[62] Given that he addresses the availability of countermeasures, one that is only the case where there is a wrongful act[63], his model of sovereignty seems to imply that the violation of state sovereignty constitutes a wrongful act and as such, sovereignty seems to be a rule. Clarification on the question of when such an act exactly constitutes a violation of sovereignty would be useful as it would offer further insights on how he understands the nature of sovereignty.

Interestingly, Roguski has more recently published a chapter in which he explicitly weighs in on the nature of sovereignty and concludes that sovereignty constitutes a self-standing rule.[64] Here, Roguski also elaborates on the threshold of when an offensive cyber operation violates the principle of sovereignty exactly, arguing this is the case not only where physical effects are caused but instead proposes an 'intrusion-based' approach, generally similar to the French model.[65] Despite the fact that Roguski envisages certain thresholds by categorising only those interferences that affect the integrity of data (e.g. by deleting or altering data), and not those that merely access them (e.g., for intended purposes or even by unauthorised access), as a violation of sovereignty, his approach remains broad.[66]

Overall, Roguski's analogy is an interesting starting point, but it would have allowed for more insights if the analogy to the layers of the law of the

61 Ibid. (n. 3), 13.

62 Ibid. (n. 3), 13.

63 ILC, 'Articles on the Responsibility of States for Internationally Wrongful Acts,' (2001) ILCYB, Vol II, Part Two, 31 ff.

64 Roguski, 'Violations of Territorial Sovereignty in Cyberspace' (n. 43), dismissing arguments that sovereignty is not a principle on page 68–69, concluding that 'sovereignty [...] forms itself a prohibitive rule of international law.,' 71.

65 Ibid. (n. 43), 73 ff.

66 Roguski, 'Violations of Territorial Sovereignty in Cyberspace' (n. 43), 79.

sea was conducted more explicitly and if the analysis provided more comprehensive assessments of how the different rights and obligations play out in these layers. Whereas the analysis of the layered approach leaves open some questions which are answered in other publications, it would be interesting to see how Roguski's understanding of sovereignty explored in his second publication mentioned here relates to the interpretation of sovereignty at sea alluded to in the first publication.

2. *Cornish and the Quantum Physics Analogy*

Cornish's approach is of a more conceptual nature, providing the reader with an analysis exploring the different understandings underlying the sovereignty debate. To illustrate the variety of interpretations of sovereignty that co-exist, Cornish applies an analogy to quantum theory's superposition principle by referring to the experiment of Schrödinger's cat in which the pet is located in a box together with radioactive material as well as a radioactive monitor and a bottle of cyanide. The bottle of cyanide will eventually break due to the radioactive material in the box measured by the radioactive monitor, and as a result, the cat will die. The decisive bit is what follows: until someone opens the box to check on the status of the cat, 'the cat is notionally both alive and dead' or perhaps neither of the two options.[67]

Cornish applies this state of superposition to cyberspace by arguing that much of cyberspace is also 'both dead and alive' depending on the perspective you take: one might argue that information is hard as it is sent through cables, yet, on the other hand, it is non-physical, soft as it merely consists of digital code. He adds more examples of such 'dualities we might wish state sovereignty to occupy at once: national and international; procedural and substantive; international and external; intangible and physical; cultural and territorial.'[68]

So far, so convincing. Yet this plurality of interpretations of state sovereignty in cyberspace can only continue to exist if 'no one opens the lid' – and there continues to be a good reason not to do so. This is where the analogy becomes more complex. The aim, so Cornish, must be 'a reasonably unified, international policy for cyberspace as a 'virtual commons,' which can only be achieved if neither of the opposing views triumphs

67 Cornish (n. 4), 166.
68 Ibid. (n. 4), 166.

over the other, 'as the result would be neither unified nor common.'[69] This means that the lid must remain closed, so the reality does not show the incompatibility of the different approaches. Basing his argument on game-theory, Cornish argues that in order for the lid to remain closed, there must be a series of concessions made by the states of opposing position.[70]

Among the concessions listed by Cornish is the acknowledgement by states such as China that 'the multi-stakeholder approach is both more realistic and inclusive [...] than intergovernmentalism'[71] and the acceptance that all norms developed 'should be respected both in letter and in spirit.'[72] In return, he sees concessions to be made by those advocating a multi-stakeholder approach, especially with respect to acknowledging that 'territorial sovereignty does bear upon many of the physical aspects of cyberspace,' respect the principle of non-intervention and that 'cyberspace is to provide a neutral medium for communication and cooperation among many different actors, rather than serving as a vehicle for the homogenisation of politics according to Western values, the enforcement of international standards of human rights around the world or the spread of liberal-democratic, rule-of-law-based systems of government,' a concession he accepts as difficult to realise.[73]

In return for these concessions, Cornish expects several benefits to arise out of this trade-off. For 'non-Western' states, it will reconfirm that states are 'at the centre of the norm- and rule-setting processes,' which thus means that these norms can be expected to reflect 'the preferences of all interested parties, rather than a small selection of them.'[74] Cornish also believes that 'by surrendering their insistence on a thin, territorial understanding of sovereignty, governments should also expect a return to a thicker and deeper understanding, in which culture and 'internal sovereignty' are acknowledged and respected.'[75]

As benefits for those supporting a multi-stakeholder approach, Cornish claims that fragmented cyberspace will become unlikely and that 'a more transparent, rules-based system' should emerge, which in turn 'should also see less tolerance for 'plausibly deniable' yet problematic behaviors in cyberspace,' ultimately making cyberspace 'more stable and predictable'

69 Ibid. (n. 4), 167.
70 Ibid. (n. 4), 167.
71 Ibid. (n. 4), 168.
72 Ibid. (n. 4), 168.
73 Ibid. (n. 4), 169.
74 Ibid. (n. 4), 168.
75 Ibid. (n. 4), 168.

which would have positive economic effects.[76] He further argues that such concessions would make it more likely to involve other stakeholders, which eventually could lead to 'the development of a normative, even cosmopolitan, framework.'[77]

Cornish's paper provides international legal scholarship with an out-of-the-box analogy and raises fundamental, highly interesting points, especially with respect to China's understanding of sovereignty. Yet difficulties arise when applying Cornish's analogy to practice. Firstly, it is questionable why it is desirable to find a reason 'not to open a lid.' This seems in clear contradiction with the aim to clarify the application of international legal norms to cyberspace,[78] an action that would – as far as the current author understands – require us to open the lid. Even though some states might prefer the current legal grey zones in cyberspace, Cornish argues that the ultimate benefit of keeping the lid shut is clarity and stability – aims that could arguably be achieved more directly by opening the lid.

Secondly, it seems highly unlikely that either side would start making any concessions. It does not seem likely China and Russia would abandon their restrictive, fragmented approach to cyberspace, nor that the West would support such restrictive interpretation, especially given that access to the internet is increasingly understood as a human right.[79]

In order to explain why states would make concessions, Cornish refers to elementary game theory and a system of cooperation in order to achieve desired benefits.[80] Here, Cornish misses a decisive element of game theory, often best explained by the Prisoner's Dilemma. In an interrogation of two prisoners, each prisoner does not know for sure if the other prisoner is also going to remain silent; a prisoner is more likely to turn on one another, despite the fact that cooperation in the form of mutual silence would be beneficial.[81] They will only remain silent if they trust one another – or

76 Ibid. (n. 4), 171–172.

77 Ibid. (n. 4), 172.

78 Often the aim to clarify norms of state behaviour is equated with leading to more stability, see e.g. Zine Homburger, 'Conceptual Ambiguity of International Norms on State Behaviour in Cyberspace,' 4 April 2019, available at: https://eucyberdirect.eu, 9. On why clarity is desirable in cyberspace, see also Robert McLaughlin and Michael Schmitt, 'The Need for Clarity in International Cyber Law,' 18 September 2017, https://www.policyforum.net.

79 Catherine Howell and Darrell M. West, 'The Internet as a Human Right,' 7 November 2016, available at: https://www.brookings.edu.

80 Cornish (n. 4), 167.

81 For more on the Prisoner's Dilemma, see Steven Kuhn, 'Prisoner's Dilemma' in: Edward Zalta (ed.), *The Stanford Encyclopedia of Philosophy* (online edn, Stanford:

have made an agreement before the interrogation to do so. With respect to Cornish's proposed concessions, the question arises why either party would start making these fundamental concessions.[82] Despite the fact that the long-term outcome might be beneficial, there is no established relationship of trust between the US and China.[83] As long as each state cannot trust the other that their concessions are binding and will be adhered to, the trade-off does not work or as the prisoner's dilemma shows: each prisoner will turn on the other. One way to establish a binding nature could, of course, be in the form of an international treaty – yet Cornish mentions no such step, although it is crucial in order for the reference to game theory to work and to find a rational incentive to keep the lid shut. Without negotiations, transparency or guarantees, these concessions seem to appear 'out of the blue,' making it difficult to see how this analogy could play out in practice.

Thirdly, the current author believes that such concessions are fundamental. Cornish sees them as an enabler to ultimately reach a 'framework for global cyber governance.'[84] It would be interesting to know more about where Cornish sees the benefit of such a model. Is keeping the lid shut merely a temporal solution to establish trust between both frontiers while they make one concession after the other? If one assumes that both sides are ultimately willing to make such fundamental concessions, would it not be more favourable to fully open the lid straight away and find a compromise as a whole? This is in line with the previous arguments, as the current author believes negotiations of a treaty to establish trust and accountability are vital to lead to concessions in the first place. Given the current state of negotiations within the UN working groups, it, of course, does not seem very likely that such negotiations would be fruitful. However, it could be argued that by keeping the lid shut, states like China and Russia will continue to work towards a fragmented model of cyberspace and violate human rights while the West will advance their

The Metaphysics Research Lab 2019), 2 April 2019, https://plato.stanford.edu/index.html.

82 Cornish (n. 4) says that 'China, [...] would first have to concede that cyberspace should not (and logically cannot) be territorialised,' 168, yet he does not explain whether this is meant as a temporal assessment and if yes, why a first step would be taken by China and if so, on what basis.

83 This was the case when Cornish wrote his analogy (2015) as well as today (2021). For more see Council on Foreign Relations, 'U.S. Relations With China – 1949–2020' (2020), https://www.cfr.org/timeline/us-relations-china.

84 Cornish (n. 4), 172.

global, multi-stakeholder model – a development that is also unlikely to lead to more trust and consequently, will not encourage either party to make concessions.

Fourthly, it does not become clear how the concession that 'China, [...] would first have to concede that cyberspace should not (and logically cannot) be territorialised'[85] does not result in the triumph of one side over the other – something, so Cornish earlier, that should be avoided.[86] Despite the fact that both sides have to make concessions that certainly can outweigh one another to some extent, it nevertheless seems that, ultimately, this specific concession would lead to triumph from a Western perspective. This argument in combination with Cornish's claim that cyberspace should not be territorialised[87] might be read as a confirmation that Cornish has indeed chosen a preference of which side should ultimately triumph.

Despite the fact that the current author finds it difficult to see how the model would apply in practice, Cornish ultimately achieves a critical point that Roguski's theoretical model does not explore to the same extent: he successfully shows that there is no agreement on the concept of state sovereignty – neither from a legal nor a cultural perspective – and that sovereignty is many – often contradictory – things according to different perspectives. Instead, Cornish shows that the difficulty in applying state sovereignty to cyberspace is not so much how we can translate 'territoriality' and 'authority' to cyberspace, but that there is no agreement on the concept of state sovereignty in the first place.

V. Remarks on the Contribution of Analogies to the Sovereignty in Cyberspace Debate

The work of the two authors examined allows the critical reader to explore key issues relating to the regulation of state sovereignty in cyberspace: the lack of a common understanding of state sovereignty and how to deal with such ambiguity, the concept of territoriality in cyberspace, and the question how current geopolitics can work towards a practical way of governing cyberspace.

---

85 Ibid. (n. 4), 168.
86 Ibid. (n. 4), 167.
87 Ibid. (n. 4), 168.

Nevertheless, the present analysis also shows the shortcomings of the two models explored. In addition to the content-related arguments raised in the previous analysis, the two analogies allow for reflections on the general contribution such analogies can make when discussing the application of international law to cyberspace as the two examples chosen are representative of two more common problems encountered when using analogies.

Firstly, the interdisciplinary analogy between international cyber law and quantum physics has artificial appeal but, in practice, compounds the complexities of an already immensely complex debate. Whereas the initial analogy between Schrödinger's cat and sovereignty is a thought-provoking comparison indeed, the further the analogy is taken, the less it helps to understand the debates around sovereignty in cyberspace. In order to fully comprehend the value and meaning of the analogies, the reader of Cornish's paper ideally is familiar with basic quantum physics, international law, particularly principles applying to cyberspace, and later game theory. It is easy to see how given the number of references and complexity of each field, respectively, one cannot see the wood for the trees. The nuances that could be conveyed with such analogy are simply hidden away behind ever more metaphors, analogies and references, and it is easy to get lost. The conclusion that must be drawn in this instance is that the interdisciplinary analogy did not contribute to clarifying a complicated matter. On the contrary, the reliance on the quantum physics analogy in combination with additional references to game theory complicated the matter further.

Secondly, almost the opposite can be said for the analogy to the law of the sea made by Roguski. Here, the reference remained of a relatively superficial nature, and the opportunity for a meaningful analogy was at least to some extent missed. The law of the sea analogy could make for a promising legal parallel. However, a deeper analysis of the understanding of sovereignty at sea and in cyberspace as well as of the idea of different zones or layers with varying degrees of rights and obligations, i.e., a closer parallel to the law of the sea analogy, could have made a bigger contribution to the analysis at hand.

This is not to say that analogies generally cannot contribute to the quality of academic debate. On the contrary, they can improve the understanding of an issue, encourage readers to look for approaches and solutions applied in different fields and benefit from the experience made elsewhere. One example of how analogies in the cyberspace debate can contribute to a meaningful analysis is where cyberspace is compared to global commons, as such analogy can lead 'to some useful comparative insights.'[88] Mueller's analysis of whether cyberspace should be a global commons like the high seas works well as it is a clear yet limited reference with the defined purpose of illustrating the relationship between the two domains.[89]

However, '[t]here are always difficulties' when using (interdisciplinary) analogies.[90] Such assessment also applies to situations where sovereignty in cyberspace is compared to other areas of international law. The challenge of finding an appropriate analogy lies in striking the right balance between mere superficial reference and becoming overwhelmed by complex details. Ultimately, 'it is only possible to analogise so far before analogy fails.'[91] In an area like sovereignty in cyberspace that is already dominated by legal grey zones, uncertainty, and the difficulty of combining legal and technical expertise, what the discourse urgently needs is clarity, comprehensible approaches and sharp analysis that ideally combines technical as well as legal perspectives instead of more analogies and metaphors.

For many years, scholars in the field regularly concluded that what is needed is more insights into state practice.[92] Although such a need remains to some extent, we have recently seen more and more states coming forward with their interpretation of how international law should apply to cyberspace.[93] Especially in the context of the two UN working groups, states have publicly stated their positions, fostering the debate on how sovereignty can be applied to cyberspace. These new statements are important,[94] and some are even of 'normative sophistication.'[95] International legal scholars have waited for such clarity for a long time – and should respond by offering the same clarity in return. To this end, adding to uncertainties by getting lost in analogies that over-complicate the matter or that are not followed through with has to be avoided. The discourse will

88 David Betz and Tim Stevens, 'Analogical Reasoning and Cyber Security,' Sec. Dialogue 44 (2013), 147–164 (151–152).

89 Milton L. Mueller, 'Against Sovereignty in Cyberspace,' International Studies Review 22 (2020), 779–801.

90 Betz and Stevens (n. 88), 156.

91 Betz and Stevens (n. 88), 158.

92 E.g. Eric Talbot Jensen, 'The Tallinn Manual 2.0: Highlights and Insights,' Geo. J. Int' l L. 48 (2017), 735–778 (743).

93 See e.g. n. 18, 19, 20.

94 Przemyslaw Roguski, 'The Importance of New Statements on Sovereignty in Cyberspace by Austria, the Czech Republic and United States,' 11 May 2020, https://www.justsecurity.org.

95 Michael Schmitt, 'Finland Sets Out Key Positions on International Cyber Law,' 27 October 2020, https://www.justsecurity.org.

only benefit from direct analysis to understand technical and legal aspects of the question of how sovereignty can play out in cyberspace. Therefore, analogies should be used with caution.

VI. Conclusion

The debate surrounding the application of state sovereignty to cyberspace is a complex one. The present analysis has shown that not only is there no authoritative definition of state sovereignty in the first place, but that its application to cyberspace is especially challenging given the discrepancy between the traditional concept of state sovereignty which is often understood to be of a territorial nature and the fact that cyberspace is commonly perceived to be a territorial. In addition, this chapter has illustrated that states approach the sovereignty in cyberspace according to their national interests, e.g. by using the principle of state sovereignty as a justification for political acts or whether they lobby for a distinctive way how to approach governance and administration of cyberspace.

With these complexities in mind, legal scholarship has tried to analyse the subject matter – often with the help of analogies. After all, analogies or references to other or related subject matters are useful to catch the reader's initial attention – hence this chapter's title: 'Error 404: No Sovereignty Analogy Found,' referring to the common error notification many internet users are familiar with. However, the two examples examined in this chapter show how difficult it is to find an analogy that actually contributes to the analysis and clarification of this complex topic. On the contrary, the two analogies examined here have illustrated that instead of striking the right balance, it is likely that a very detailed analogy adds further complexity to the topic and leads to additional confusion and that, in contrast, a superficial analogy does not lead to useful comparative insights either. Therefore, the chapter concludes that where an appropriate balance cannot be struck and an (inter-disciplinary) analogy does not contribute to the analysis at hand, scholars should consider writing their analysis on sovereignty in cyberspace without using analogies and instead, favour clear and straight-forward analysis. In that sense, at least in the light of the two examples studied, no adequate analogy clarifying the sovereignty in cyberspace debate could be found.

The Constitutionalisation of the Digital Ecosystem: Lessons from International Law

Edoardo Celeste

Abstract A complex process of constitutionalisation is currently underway within contemporary society. A multiplicity of normative counteractions is emerging to address the challenges of the digital revolution. However, there is no single constitutional framer. In a globalised environment, constitutionalisation simultaneously occurs at different societal levels. Not only in the institutional perimeter of nation-states but also beyond: on the international plane, in the fiefs of the private actors, within the civil society. This chapter examines to what extent international law scholarship may offer a useful theoretical toolbox to understand the multilevel phenomenon of constitutionalisation of the digital ecosystem. International law theory indeed already projected the notion of constitution beyond the state dimension, helping explain how the emergence of globalised problems in the digital ecosystem necessarily engenders the materialisation of a plurality of constitutional responses. It will be argued that the sense of this Gordian knot can be deciphered only if these emerging constitutional fragments are interpreted as complementary tesserae of a single mosaic. Each one is surfacing with a precise mission within the constitutional dimension, each one compensating the shortcomings of the others to achieve a common aim: translating the core principles of contemporary constitutionalism in the context of the digital ecosystem. Constitutionalising the digital ecosystem is not synonymous with *en bloc* codification but rather represents a gradual process of translation of principles and values. Constitutionalisation does not merely imply the imposition of new constitutional rules but also includes a substantial bottom-up societal input. All the various scattered components of the process of constitutionalisation of the digital ecosystem equally contribute to substantiating the ideals and values of digital constitutionalism, which represents a new theoretical strand within contemporary constitutionalism aiming to adapt its core values to the needs of the digital ecosystem.

I. Introduction

There is a link between the constitutional dimension, both at the state level and beyond, and technological advancement.[1] Technology has always profoundly transformed society and the role of individuals within it. Over

---

1 This chapter draws on Chapter 4 of my doctoral thesis 'Digital Constitutionalism: The Role of Internet Bills of Rights' (University College Dublin, 2020), now published, with the same title, by Routledge (2022). I would like to thank the participants of the workshop 'International Law and the Internet' hosted by the Max Planck Institute for Comparative Public Law and International Law on 16th October 2020, and in particular Gunther Teubner, Chien-Huei Wu, Thiago Almeida, and the Editors of this Volume for their comments on this paper.

the past few centuries, new technologies have altered power relations, created new tools of societal control and generated socio-economic expectations. These changes have been reflected in major constitutional upheavals. The great constitutional revolutions that occurred in Europe and America at the end of the eighteenth century were the heir of two centuries of a scientific revolution.[2] Similarly, today, constitutional law both within and beyond the state is not remaining inert vis-à-vis the challenges of the digital revolution. It is true – in contemporary society, the constitutional dimension struggles on multiple fronts.[3] Its state-centric origin demands a conceptual rethinking when applied to the global digital ecosystem, where private multinational companies emerge as dominant actors beside nation-states. Yet, the constitutional dimension is slowly reacting, progressively changing and evolving through a series of targeted transformations.

These transformations take the form of normative responses, seeking to protect fundamental rights and to balance the relationship between powerful and weak actors in the mutated contest of the digital ecosystem. One can mention as examples new provisions added to national constitutions that aim to guarantee the right to participate in the information society, such as the new Article 5A of the Greek Constitution.[4] Judicial decisions affirming the right to Internet access: in 2009, the French *Conseil constitutionnel* explicitly recognised this right, followed in 2010 by the Costa Rican *Sala Constitucional*.[5] Sets of legislation detailing the guarantees for our 'digital body,' personal data: here, the compulsory reference is to the General Data Protection Regulation.[6] Dozens of declarations of rights for the Internet age issued by civil society groups around the globe: one example for all, the Charter of Human Rights and Principles

---

2 See Chris Thornhill, *A Sociology of Constitutions: Constitutions and State Legitimacy in Historical-Sociological Perspective* (Cambridge: Cambridge University Press 2013), 181 ff.; Thomas S Kuhn, *The Structure of Scientific Revolutions* (4th edn, Chicago, London: University of Chicago Press 2012).

3 See Petra Dobner and Martin Loughlin (eds), *The Twilight of Constitutionalism?* (Oxford: Oxford University Press 2010).

4 Greek Constitution, http://www.hellenicparliament.gr/UserFiles/f3c70a23-7696-49db-9148-f24dce6a27c8/001-156%20aggliko.pdf.

5 Conseil constitutionnel, décision n° 2009–580 DC du 10 juin 2009, https://www.conseil-constitutionnel.fr/decision/2009/2009580DC.htm; Sala Constitucional de la Corte Suprema de Justicia, sentencia n° 12790 de 30 de Julio de 2010, https://www.poder-judicial.go.cr/salaconstitucional/index.php/servicios-publicos/759-10-012790.

6 Regulation 2016/679/EU.

for the Internet, currently translated in more than ten languages.[7] New procedural safeguards instilled within internal governance mechanisms of private companies: there is still much work to do, but we can certainly refer to the new online content moderation principles and practices of social media companies like Facebook or Twitter.[8] And as the last, but certainly not least examples of normative response to the challenges of the digital revolution, one can list the emergence of case-law from sector-specific adjudicating mechanisms, such as the ICANN dispute resolution service providers,[9] as well as the institution by online private companies of semi-judicial internal bodies with the duty to decide issues related to the validity of content published on these platforms.[10]

By adopting a functional approach, looking beyond the formal character of norms, one can identify the emergence of these constitutional responses both within and beyond the state dimension, involving also private companies as main actors of constitutionalising trends.[11] The reaction of the constitutional dimension to the digital revolution does not only materialise in national constitutions, statutes and judicial decisions. Civil society groups affirm their digital rights in non-binding declarations. Multinational technology corporations are pushed to introduce individual rights safeguards in their internal rules. Private companies' decision-making bodies progressively establish principles to protect users' rights in their own case-law.

---

7 Charter of Human Rights and Principles for the Internet https://internetrightsandprinciples.org/charter/.

8 See Edoardo Celeste, 'Terms of Service and Bills of Rights: New Mechanisms of Constitutionalisation in the Social Media Environment?,' International Review of Law, Computers & Technology 33 (2019), 122-138.

9 See Lars Viellechner, 'Constitutionalism as a Cipher: On the Convergence of Constitutionalist and Pluralist Approaches to the Globalization of Law,' Göttingen Journal of International Law 4 (2012), 599-623. See also Cäcilia Hermes, 'Cyberspace as an Example of Self-Organisation from a Network Perspective,' HJIL 81 (2021).

10 See Matthias C. Kettemann and Wolfgang Schulz, 'Setting Rules for 2.7 Billion. A (First) Look into Facebook's Norm-Making System: Results of a Pilot Study,' Working Papers of the Hans-Bredow-Institut, January 2020, https://www.hans-bredow-institut.de/uploads/media/default/cms/media/k0gjxdi_AP_WiP001InsideFacebook.pdf.

11 For an analysis that focuses on the digital context see Edoardo Celeste, 'Digital Constitutionalism: A New Systematic Theorisation,' International Review of Law, Computers & Technology 33 (2019), 76-99; more generally on the point, see Gunther Teubner, *Constitutional Fragments: Societal Constitutionalism and Globalization* (Oxford: Oxford University Press 2012).

The panorama of constitutional counteractions to the challenges of the digital revolution appears fragmented, plural, polycentric. Constitutional patterns emerge both in legally binding and non-binding legal sources, through democratic and institutionalised processes, and through spontaneous deliberation of non-organised groups. Counteractions developing in the national dimension address the relationship between the state and individuals and apply within circumscribed territories, while transnational constitutional instruments focus on the power that private corporations exercise on their users on a global scale. The constitutional discourse is no longer uniform and unitary. Nor is it possible to refer to single legal orders. Each constitutional instrument is a 'fragment,'[12] a 'partial constitution,'[13] We face a scenario of constitutional pluralism, a complex mosaic not only combining multiple sources but also intersecting different legal orders.[14] If one were able to gain an aerial view of this phenomenon in motion, one would not simply see the static image of a set of constitutional fragments but would observe a lively and effervescent scenario: what this chapter calls a process of constitutionalisation.

The image of the medieval feudal system, where the power is layered and fragmented, where kings are such in one territory but subjects in others, and the distinction between private and public blurs, once again comes to mind. However, it is not necessary to go back to the Middle Ages to retrace an analogous phenomenon.[15] Interestingly, in international law, there is a long-standing tradition of scholars embracing a constitutionalist approach. Recent studies explain that constitutional pluralism is a general phenomenon of our age, a consequence of a specific contemporary trend: globalisation. This chapter does not aim to advance a normative call in favour of the emergence of these constitutional counteractions but rather seeks to investigate to what extent international law can offer a useful theoretical toolbox to analyse this multifaceted trend as a single phenomenon of constitutionalisation of the digital ecosystem.

12 See Teubner, *Constitutional Fragments* (n. 11).

13 See Viellechner (n. 9); Anne Peters, 'The Globalization of State Constitutions' in: Janne E. Nijman and André Nollkaemper (eds), *New Perspectives on the Divide Between National and International Law* (Oxford: Oxford University Press 2007), 251-308.

14 See the extremely accurate overview provided in Matthias C. Kettemann, *The Normative Order of the Internet: A Theory of Rule and Regulation Online* (Oxford: Oxford University Press 2020); on the notion of 'constitutional pluralism,' see Neil Walker, 'The Idea of Constitutional Pluralism,' MLR 65 (2002), 317-359.

15 See Viellechner (n. 9).

This contribution is divided into two main sections. Section 2 analyses the conceptual instruments that international law offers to interpret the current phenomenon of constitutionalisation of the digital ecosystem. It will start by explaining how international law theory projected the notion of constitution beyond the state dimension and will argue that the emergence of globalised problems necessarily engenders the materialisation of a plurality of constitutional responses (II.1). Such a process, which will be denoted as constitutionalisation, may take different forms. Section II.2 will present a notorious example focusing on the constitutionalisation of the European Union. This context will not be used as a model of the process of constitutionalisation of the digital ecosystem but will be analysed from a theoretical standpoint to show that the appearance of constitutional patterns beyond the nation-state does not neuter but rather complement parallel constitutionalising processes at multiple levels (II.3). This argument will be finally supported by referring to the socio-legal scholarship on the topic (II.4).

Section III will investigate how the conceptual framework analysed in Section II can be applied to interpret the process of constitutionalisation of the digital ecosystem. Such process, too, is engendered by the globalised issues generated by the digital revolution and consequently comprises a plurality of fragmented constitutional counteractions (III.1). Constitutionalising the digital ecosystem is not synonymous with *en bloc* codification but rather represents a gradual process of translation of principles and values (III.2). Constitutionalisation does not merely imply the imposition of new constitutional rules but also includes a substantial bottom-up societal input (III.3). All the various scattered components of the process of constitutionalisation of the digital ecosystem equally contribute to substantiating the ideals and values of digital constitutionalism, which represents a new theoretical strand within contemporary constitutionalism aiming to adapt its core values to the needs of the digital ecosystem (III.4).

II. The International Law Toolbox on the Concept of Constitutionalisation

1. Globalisation and Pluralism: The Legacy of International Constitutional Law

Interestingly, in international law, there is a long-standing tradition of scholars embracing a constitutionalist approach.[16] In fact, the roots of what has been called 'international constitutional law' date back to the first half of the past century.[17] In 1926, Alfred Verdross wrote a book entitled *The Constitution of the International Legal Community*, in which he argued that the norms regulating the sources, scope, and jurisdiction of international law represent its 'constitution.'[18] For the sake of simplification, a first strand of the international constitutional law doctrine insisted on this analogic and hierarchical approach.[19] According to this vision, the meta-rules of international law, i.e. the rules which regulate international rule-making, would present some characters similar to domestic constitutions.[20] On the one hand, they would represent 'higher' norms establishing procedural constraints, as, for example, the Charter of the United Nations does by setting the rules related to the sources, scope and jurisdiction of international law.[21] On the other hand, they would provide substantive limitations in relation to primary values worthy of protection, such as, for

16 For a general overview, see Andrea Bianchi, *International Law Theories: An Inquiry into Different Ways of Thinking* (Oxford: Oxford University Press 2016), 44-71; for a critique on the use of a constitutionalist approach in international law, see Martti Koskenniemi, 'Constitutionalism as Mindset: Reflections on Kantian Themes About International Law and Globalization,' Theoretical Inquiries in Law 8 (2006), 9-35.

17 This expression first appeared in Wolfgang Friedmann, *The Changing Structure of International Law* (New York: Columbia University Press 1964).

18 Alfred Verdross, *Die Verfassung der Völkerrechtsgemeinschaft* (Wien: Springer 1926); see Bardo Fassbender, 'The Meaning of International Constitutional Law' in: Ronald St. John Macdonald and Douglas M. Johnston (eds), *Towards World Constitutionalism: Issues in the Legal Ordering of the World Community* (Leiden: Nijhoff 2005), 837-851.

19 See, in particular, Bardo Fassbender, 'The United Nations Charter as the Constitution of the International Community,' Colum. J. Transnat'l L.36 (1998), 529-619; Fassbender, 'The Meaning of International Constitutional Law' (n. 18).

20 See Verdross (n. 18); Fassbender, 'The Meaning of International Constitutional Law' (n. 18).

21 See Fassbender, 'The United Nations Charter as the Constitution of the International Community' (n. 19).

instance, in the case of the principles of *jus cogens* or *erga omnes* obligations prohibiting slavery and genocide.[22]

Starting from these premises, a stream of scholars went even further. They argued that core international values and principles would not be merely *analogically* constitutional, as the fundamental rules of an autonomous legal order – that of interstate relationships – that is deemed to be distinct from domestic systems. These norms would really perform a constitutional function *in conjunction with* domestic constitutional law.[23] The international legal order is no longer seen as an interstate, state-centric normative architecture. According to this vision, the weathercock of international law would have turned towards the individual dimension.[24] The entirety of constitutional law, both on an international and domestic plane, would share its primary aim. International constitutional norms, too, become inviolable principles seeking to protect individual rights, a series of norms that would be even superior to the will of the states.[25] States would still be the chief characters but would act 'in a play written and directed by the international community.'[26]

Such a novel reading of the role of international law was explained in the context of the globalisation phenomenon. Globalisation is the process of progressive 'appearance of global, de-territorialised problems.'[27] Issues such as climate change, international terrorism, or mass migration cannot be addressed on the international plane by single nation-states but would require the cooperation of a multiplicity of actors.[28] Such enhanced inter-

---

22 See Fassbender, 'The Meaning of International Constitutional Law' (n. 18).

23 See, in particular, Christian Tomuschat, 'International Law: Ensuring the Survival of Mankind on the Eve of a New Century: General Course on Public International Law,' Collected Courses of The Hague Academy of International Law 281 (1999), 9-438; further on Tomuschat's vision, see Armin von Bogdandy, 'Constitutionalism in International Law: Comment on a Proposal from Germany,' Harv. Int'l. L.J. 47 (2006), 223-242.

24 See Anne Peters, 'Humanity as the A and Ω of Sovereignty,' EJIL 20 (2009), 513-544.

25 Christian Tomuschat, 'Obligations Arising for States without or against Their Will,' Collected Courses of The Hague Academy of International Law 241 (1993), 195-374; cf. Fassbender, 'The Meaning of International Constitutional Law' (n. 18).

26 Von Bogdandy (n. 23), 228.

27 Anne Peters, 'Compensatory Constitutionalism: The Function and Potential of Fundamental International Norms and Structures,' LJIL 19 (2006), 579-610 (580).

28 See Jost Delbrück, 'Structural Changes in the International System and Its Legal Order: International Law in the Era of Globalization,' Swiss Review of International and European Law 11 (2001), 1-36; Anne Peters, 'The Refinement of Inter-

dependence concretely manifests itself in a double, vertical shift of power. Part of nation-states' functions are, on the one hand, absorbed by higher level, supranational entities; on the other hand, entrusted to a lower level, multinational non-state actors.[29] Dobner and Loughlin talk of an 'erosion of statehood.'[30] The nation-state is no longer the monopolist of power. A series of dominant actors emerge beyond the state dimension, creating new transnational contexts in which individual rights need to be protected and the powers of the players involved balanced.

This novel circumstance generates a new constitutional question.[31] Domestic constitutions, only binding single nation-states, cannot address this issue alone. Global problems ultimately require constitutional pluralism.[32] The dispersion of power among various actors engenders the emergence of new constitutional mechanisms beyond the state: a series of phenomena that have been called 'constitutionalisation.'

2. *Forms of Constitutionalisation: The EU as a Case Study*

The European Union is one of the transnational contexts in which the scholarship has more extensively analysed and vigorously debated the effective existence of a process of constitutionalisation. This context will not be used as an example of the process of constitutionalisation of the digital ecosystem but will be analysed from a theoretical standpoint to demonstrate that the appearance of constitutional patterns beyond the nation-state does not neuter but rather complement parallel constitutionalising processes at multiple levels.

national Law: From Fragmentation to Regime Interaction and Politicization,' I CON 15 (2017), 671-704.

29 Peters, 'Compensatory Constitutionalism' (n. 27).

30 Dobner and Loughlin (n. 3), pt. 1.

31 See Gunther Teubner, 'Societal Constitutionalism: Alternatives to State-centred Constitutional Theory?' in: Christian Joerges, Inger-Johanne Sand and Gunther Teubner (eds), *Transnational Governance and Constitutionalism. International Studies in the Theory of Private Law* (Oxford: Hart Publishing 2004), 3-28.

32 Cf. Daniel Halberstam, 'Constitutional Heterarchy: The Centrality of Conflict in the European Union and the United States' in: Jeffrey L. Dunoff and Joel P. Trachtman (eds), *Ruling the World?: Constitutionalism, International Law, and Global Governance* (Cambridge: Cambridge University Press 2009), 326-355.

In 1951, six European countries created the European Coal and Steel Community.[33] In 1957, the same founding states established the European Economic Community (EEC) and the European Atomic Energy Community (Euratom). From a formal point of view, these three entities, which only in 1967 merged together to become the European Communities, were nothing but new international organisations established by a series of classical multilateral treaties. International agreements that were really called 'treaties,' and not charged with a constitutional flavour, as in the case of the statutes of the International Labour Organisation (ILO), the Food and Agriculture Organisation (FAO), or the United Nations Educational, Scientific and Cultural Organization (UNESCO), which had been formally denominated as 'constitutions.'[34]

Yet, in less than four decades, the very peculiarities of these apparently ordinary multilateral agreements would have allowed a seemingly conventional interstate organisation to become autonomous, 'constitutional legal order.'[35] Indeed, the scholarship soon acknowledged that precisely the power conferred by the treaties to the European Court of Justice had been the key factor of this transformation.[36] In 1963, in the *Van Gend en Loos* case, the court recognised the right of individuals to rely on the provisions of what at the time was Community law before national jurisdictions (so-called 'direct effect'), even if technically the treaty had been signed by, and therefore only bound, Member States.[37] The following year, in the

33 On the history of the European Union, see Wim F. V. Vanthoor, *A Chronological History of the European Union 1946-1998* (Cheltenham: Edward Elgar Publishing 1999).

34 See ILO, 'International Labour Organisation Constitution,' (1919), https://www.ilo.org/dyn/normlex/en/f?p=1000:62:0::NO:62:P62_LIST_ENTRIE_ID:2453907:NO; FAO, 'Constitution of the Food and Agriculture Organization of the United Nations,' (16 October 1945), http://www.fao.org/3/x5584e/x5584e0i.htm; UNESCO, 'Constitution of the United Nations Educational, Scientific, and Cultural Organization,' (16 November 1945), http://portal.unesco.org/en/ev.php-URL_ID=15244&URL_DO=DO_TOPIC&URL_SECTION=201.html.

35 See Paul Craig, 'Constitutions, Constitutionalism, and the European Union,' ELJ 7 (2001), 125-150; J.H.H. Weiler and Ulrich R. Haltern, 'The Autonomy of the Community Legal Order - Through the Looking Glass,' Harv. Int'l L.J. 37 (1996), 411-448 37.

36 See Eric Stein, 'Lawyers, Judges, and the Making of a Transnational Constitution,' The American Journal of International Law 75 (1981), 1-27; G. Federico Mancini, 'The Making of A Constitution For Europe,' CML Rev. 26 (1989), 595-614.

37 ECJ, *NV Algemene Transport- en Expeditie Onderneming van Gend & Loos v. Netherlands Inland Revenue Administration*, judgment of 5 February 1963, case no. 26/62, ECLI:EU:C:1963:1.

case *Costa v. Enel*, the European judges held that Community law prevails on national law, even if the latter is adopted subsequently (so-called 'supremacy of EU law').[38] In a series of cases from the early 1970s, the Court distinguished areas of exclusive Community competence and areas in which Member States were prevented from legislating unless the Community had not taken any positive action (so-called principles of 'exclusivity' and 'pre-emption').[39] In *Nold v. Commission*, the Luxembourg judges affirmed to be bound by fundamental rights, as recognised by Member States' constitutions and by international human rights treaties.[40] In *Les Verts*, the court, by acknowledging that the European Economic Community is founded on the rule of law, asserted that the treaty is the Community's 'basic constitutional charter.'[41] Last but certainly not least, in *Kadi*, the Court affirmed the need to protect EU fundamental rights also when giving effect to UN Security Council measures, *de facto* subjecting the latter to a sort of control of constitutionality against EU internal standards.[42]

This selection of examples provides an idea of how the European Court of Justice *constitutionalised* the European legal order. The Luxembourg judges, to use the words of Judge Mancini, read 'an unwritten bill of rights into Community law.' They elaborated a European constitution to complement a conventional international treaty. Weiler compares the set of rules elaborated by the Court with Microsoft Windows: they would be the operating system created to 'overlay' the European Community's Disk Operating System (DOS), public international law.[43] The European Court of Justice would have transformed an interstate organisation into a *sui generis* regime where *both* individuals *and* Member States are subject

38 ECJ, *Flaminio Costa v. ENEL*, judgment of 15 July 1964, case no. 6/64, ECLI:EU:C:1964:66.

39 Mancini (n. 36); J.H.H. Weiler, *The Constitution of Europe: 'Do the New Clothes Have An Emperor?' and Other Essays on European Integration* (Cambridge: Cambridge University Press 1999), 10-101.

40 ECJ, *J. Nold, Kohlen- und Baustoffgroßhandlung v. Commission of the European Communities*, judgment of 14 May 1974, case no. 4/73, ECLI:EU:C:1974:51.

41 ECJ, *Parti écologiste 'Les Verts' v. European Parliament*, judgment of 23 April 1986, case no. 294/83, ECLI:EU:C:1986:166.

42 ECJ (Grand Chamber), Yassin Abdullah Kadi and Al Barakaat International Foundation v. Council of the European Union and Commission of the European Communities, judgment of 3 September 2008, case no. C-402/05 P and C-415/05 P, ECLI:EU:C:2008:461.

43 J.H.H. Weiler and Joel P. Trachtman, 'European Constitutionalism and Its Discontents,' Nw. J. Int'l L. & Bus. 17 (1996-1997), 354-397 (357). The acronym 'DOS' refers to the basic Disk Operating System for personal computer.

to a common set of rules.[44] Constitutionalisation would mean not only a 'horizontal,' infra-institutional, re-distribution of power but also the configuration of a 'vertically integrated' legal order.[45]

In one of his papers, Francis Snyder investigated to what extent the EU has a 'constitution,' and observed that the answer to this question depends on what one means by such a term.[46] He recognised that, while the EU can be said to have a constitution in an empirical and material sense, respectively meaning a factual organisation and a set of norms ordering the polity, it is arguable that the EU has a formal constitution, and it is certain that the EU still lacks a subjective constitution, intended as a fundamental law approved by its people.[47] This observation allows us to better understand why the scholarly debate about the constitutionalisation of the EU did not confine itself to the analysis of the judicial activism that led the Court of Justice to distil a set of constitutional principles from an apparently conventional multilateral treaty, what in Snyder's terms would be the EU 'material' constitution. Indeed, the notion of constitutionalisation was also used to refer to the process of adoption of a 'formal' constitution of the EU and to the progressive democratisation of the European constitutional architecture, Snyder's 'subjective' constitution. Ingolf Pernice wrote: 'If we talk about the 'constitutionalisation' of the EU, in my view, this means talking about the citizens of the Union taking ownership of the Union […].'[48]

However, the problem for many authors is: who are the citizens of the Union? Can we have a European constitution without European *demos*?[49] These questions highlight one of the major difficulties that characterise

---

44 Weiler and Trachtman (n. 43).

45 Ibid., 356; see also Koen Lenaerts, 'Constitutionalism and the Many Faces of Federalism,' Am. J. Comp. L. 38 (1990), 205-264.

46 Francis Snyder, 'The Unfinished Constitution of the European Union: Principles, Processes and Culture' in: J.H.H. Weiler and Marlene Wind (eds), *European Constitutionalism Beyond the State* (Cambridge: Cambridge University Press 2003), 55-73.

47 See also Craig (n. 35).

48 Ingolf E. A. Pernice, 'The Treaty of Lisbon: Multilevel Constitutionalism in Action,' Columbia Journal of European Law 15 (2009), 349-407 (369).

49 See Dieter Grimm, 'Does Europe Need a Constitution?,' ELJ 1 (1995), 282-302; Jürgen Habermas, 'Remarks on Dieter Grimm's 'Does Europe Need a Constitution?'', ELJ 1 (1995), 303-307; see also Craig (n. 35); J.H.H. Weiler, 'In Defence of the Status Quo: Europe's Constitutional Sonderweg' in: J.H.H. Weiler and Marlene Wind (eds), *European Constitutionalism Beyond the State* (Cambridge: Cambridge University Press 2003), 7-24.

the constitutional discourse in the transnational context: translating the concept of the constitution beyond the state dimension.[50] This issue is currently one of the main subjects of investigation of the scholarly stream that studies phenomena of 'global constitutionalism.'[51] As is evident from those who support the idea that the EU should have a subjective constitution, the objective of analysing processes of constitutionalisation is not only to identify the emergence of constitutional patterns at the transnational level but also to normatively suggest potential avenues to instil constitutional values and mechanisms beyond the state. To this purpose, an exercise of translation is needed. One cannot simply reason with categories belonging to domestic constitutional theory. One would need a 'post-national' concept of the constitution.[52] It is in this way that, for example, Pernice salvages the idea of a European constitution without a homogenous European people.[53] A post-national constitution would differ from a domestic constitution, firstly, because it would *not* be an 'exclusive,' total constitution, comprehensively regulating the exercise of power within a territory, and, secondly, because it would not presuppose the pre-existence of a people living in a specific territory, given the fact that a post-national constitution does not necessarily need to 'constitute' a state. Transnational constitutions, such as the European one, would not aim to annihilate domestic constitutions but rather to integrate and/or compliment them within a 'multilevel' constitutional order.

50 Specifically on the issue of transferring democracy in transnational constitutions, see Gunther Teubner, 'Quod Omnes Tangit: Transnational Constitutions Without Democracy?,' J. L. & Soc. 45 (2018), 5-29; cf. Armin von Bogdandy and Sergio Dellavalle, 'The Lex Mercatoria of Systems Theory: Localisation, Reconstruction and Criticism from a Public Law Perspective,' Transnational Legal Theory 4 (2013), 59-82.

51 See Anne Peters, 'Global Constitutionalism' in: Michael T. Gibbons (ed), *The Encyclopedia of Political Thought* (Chichester: Wiley-Blackwell 2014), 1484-1487; Christine E. J. Schwöbel, 'Situating the Debate on Global Constitutionalism,' I.CON 8 (2010), 611-635; Antje Wiener et al., 'Global Constitutionalism: Human Rights, Democracy and the Rule of Law,' Global Constitutionalism 1 (2012), 1-15.

52 See Neil Walker, 'Postnational Constitutionalism and the Problem of Translation' in: J.H.H. Weiler and Marlene Wind (eds), *European Constitutionalism Beyond the State* (Cambridge: Cambridge University Press 2003), 27-54.

53 Pernice, 'The Treaty of Lisbon' (n. 48), 365 ff.

3. *Multilevel Theory: Reconciling Constitutional Dimensions*

Interestingly, in the study of phenomena of constitutionalisation, constitutional principles, the existence of which is identified or advocated at the transnational level, are not examined in isolation. The scholarship also investigated the nature of the link between domestic and transnational constitutional dimensions. These two constitutional levels would not amount to watertight legal orders but could rather be seen as two communicating vessels. Working in tandem, when the domestic constitutional law vessel reaches its point of saturation due to the materialisation of global challenges beyond its reach, the inner fluid would start flowing in the international constitutional law container.

This relationship has been described by the scholarship in different ways. Christian Tomuschat analysed the role of international treaties in terms of 'völkerrechtliche Nebenverfassungen,' literally translated as international law supplementary (or auxiliary) constitutions.[54] According to this vision, international and domestic law would no longer have different aims but would both share the goal of protecting individual rights.[55] International law's focus would be on human rights rather than on interstate relations. Therefore, one can conceive one single integrated 'individual-oriented' system composed of multiple levels.[56] In this way, international law acquires a new constitutional function, supplementing domestic law vis-à-vis global challenges and even imposing a series of principles superior to the will of the states.[57] In this way, Tomuschat eventually postulated a new hierarchy of legal sources, where international law acquires a foundational value for domestic constitutional law.[58]

54 Christian Tomuschat et al. (eds), *Veröffentlichungen der Vereinigung der Deutschen Staatsrechtslehrer, Heft 36: Der Verfassungsstaat im Geflecht der internationalen Beziehungen. Gemeinden und Kreise vor den öffentlichen Aufgaben der Gegenwart: Berichte und Diskussionen auf der Tagung der Vereinigung der Deutschen Staatsrechtslehrer in Basel vom 5. bis 8. Oktober 1977* (eBook, Berlin: De Gruyter 2013), 51; see von Bogdandy (n. 23).

55 For a comprehensive outline of Tomuschat's position, see von Bogdandy (n. 23); see also Anne Peters, *Beyond Human Rights: The Legal Status of the Individual in International Law* (Cambridge: Cambridge University Press 2016); Peters, 'Humanity as the A and Ω of Sovereignty' (n. 24).

56 Tomuschat, 'International Law: Ensuring the Survival of Mankind' (n. 23), 237.

57 See Tomuschat, 'Obligations Arising for States without or against Their Will' (n. 25).

58 Tomuschat, 'International Law: Ensuring the Survival of Mankind' (n. 23).

Other scholars, although sharing similar premises, did not support the view of a hierarchical relationship between transnational and domestic constitutional law. In the context of the European Union, for example, EU law and Member States' constitutions have rather been seen as complementary sources. According to Pernice, EU and national law would represent two 'formally autonomous systems,' which, however, in contrast to what happens in federal states, would mutually affect each other without implying the existence of a hierarchy.[59] For Pernice, both these sources would aim to protect citizens' rights and, as such, would form a *Verfassungsverbund*, a composed 'constitutional unit,' though being 'in permanent interdependency.'[60] Pernice baptises this complex architecture 'multilevel constitutionalism,' stressing that the presence of multiple layers does not necessarily imply the existence of a hierarchy.[61] Complementation between EU and national law would be a form of symbiotic interdependence.[62]

Lastly, Anne Peters further characterises the relationship between transnational and domestic law in a different way. Globalisation would have put national constitutions under pressure.[63] Principles of national constitutional law appear 'dysfunctional' or 'empty' vis-à-vis phenomena which transcend the territory of the state.[64] A significant portion of state power is progressively transferred to the transnational level. Both supranational

59 Pernice, 'The Treaty of Lisbon' (n. 48), 383.

60 Ibid., 352, 373, 379.

61 Ibid.; see also Ingolf Pernice, 'Multilevel Constitutionalism and the Treaty of Amsterdam: European Constitution-Making Revisited,' CML Rev. 36 (1999), 703-750. Pernice will subsequently apply the theory of multilevel constitutionalism to the broader context of the contemporary society amidst the challenges of the digital revolution: see Ingolf Pernice, 'Global Constitutionalism and the Internet. Taking People Seriously' in: Stefan Kadelbach and Rainer Hofmann (eds), *Law Beyond the State: Pasts and Futures* (Frankfurt a.M/New York: Campus Verlag 2016), 151-206; Ingolf Pernice, 'Risk Management in the Digital Constellation – A Constitutional Perspective,' October 2017, HIIG Discussion Paper Series No 2017-07.

62 See Weiler and Trachtman (n. 43).

63 Peters, 'Global Constitutionalism' (n. 51).

64 Jan Klabbers, Anne Peters and Geir Ulfstein, *The Constitutionalization of International Law* (Oxford: Oxford University Press 2009), 347; see also Peters, 'The Globalization of State Constitutions' (n. 13); cf. also Anneli Albi and Samo Bardutzky (eds), *National Constitutions in European and Global Governance: Democracy, Rights, the Rule of Law. National Reports* (The Hague/Berlin: Asser Press/Springer Open 2019), taking Peter's analysis as a starting point for an in-depth analysis focusing on the national constitutions of EU Member States.

organisations and multinational private actors emerge as new dominant players, but at the same time, domestic constitutions are no longer 'total constitutions,' capable of facing this mutated transnational scenario.[65] According to Peters, globalisation would not alter the assumption that the 'achievements of constitutionalism are to be preserved.'[66] She, therefore, affirms that this 'de-constitutionalisation' at the domestic level normatively requires a 'compensatory constitutionalisation on the international plane.'[67] The final result, as in the previous case, is always a constitutional conglomerate composed of *both* domestic and transnational constitutional instruments. However, the rationale behind the symbiosis between these two sources of law changes: national constitutional law has lost its centrality, it is no longer effective, and consequently needs to be compensated by a series of normative instruments emerging at the transnational level.

4. *Double Reflexivity: A Socio-legal Perspective*

In the first act of Rossini's *The Barber of Seville*, Figaro, the hairdresser of the title, enters the stage on the notes of the famous aria 'Largo al factotum della città.' Cesare Sterbini, the libretto's author, writes 'make the way for the factotum of the city' because effectively, in the eighteenth century, the barber was a man of all work: coiffeur, clock repairer, dentist and even surgeon. A role with a wide-ranging set of competencies that today – luckily – are exercised by several other professionals.

The nation-state, before the advent of globalisation, somehow resembled Figaro: it was like the eighteenth century's barber, the factotum of both domestic and interstate affairs. Interestingly, similarly to what has happened to the one-time multifaceted profession of the barber, the state, too, has progressively lost its societal centrality. Functions once exclusively exercised by the state are today delegated to transnational entities. Consequently, constitutional law is no longer exclusively national, rooted in a territory, linked to a specific people. Conversely, it is necessarily plural, and it appears as a complex conglomerate of several legal sources also emerging beyond the state dimension.

65 Peters, 'Compensatory Constitutionalism' (n. 27), 580.

66 Peters, 'Global Constitutionalism' (n. 51), 2.

67 Peters, 'Compensatory Constitutionalism' (n. 27), 580; see also Peters, 'The Refinement of International Law' (n. 28), 688 ff. on 'rapprochement' techniques in international norms.

The explanation of such a phenomenon provided by legal sociologists reflects the dynamics underlying the evolution of the role of the barber in the last three centuries. In the globalised society, boundaries no longer follow national frontiers but are defined according to functional specialisation.[68] One can identify 'a multiplicity of autonomous sub-systems.'[69] The economy, media, health, science: each one represents an independent regime. The barber is no longer, at the same time, the clock repairer, dentist and surgeon because these figures have emerged as autonomous, specialised professions. In the same way, vis-à-vis global phenomena which engender a sectoral differentiation, some prerogatives once concentrated in the hands of the state are today assumed by specialised transnational entities.

Such displacement of power at the transnational level generates a series of constitutional questions to which national constitutional law cannot, alone, provide an answer. Niklas Luhmann argued that the emergence of a 'world society' is not compensated by the emergence of world politics, and this circumstance would generate a twilight of constitutionalism at a global level.[70] Conversely, David Sciulli contended that in spite of rampant authoritarianism at the societal level, a constitutionalising trend was emerging in a plurality of societal institutions, such as those setting norms for specific professions in a collegial way.[71] Following this line, Gunther Teubner insisted that the functional differentiation of society would generate a 'societal' constitutionalisation: each societal sub-system would be able to develop its own constitutional norms.[72] According to this vision, constitutional law-making would not only involve traditional centres of

---

68 See Niklas Luhmann, *Theory of Society, Volume 1* (Stanford: Stanford University Press 2012); Teubner, 'Societal Constitutionalism: Alternatives to State-centred Constitutional Theory?' (n. 31).

69 Ibid., 8; for an overview of Teubner's position, see also Bianchi (n. 16), 44-71.

70 Niklas Luhmann, *Law as a Social System* (Oxford: Oxford University Press 2004).

71 See David Sciulli, *Theory of Societal Constitutionalism: Foundations of a Non-Marxist Critical Theory* (Cambridge: Cambridge University Press 1992); David Sciulli, *Corporate Power in Civil Society: An Application of Societal Constitutionalism* (New York: NYU Press 2001).

72 See Teubner, 'Societal Constitutionalism: Alternatives to State-centred Constitutional Theory?' (n. 31); Teubner, *Constitutional Fragments* (n. 11); Angelo Golia and Gunther Teubner, 'Societal Constitutionalism (Theory Of),' Max Planck Institute for Comparative Public Law & International Law Research Paper No. 2021-08, 15 March 2021, https://www.ssrn.com/index.cfm/en/; cf. Karl-Heinz Ladeur, 'The evolution of the law and the possibility of a 'global law' extending beyond the sphere of the state – simultaneously, a critique of the 'self-constitutionalisation' thesis,' Ancilla Iuris (2012), 220-255.

power but would flood into the 'peripheries of law.'[73] Constitutional law would no longer be relegated to the state dimension. On the contrary, domestic constitutions would become 'a sub-constitution among others.'[74]

A socio-legal perspective allows us to understand that the 'fragments' of this plural constitutional scenario are not only represented by norms developed in a state-centric dimension, be they at the national or supranational level, but also by principles shaped in the social context.[75] Teubner talks of the emergence of 'civil constitutions.'[76] A world unitary constitution is a utopia, as is to think that the activities of states and supranational organisations exhaust the potential articulations of global society's constitutionalisation. Such a process would be incremental, but, above all, hybrid and composite: 'a mix of autonomous and heteronomous law-making.'[77] Constitutionalisation is therefore understood as a legal *and* social process.[78] Teubner articulates it into several steps.[79]

The constitutional norms self-produced by autonomous sub-systems of society, such as the economy, media, health or science, would be initially only of 'constitutive,' and not 'limitative,' nature: they would amount to the fundamental rules which do not limit, but articulate the power of the dominant actors (e.g. private corporations), what Teubner calls the 'organised-professional' sphere of the society.[80] This situation triggers a reaction from its societal counterpart, the 'spontaneous' sector, which includes governmental agencies, civil society groups, trade unions, consumer protection organisations and alike. The latter generates 'constitutional learning impulses' by manifesting its expectations.[81] In a variety of ways,

73 Teubner, 'Societal Constitutionalism: Alternatives to State-centred Constitutional Theory?' (n. 31), 17.
74 Ibid., 15.
75 See Teubner, *Constitutional Fragments* (n. 11).
76 Teubner, 'Societal Constitutionalism: Alternatives to State-centred Constitutional Theory?' (n. 31).
77 Ibid., 17.
78 Teubner even argues that constitutionalisation is 'primarily a social process,' see Teubner, *Constitutional Fragments* (n. 11), 104.
79 See ibid.; for a clear schematisation of Teubner's conception of constitutionalisation, see Christoph B. Graber, 'Bottom-up Constitutionalism: The Case of Net Neutrality,' Transnational Legal Theory 7 (2016), 524-552.
80 Teubner, *Constitutional Fragments* (n. 11), 75 ff.; see also Gunther Teubner, 'Self-Constitutionalizing TNCs? On the Linkage of 'Private' and 'Public' Corporate Codes of Conduct,' Ind. J. Global Legal Stud. 18 (2011), 617-638; cf. Nicolas Suzor, *Lawless. The Secret Rules That Govern Our Digital Lives* (Cambridge: Cambridge University Press 2019).
81 Teubner, *Constitutional Fragments* (n. 11), 94 ff.

the spontaneous societal sphere exercises pressure on the organised-professional sector until those impulses are 'reflected,' translated in 'limitative' constitutional norms, rules which aim to restrict the power of dominant actors.[82]

Subsequently, the constitutional principles generated at the societal level are progressively 'juridified' under the form of secondary norms, rules about rule-making.[83] They become an integral part of the legal system through a process that Teubner defines as 'reflexive' due to a 'structural coupling' between law and society.[84] In other words, legal norms start to mirror societal rules, which, at their turn, reflect societal expectations. Lastly, legal rules within their own legal system can surge to the level of constitutional norms.[85] Either by directly being inserted in the text of the constitution or by testing in court their compatibility with the constitution.

Teubner's reconstruction, therefore, reveals that the process of constitutionalisation is characterised by a 'double reflexivity.'[86] The social and legal systems are mutually interwoven: their interaction could be metaphorically illustrated as 'an exchange of fluids between porous and permeable materials,' at the same time bottom-up and top-down.[87] Not only the national and transnational dimensions but also the social and legal planes are part of a unique set of 'communicating vessels.'[88] In contrast to natural law theory, one realises that constitutional principles are the product of a process of societal elaboration and, at the same time, that social norms are shaped and oriented by legal rules.[89]

---

82 Ibid., 94 ff.; cf. the concept of 'inclusionary pressures' in Thornhill (n. 2).

83 Teubner, *Constitutional Fragments* (n. 11), 105 ff.

84 Ibid., 102 ff.

85 Ibid., 110 ff.

86 Ibid., 102 ff.

87 Celeste, 'Digital Constitutionalism' (n. 11), 87; see Gunther Teubner, *Law as an Autopoietic System* (Oxford/Cambridge: Blackwell Publishers 1993); Graber (n. 79).

88 See Graber (n. 79), 551.

89 See Teubner, *Constitutional Fragments* (n. 11), 112; on the same line, see also Norberto Bobbio, *The Age of Rights* (Cambridge: Polity Press 1996).

III. Conceptualising the Process of Constitutionalisation of the Digital Ecosystem

This brief overview of how international law scholars have conceptualised phenomena of constitutionalisation helps us contextualise the emergence of constitutional counteractions to the challenges of digital technology. Recent technological advancements are an integral part of the process of globalisation, not to say that they represent one of its main triggers.[90] The incessant development of digital technology generates a series of challenges that are no longer confined to a specific territorial dimension but involve global realities. In this context, nation-states do not hold the monopoly of power anymore because global issues require forms of cooperation with a multiplicity of transnational actors, both supranational organisations and multinational private entities.

This complex, layered governance system is reflected at the constitutional level. National constitutions are no longer able, alone, to face the challenges of the digital revolution. The dispersion of power in the transnational dimension triggers the emergence of constitutional mechanisms beyond the state. Constitutional pluralism is a direct consequence of the phenomenon of globalisation. There is no single constitution for the digital ecosystem. The constitutional discourse is necessarily composite because no constitutional fragment, singularly taken, is able to address all the different portions of power. However, precisely this fragmentation becomes a new technique to provide a constitutional response to the issues of the global digital ecosystem.[91] The multifarious constitutional counteractions which are emerging to face the challenges of the digital revolution can eventually be regarded as the miscellaneous tesserae of a single mosaic. The different levels of this complex constitutional picture complement each other: like in a puzzle, the holes and bulges of each piece.

If one were able to gain an aerial view of this phenomenon in motion, one would not simply see the static image of a set of constitutional fragments, but one would observe a lively and effervescent phenomenon of constitutionalisation, intended, as seen in the previous sections, as

90 See Manuel Castells, *The Rise of the Network Society* (2nd edn, Oxford; Malden, MA: Blackwell Publishers 2000), 77-162; Manuel Castells, *The Power of Identity* (2nd edn, Chichester: Wiley-Blackwell 2010), 303-366.

91 See Andrzej Jakubowski and Karolina Wierczyńska (eds), *Fragmentation vs the Constitutionalisation of International Law: A Practical Inquiry* (London: Routledge 2016), pt. 3 who talk of 'constitutionalisation through fragmentation' in the context of international law.

the progressive introduction of constitutional values and principles in a dimension which formerly did not possess them.[92] Let us explore its main characteristics.

1. *Plurality and Fragmentation*

Firstly, such a phenomenon would not be uniform and unitary but articulated, plural and fragmented. The series of constitutional counteractions which have so far emerged to address the challenges of the digital revolution does not share the same level of elaboration. They materialise in a variety of contexts, adopting a multiplicity of forms and involving different actors, including private companies. Constitutional pluralism in the digital ecosystem goes beyond the scenario of interaction between national and supranational entities denoted with this name in the context of the EU.[93] Constitutional plurality in the Internet age involves also, and especially, non-state actors, such as the powerful multinational companies producing, managing and selling online products and services.[94]

However, notwithstanding this plurality, one cannot ignore that this composite scenario rotates around a common aim. All these different constitutional counteractions seek to instil basic constitutional principles and values in the mutated context of the digital ecosystem. In light of this observation, more accurate analysis of this phenomenon reveals that these constitutional counteractions do not simply emerge spontaneously in different contexts, as in an extemporaneous mushrooming phenomenon. One can argue that they are all necessary components of a single, coordinated system. Indeed, drawing inspiration from the multilevel theory developed in international law and EU law, one could claim that each of these constitutional fragments is needed to complement the action of the

92 Cf. Anne-Claire Jamart, 'Internet Freedom and the Constitutionalization of Internet Governance' in: Roxana Radu, Jean-Marie Chenou and Rolf H. Weber (eds), *The Evolution of Global Internet Governance* (Berlin/Heidelberg: Springer 2014), 57-76; for a critical analysis see Kettemann (n. 14).

93 See Armin von Bogdandy, 'Common Principles for a Plurality of Orders: A Study on Public Authority in the European Legal Area,' I.CON 12 (2014), 980-1007; for a succint overview of Weiler's position see J.H.H. Weiler, 'Prologue: Global and Pluralist Constitutionalism – Some Doubts' in: Gráinne de Búrca and J.H.H. Weiler (eds), *The Worlds of European Constitutionalism* (Cambridge: Cambridge University Press 2011), 8-18.

94 Following this line, see Teubner, *Constitutional Fragments* (n. 11).

other constitutional instruments.[95] They would represent the pieces of a single puzzle, in which each one interacts with, informs and complements the others.[96]

The existing scholarship analysed many of these counteractions singularly, sometimes normatively claiming in favour of their allegedly pivotal role in constitutionalising the digital ecosystem.[97] For instance, Berman advocated the importance of national constitutions in this context;[98] Fitzgerald and Suzor recognised the significance of private law as a way to instil constitutional values in the rules of private actors;[99] Karavas praised the ability of digital communities to self-constitutionalise themselves;[100] and Redeker, Gill and Gasser, lastly, underlined the potential constitutionalising function of Internet bills of rights.[101] Conversely, the reconstruction presented in this paper does not support any hierarchical vision.[102] The constitutional counteractions to the challenges of the digital revolution would work in tandem. Their ultimate value could only be appreciated if globally assessed in conjunction with the achievements of the other constitutional counteractions involved.

95 On the same line, see Pernice, 'Global Constitutionalism and the Internet. Taking People Seriously' (n. 61); Pernice, 'Risk Management in the Digital Constellation – A Constitutional Perspective' (n. 61).

96 This position would reflect what in international law has been presented as 'pluralisme ordonné': see Mireille Delmas-Marty, *Le Pluralisme Ordonné. Les Forces Imaginantes Du Droit (II)* (Paris: Éditions du Seuil 2006); see also Peters, 'The Refinement of International Law' (n. 28); further on the point, see Kettemann (n. 14).

97 See Celeste, 'Digital Constitutionalism' (n. 11).

98 Paul Berman, 'Cyberspace and the State Action Debate: The Cultural Value of Applying Constitutional Norms to 'Private' Regulation,' U. Colo. L. Rev. 71 (2000), 1263-1310.

99 Brian Fitzgerald, 'Software as Discourse? The Challenge for Information Law,' European Intellectual Property Review 22 (2000), 47-50; Nicolas Suzor, 'The Role of the Rule of Law in Virtual Communities,' Berkeley Technology Law Journal 25 (2010), 1817-1886.

100 Vaios Karavas, 'Governance of Virtual Worlds and the Quest for a Digital Constitution' in: Christoph B. Graber and Mira Burri-Nenova (eds), *Governance of Digital Game Environments and Cultural Diversity: Transdisciplinary Enquiries* (Cheltenham: Edward Elgar Publishing 2010), 153-169.

101 Dennis Redeker, Lex Gill and Urs Gasser, 'Towards Digital Constitutionalism? Mapping Attempts to Craft an Internet Bill of Rights,' International Communication Gazette 80 (2018), 302-319.

102 See Celeste, 'Digital Constitutionalism' (n. 11).

2. *Progressive Translation*

Secondly, the phenomenon of constitutionalisation of the digital ecosystem would not merely consist in a transfer of constitutional values and principles from one context to another. Such a process would unavoidably presuppose a progressive adaptation, translation of those values and principles in light of the characteristics of their context of destination – Teubner talks of a process of 'generalisation' and 're-specification.'[103] Key principles of contemporary constitutionalism cannot be simply transplanted in the transnational, global context to address the challenges of the digital revolution. One first needs to identify their quintessence and then implement it in the context of the digital ecosystem.

It is, therefore, apparent that the phenomenon of constitutionalisation does not temporally denote a *fait accompli* but rather describes – as the suffix -isation shows – a process. As an example, one could mention the introduction of rules about the protection of personal data, a set of legislation that in the past fifty years has evolved and is still evolving today. More generally, constitutional counteractions do not end with their conceptual spring but constantly ripe, develop, and change themselves. Consequently, the process of constitutionalisation does not merely correspond to the phase of formal codification of legal principles. It encompasses a broader process, which does not necessarily end with a codification in a formal constitution but could involve the stabilisation of a norm within different sets of rules, such as, for instance, at the level of corporate policy.

3. *Societal Input*

Finally, the process of constitutionalisation of the digital ecosystem is not uniquely top-down but also implicates bottom-up instances.[104] As the socio-legal scholarship on the phenomena of constitutionalisation shows, constitutional norms are first elaborated at the societal level. Law and society are not two airtight containers. The evolution of the law is closely connected to societal developments: it represents the result of the juridification of social norms, which are at their turn a reflection of societal pressures. If one adopts an empirical-functional approach, looking beyond

103 Teubner, 'Societal Constitutionalism: Alternatives to State-centred Constitutional Theory?' (n. 31).

104 See Graber (n. 79).

what is formally constitutional, it is possible to identify the emergence of constitutional counteractions even at the societal level. The process of constitutionalisation, therefore, cannot be exclusively confined to what is formally legal or, conversely, be uniquely characterised as a societal phenomenon.[105] Such compartmentalisation would simply not correspond to reality. The concept of constitutionalisation of the digital ecosystem pragmatically encompasses the full range of possible constitutional counteractions. Not only those are emerging in the legal dimension, but also mere societal initiatives: all the tesserae of the contemporary constitutional mosaic.

4. *Implementing Digital Constitutionalism*

Constitutionalisation and constitutionalism are not two interchangeable concepts. Unfortunately, the scholarship sometimes uses these two terms as synonyms.[106] However, the concept of constitutionalisation denotes a process.[107] The suffix -isation characterises a procedure, an operation; it implies the idea of advancement, progression, and evolution. It may have occurred in the past, be still ongoing, or be advocated in a normative sense for the future. Conversely, constitutionalism is a 'theory,'[108] a 'movement of thought,'[109] a 'conceptual framework,'[110] a 'set of values,'[111] an 'ideolo-

---

105 As some scholars seem to contend, see Celeste, 'Digital Constitutionalism' (n. 11).

106 Rossana Deplano, 'Fragmentation and Constitutionalisation of International Law: A Theoretical Inquiry,' European Journal of Legal Studies 6 (2013), 67-89.

107 See Girardeau A. Spann, 'Constitutionalization,' Saint Louis University Law Journal 49 (2005), 709-747; Karolina Milewicz, 'Emerging Patterns of Global Constitutionalisation: Towards a Conceptual Framework,' Ind. J. Global Legal Stud. 16 (2009), 413-436; Wiener et al. (n. 51); Jamart (n. 92).

108 Jeremy Waldron, 'Constitutionalism: A Skeptical View,' Philip A. Hart Memorial Lecture (2010), https://scholarship.law.georgetown.edu/hartlecture/4; see also Pernice, 'Global Constitutionalism and the Internet. Taking People Seriously' (n. 61), 7, according to whom constitutionalism is a form of 'theoretical thinking'.

109 Marco Bani, 'Crowdsourcing Democracy: The Case of Icelandic Social Constitutionalism,' (2012) SSRN Scholarly Paper ID 2128531.

110 Peer Zumbansen, 'Comparative, Global and Transnational Constitutionalism: The Emergence of a Transnational Legal-Pluralist Order,' Global Constitutionalism 16 (2012), 16-52.

111 Aoife O'Donoghue, *Constitutionalism in Global Constitutionalisation* (Cambridge: Cambridge University Press 2014).

gy.'[112] The suffix -ism does not imply the idea of the process; it denotes a more static concept.[113] An ism is 'a distinctive practice, system, or philosophy, typically a political ideology or an artistic movement.'[114] Constitutional-*isation* is the *process* of implementation of constitutional-*ism*. Constitutionalisation would put into effect the values of constitutionalism or, regarded the other way around; constitutionalism would provide the principles that permeate, guide, inform constitutionalisation.[115]

The constitutional counteractions that have emerged so far to address the challenges of the digital ecosystem are driven by the values of contemporary constitutionalism. Constitutionalism evolves. Its underlying values, ideals, principles have changed over time. Constitutionalism is today synonymous with key principles such as the values of democracy, the rule of law and the separation of powers.[116] Constitutionalism is associated with the idea of the protection of all fundamental rights that have been gradually recognised over the past few centuries, be they civil, political, socio-economic or cultural.[117] However, what today no longer holds true is the necessary connection of the idea of constitutionalism with the nation-state.

The values of constitutionalism historically ripened in the context of the state.[118] However, over the past few decades, in a society that has become increasingly more global, the centrality of the state has faded due to the emergence of other dominant actors in the transnational context.[119] The scholarship has therefore started to transplant the constitutional conceptual machinery beyond the state, including the concept of constitutionalism.[120] The myth of the compulsory link between constitutionalism

112 Celeste, 'Digital Constitutionalism' (n. 9); see Maurice Cranston, 'Ideology' https://www.britannica.com/topic/ideology-society; cf. Viellechner (n. 9).

113 See Waldron (n. 108); Milewicz (n. 107).

114 *Oxford Dictionary of English* (3rd edn, Oxford: Oxford University Press 2010).

115 Celeste, 'Digital Constitutionalism' (n. 11); on the same line, but more concretely, Martin Loughlin, 'What Is Constitutionalisation?' in: Petra Dobner and Martin Loughlin (eds), *The Twilight of Constitutionalism?* (Oxford: Oxford University Press 2010).

116 Cf. von Bogdandy (n. 93).

117 See András Sajó and Renáta Uitz, *The Constitution of Freedom: An Introduction to Legal Constitutionalism* (Oxford: Oxford University Press 2017), chs 1 and 10.

118 See Dieter Grimm, *Constitutionalism: Past, Present, and Future* (Oxford: Oxford University Press 2016).

119 See Dobner and Loughlin (n. 3).

120 See Grimm (n. 118), ch VII and VIII.

and the state is debunked.[121] As Hamann and Ruiz Fabri state, today 'it appears that any polity can be endowed with or can acquire constitutional features.'[122] Consequently, the constitutional dimension becomes plural, composite and fragmented.[123] If the values of constitutionalism remain the same in their essence, their articulation in specific contexts, within and beyond the state, necessarily becomes 'polymorphic.'[124]

Today, existing constitutional principles cannot anymore solve all the challenges of contemporary society. The external shape of constitutionalism necessarily changes again. New constitutional layers are progressively added to those already in existence. Novel principles emerge to articulate the fundamental values of constitutionalism in light of the problematic issues of contemporary society, including, but not limited to, the challenges of the digital revolution.[125] Constitutionalism is undergoing a mutation on multiple fronts. However, the scale of transformation prompted by the advent of the digital revolution is such that one can neatly distinguish the multiplicity of new normative layers addressing this phenomenon. A fresh sprout within the constitutionalist theory: what one could call 'digital constitutionalism.'[126]

---

121 See Ulrich K. Preuss, 'Disconnecting Constitutions from Statehood: Is Global Constitutionalism a Viable Concept?' in: Petra Dobner and Martin Loughlin (eds), *The Twilight of Constitutionalism?* (Oxford: Oxford University Press 2010).

122 Andrea Hamann and Hélène Ruiz Fabri, 'Transnational Networks and Constitutionalism,' International Journal of Constitutional Law 6 (2008), 481–508, 503.

123 Walker (n. 12); Teubner, *Constitutional Fragments* (n. 9); see also Paul Blokker, 'Modern Constitutionalism and the Challenges of Complex Pluralism' in: Gerard Delanty and Stephen P. Turner (eds), *Routledge International Handbook of Contemporary Social and Political Theory* (London: Routledge 2011).

124 See Walker (n. 14).

125 An example is the constitutionalisation of principles related to the protection of the environment, see David Marrani, 'The Second Anniversary of the Constitutionalisation of the French Charter for the Environment: Constitutional and Environmental Implications,' Environmental Law Review 10 (2008), 9-27, 9; see also Stefano Rodotà, *Il diritto di avere diritti* (Rome: Laterza 2012), 70.

126 First formulated in this sense in Edoardo Celeste, 'Digital Constitutionalism: Mapping the Constitutional Response to Digital Technology's Challenges,' 2018, HIIG Discussion Paper Series No. 2018-02; subsequently revised and amplified in Celeste, 'Digital Constitutionalism' (n. 9). In this last paper, at 88, I defined 'digital constitutionalism' as 'the ideology which aims to establish and to ensure the existence of a normative framework for the protection of fundamental rights and the balancing of powers in the digital environment'.

IV. Conclusion

A complex process of constitutionalisation is currently underway within contemporary society. A multiplicity of normative counteractions is emerging to address the challenges of the digital ecosystem. However, there is no single constitutional framer. As in a vast construction site, there are several contracting companies working at the same time, so, in a globalised environment, constitutionalisation simultaneously occurs at different societal levels. This is not only in the institutional perimeter of nation-states but also beyond: on the international plane, in the fiefs of the private actors, within the civil society. The sense of this Gordian knot of normative responses can be deciphered only if these emerging constitutional fragments are interpreted as complementary tesserae of a single mosaic. Each one is surfacing with a precise mission within the constitutional dimension, each one compensating for the shortcomings of the others in order to achieve a common aim: translating the core principles of contemporary constitutionalism in the context of the digital ecosystem.

International law scholarship offers a useful theoretical toolbox to understand the phenomenon of constitutionalisation of the digital ecosystem. International constitutional law first projected the notion of constitution beyond the state dimension by taking a functional approach, looking beyond the formal constitutional character of norms. International law scholarship understands that, in a globalised environment, national constitutional law faces a plurality of issues when projected in a transnational dimension. State constitutions cannot cope alone with transnational legal issues but necessitate the emergence of a plurality of parallel responses. The constitutional dimension becomes plural and composite, acting at the same time on multiple levels in a complementary fashion. Constitutionalisation is, therefore, a fragmented phenomenon, which finds its unity in its aim to instil constitutional values in an environment that is challenged by global legal issues.

Digital constitutionalism is the theoretical strand of contemporary constitutionalism that is adapting core constitutional values to the needs of the digital ecosystem. An evolution and not a revolution of contemporary constitutionalism. Digital constitutionalism advocates the perpetuation of foundational principles, such as the rule of law, the separation of powers, democracy and the protection of human rights, in the mutated scenario of the digital ecosystem. It triggers a complex process of constitutionalisation of the virtual environment, which occurs through a multiplicity of constitutional counteractions, within and beyond the state, through top-down and bottom-up complementary instances. Century-old values are translated into normative principles that can speak to the new social reality. Digital constitutionalism reiterates that digital technology does not create any secluded world where individuals are not entitled to their quintessential guarantees.

Part II
Security

Rethinking the African Union Non-Aggression Treaty as a Framework for Promoting Responsible State Behavior in Cyberspace

Uchenna Jerome Orji

Abstract In Africa, regional organisations have established legal measures with a view to promoting norms for cybersecurity governance. However, such measures do not explicitly address State aggression in cyberspace. This appears to create legal uncertainty in determining the behavior of States with respect to activities that can constitute aggression in cyberspace. In 2005, the African Union established the Non-Aggression and Common Defense Pact to put an end to 'conflicts of any kind within and among States in Africa.' Given the absence of an explicit regime to govern the behavior of Member States with respect to activities that can constitute aggression in cyberspace, the question arises as to whether it is possible to apply the AU Non-Aggression and Common Defense Pact for such purposes. This chapter considers the prospects and challenges of applying the Pact to State behavior in cyberspace. It makes a case for the application of the Pact's principles to promote responsible State behavior in cyberspace and suggests that such an approach will enhance legal certainty with respect to activities that can constitute aggression in cyberspace.

I. Introduction

It is no longer in doubt that cyber capabilities can be deployed to achieve objectives that endanger international peace and security.[1] Accordingly, there are growing concerns that malicious activities by State actors in cyberspace can harm the critical infrastructure and information systems of other States.[2] States are also increasingly developing offensive cyber capabilities for military objectives.[3] Consequently, there have been several calls for international norms and legal regimes to govern the conduct of

1 Alexander Kosenkov, 'Cyber Conflicts as a New Global Threat,' Future Internet, 8 (2016), 1–9.

2 Martin Rudner, 'Cyber – Threats to Critical National Infrastructure: An Intelligence Challenge,' International Journal of Intelligence and CounterIntelligence 3 (2013), 453–481.

3 James A. Lewis and Katrina Timlin, *Cybersecurity and Cyberwarfare: Preliminary Assessment of National Doctrine and Organization* (Washington, D.C.: CSIS 2012), 3–4; Paul Cornish et al., *On Cyber Warfare* (London: Chatham House 2010).

States with respect to cyber activities that can endanger international peace and security.[4]

Such calls have sought to promote international peace and stability by proposing the establishment of rules to ensure responsible State behavior in cyberspace.[5] More importantly, such calls have led to the establishment of international initiatives to promote cyber stability. For example, between 2004 and 2017, the United Nations convened the Group of Governmental Experts on Developments in the Field of Information and Telecommunications in the Context of International Security (UN GGE) to examine 'existing, and potential threats arising from the use of ICTs [information and communication technologies] by States' and also propose measures to address them, including norms, rules, principles and confidence-building measures.[6] Also, between 2009 and 2012, the Tallinn based NATO Cooperative Cyber Defence convened an international group of distinguished international law academics to study how international law applies to cyber oppressions conducted by States.[7] The study resulted in the publication of an academic and non-binding treatise known as the Tallinn Manual in 2013,[8] with the second edition in 2017.[9] Generally, the Manual clearly advances the position that general principles of existing international law apply to cyber operations without the need for new international legal regimes. At the regional level, intergovernmental organisations such as the Council of Europe, the European Union, the League of Arab States and the Shanghai Cooperation have sought to promote cyber stability by establishing legal and policy regimes on cybersecurity

4 Camino Kavanagh, *The United Nations, Cyberspace and International Peace and Security: Responding to Complexity in the 21st Century* (Geneva: UNIDR 2017), 15–36.

5 Uchenna J. Orji, *Cybersecurity Law and Regulation* (The Netherlands: Wolf Legal Publishers 2012), 75–76.

6 UN General Assembly, *Report of the Groups of Governmental Experts on Developments in the Field of Information and Telecommunications in the Context of International Security*, A/70/174 (22 July 2015), 2; UN Office for Disarmament, Fact Sheet – Developments in the Field of Information and Telecommunications in the Context of International Security (July 2018), 2.

7 The NATO Cooperative Cyber Defence Centre of Excellence, *The Tallinn Manual*, available at: https://cdcoe.org/research/tallinn-manual/.

8 Michael N. Schmitt (ed.), *Tallinn Manual on International Law Applicable to Cyber Warfare* (Cambridge: Cambridge University Press 2013).

9 Michael N. Schmitt (ed.), *Tallinn Manual 2.0 on the International Law Applicable to Cyber Operations* (Cambridge: Cambridge University Press 2017).

governance and the control of cybercrime.[10] In addition, bilateral arrangements that aim to promote cyber stability and responsible State behavior in cyberspace are beginning to feature prominently in the dialogue on international cyber stability.[11]

However, existing initiatives to promote cyber stability have not established binding rules that explicitly address the issue of State aggression in cyberspace. For example, the UN GGE addressed issues relating to State aggression in terms of its recommendation that a State should not conduct or knowingly support ICT[12] activity contrary to its obligations under international law, that intentionally damages or impairs the operation of critical infrastructure used to provide services to the public.[13] This recommendation is, however, not legally binding on States but rather provides a framework of international best practices that States should consider with a view to promoting cyber stability.

Similarly, in Africa, regional organisations have established legal measures with a view to promoting norms for cybersecurity governance. For example, the Economic Community of West African States (ECOWAS), the Common Market for Eastern and Southern Africa (COMESA), the Southern African Development Community (SADC) and the African Union (AU) have all adopted regional legal instruments requiring the Member States to establish cybersecurity governance measures.[14] Thus, in 2011, the ECOWAS adopted a Directive to fight cybercrime within the ECOWAS

10 The Council of Europe Convention on Cybercrime, 41 I.L.M. 282 (Budapest, 23 November 2001); Directive 2013/40/EU of 12 August 2013 on Attacks against Information Systems; Arab Convention on Combating Information Technology Offences (2010); Agreement between the Governments of Member States of the Shanghai Cooperation Organization on Cooperation in the Field of international Information Security (2009).

11 Alex Grigby, 'Overview of Cyber Diplomatic Initiatives' in: Global Commission on the Stability of Cyberspace, *Briefings from the Research Advisory Group to the Global Commission on the Stability of Cyberspace: Issue Brief No.1* (The Hague, NL: The Hague Centre for Strategic Studies 2018), 6–38 (24–26).

12 Information and communication technologies.

13 UN General Assembly, *Report of the Group of Government Experts on Developments in the Field of Information and Telecommunications in the Context of International Security*, A/70/174 (22 July 2015), 8 at paragraph 13(f).

14 ECOWAS Directive C/DIR.1/08/11 on Fighting Cybercrime (2011); Official Gazette of the Common Market for Eastern and Southern Africa (COMESA) 16 (2011); SADC Model Law on Computer Crime and Cybercrime (2012), available at https://www.itu.int/en/ITU-D/Cybersecurity/Documents/SADC%20Model%20Law%20Cybercrime.pdf; AU Convention on Cybersecurity and Personal Data Protection, EX.CL/846 (XXV) (2014).

region.[15] Also, in October 2011, COMESA developed a Model Cybercrime Bill with a view to providing a uniform framework that would serve as a guide for the development of cybercrime laws in the Member States.[16] In 2012, the SADC adopted a Model Law on Computer Crime and Cybercrime to serve as a guide for the development of cybersecurity laws in the SADC Member States.[17] And in 2014, the AU adopted the Convention on Cyber Security and Personal Data Protection to harmonize the laws of African States on electronic commerce, data protection, cybersecurity promotion and cybercrime control.[18]

The above regional instruments have been adopted following the increasing penetration of information ICTs in Africa[19] and their growing integration in critical national sectors.[20] However, Africa is yet to achieve a high level of digitalisation that is comparable to developed countries. Nevertheless, the rise of digitalisation in Africa has increased the reliance of critical national sectors on information infrastructure to the extent that the disruption of such infrastructure by accidents or cyber attacks will also cause the disruption of economic and social activities and public services in a manner that could trigger serious national security concerns.[21]

Recent research indicate that attacks on critical infrastructure are becoming 'frequent' in Africa, with banks particularly being the common targets and losing billions of dollars to theft and service disruption.[22] There are also reports of the critical infrastructure of African regional organisati-

---

15 ECOWAS Directive C/DIR.1/08/11 on Fighting Cybercrime, adopted at the Sixty-Sixth Ordinary Session of the ECOWAS Council of Ministers at Abuja, Nigeria (August 2011).

16 Official Gazette of the Common Market for Eastern and Southern Africa (COMESA) 16 (15 October 2011).

17 SADC Model Law on Computer Crime and Cybercrime (n.14).

18 African Union (AU) Convention on Cyber Security and Personal Data Protection, EX.CL/846(XXV), adopted at the 23rd Ordinary Session of the Assembly of the African Union (Malabo, 27 June 2014).

19 See the regional reports provided by GSMA, available at: https://www.gsma.com/mobileeconomy/.

20 Blessings T. Mbatha Dennis Ocholla and Cjb Le Roux, 'Diffusion and adoption of ICTs in Selected Government Departments in KwaZulu-Natal, South Africa,' Information Development 27 (2011), 51–263.

21 Uchenna J. Orji, 'Moving Beyond Criminal Law Responses to Cybersecurity Governance in Africa,' International Journal of Criminal Justice 3 (2021), 60–98 (70).

22 Nathaniel Allen, 'Africa's Evolving Cyber Threats,' African Center for Strategic Studies, 19 January 2021, available at https://africacenter.org/spotlight/africa-evolving-cyber-threats/.

ons being targets of hacking. For example, in January 2018, China denied that the computer network equipment it had supplied to the AU allowed it access to confidential information from the AU.[23] In December 2020, it was reported that Chinese hackers had been accessing the security footage from cameras installed at the AU headquarters.[24] Also, in December 2020, it was reported that Facebook found that Russians and individuals affiliated with the French military were using fake Facebook accounts to conduct dueling political information operations in Africa.[25]

However, to a large extent, the focus on cybersecurity governance in Africa appears to be mainly directed towards curbing cybercrimes.[26] Accordingly, although African regional cybersecurity governance measures aim to promote cyber stability, they do not explicitly address the issue of State aggression in the cyber domain. This appears to create legal uncertainty in terms of determining the behavior of African States with respect to activities that can constitute aggression in cyberspace. In 2005, the AU established the Non-Aggression and Common Defense Pact[27] with a view 'to putting an end to *conflicts of any kind within and among States in Africa*' and 'promoting cooperation in the area of non-aggression and common defense.'[28] Could this instrument thus fill the gap and be applied in the context of cyberspace? The aim of this chapter is to consider the prospects and challenges of applying the Pact to State behavior in cyberspace. In so doing, the chapter will make a case for the application of the Pact's principles to promote responsible State behavior in cyberspace. It will suggest that the application of the Pact's principles to promote responsible State behavior in cyberspace would enhance legal certainty with regard to respect to activities that can constitute aggression in cyberspace.

This chapter comprises four sections. Following this introduction, the second section explores the concept of cyber stability within the context of promoting responsible State behavior. The third section discusses the principles of the Pact and considers how they can be applied as a frame-

---

23 Center for Strategic and International Studies (CSIS), *Significant Cyber Incidents* (Washington, D.C.: CSIS 2021), 35, available at https://www.csis.org/programs/strategic-technologies-program/significant-cyber-incidents.

24 Ibid, 7.

25 Ibid.

26 Orji (n. 21), 60–98.

27 AU Non-Aggression and Common Defense Pact (Addis Ababa, 2005), opened for signature 31 January 2005 (entered into force 18 December 2009).

28 Preamble, AU Non-Aggression and Common Defense Pact (2005), (emphasis added).

work to govern activities that can constitute aggression in cyberspace. It also considers the limits of the Pact in governing cyber activities that can constitute aggression. The fourth section concludes the chapter.

II. Cyber Stability and Responsible State Behavior in Cyberspace

The concept of 'cyber stability' has been defined in various contexts. For example, 'cyber stability' has been defined as 'the ability of all countries to utilize the Internet for both national security purposes and economic, political and social benefit while refraining from activities that could cause unnecessary suffering and destruction.'[29]

Another definition refers to 'cyber stability' as 'a geostrategic condition whereby users of the cyber domain enjoy the greatest possible benefits of political, civil, social and economic life while preventing and managing conduct that may undermine those benefits at the national, regional and international level.'[30] It has been observed that this definition creates a basis from which to identify when stability is the goal and also to discern what is potentially relevant, useful and strategic information about activity in the cyber domain from what is not.[31]

'Cyber stability' has also been defined as referring to 'a state of relations between States characterised by the absence of serious hostile cyber actions against one another, where the States have a sufficient common understanding of each other's capabilities and intentions so as to be inclined generally to avoid such actions, likely associated with a common belief that the costs of such conduct would outweigh the benefits.'[32]

The Report on a Framework for International Cyber Stability which was commissioned by the United States, refers to 'cyber stability' as 'an environment where all participants, including nation-States, non-governmental organisations, commercial enterprises, and individuals, can positively and dependably enjoy the benefits of cyberspace; where there are benefits

---

29 Jody R. Westby, 'Cyber War v. Cyber Stability,' presented at the 42nd session of the World Federation of Scientists International Seminars on Planetary Emergencies (Eric, Italy, 19–22 August 2009), 1.

30 Lisa Rudnick, Derek B. Miller and Leeor Levy, *Towards Cyber Stability: A User Centered Tool for Policy Makers* (Geneva: UNIDR 2015), 7.

31 Ibid.

32 R. Gorchayev et al., *Cyber Deterrence and Stability: Assessing Cyber Weapon Analogues through Existing WMD Deterrence and Arms Control Regimes* (Washington D.C.: US Department of Energy, 2017), 1.16.

to cooperation and to avoidance of conflict, and where there are disincentives for these actors to engage in malicious cyber activity.'[33]

A common thread that appears to run through the above definitions of cyber stability is that the concept aims to prevent conflict or hostilities in cyberspace. Therefore, the concept can be used to generally classify measures that aim to prevent or minimize conflict between actors, including States in cyberspace. As such, the concept aims to minimize cyber activities that can escalate tensions between States. However, despite the above definitions of cyber stability, the concept is to a large extent regarded as an emerging concept that has not been developed as an analytic category.[34]

On the other hand, the concept of 'responsible State behavior' is regarded as vague, and its definition is generally dependent on the context in which it is used and therefore varies in each context.[35] For example, the general concept of responsible behavior in cyberspace has been defined as 'behavior by a given actor in a given set of circumstances that can be said to conform to the laws, customs and norms generally expected from that actor in those circumstances.'[36] If the elements of the above definition were to be adapted to the context of State behavior in cyberspace, 'responsible State behavior' would simply refer to a State's compliance with established laws, customs and norms generally expected of such State in cyberspace. The concept of responsible State behavior in cyberspace aims to promote cyber stability by requiring States to ensure that cyber activities which are conducted within their jurisdiction do not cause harm to other individuals or infrastructure located in another jurisdiction. This implies that a State should ensure that cyber activities conducted within its jurisdiction or on the basis of its authority do not escalate cyber instability or create conflicts.

Generally, the need to promote cyber stability through responsible State behavior arises from the increasing interconnectedness of information networks in different countries. This state of affairs has ushered in a new age of network interdependence where the security of each country's network is also dependent on the actions of State and non-State actors around the

33 International Security Advisory Board, *Report on a Framework for International Cyber Stability* (US Department of State, 2014) Appendix B.1, 33.

34 Rudnick (n. 30), 7.

35 Andrijana Gavrilovic, 'What is Responsible Behavior in Cyberspace,' Diplo, 30 October 2018, available at https://www.diplomacy.edu/blog/webinar-what-responsible-behaviour-cyberspace/.

36 Gavrilovic (n. 35).

world.[37] Hence, malicious cyber activities conducted in a particular State can harm individuals or infrastructure located in another State. This also has the potential to affect relations between States in a manner that endangers international peace and security. Therefore, the concept of responsible State behavior in cyberspace requires States to promote cyber stability by ensuring governance responsibility for cyber activities on their territory.

Within the context of cyber stability, the concept of responsible State behavior can be seen as enshrining elements of the international law principle on State responsibility for transboundary harm. This principle has been recognised in different contexts in the *Corfu Channel Case*, where the International Court of Justice (ICJ) held that a State might not 'allow knowingly, its territory to be used for acts contrary to the rights of other States,'[38] and also in the *Trail Smelter Case*.[39] This principle has been recognised in international law that applies to the regulation of communication networks. For example, Article 38.5 of the Constitution of the International Telecommunication Union (ITU) requires Member States not to cause harm to the operation of telecommunication installations in other States.[40] However, while existing principles of international law on State responsibility can be broadly interpreted to promote responsible State behavior in cyberspace, they do not explicitly address activities that can constitute aggression in cyberspace. In the next section, the chapter will consider how the AU Non-Aggression and Common Defense Pact can be applied to govern the behavior of African States with respect to activities that can constitute aggression in cyberspace.

III. The AU Non-Aggression and Common Defense Pact

Africa comprises 55 sovereign States and is classified as the world's second-largest and second most-populous continent after Asia, with a terrestrial mass of 30,2044,049 million square kilometers and a human population of

---

37 Harry D. Raduege, 'Fighting Weapons of Mass Disruption: Why America Needs a 'Cyber Triad' in: Andrew Nagorski (ed.), *Global Cyber Deterrence: Views from China, U.S., Russia, India, and Norway* (New York: East West Institute 2010), 5.

38 ICJ, *Corfu Channel Case* (UK v. Albania), merits, judgement of 9 April 1949, ICJ Reports 1949, 4, at paragraph 22.

39 *The Trail Smelter Arbitration Case (United States of America v. Canada)*, (1938) 3R.I.A.A 1905; Judicial Decision, 'The Trail Smelter Arbitral Decision,' AJIL *35* (1941), 684.

40 Art. 38.5 Constitution of the ITU (2010).

over one billion people.[41] The African Union (AU) is the most prominent regional intergovernmental organisation in Africa, and its membership comprises and unites all the 55 sovereign States in Africa.[42]

The African continent has been challenged by incidents of inter-state conflicts.[43] This state of affairs led the AU to declare that 'the scourge of conflicts in Africa constitutes a major impediment to the socio-economic development of the continent.'[44] Some causes of Africa's interstate conflicts have been traced to colonialism and the subsequent processes of decolonisation and State formation, as well as the ensuring crisis of nation-building.[45] In this regard, it has been observed that 'modern Africa was created by colonial powers out of ethnic and regional diversities [with] gross inequalities in power relations and in the uneven distribution of national wealth and development opportunities.'[46] In some cases, colonial boundaries 'forced starkly different rival cultures to cohabit within the confines of a single State.'[47] This resulted in the creation of fragile political units which divided ethnic groups in several cases while also combining many warring ethnic groups in many cases. Given this state of affairs, most inter-state conflicts in post-colonial Africa have arisen as a result of the boundaries set by colonial powers to demarcate the continent into States.[48]

In order to address the incidence of inter-state conflicts in Africa, the Constitutive Act of the AU recognizes the need to promote peace, security and stability as a prerequisite for implementing Africa's development and integration agenda.[49] Accordingly, the core objectives of the AU include to 'achieve greater unity and solidarity between African countries and the

41 Matt Rosenberg, *The 7 Continents Ranked by Size and Population* (April 2020), available at https://www.thoughtco.com/continents-ranked-by-size-and-population-4163436.

42 'AU Member States,' available at https://au.int/en/member_states/countryprofiles2.

43 Aremu J. Olaosebikan, 'Conflicts in Africa: Meaning, Causes, Impact and Solution,' Africa Research Review 4 (2010), 551.

44 Preamble to the Constitutive Act of the African Union (2000).

45 Herman J. Cohen, 'What Should We Do When Nations Get Angry?,' *Nexus Africa*, 1 (1995), 11–14; Fonken Achankeng, 'Conflict Resolution in Africa: Engaging the Colonial Factor,' AJCR, 2 (2013), available at https://www.accord.org.za/ajcr-issues/%Ef%BFbconflict-and-conflict-resolution-in-Africa/.

46 Cohen (n. 45).

47 Olaosebikan (n. 43), 551.

48 Timothy Gachanga, 'Inter-State Conflicts in Africa,' 7 January 2018, available https://medium.com/@gachannga/inter-state-conflicts-in-africa-2f378a03fa8.

49 Preamble to the Constitutive Act of the AU.

peoples of Africa,'[50] and to 'promote peace, security and stability on the continent.'[51] In addition, the Constitutive Act of the AU establishes a range of principles to prevent inter-state conflicts. These principles include: a) the prohibition of the use of force among the Member States;[52] b) the peaceful co-existence of the Member States and their right to live in peace and security;[53] c) the peaceful resolution of conflicts among the Member States;[54] and d) the establishment of a common defense policy for the AU.[55]

On the basis of the above objectives and principles, the AU has adopted a range of related regional security instruments such as the Protocol Relating to the Establishment of the Peace and Security Council of the African Union,[56] the Common African Defense and Security Policy,[57] and the Non-Aggression and Common Defense Pact. The Protocol Relating to the Establishment of the Peace and Security Council of the African Union creates a framework for the prevention and resolution of conflicts and also establishes the AU Peace and Security Council as collective security and early-warning arrangement to facilitate timely and efficient response to conflict and crisis situations in Africa.[58] The Common African Defense and Security Policy aims to ensure collective responses to both internal and external security threats that affect Africa and serve as a framework for promoting defense cooperation between the African States.[59] On the other hand, the Non-Aggression and Common Defense Pact aims to prevent aggression among African States while also promoting cooperation amongst them in the areas of common defense.[60] However, the discussion in this chapter will focus on the Non-Aggression and Common Defense Pact.

The AU Non-Aggression and Common Defense Pact recognizes the devastating impact of intra and inter-state conflicts on peace, security,

---

50 Art. 3 lit. a) Constitutive Act of the AU.
51 Art. 3 lit. f) Constitutive Act of the AU.
52 Art. 4 lit. f) Constitutive Act of the AU.
53 Art. 4 lit. i) Constitutive Act of the AU.
54 Art. 4 lit. f) Constitutive Act of the AU.
55 Art. 4 lit. d) Constitutive Act of the AU.
56 Protocol Relating to the Establishment of the Peace and Security Council of the AU.
57 Solemn Declaration On A Common African Defense and Security Policy.
58 Art. 2 Protocol Relating to the Establishment of the Peace and Security Council of the AU.
59 Protocol Relating to the Establishment of the Peace and Security Council of the AU.
60 Art. 2 AU Non-Aggression and Common Defense Pact.

stability and economic development in Africa and therefore seeks 'to put an end *to conflicts of any kind within and among States in Africa* in order to create conditions for socio-economic development and integration of the continent as well as the fulfillment of the aspirations of [African] peoples.'[61] As such, the Pact aims to address threats to peace, security and stability in the continent so as to ensure the wellbeing of African peoples.[62] The Pact entered into force on 18 December 2009 after its ratification by 15 Member States of the AU. As of August 2021, 44 Member States of the AU had signed the Pact, while 22 Member States had ratified it.[63] To a large extent, the Pact is regarded as containing by far 'the most elaborate political commitment of African States not to commit aggression against each other.'[64] To minimize ambiguity in its interpretation, the Pact provides elaborate definitions of terms such as 'aggression,'[65] 'acts of subversion,'[66] 'non-aggression,'[67] 'destabilisation,'[68] 'threat of aggression,'[69] and 'transnational organised criminal group.'[70]

The objectives of the Pact include: a) to promote cooperation among the African States in the areas of non-aggression and common defense; b) to promote peaceful co-existence in Africa; c) to prevent intra and inter-state conflicts; and d) to ensure that disputes between the Member States, including a breach of the peace and security within the AU, are resolved by peaceful means.[71]

In line with the above objectives, the Pact defines a framework for the AU to address situations of aggression in accordance with African regional instruments such as the Constitutive Act of the AU, the Protocol on the Establishment of the Peace and Security Council and the Common African Defense and Security Policy.[72]

---

61 Preamble AU Non-Aggression and Common Defense Pact.

62 Ibid.

63 The Status List AU Non-Aggression and Common Defense Pact, https://au.int.

64 Global Institute for the Prevention of Aggression, *Preventing Aggression in the African Context*, available at: https://crimeofaggression.info.

65 Art. 1 lit. c) Non-Aggression and Common Defense Pact.

66 Art. 1 lit. a) Non-Aggression and Common Defense Pact.

67 Art. 1 lit. p) Non-Aggression and Common Defense Pact.

68 Art. 1 lit. i) Non-Aggression and Common Defense Pact.

69 Art. 1 lit. w) Non-Aggression and Common Defense Pact.

70 Art. 1 lit.x) Non-Aggression and Common Defense Pact.

71 Art. 2 lit. a) Non-Aggression and Common Defense Pact.

72 Art. 2 lit. b) Non-Aggression and Common Defense Pact.

1. *The Concept of 'Aggression' and 'Collective Security' under the Pact*

The Pact elaborately defines 'aggression' as 'the use, intentionally, and knowingly, of an armed force or *any other hostile act* by a State, a group of States, an organisation of States or non-State actor(s) or by any foreign or external entity, against the sovereignty, political independence, territorial integrity and human security of the population of a State party to this Pact, which are incompatible with the Charter of the United Nations or the Constitutive Act of the African Union...'[73] To some extent, the above definition of aggression appears to mirror elements of the definition of aggression under UN Resolution 3314 (XXIX) due to its adoption of elements such as 'the use ... of armed force,' 'against the sovereignty,' 'territorial integrity,' or 'political independence of a State.'[74] However, the definition under the Pact goes beyond Resolution 3314 (XXIX) because it encompasses more elements and appears more extensive in its elaboration of the meaning of aggression. Some elements of the above definition of aggression under the Pact appear to create a broad scope for classifying hostile cyber activities conducted by a Member State against another Member State within the meaning of aggression. For example, the Pact does not restrict the definition of aggression to the use of 'armed force' but includes 'any other hostile act' conducted by a State or non-State actor against the 'sovereignty' and 'human security' of the population of a Member State. In modern times, hostile acts against the sovereignty of a State would include the disruption of its critical information infrastructure given the strategic importance of such infrastructure to national security.[75] As such, under the Pact, there is scope for classifying a Member State's cyber activities that disrupt another Member State's critical information infrastructure as a hostile act that fits into the definition of aggression under the Pact.

The Pact's definition of 'human security' further provides the basis for qualifying a Member State's hostile cyber activities that affect another Member State's population as fitting within the definitional scope of aggression. In this regard, the Pact defines 'human security' as 'the security of the individual in terms of satisfaction of his/her basic needs. It also includes the creation of social, economic, political, environmental and cultural conditions necessary for the survival and dignity of the individual,

73 Art. 1 lit. c) Non-Aggression and Common Defense Pact (Emphasis added).
74 UNGA Res 3314 (XXIX) of 14 December 1974, A/RES/3314 (XXIX), Art. 1.
75 Art. 1 AU Convention on Cyber Security and Personal Data Protection.

the protection of and respect for human rights, good governance and the guarantee for each individual of opportunities and choices for his/her full development.'[76] Within the context of the above definition, a Member State's hostile cyber acts (such as denial of service attacks, attacks on personal data, or cyber attacks that target critical sectors, including banking and financial systems, health institutions or other critical services) against the population of another Member State would qualify as a hostile act against the human security of the targeted Member State's population. This is because such cyber attacks have the potential to make individuals insecure in the information society while also reducing opportunities for the protection of human rights such as the right to privacy and freedom of expression, which are guaranteed under the Universal Declaration of Human Rights[77] and the International Convention on Civil and Political Rights (ICCPR).[78] In addition, such attacks can hinder the potential of ICTs to enhance social and economic development and promote living standards, which would ultimately affect human security.

The Pact classifies specific acts that will constitute 'acts of aggression.' In this regard, it provides that 'the following shall constitute acts of aggression, *regardless of a declaration of war by a State, group of States, organization of States, or non-State actor(s) or by any foreign entity*:

(i) the use of armed forces against the sovereignty, territorial integrity and political independence of a Member State, or any other action inconsistent with the provisions of the Constitutive Act of the African Union and the Charter of the United Nations;
(ii) the invasion or attack by armed forces against the territory of a Member State, or military occupation, however temporary, resulting from such an invasion or attack, or any annexation by the use of force of the territory of a Member State or part thereof;
(iii) the bombardment of the territory of a Member State *or the use of any weapon against the territory of a Member State*;
(iv) *the blockade of the ports, coasts or airspace of a Member State*;
(v) the attack on the land, sea or air forces, or marine and fleets of a Member State;

76 Art. 1 lit. k) AU Non-Aggression and Common Defense Pact.
77 Universal Declaration on Human Rights, UNGA Res 217A (III) of 10 December, 1948, A/RES/217(III),) Arts. 12 and 19.
78 Arts. 12 and 19 International Covenant on Civil and Political Rights (ICCPR).

(vi) the use of the armed forces of a Member State which are within the territory of another Member State with the agreement of the latter, in contravention of the conditions provided for in this Pact;

(vii) *the action of a Member State in allowing its territory to be used by another Member State for perpetrating an act of aggression against a third State*;

(viii) *the sending by, or on behalf of a Member State or the provision of any support to armed groups, mercenaries, and other organized transnational criminal groups which may carry out hostile acts against a Member State*, of such gravity as to amount to the acts listed above, or its substantial involvement therein;

(ix) *the acts of espionage which could be used for military aggression* against a Member State;

(x) *technological assistance of any kind*, intelligence and training to another State for use in committing acts of aggression against another Member State; and,

(xi) the encouragement, support, harbouring or provision of any assistance for the commission of terrorist acts and other violent trans-national organized crimes against a Member State.'[79]

While the above classification of acts that constitute aggression under the Pact adapt several elements from UN Resolution 3314 (XXIX), the Pact however includes additional elements such as acts of espionage, technological assistance and the support of violent transnational organized groups by a Member State.

Article 2(c) of the Pact declares that 'any aggression or threat of aggression against any Member State shall be deemed to constitute a threat or aggression against all Member States of the Union.'[80] This provision implies that the Pact operates a collective security principle. The concept of collective security has several definitions.[81] For example, 'collective security' has been defined as 'a system whereby States commit not to use force unilaterally in their mutual relations by preferring the peaceful settlement of disputes and to support a collective decision aimed at stopping any

79 Art. 1 lit. c) AU Non-Aggression and Common Defense Pact (Emphasis added).

80 Art. 2 lit. c) AU Non-Aggression and Common Defense Pact.

81 Joseph C. Ebegulem, 'The Failure of Collective Security in the Post World Wars I and II International System,' *Transcience*, 2 (2011), 23–29 (23 f.).; Stefan Aleksovski, Oliver Bakreski and Biljana Avramovska, 'Collective Security – The Role of International Organizations- Implications in the International Security Order,' Mediterranean Journal of Social Sciences 5 (2014), 274–282 (274 f.).

act of aggression or common threat to peace.'[82] Following this definition, within the context of Article 2(c), hostile cyber activities conducted by one or more Member States against another Member State would be considered as aggression against all Member States of the AU and would therefore trigger a response from all Members of the Union. In this regard, the Pact imposes obligations on the Member States 'to provide a mutual assistance towards their common defense and security [with respect to] any aggression or threats of aggression,'[83] and 'individually and collectively respond by *all available means* to aggression or threats of aggression against any Member State.'[84]

The Pact does not define the meaning of 'by all available means.' However, literally, the phrase would imply that the Member States are to adopt all means at their disposal, including military, diplomatic and economic measures in responding to aggression or threats of aggression against any Member State. The collective security principle under the Pact appears largely similar to Article 5 of the North Atlantic Treaty, which provides that:

> 'The Parties agree that an armed attack against one or more of them in Europe or North America shall be considered an attack against them all, and consequently, they agree that, if such an armed attack occurs, each of them, in the exercise of the right of individual or collective self-defence recognised by Article 51 of the Charter of the United Nations, will assist the Party or Parties so attacked by taking forthwith, individually and in concert with the other Parties, such action as it deems necessary, including the use of armed force, to restore and maintain the security of the North Atlantic area. *Any such armed attack and all measures taken as a result thereof shall immediately be reported to the Security Council. Such measures shall be terminated when the Security Council has taken the measures necessary to restore and maintain international peace and security.*'[85]

82 Balingene Kahombo, 'The Peace of and Security Council of the African Union: Rise or Decline of Collective Security in Africa,' *KFG Working Paper Series* 23 (2018), 5. See also Evert Jordan, 'Collective Security in Africa: The Tension between Theory and Practice,' *Strategic Review for Southern Africa*, 39 (2017), 160–184 (163 f.).

83 Art. 4 lit. a) AU Non-Aggression and Common Defense Pact.

84 Art. 4 lit.b) AU Non-Aggression and Common Defense Pact.

85 Art. 5 NATO (emphasis added).

However, unlike the North Atlantic Treaty, the Pact does not include a provision that measures taken by the Member States when individually and collectively responding to aggression or threats of aggression against any Member State shall be reported to the United Nations Security Council or terminated upon measures taken by the Council to restore and maintain peace and security. In practice, the collective security regime in Article 5 of the North Atlantic Treaty has been invoked once on 12 September 2001, following the terrorist attacks on the United States on September 11, 2001;[86] however, there is no record that the collective security in AU Non-Aggression and Common Defense Pact has ever been invoked.

2. *Prospects of Applying the Pact to Promote Responsible State Behavior in Cyberspace*

A major basis for considering the application of the Pact as a framework for promoting responsible State behavior in cyberspace arises from its declaration to end '*conflicts of any kind within and among States in Africa* and promote cooperation in the areas of non-aggression and common defense.'[87] By this explicit declaration, the Pact appears to have been drafted with foresight to include and accommodate future technological developments that can create conflicts among States in Africa. This makes the Pact relevant in the context of State aggression in cyberspace. In addition, the Pact's broad definition of aggression to include '*...any other hostile act* by a State, a group of States, an organization of States or non-State actor(s) or by any foreign or external entity...'[88] provides another major basis for considering the application of the Pact as an African framework for promoting responsible State behavior in cyberspace. As noted earlier, hostile acts that violate the sovereignty of a State would include attacks that target its critical information infrastructure, given the strategic importance of such infrastructure to national security.

Furthermore, the Pact's definition of aggression includes elements such as 'the *use of any weapon against the territory of a Member State*;' 'the blockade of the ports, coasts or airspace of a Member State;' 'attack on the land, sea or air forces, or marine and fleets of a Member State;' 'acts of espionage

---

86 North Atlantic Treaty Organisation, 'Collective Defence – Article 5,' available at: https://www.nato.int.

87 Preamble AU Non-Aggression and Common Defense Pact (emphasis added).

88 Art. 1 lit. c) AU Non-Aggression and Common Defense Pact (emphasis added).

which could be used for military aggression against a Member State;' 'technological assistance of any kind;' 'the action of a Member State in allowing its territory, to be used by another Member State for perpetrating an act of aggression against a third State;' and, 'the provision of any support to armed groups, mercenaries, and other organized transnational criminal groups which may carry out hostile acts against a Member State.'[89]

The above elements provide a broad scope for considering the Pact as a framework for promoting responsible State behavior in cyberspace. For example, 'any weapon' within the context of the Pact would technically include a cyber weapon such as malware, given that such weapon can be used to execute an attack against critical information infrastructure located in the territory of a Member State. Also, cyber attacks can be used to conduct a blockade of Member State's ports, coasts or airspace,[90] while the use of a cyber weapon to immobilize the armed forces or marine and fleets of a Member State would technically fit within the Pact's definition of aggression. This also applies where a Member State engages in acts of cyber espionage which could be used for military aggression against another Member State or provides another Member State with technological assistance of any kind, such as providing cyber capability to conduct aggression against another Member State. In addition, a Member State that allows its territory to be used by another Member State to conduct cyber attacks against another Member State or provides support to mercenaries or criminal groups to carry out such attacks against another Member State would fit within the Pact's definition of aggression.

Other bases for considering the application of the Pact as a framework for promoting responsible State behavior in cyberspace arise from the interpretation of a range of obligations which it imposes on the Member States. For example, Article 5(a) of the Pact requires the Member States to cooperate in preventing acts aimed at the 'destabilization of any Member State.' The Pact defines 'destabilization' as 'any act that disrupts the peace and tranquility of any Member State or which may lead to mass social and political disorder.'[91]

Following the emergence of the information society, it is possible for hostile cyber acts to disrupt critical services and cause mass social and political disorder in a State. Therefore, the Pact's definition of 'destabilization'

89 Art. 1 lit. c) AU Non-Aggression and Common Defense Pact (emphasis added).

90 Christopher C. Joyner and Catherine Lotrionte, 'Information Warfare as International Coercion: Elements of a Legal Framework,' EJIL 12 (2001), 825–865 (838).

91 Art. 1 lit. i) AU Non-Aggression and Common Defense Pact.

along with the obligation under Article 5(a), provides scope for applying the Pact to cyber attacks that can cause mass social and political disorder in a State. In addition, Article 5(b) of the Pact requires the Member States 'to prevent its territory and its people from being used for encouraging or committing *acts of subversion*, hostility, aggression and other harmful practices that might threaten the territorial integrity and sovereignty of a Member State or regional peace and security.' Under the Pact 'acts of subversion' refers to 'any act that incites, aggravates or creates dissension within or among the Member States with the intention or purpose to destabilize or overthrow the existing regime or political order by, among other means, fomenting racial, religious, linguistic, ethnic and other differences…'[92]

To a large extent, the obligation under Article 5(b) provides a broad scope for applying the Pact as a framework for promoting responsible State behavior. This is because acts of subversion can be carried out through the use of cyberspace. For example, cyberspace can be used to spread disinformation or hate speech with the aim of creating dissension and destabilising a Member State. Therefore, the obligation would require a Member State to prevent its territory and its people from being used to encourage or commit acts of subversion through cyberspace.

3. *Limits of Applying the Pact to Promote Responsible State Behavior in Cyberspace*

There are several limitations that would impede the Pact's application as a framework for promoting responsible State behavior in cyberspace. A major limitation in this regard is the issue of attribution. The challenge of accurately attributing cyber attacks to a particular entity affects the classification of cyber attacks as an act of State aggression. Various incidents of cyber attacks in several countries have been categorised as acts of cyberwarfare.[93]

---

92 Art. 1 lit. a) AU Non-Aggression and Common Defense Pact.

93 Jordan Robertson and Laurence Arnold, 'Cyberwar: How Nations Attack without Bullets or Bombs,' *Washington Post,* (8 June 2021), available at: https://www.washingtonpost.com; Stephen Blank, 'Cyber War and Information War à la Russe' in George Perkovich and Ariel E. Levite (eds), *Understanding Cyber Conflict: Fourteen Analogies* (Georgetown: Georgetown University Press 2017), 81–98 (85); Damien McGuinness, 'How a Cyber Attack Transformed Estonia,' *BBC News* (27 April 2017), available at: https://www.bbc.com; Susan Landau, 'National Security on the Line,' JTHTL 4 (2006), 409–447 (429).

For example, in May 2007, Estonia experienced a series of massive and coordinated cyber attacks which targeted the country's public and private critical information infrastructure.[94] The attacks deployed botnets of over one million computers located in over 50 countries around the world[95] and are classified as the world's first cyberwar and linked to Russia.[96] In 2008, during the brief Russian-Georgia conflict, Georgia alleged that Russia had carried out cyber attacks against its government.[97] Similar attacks were also launched against Georgia in 2019.[98] The 2010 Stuxnet attack, which targeted and destroyed Iran's nuclear centrifuges, was reported to be a joint cyber operation between the United States and Israel code-named Olympic games.[99] In 2015, it was alleged that Russia had launched cyber attacks against Ukraine.[100] Following bilateral tensions between China and India, it was reported in 2021 that China-linked groups were carrying out cyber attacks against India's critical infrastructure.[101] However, given that the above attacks were not traced with certainty to a particular State, it becomes difficult to classify such incidents as cyber warfare.[102] With the challenge of attribution, criminal actors or non-State actors can loop through different computer systems in the process of perpetrating cyber

---

94 Cooperative Cyber Defence Centre of Excellence Legal Task Team, *Case Study Estonia: Legal Lessons Learned from the April-May 2007 Cyber Attacks against Estonia* (NATO CCD COE, 2008).

95 Ibid.

96 Kertu Ruus, 'Cyber War I: Estonia Attacked from Russia,' *European Affairs* 9 (2008), available at: https://www.europeaninstitute.org; Paul Meller, 'Cyberwar: Russia vs Estonia,' *Networkworld.com*, (Maz 24 2007), available at: http://www.networkworld.coml.

97 'UK says Russia's GRU behind massive Georgia Cyber-Attack,' *BBC News (20 February 2020)*, available at: https://www.bbc.co.uk.

98 Przemyslaw Roguski, 'Russian Cyber Attacks Against Georgia, Public Attributions and Sovereignty in Cyberspace,'*Just Security* (6 March 2020), available at: https://www.justsecurity.org.

99 David E. Sanger, *Confront and Conceal: Obama's Secret Wars and Surprising Use of American Powers* (New York, NY: Crown 2012), 188–225; David E. Sanger, 'Obama Order Sped up Wave of Cyberattacks against Iran,' *New York Times* (1 June 2012), available at: https://www.nytimes.com/.

100 Andy Greenberg, 'How an Entire Nation Became Russia's Test Lab for Cyberwar,' *Wired* (20 June 2017), available at: https://www.wired.com.

101 'China's Cyber-War with India,' *ANI News* (18 March 2021), available at: https://www.aninews.in.

102 Lorraine Finlay and Christian Payne, 'The Attribution Problem and Cyber Armed Attacks,' AJIL 113 (2019), 202–206 (203ff.); Chris Morgan, 'Cyber Attacks: The Challenge of Attribution,' *Digital Shadows* (June 2021), available at: https://www.digitalshadows.com.

attacks or even orchestrate attacks to appear to originate from government computers in another country. Thus, the problem of attribution creates uncertainty in identifying the origin of cyber attacks or the motive behind such attacks.[103] The challenge of attribution appears more pervasive in Africa given the absence of capacity to address cyber threats and would therefore limit the ability of African States to attribute cyber attacks whether such attacks emanate from an African State or a foreign entity. For example, as of December 2021, only 23 African States had national Computer Emergency Response Teams (CERTs),[104] while many African States still require technical assistance to address cyber threats.[105]

Another limitation is the seemingly weak position of the African Peace and Security Council in implementing the Pact and the Common African Defense and Security Policy.[106] The African Peace and Security Council was established in 2002 to serve as a standing decision-making organ for the prevention, management and resolution of conflicts within the African Union. The Council functions as a collective security and early-warning arrangement to facilitate timely and efficient response to conflict and crisis situations in Africa.[107] In exercising its mandate, the Council is required to be guided by the principles enshrined in the Charter of the United Nations[108] and also cooperate and work closely with the United Nations Security Council, which has 'the primary responsibility for the maintenance of international peace and security.'[109] The Peace and Security Council

---

103 Uchenna J. Orji, 'Deterring Cyberterrorism in the Global Information Society: A Case for the Collective Responsibility of States,' DATR 6 (2014), 31- 45 (35, 41).

104 Orji (n. 21), 78-81; ITU, *Cybersecurity Country Profiles*, available at https://www.itu; African Union and Symantec Corporation, *Cyber Crime & Cyber Security Trends in Africa* (Tempa, AR: Symantec Corporation 2016), 53–56.

105 UNODC, *Comprehensive Study on Cybercrime* (New York, NY: United Nations 2013), 178.

106 AU, 'Main Successes of the AU in Peace and Security Challenges and Mitigation Measures in Place,' available at: https://au.int; Kristiana Powell, *The African Union's Emerging Peace and Security Regime: Opportunities and Challenges for Delivering on the Responsibility to Protect* (Ottawa: The North-South Institute 2005).

107 Art. 2 Protocol Relating to the Establishment of the Peace and Security Council of the African Union.

108 Art. 4 Protocol Relating to the Establishment of the Peace and Security Council of the African Union.

109 Art. 17 Protocol Relating to the Establishment of the Peace and Security Council of the African Union: Kwesi Aning, 'The African Union's Peace and Security Architecture: Defining an Emerging Response Mechanism,' *Lecture Series on African Security* 3 (2008), 1–13.

is responsible for implementing the Pact[110] and is required to periodically update the Pact so as to enhance its implementation in light of contemporary security challenges.[111] However, the Council has not carried out any update to reflect cyber security challenges that can constitute State aggression under the Pact. More importantly, a critical limitation that will impede the Pact's application for promoting responsible State behavior in cyberspace is the fact that its application is restricted to the African States. However, given the nature of cyberspace, acts that qualify as State aggression in cyberspace against an African State can emanate from outside the continent, thereby making the application of the Pact impossible.

IV. Concluding Remarks

The adoption of regional cybersecurity governance instruments in Africa indicates a collective interest to promote cyber stability. Although existing cybersecurity governance instruments do not address the issue of State aggression in cyberspace and thereby create legal uncertainty with respect to the governance of responsible State behavior, a broad interpretation of the AU Non-Aggression Pact in the light of contemporary cyber challenges appears to address this vacuum.

Despite its limitations, the Pact provides a framework that can promote responsible State behavior among the African States in cyberspace. Its application to acts of cyber aggression would promote legal certainty on the governance of State behavior in cyberspace in Africa while also contributing an example for the development of norms for responsible State behavior in cyberspace. Achieving this prospect will, however, require responses including rising awareness within the AU and its Peace and Security Council on issues bordering on cyber aggression and responsible behavior State behavior in cyberspace.

This step appears imperative given that the African States and regional institutions appear to have focused on curbing cybercrimes while having low levels of awareness of cyber aggression. In concluding, it is important to highlight that although the Pact in its present form can be broadly interpreted to promote responsible State behavior in cyberspace, the AU Peace and Security Council, in the exercise of its mandate, should nevertheless consider making updates to the Pact so as to clearly reflect elements

110 Art. 9 AU Non-Aggression and Common Defense Pact.

111 Art. 21 AU Non-Aggression and Common Defense Pact.

of cyber operations that can constitute State aggression. Such an update will further enhance legal certainty and also go a long way to increase the needed awareness amongst the African States and regional institutions.

The Changing Nature of Sanctions in the Digital Age

Alena Douhan

Abstract Cyber technologies have already changed our lives drastically. Nearly every area of social relations is currently being digitalized both nationally and internationally. The UN Security Council, in its resolutions 2419 (2018), 2462 (2019), and 2490 (2019), and many others, recognizes that the activity of individuals and non-state entities in the cyber area may constitute a threat to international peace and security. Cyber attacks on critical infrastructure; the impossibility to use online payment systems; blocking access to the Internet, Twitter and Instagram accounts, Zoom and other services; and the application of cyber measures in response to cyber threats and many others have started to be actively discussed today with regard to the problem of sanctions. This chapter seeks to provide an overview of developments and situations, when the application of sanctions is affected by the development of cyber means. It also focuses on the changes in and legal qualifications for the grounds, subjects, targets, means and methods of introduction and implementation of sanctions regimes in the digital age.

I. Introduction

The information communication infrastructure, as well as digital devices, have already become an integral part of today's reality. Digitalization has a huge impact on the development and observance of human rights, as well as on the very status of the individual. The changes are so drastic that sometimes it is even maintained that, despite the general perception of the need to apply online the same rules that are applied offline (UN General Assembly resolution A/RES/68/167 of 18 December 2013, para. 3),[1] the very notion and concept of sovereignty are outdated.[2] Individuals become all the more active in the international arena. Threats caused by the use of cyber technologies by terrorist and extremist groups had already been recognized by the UN General Assembly in 1999 (resolution 53/70 of 4

---

1 UNGA Res 68/167 of 18 December 2013, A/RES/68/167, para. 3.

2 Nicola Wenzel, 'Opinion and Expression, Freedom of, International Protection' in: Rüdiger Wolfrum (ed.), *MPEPIL* (online edn, Oxford: Oxford University Press 2014), available at: https://opil.ouplaw.com/view/10.1093/law:epil/978019923169 0/law-9780199231690-e855; Johann-Christoph Woltag, 'Cyber warfare' in: Rüdiger Wolfrum (ed.), *MPEPIL* (online edn, Oxford: Oxford University Press 2015), available at: http://opil.ouplaw.com/view/10.1093/law:epil/9780199231690/law-9780199 231690-e280?rskey=eCCfoY&result=7&prd=EPIL&print.

January 1999)[3] and elaborated in detail in later resolutions of the UN Security Council (resolutions 2419 (2018) of 6 June 2018,[4] 2462 (2019) of 28 March 2019[5] and 2490 (2019) of 20 September 20199.[6] The UN Security Council also mentions that young people become frequent targets of terrorist online propaganda and recruiting.[7]

Thus, it does not come as any surprise that the development of cyber means is affecting the purposes, means, mechanisms and targets of sanctions applied by the UN Security Council, regional organizations and individual states. An attack with the use of ten drones over Saudi Arabian oil extraction stations on 14 September 2019,[8] allegedly by a non-state actor from the territory of Yemen, resulted in a 60 per cent drop in oil extraction in Saudi Arabia, a 6 per cent drop in the world's oil extraction and a rise in oil prices of 15 per cent.[9] Eight individuals and four legal entities from Russia, China and North Korea have been declared to 'provide support for or [be] involved in, or facilitated cyber attacks or attempted cyber attacks publicly known as 'WannaCry' and 'NotPetya,' as well as 'Operation Cloud Hopper'.'[10]

Today, the legal scholarship pays much attention to the general aspects of cyber security,[11] the use of cyber means and methods of warfare[12] and its effects on the enjoyment of the rights to privacy and freedom

3 UNGA Res 53/70 of 4 January 1999, A/RES/53/70.

4 UNSC Res 2419 of 6 June 2018, S/RES/2419.

5 UNSC Res 2462 of 28 March 2019, S/RES/2462.

6 UNSC Res 2490 of 20 September 2019, S/RES/2490.

7 UNSC Res 2419 (n. 4), paras 9, 12.

8 'Drone attacks on Saudi oil sites disrupt supplies,' France 24 (2019), available at: https://www.france24.com/en/20190915-drone-attacks-saudi-aramco-sites-disrupt-oil-supplies-us-blames-iran.

9 Frank Gardner, 'Saudi oil facility attacks: Race on to restore supplies,' BBC (2019), available at: https://www.bbc.com/news/world-middle-east-49775849.

10 Council Implementing Regulation 2020/1125 of 30 July 2020 implementing Regulation 2019/796 concerning restrictive measures against cyber-attacks threatening the Union or its Member States ST/9568/2020/INIT OJ L 246, 2020, 4–9.

11 Elias G Carayannis, David FJ Campbell, Marios Panagiotis Efthymiopoulos (eds), *Handbook of Cyber-Development, Cyber-Democracy, and Cyber-Defense* (New York: Springer International Publishing 2018); Fabio Rugge, *Confronting an 'Axis of Cyber'? China, Iran, North Korea and Russia in Cyber Space* (Milano: Ledizioni 2018).

12 Woltag (n. 2); Michael Schmitt, "Attack' as a Term of Art in International Law: The Cyber Operations Context' in: Christian Czosseck, Rain Ottis and Katharina Ziolkowski (eds), *Proceedings of the 4th International Conference on Cyber Conflict* (NATO CCD COE 2012), 287–288; Marco Roscini, 'World Wide Warfare – *Ius*

of expression,[13] the emerging right to be forgotten[14] and the violation of human rights in the digital age[15] or by being cut off from the Internet by governments.[16] Recent publications attempt to analyze specific situations relevant to the use of digital means in the course of sanctions[17] or as sanctions to limit unwelcomed online behavior.[18] However, no comprehensive overview of the impact of cyber technologies on the application and implementation of sanctions has been done in the international legal doctrine yet.

Despite the diversity of possible uses of cyber means in the modern world and the mutual impact of sanctions and the use of cyber technologies, the present article focuses on the use of cyber means as a ground for the introduction of sanctions by international and unilateral actors; blocking on-line commerce; the specifics of sanctions on trade in software; reputational risks; and blocking online educational platforms, messengers and social networks both directly and indirectly. In this regard, it is important not only to identify existing threats and challenges but to qualify them from the standpoint of international law, including for their impact on the law of human rights.

---

ad bellum and the Use of Cyber Force' in: Armin von Bogdandy and Rüdiger Wolfrum (eds), Max Planck UNYB 14 (2010), 85–130.

13 HRC, 'Report of the Special Rapporteur on the Promotion and Protection of the Right to Freedom of Opinion and Expression,' A/HRC/35/22 of 30 March 2017; UNGA, 'Report of the Special Rapporteur to the General Assembly on the Temporary Challenges to Freedom of Expression,' A/HRC/71/373 of 6 September 2016.

14 Ineta Ziemele, 'Privacy, Right to, International Protection' in: Rüdiger Wolfrum (ed.), *MPEPIL* (online edn, Oxford: Oxford University Press 2008); Janne Hagen and Olav Lysne, 'Protecting the Digitized Society: The Challenge of Balancing Surveillance and Privacy,' The Cyber Defense Review 1 (2016), 75–90.

15 Alena F. Douhan, 'Adapting the Human Rights System to the Cyber Age,' Max Planck UNYB 23 (2019), 249–289; Kai Möller 'Beyond Reasonableness: The Dignitarian Structure of Human and Constitutional Rights' CJLJ 34 (2021), 341–364.

16 Sage Cheng and Berhan Taye, 'Targeted, Cut Off, and Left in the Dark: The #KeepItOn report on internet shutdowns in 2019,' available at: https://www.accessnow.org/keepiton-2019-report.

17 Philipp Lutscher, 'Digital Retaliation? Denial-of-Service Attacks after Sanction Events' JoGSS 6 (2021), 1–11.

18 Enguerrand Marique and Yseult Marique, 'Sanctions on Digital Platforms: Balancing Proportionality in the Modern Public Square,' CLSR 36 (2020), 105372.

II. The Expanding Nature of Sanctions in International Law

The notion of sanctions is one of the most controversial ones in contemporary international law.[19] It is so often employed today in politics, criminal law, news and even everyday life and is applied to so many diverse types and categories of measures taken by entirely different subjects that neither the legality of each particular type of sanction nor its humanitarian impact are sought to be assessed anymore.

In international law, sanctions may be viewed as a power (possibility) to ensure the law,[20] an analogy of responsibility for internationally wrongful acts,[21] punishment,[22] a complex of enforcement measures (countermeasures) applied to a delinquent state,[23] a method to make someone comply,[24]

---

19 ILC, 'Articles on the Responsibility of States for Internationally Wrongful Acts with Commentaries,' (2001) ILCYB, Vol. II, Part Two, 31, 128.

20 Gerald Sparrow, *Sanctions* (London: Knightly Vernon Ltd. 1972), 11–12.

21 Aleksandr A. Kovalev and Stanislav V. Chernichenko (eds), *Mezhdunarodnoe pravo*, (3rd edn, Moscow: Prospekt 2008), 237–238 (in Russ.).

22 Ademola Abass, *Regional Organisations and the Development of Collective Security* (London: Hart Publishing 2004), 49; Ramesh Thakur, *The United Nations, Peace and Security* (Cambridge: Cambridge University Press 2010), 135. This approach is, however, disputed by the UN Secretary-General in the UN, 'Supplement to an Agenda for Peace: Position Paper,' (1995) UNGA, UNSC, A/50/60, S/1995/1 of 25 January 1995, para. 66. However, the punitive nature of sanctions has been rejected by most states: see UNSC, 'Report, 4128th Meeting,' (2000) S/PV.4128 of 17 April 2000; Johan Galtung, 'On the Effects of International Economic Sanctions' in: Miroslav Nincic and Peter Wallensteen (eds), *Dilemmas of Economic Coercion: Sanctions in World Politics* (New York: Praeger Publishers 1983), 19; Chukwudi V. Odoeme and Collins O. Chijioke, 'Sanctions in International Law: Morality and Legality at War,' CLRJ 7 (2021), 102–120 (103).

23 Gennady V. Ignatenko and Oleg I. Tiunov, *Mezhdunarodnoe pravo* (Moscow: Norma Publ. 2005), 202; Ruben Kalamkaryan and Yury Migachev, *International Law* (Moscow: Norma Publ. 2004), 182; Elena A. Shibaeva, 'International Organizations in the System of International Legal Regulation,' Soviet Yearbook of International Law 1978 (1980), 214–224 (in Russ.); Fred Grunfeld, 'The Effectiveness of United Nations Economic Sanctions' in Willem J. van Genugten and Gerard A de Groot (eds), *United Nations Sanctions: Effectiveness and Effects, Especially in the Field of Human Rights: A Multidisciplinary Approach* (Antwerp: Intersentia 1999), 115; Lori F. Damrosch, 'The Legitimacy of Economic Sanctions as Countermeasures for Wrongful Acts,' Ecology L.Q. 46 (2019), 95–110.

24 Galtung (n. 22), 19; Natalino Ronzitti, 'The Report of the High-Level Panel on Threats, Challenges and Change, the Use of Force and the Reform of the United Nations,' Italian Yearbook of International Law XIV (2004), (Leiden/Boston: Martinus Nijhoff Publishers 2005), 11.

negative consequences in the case of violation,[25] measures of protection of the international legal order,[26] measures not involving the use of armed force in order to maintain or restore international peace and security,[27] a means of implementation of international responsibility (countermeasures),[28] or measures taken by international organizations against its Member States or other actors,[29] mechanism of prompting citizens of a state to put pressure on its government.[30]

The above approaches do not specify whether they refer to universal sanctions adopted by the UN Security Council under Chapter VII of the UN Charter[31] for the maintenance of international peace and security or to unilateral measures of pressure, both military or non-military, taken without or beyond the authorization of the Security Council (unilateral sanctions). Moreover, the use of the term 'sanctions' does not automatically qualify a situation as legal or illegal.

The situation appears to be even more complicated due to the existence of other terms identifying the application of unilateral means of pressure. In particular, numerous resolutions of the UN Human Rights Council (resolutions 15/24 of 6 October 2010;[32] 19/32 of 18 April 2012;[33] 24/14 of 8 October 2013;[34] 30/2 of 12 October 2015;[35] 34/13 of 24 March 2017;[36] and

25 Igor I. Lukashuk, *Law of International Responsibility* (Moscow: Wolters Kluwer 2004), 309 (in Russ.); Tatiana N. Neshataeva, *International Legal Sanctions of the UN Specialized Agencies* [extended abstract of PhD dissertation] (Moscow: Moscow State University 1985), 9, 12, 14 (in Russ.).

26 Neshataeva (n. 25), 17.

27 UN, 'Supplement to an Agenda for Peace: Position Paper' (n. 22). The same approach was taken by states that participated in the discussion of the problem in the UNSC, 'UN Security Council Report oft he Agenda to the 4128th meeting,' (2000), S/PV.4128 of 17 April 2000.

28 Lukashuk (n. 25), 306, 308; The same approach is supported by Grigory I. Tunkin, Nikolai A. Ushakov, Pranas Kuris, cited by Tatiana N. Neshataeva, 'The Notion of Sanctions of International Organizations,' Jurisprudence 6 (1984), 94; Abass (n. 22), 49, 51.

29 Tom Ruys, Sanctions, Retorsions and Countermeasures: Concepts and International Legal Framework' in Larissa van den Herik (ed.), *Handbook on UN Sanctions and International Law* (Cheltenham: Edward Elgar Publishing 2017), 19–51.

30 Odoeme and Chijioke (n. 22), 105.

31 United Nations, Charter of the United Nations, 24 October 1945, 1 UNTS XVI, Chapter VII.

32 HRC Res 15/24 of 6 October 2010, A/HRC/RES/15/24, paras 1–3.

33 HRC Res 19/32 of 18 April 2012, A/HRC/RES/19/32, paras 1–3.

34 HRC Res 24/14 of 8 October 2013, A/HRC/RES/24/14, paras 1–3.

35 HRC Res 30/2 of 12 October 2015, A/HRC/RES/30/2, paras 1–2, 4.

36 HRC Res 34/13 of 24 March 2017, A/HRC/RES/34/13, paras 1–2, 4.

45/5 of 6 October 2020)[37] and the General Assembly (resolutions 69/180 of 18 December 2014;[38] 70/151 of 17 December 2015;[39] and 71/193 of 19 December 2016)[40] refer to unilateral coercive measures including but not limited to military, economic and political measures taken without or beyond the authorization of the UN Security Council, and qualify them as illegal. These resolutions, however, do not use the term sanctions. Thus, until now, there is no established distinction between sanctions, especially unilateral ones, and unilateral coercive measures.

At the same time, given the absence of a definition of unilateral coercive measures and their presumably illegal character, States prefer to present their unilateral activities as not constituting unilateral coercive measures and to use therefore other terms, like 'sanctions,' 'restrictive measures'[41] and 'unilateral measures not in accordance with international law,'[42] 'security measures,' 'countermeasures' and many others.[43] The States involved are thus also identified in various ways, including as sanctioning/sanctioned, targeting/targeted or sender/source States.[44]

It is thus possible to state that in the face of the expanded application of unilateral and multilateral measures, there is no general consent about the notion and scope of sanctions in the absence of a consensus about their application and relevant legal grounds, in the presence of multiple similar or adjunct terminology. The term 'sanctions' is used so often today without due assessment of their legality and the humanitarian impact that it starts to feel 'generally accepted.' Sanctions are presented as having a certain presumption of legality, even though they are taken in a decentralized fashion with no independent body qualifying or assessing them. The development of cyber means is affecting various aspects of the use of means of pressure.

---

37 HRC Res 45/5 of 6 October 2020, A/HRC/RES/45/5, preamble.

38 UNGA Res 69/180 of 18 December 2014, A/RES/69/180, paras 5–6.

39 UNGA Res 70/151 of 17 December 2015, A/RES/70/151, paras 5–6.

40 UNGA Res 71/193 of 19 December 2016, A/RES/71/193, paras 5–6.

41 Council of the European Union, 'Guidelines on the implementation and evaluation of restrictive measures (sanctions) in the framework of the EU Common Foreign and Security Policy' of 4 May 2018, doc No. 5664/18.

42 UNGA Res 70/151 (n. 31), para. 1; UNGA Res 71/193 (n. 32), para. 2.

43 HRC Res 48/59 of 25 June 2021, 'Unilateral Coercive Measures: Notion, Types and Qualification,' Report of the Special Rapporteur on the negative impact of unilateral coercive measures on the enjoyment of human rights (2021).

44 HRC, 'Report of the Special Rapporteur on the negative impact of unilateral coercive measures on the enjoyment of human rights,' (2017), A/HRC/36/44 of 26 July 2017.

The present chapter does not aim at an in-depth terminological discussion, and therefore it views sanctions as any means of pressure applied by a state or international organization, including the UN Security Council, against other states, their nationals or legal entities to change the policy or behavior of the latter without any prejudice to the legality or illegality of such activity.

III. Malicious Use of Cyber Means as a Ground for Introduction of Sanctions by International and Unilateral Actors

1. The Use of Cyber Means as a Threat to International and National Security

As mentioned above, the UN Security Council and UN General Assembly, in their resolutions,[45] have recognized that the use of new information and communication technologies even by individuals and non-State entities may constitute a threat to international peace and security.

A similar position is taken by the Group of Governmental Experts on Developments in the Field of Information and Telecommunications in the Context of International Security, which refers to the 'dramatic increase in incidents involving the malicious use of information and communication technologies by State and non-State actors' in its report 70/174.[46] Experts uphold the opinion that the misuse of ICT (including by individuals and private entities) may harm or threaten international peace and security (para. 3).

As of the end of 2020, the UN Security Council had never imposed sanctions on states, individuals or legal entities in response to the malicious use of cyber means. It has, however, stressed that states have an obligation to control information flows, to prevent the use of the Internet for money laundering and terrorism financing, to control virtual finance and to exchange the necessary financial intelligence information[47] or aviation and passenger name data.[48] A similar call 'to prevent the use of the

45 UNSC Res 2462 (n. 5), preamble, paras 19, 21; UNSC Res 2419 (n. 4), preamble, para. 5; UNGA Res 72/246 of 24 December 2017 A/RES/72/246, paras 7–8. See also UNODC, *The Use of the Internet for Terrorist Purposes* (New York: United Nations 2012), 3–11, 32–34.

46 UNGA Res 70/174 of 22 July 2015, A/RES/70/174. 'ICT' refers to 'information and communications technology'.

47 UNSC Res 2462 (n. 5), para. 19.

48 UNSC Res 2482 of 19 July 2019, S/RES/2482, para. 15(c).

Internet to advocate, commit, incite, recruit for, fund or plan terrorist acts' has been made by the UN General Assembly.[49]

The number of people involved in terrorist activity via the Internet is enormous today. While being aware of existing skeptical approaches towards the role of the Internet in terrorism radicalization, I would join here the position of many others that large amounts of easily available violent extremist content online may have radicalizing effects in various forms.[50] Statistics show that up to 30,000 foreigners were involved in the Al Qaeda and ISIL groups by the end of 2015.[51] The UN Security Council maintains that some of the terrorist activity can be qualified not only as violating the right to life but also as war crimes, crimes against humanity or genocide.[52]

It is also generally agreed both in practice and in the legal doctrine that under certain conditions, a cyber operation may constitute an armed attack or part of an armed attack[53] or be part of a military operation in the course of a non-international military conflict.[54] As such, it may endanger the very existence of a state;[55] cause the loss of human lives (death or injury of combatants or civilians); cause the destruction or damaging of property

---

49 UNGA Res 73/174 of 17 December 2018, A/RES/73/174, paras 30–31.

50 Maura Conway, 'Determining the Role of the Internet in Violent Extremism and Terrorism: Six Suggestions for Progressing Research,' Studies in Conflict &Terrorism 40 (2017), 77–98 (77); Ines von Behr, Anaïs Reding, Charlie Edwards and Luke Gribbon, *Radicalisation in the Digital Era: The Use of the Internet in 15 Cases of Terrorism and Extremism* (online edn, Santa Monica, CA: RAND 2013).

51 UNGA, 71/384, 'Report of the Special Rapporteur on the promotion and protection of human rights and fundamental freedoms while countering terrorism,' (2016), A/71/384 of 13 September 2016, para. 12.

52 UNSC Res 2490 (n. 6), para. 2.

53 ICRC, 'Article 2: Application of the Convention,' Convention (I) for the Amelioration of the Condition of the Wounded and Sick in Armed Forces in the Field (12 August 1949) (Commentary of 2016), available at: https://ihl-databases.icrç.org/applic/ihl/ihl.nsf/Comment.xsp?action=openDocument&documentId=BE2D518CF5DE54EAC1257F7D0036B518, paras 253–256.

54 ICRC, 'Article 3: Conflicts not of an international character,' Convention (I) for the Amelioration of the Condition of the Wounded and Sick in Armed Forces in the Field (12 August 1949) (Commentary of 2016), available at: https://ihl-databases.icrc.org/applic/ihl/ihl.nsf/Comment.xsp?action=openDocument&documentId=BE2D518CF5DE54EAC1257F7D0036B518, paras 436–437.

55 Woltag (n. 2); Yoram Dinstein, *War, Aggression and Self-Defence* (Cambridge: Cambridge University Press 2001), 175–176. Jochen A. Frowein, 'Legal Consequences for International Law Enforcement in the Case of Security Council Inaction' in: Jost Delbrück (ed.), *The Future of International Law Enforcement: New Scenarios – New Law* (Berlin: Dunker and Humblot 1993), 114–115.

(civilian or military), including critical infrastructure;[56] or cause the loss of part of a state's territory.[57] The existence of a causal link between a cyber attack and the immediacy of negative consequences can be established (seconds or minutes between the attack and its results).[58]

Special attention is also traditionally paid to so-called 'attacks on critical infrastructure' that are attacks against dams, nuclear electricity stations, arms control systems, bank accounts and operations, gas and oil pipelines, electricity lines, taxation systems, governmental servers and computer networks,[59] as well as other critical infrastructure; and the interception of control over air defense systems,[60] floodgates of dams, aircraft or trains (which can cause them to collide),[61] etc.

If such attacks meet the above criteria, they may give rise to acts of self-defense in accordance with Article 51 of the UN Charter. The above-mentioned attack accomplished with the use of ten drones over Saudi Arabian oil extraction stations on 14 September 2019[62] can serve as a good illustration that the well-being and even the very existence of states may be endangered by cyber means by a group of individuals. It appeared impossible to identify the actual perpetrators of this attack, although the UN Secretary-General, in his report to the UN Security Council S/2020/531, noted that some items subsequently seized by the United States were identified as having Iranian origin and 'were identical or similar to those found in the debris of the cruise missiles and the delta-wing uncrewed aerial vehicles used in the attacks on Saudi Arabia in 2019.'[63] In such situations, the UN Security Council will face serious problems when trying to attribute an act or acts to a specific state in order to be able to take

56 Schmitt (n. 12), 287–288; Roscini (n. 12), 106–107.

57 Pauline C. Reich, Stuart Weinstein, Charles Wild and Allan S. Cabanlong, 'Cyber Warfare: A Review of Theories, Law, Policies, Actual Incidents – and the Dilemma of Anonymity,' EJLT 1 (2010), 1–58 (26).

58 Heather Harrison, *Cyber Warfare and the Laws of War* (Cambridge: Cambridge University Press 2014), 63–73.

59 Reich et al. (n. 57), 12–17.

60 International Law Association, 'Draft Report on Aggression and the Use of Force' (May 2016), available at: https://ila.vettoreweb.com/Storage/Download.aspx?DbStorageId=1055&StorageFileGuid=c911005c-6d63-408e-bc2d-e99bfc2167e4, 18.

61 ICRC, 'Article 3: Conflicts not of an international character' (n. 54), para. 437.

62 'Drone attacks on Saudi oil sites disrupt supplies,' France 24 (2019), available at: https://www.france24.com/en/20190915-drone-attacks-saudi-aramco-sites-disrupt-oil-supplies-us-blames-iran.

63 UNSC, 'Implementation of Security Council resolution 2231(2015),' Ninth report of the Secretary-General S/2020/531 of 11 June 2020, available at: https://undocs.org/S/2020/531, paras 11–14.

appropriate sanctions towards states. It is very probable that it will have to limit itself to general recommendations or to impose targeted sanctions, for example, within the framework of sanctions against individuals and organizations involved in terrorist activity, or it may consider establishing a mixed criminal tribunal with the consent of a state concerned.

In cases when an attack on critical infrastructure does not reach the level of an armed attack but is brought in breach of international obligations or violates the rights and interests of states, the latter usually refers to the possibility to take unilateral sanctions independently or via corresponding regional international organizations. It follows from the above that cyber attacks or other offensive uses of information and communication technologies may be qualified under certain conditions as a threat to peace, a breach of the peace or an act of aggression by the UN Security Council and may thus give rise to UN sanctions against states, individuals or legal entities.

States and regional organizations also look for the framework of possible reactions to the use of the Internet for malicious activity. The Security Council in particular persistently refers to the obligation of states to 'ensure that all measures taken to counter-terrorism, including measures taken to counter the financing of terrorism as provided for in this resolution, comply with their obligations under international law, including international humanitarian law, international human rights law and international refugee law' and to 'take into account the potential effect of those measures on exclusively humanitarian activities, including medical activities, that are carried out by impartial humanitarian actors.'[64] Also, the OSCE's recommendations on countering the use of the Internet for terrorism purposes focus on domestic investigation and judicial processes.[65]

64 See UNSC Res 2462 (n. 5), paras 6, 24; UNSC Res 2482 (n. 48), preamble, para. 15(c); UNSC Res 2501 of 16 December 2019, S/RES/2501, preamble; UNSC Res 2535 of 14 July 2020, S/RES/2535, para. 7.

65 Decision 7/06 of 5 December 2006 'Countering the Use of the Internet for Terrorist Purposes,' OSCE, MC.DEC/7/06; Regional Workshop on Countering the Use of the Internet for Terrorist Purposes for Judges, Prosecutors and Investigators from South Eastern Europe of 8 February 2017, CIO.GAL/224/16, OSCE (2016), available at: https://www.osce.org/files/f/documents/7/e/299091.pdf.

2. *Overview of State Practice of Imposing Sanctions in Response to Malicious Cyber Activities*

State practice of imposing sanctions in response to real or alleged malicious cyber activities is rather extensive. In particular, United States Executive Order (EO) 13694 of 1 April 2015, as amended by later documents,[66] introduced and expanded the list of 'cyber-enabled activities subject to sanctions'[67] such as blocking property and interests in property in a broad number of cases, to include attacks on critical infrastructure, interference in the election process, disruption of networking or computer operations, misappropriation of financial funds and personal information, etc.

Some of these measures in response to malicious cyber activity are taken by the United States with reference to implementing UN Security Council resolutions against North Korea (hereafter – DPRK) in the struggle against the proliferation of weapons of mass destruction (from resolution 1718 (2006) of 14 October 2006[68] to resolution 2397 (2017) of 22 December 2017).[69] They aim to suppress attempts by North Korea to use cyber technologies to circumvent sanctions imposed both by the UN Security Council and the United States.[70]

In its Guidance on the North Korean Cyber Threat of 15 April 2020, the United States refers to disruptive or destructive cyber activities affecting critical US infrastructure: cybercrimes, espionage, cyber-enabled financial theft and money laundering, extortion campaigns and crypto-jacking. This activity may be prosecuted by the United States with a penalty of 'up to 20 years of imprisonment, fines of up to $1 million or totaling twice

66 For example, Executive Order 13757 of 28 December 2016, 'Taking Additional Steps to Address the National Emergency With Respect to Significant Malicious Cyber-Enabled Activities,' available at: https://home.treasury.gov/system/files/126/cyber2_eo.pdf.

67 Executive Order 13694 of 1 April 2015, 'Blocking the Property of Certain Persons Engaging in Significant Malicious Cyber-Enabled Activities,' available at: https://www.govinfo.gov/content/pkg/CFR-2016-title3-vol1/pdf/CFR-2016-title3-vol1-eo13694.pdf. See also Silvina M. Romano, 'Psychological War Reloaded: Cyber-Sanctions, Venezuela and Geopolitics,' Revista Internacional de Pensamiento Politico 12 (2017), 105–126 (113–115).

68 UNSC Res 1718 of 14 October 2006, S/RES/1718.

69 UNSC Res 2397 of 22 December 2017, S/RES/2397.

70 North Korea Committing Cybercrimes to Avoid US Sanctions (2019), available at: https://beincrypto.com/north-korea-cybercrimes-us-sanctions/; DPRK Cyber Threat Advisory, 'Guidance on the North Korean Cyber Threat,' (2019), available at: https://home.treasury.gov/system/files/126/dprk_cyber_threat_advisory_20200415.pdf.

the gross gain, whichever is greater, and forfeiture of all funds involved in such transactions' against those who violate the US sanctions laws[71] (applying secondary sanctions). The United States also offers rewards of up to 5 million US dollars for information that 'leads to the disruption of financial mechanisms of persons engaged in certain activities that support North Korea, including money laundering, sanctions evasion, cyber-crime' via the Rewards for Justice program.[72]

A Panel of Experts, established by the UN Security Council to make recommendations to the Council, Member States and the corresponding Sanctions Committee as regards the implementation of resolutions on North Korea,[73] has repeatedly noted the evasion of financial sanctions by North Korea through cyber means, including crypto-currency operations[74] and recommended the Security Council to 'consider explicitly addressing the DPRK's evasion of sanctions through cyber means if drafting additional sanctions measures' and to enhance control of the UN Member States in the sphere of cryptocurrency.[75] At the same time, no resolution of the UN Security Council authorizes any additional measures in response to DPRK cyber activity.

In this regard, it is also worth mentioning that on 21 September 2021, the United States designated SUEX OTC, S.R.O. (SUEX) as a malicious cyber actor, the first designation against a virtual currency exchange.[76] Some measures in response to serious or attempted cyber attacks, understood as actions involving access to information systems, information systems interference, data interference or data interception, have been taken by the European Union and the United Kingdom since 17 May 2019.[77] Both have

71 DPRK Cyber Threat Advisory, 'Guidance on the North Korean Cyber Threat,' (2019), available at: https://home.treasury.gov/system/files/126/dprk_cyber_threat_advisory_20200415.pdf, 8.

72 See at: https://rewardsforjustice.net/english/about-rfj/north_korea.html.

73 See UNSC Res 1874 of 12 June 2009, S/RES/1874, para. 26; and UNSC Res 2515 of 28 July 2020, S/RES/2515, para. 1.

74 UNSC, 'Report of the Panel of Experts established pursuant to resolution 1874(2009),' S/2019/691 of 29 August 2019, paras 57–71.

75 Ibid., conclusions, paras 8–11; and UNSC, 'Final report of the Panel of Experts submitted pursuant to resolution 2464 (2019),' S/2020/151 of 7 February 2020, recommendations, Annex 73, paras 26–28.

76 See 'Treasury Takes Robust Actions to Counter Ransomware,' Press Release, 21 September 2021, available at: https://home.treasury.gov/news/press-releases/jy0364.

77 Until 31 December 2020, the United Kingdom will apply the European Union cybersanctions. See at: https://assets.publishing.service.gov.uk/government/upload

introduced visa and entry prohibitions and requested the freezing of assets of listed persons or the refusal to make assets or funds available to them.[78]

In July 2020 and October 2020, eight individuals and four legal entities from Russia, China and North Korea were listed for being considered to have 'provided support for or were involved in, or facilitated cyber attacks or attempted cyber attacks, including the attempted cyber attack against the OPCW and the cyber attacks publicly known as 'WannaCry' and 'NotPetya,' as well as 'Operation Cloud Hopper''[79] and to have been 'involved in cyber attacks with a significant effect which constitutes an external threat to the Union or its Member States, in particular, the cyber attack against the German federal parliament (Deutscher Bundestag) which took place in April and May 2015'[80] correspondingly.

3. *Legality of Unilateral Sanctions Taken in Response to Malicious Cyber Activities*

The above practice clearly demonstrates that measures taken by states and the European Union in response to malicious cyber activities include measures aimed to enhance the internal capacity of states to suppress cyber threats as well as the application of targeted sanctions to listed individuals and companies.

The possibility to impose unilateral sanctions with the purpose of implementing relevant decisions of the UN Security Council formed a ground for extensive scholarly debate since the early 1990s. The very idea of implicit, tacit or general authorization[81] or the possibility to use

---

s/system/uploads/attachment_data/file/813212/HM_Treasury_Notice__CA_regime.pdf.

78 Council Regulation 2019/796 of 17 May 2019 concerning restrictive measures against cyber-attacks threatening the Union or its Member States OJ L 129I 2019, 1.

79 Council Implementing Regulation 2020/1125 (n. 10), 4–9.

80 Regulation 2020/1125 (n. 10), 1–4.

81 Vera Gowlland-Debbas, 'The Limits of Unilateral Enforcement of Community Objectives in the Framework of UN Peace Maintenance,' EJIL 11 (2000), 373; Peter Malanczuk, *Humanitarian Intervention and the Legitimacy of the Use of Force* (The Hague: Het Spinhuis 1993), 17–19; Rein Müllerson, 'Jus ad Bellum and International Terrorism' in: Fred L. Borch and Paul S. Wilson (eds), *International Law and the War on Terror* (Newport, R.I.; Naval War College 2003), 175; Michael Byers, 'Terrorism, the Use of Force and International Law after 11 September 2001,' ICLQ 51 (2002), 401; Alexander Orakhelashvili, 'The Impact of Peremptory

enforcement measures unilaterally, when the decisions of the Security Council are not observed,[82] have been repeatedly condemned in the international legal scholarship.[83] Already in 1998, the UN General Assembly urged the international community 'to eliminate the use of unilateral coercive economic measures ... which are not authorized by relevant organs of the United Nations.'[84]

Taking into account that the above measures are not authorized directly by the UN Security Council and that the UN Charter does not provide for any possibility or mechanism for states and regional organizations to take any enforcement measures unilaterally, sanctions in response to malicious cyber activity can only be legal if they do not breach any international obligation of states, including, as referred to above, obligations in the sphere of human rights; or if their wrongfulness is excluded in accordance with international law in the course of countermeasures.[85]

The above documents clearly demonstrate that sanctions are imposed by the United States, the European Union and the United Kingdom by executive bodies in the absence of court hearings or due process guarantees such as access to courts. Moreover, the reference to cyber-threats makes the acquisition and disclosure of evidence problematic and all allegations rather ill-founded. This results in the aggravation of violations that traditionally occur with targeted sanctions, in particular, of property rights, freedom of movement, the right to privacy, the right to reputation and even in some cases, labor and social rights of targeted individuals with very little possibility to protect their rights in judiciary bodies.[86]

The recent practice of the United States is rather remarkable in this regard. In June 2020, six Nigerians were listed by the Department of the Treasury's Office of Foreign Assets Control (OFAC) for stealing 'over six

---

Norms,' EJIL 16 (2005), 59–88 (63–64); Hartmut Körbs, *Die Friedensdicherung duech die Vereinten Nationen und Regionalorganizationen* (Bochum: Brockmeyer 1997), 538.

82 Rainer Hofmann, 'International Law and the Use of Military Force against Iraq,' GYIL 45 (2002), 9–34 (13–15); Edward McWhinney, 'International Law-based Responses to the September 11 International Terrorist Attacks,' Chin. J. Int. Law 1 (2002), 280–286 (282); Christian Schaller, 'Massenvernichtungswaffen und Präventivkrieg. Möglichkeiten der Rechtvertigung einer militärischen Intervention im Irak aus völkerrechtlicher Sicht,' HJIL 62 (2002), 641–668 (654).

83 See e.g. Schaller (n. 82), 654; McWhinney (n. 82), 282; Hofmann (n. 82), 13–15.

84 UNGA Res 52/181 of 4 February 1998, A/RES/52/181, para. 2.

85 See Alena F. Douhan, *Regional Mechanisms of Collective Security: The New Face of Chapter VIII of the UN Charter?* (Paris: L'Harmattan 2013), 98–112.

86 Ibid., 98–112.

million dollars from victims across the United States' with the use of fraud involving cyber schemes.[87] A press release provides information about the alleged activity of each of the individuals, their photos and other personal data, as well as the presumed fraudulent schemes as if they were confirmed facts. The same approach was taken towards two Russian nationals in September 2020.[88]

While recognizing that states are under the obligation to take measures to suppress cyber crimes against the state, its nationals and legal entities, such measures shall remain within the recognized international intercourse: joining international treaties, developing legislation, starting criminal investigations and prosecutions, and judicial cooperation.[89] It is thus not clear why no criminal case has been initiated in response to the alleged cybercrimes, which would provide for the possibility to freeze assets, initiate criminal investigations, involve relevant international criminal police cooperation bodies and gather evidence. Instead, measures were taken in the form of unilateral sanctions upon the decision of the executive body, OFAC, without any identification of the beginning of criminal proceedings, any court hearing or any possibility for the listed individuals to access courts in order to protect their rights, reputations or personal data.

Moreover, the imposition of economic sanctions and entry bans, besides violating property and other rights, goes counter to the requirement of the presumption of innocence set forth in Article 14(2) of the International Covenant on Civil and Political Rights (ICCPR),[90] which is viewed by the Human Rights Committee as a guarantee 'that States parties must respect, regardless of their legal traditions and their domestic law.'[91] Paragraph 30 of the General Comment No. 32 expressly notes that 'no guilt can be presumed until the charge has been proved beyond a reasonable

87 'Treasury Sanctions Nigerian Cyber Actors for Targeting U.S. Businesses and Individuals,' Press Releases of 16 June 2020, available at: https://home.treasury.gov/news/press-releases/sm1034.

88 'Treasury Sanctions Russian Cyber Actors for Virtual Currency Theft,' Press Releases of 16 September 2020, available at: https://home.treasury.gov/news/press-releases/sm1123.

89 Decision 7/06 (n. 65); Regional Workshop on Countering the Use of the Internet for Terrorist Purposes for Judges, Prosecutors and Investigators from South Eastern Europe (n. 65).

90 UNGA, International Covenant on Civil and Political Rights, 16 December 1966, UNTS 999, 171.

91 Human Rights Committee, General Comment No. 32 of 23 August 2007, 'Article 14: Right to equality before courts and tribunals and to a fair trial,' CCPR/C/GC/32, para. 4.

doubt, ensures that the accused has the benefit of doubt' and requests governments to abstain from making public statements affirming the guilt of the accused.[92]

The Treaty on the Functioning of the European Union, unlike the US legislation, provides for the possibility to appeal to the European Court of Justice to review the legality of decisions allowing for restrictive measures against natural or legal persons adopted by the Council (Article 275[93]). The European Court of Justice has been active in the sphere of so-called 'sanctions cases,' making more than 360 judgements by December 2020.[94] No review of a cyber sanctions case has taken place until now.

Another aspect that deserves careful attention is the possibility to apply unilateral measures in response to cyber attacks and cyber threats in the course of countermeasures. In accordance with Article 49(1) of the Draft Articles on Responsibility of States for Internationally Wrongful Acts of 2001 (ARSIWA), 'An injured State may only take countermeasures against a State which is responsible for an internationally wrongful act in order to induce that State to comply with its obligations.'[95] Therefore, measures that constitute countermeasures can only be taken in response to the violation of a specific international obligation by a specific state and may be directed only against that state[96] to induce it to comply with the obligation.

Countermeasures thus can only be applied against individuals immediately responsible for the policy or activity of a state in breach of an international obligation, in order to change that policy or activity, or against states as such with due account of the attribution of the malicious cyber activity to the corresponding state (ARSIWA, Articles 4–11). Countermeasures thus are not applicable to other categories of persons or entities accused in particular of committing cybercrimes. The same approach is taken

92 Ibid., para. 30.

93 Consolidated version of the Treaty on the Functioning of the European Union OJ C 326, 2012, 47390.

94 EU sanctions. Court Judgements (2020), available at: https://www.europeansanctions.com/judgment/.

95 ILC, ARSIWA (n. 19), 43–59. See also Institut de Droit International, 'The Protection of Human Rights and the Principle of Non-Intervention in Internal Affairs of States,' Session in Santiago de Compostela (1989), available at: https://www.idi-iil.org/app/uploads/2017/06/1989_comp_03_en.pdf.

96 In support, see Dorothee Geyrhalter, *Friedenssicherung durch Regionalorganisationen ohne Beschluß des Sicherheitsrates* (Cologne: LIT 2001), 66.

by the drafters of Tallinn manual 2.0 on the international law applicable to cyber operations (Rules 20–21).[97]

In this regard, a provision of Article 1(6) of Council Regulation (EU) 2019/796 of 17 May 2019 does not fit the requirement of Article 49(1) of ARSIWA as it speaks about the possibility to impose sanctions 'where deemed necessary to achieve common foreign and security policy (CFSP) objectives' rather than in response to an internationally wrongful act. Moreover, the possibility to apply restrictive measures 'in response to cyber attacks with a significant effect against third States or international organisations' rather than the EU or its Member States provides for the possibility of any action in the course of countermeasures only if underlying violations have a so-called collective nature in accordance with Article 48 ARSIWA.

Another aspect which comes into discussion of the possibility to apply unilateral sanctions as countermeasures is the difficulty of attributing the activity of specific individuals or other non-state entities to a specific state for the purposes of holding it responsible, as shown above in the case of the cyber attack against Saudi oil installations. The traditional approach refers to the need for 'effective'[98] or 'overall'[99] control from the side of the specific state. I would align myself here with the position of the drafters of the Tallinn manual 2.0 that the same rules of attribution of activity of non-state actors to states (acting under direction and control) shall be applied to the activity in the cybersphere as international law does not provide any additional or different regulation.[100]

Therefore, unilateral sanctions against allegedly malicious cyber activity can only be taken if they do not violate any obligation of a state, including in the sphere of human rights (retortion) or as countermeasures in full compliance with international law in accordance with basic principles of the law of international responsibility, with the purpose to restore the observance of international obligations, prior notice, and observance of the rule of law, including legality, legitimacy, humanity and proportionality to

---

97 Michael N. Schmitt (ed), *Tallinn manual 2.0 on the International Law Applicable to Cyber Operations* (2nd edn, Cambridge: Cambridge University Press 2017), 111- 122.

98 ICJ, *Military and Paramilitary Activities in and against Nicaragua* (Nicaragua v. United States of America), merits, judgment of 27 June 1986, ICJ Reports 1986, 14, (paras 113–115).

99 ICTY, Appeals Chamber, *The Prosecutor v. Dusko Tadić*, 15 July 1999 (case no. IT-94-1-A), paras 120–124, 146.

100 Tallinn manual 2.0 (n. 97), 94–96.

the harm suffered (ARSIWA, Articles 49–51),[101] with due account for the precautionary approach as concerns the humanitarian impact of measures taken. Under Article 50(1)(b) ARSIWA, the obligations for the protection of fundamental human rights can never be affected by countermeasures. As correctly noted by Alexander Kern, punitive sanctions have mostly been geared towards the past,[102] and in the contemporary world, shall be taken in accordance with international law standards.

IV. Blocking On-line Commerce

The blocking of online commerce has turned into one of the frequently used forms of unilateral sanctions today – a means of implementation of economic and financial sanctions, as far as international transactions are mostly happening online. Today, blocking online payments constitutes an integral part of the implementation of UN Security Council sanctions[103] and of the Financial Action Task Force (FATF) recommendations aimed to suppress money laundering and terrorism financing.[104] Today funds and assets are understood by the FATF to include also those existing in electronic and digital form.[105] Further, recommendation 16 of the FATF imposes on financial institutions obligations aimed to facilitate 'identification and reporting of suspicious transactions and to implement the requirements to take freezing action and comply with prohibitions from conducting transactions with designated persons and entities'[106] *inter alia* via virtual means.

The impossibility to make financial transfers to/from targets of sanctions has been cited *inter alia* as a part of trade and financial sanctions

101 Even so, Geyrhalter, for example, claims it is possible that economic sanctions may be applied to states responsible for mass violations of fundamental human rights; see Geyrhalter (n. 96), 66; ILC, ARSIWA (n. 19), para. 6. See also Antonios Tzanakopoulos, 'State Responsibility for Targeted Sanctions,' AJIL 113 (2019), 135–139 (136–137).

102 Alexander Kern, *Economic Sanctions: Law and Public Policy* (New York: Palgrave Macmillan 2009), 62.

103 UNSC Res 1874 (n. 73), paras 18–19; UNSC Res 2462 (n. 5), paras 2–4.

104 Recommendation 36 FATF, 'International Standards on Combating Money Laundering and the Financing of Terrorism & Proliferation,' adopted by the FATF plenary in February 2012 (Updated October 2021), available at: www.fatf-gafi.org/recommendations.html, 27.

105 Ibid., 124, 130.

106 Ibid., 78.

as concerns transactions with Cuba,[107] Iran, Venezuela, Syria and other states.[108] In particular, any transactions, including online transactions made by US persons (individuals and legal entities) or made in or involving the United States relating to the property or interests in property of sanctioned individuals, are prohibited unless authorized or exempted.[109]

The situation is aggravated by the fact that the majority of the elements that enable any individual, corporation or government to trade are concentrated either within the United States or the European Union. This jurisdiction provides the United States in particular with the possibility to control and block all payments in US dollars via Visa, MasterCard, American Express, Western Union and PayPal.[110] Another illustrative example could be seen in the repeated calls to cut off SWIFT – the information exchange system connecting more than 11,000 financial institutions from 200 countries and territories –[111] as part of sanctions against Iran, Israel, the Russian Federation Belarus and China.[112] On the other hand, using SWIFT to block transactions as a countermeasure to the US sanctions has also been considered within the EU.[113]

---

107 Luis Rondon Paz, 'The External Blockade and Internet Sanctions on Cuba,' Havana Times (2015), available at: https://havanatimes.org/opinion/the-external-blockade-and-internet-sanctions-on-cuba/.

108 Statements of states during the Virtual Arria meeting of the UN Security Council of 25 November 2020 (2020), available at: http://webtv.un.org/live/watch/part-12-virtual-arria-meeting-on-%E2%80%9Cend-unilateral-coercive-measures-now%E2%80%9D/6212373519001/?term=. See also Call for submissions: UCM-Study on impact of unilateral sanctions on human rights during the state of emergency amid COVID-19 pandemic (2020), available at https://www.ohchr.org/EN/Issues/UCM/Pages/call-covid.aspx.

109 United States, Cyber-Related Sanctions Program, available at: www.treasury.gov/resourcecenter/sanctions/
Programs/Documents/cyber.pdf.

110 See Renata Avila Pinto, 'Digital Sovereignty or Digital Colonialsim,' Sur – International Journal on Human Rights 27 (2018), 15–28 (20).

111 SWIFT. About us (2020), available at: https://www.swift.com/about-us.

112 Brian O'Toole, 'Don't believe the SWIFT China sanctions hype,' Atlantic Council (2020), available at: https://www.atlanticcouncil.org/blogs/new-atlanticist/dont-believe-the-swift-china-sanctions-hype/; 'SWIFT Says It 'Has No Authority' To Unplug Russia Or Israel,' PYMNT (2014), available at: https://www.pymnts.com/in-depth/2014/swift-says-it-has-no-authority-to-unplug-russia-or-israel/; 'Economist: Disconnecting from SWIFT Will Be a Bomb for the Regime' (2020), available at: https://charter97.org/en/news/2020/11/25/401835/.

113 Tobias Stoll, 'Extraterritorial sanctions on trade and investments and European responses Policy Department for External Relations,' Directorate General for External Policies of the Union PE 653.618 (2020), available at: https://www.europa

It has been generally recognized in economic and legal scholarship that a limited number of service providers, as well as the interdependence or dependence on a specific resource (financial system, currency, etc.), results in a special vulnerability of both non-controlling countries and the end-users,[114] while digital platforms may be used not only for transactions but for many other purposes.[115] In the contemporary interdependent world, being disconnected from the single bank payment system would have not a targeted but rather a comprehensive impact, affecting the country as a whole, every single individual and company on its territory, as well as every third-country national and company involved in economic transactions with the latter, resulting in an economic crisis. That is why Russia, China and India not only developed national payment systems but are exploring the possibility to establish an alternative to SWIFT.[116]

Other types of blocking online commerce through the implementation of sectoral or targeted sanctions generally result in the extension of the time necessary to complete transactions, increasing bank costs and entrepreneurial risks, the shutting down of investments and the impossibility to buy or order even essential goods, including medicine, medical equipment, food, electricity, etc.[117] This badly affects a number of fundamental human rights, including the right to health, the right to food and economic rights; it gives rise to poverty and, in some cases, may result in the violation of the right to life.

Additional sanctions imposed by the United States on 18 Iranian banks on 8 October 2020 prevent any possibility for online transactions involving

rl.europa.eu/thinktank/en/document.html?reference=EXPO_STU(2020)653618, 12.

114 Allan E. Gotlieb, 'Extraterritoriality: A Canadian Perspective,' Nw. J. Int'l L. 5 (1983), 449 (451).

115 Marique and Marique (n. 18), 5.

116 Dipanjan Roy Chaudhury, 'India-Russia-China explore alternative to SWIFT payment mechanism,' The Economic Times (2019), available at: https://economictimes.indiatimes.com/news/economy/foreign-trade/india-russia-china-explore-alternative-to-swift-payment-mechanism/articleshow/72048472.cms?utm_source=contentofinterest&utm_medium=text&utm_campaign=cppst.

117 UNGA, 'Negative impact of unilateral coercive measures on the enjoyment of human rights in the coronavirus disease pandemic,' Report of the Special Rapporteur on the negative impact of unilateral coercive measures on the enjoyment of human rights, Alena Douhan. A/75/209 of 21 July 2020, available at: https://www.undocs.org/en/A/75/209; Joint Communiqué, 'Unilateral Coercive Measures (UCMs) and their Impacts in the Context of COVID-19,' Vienna, 30 November 2020, available at: https://viennaun.mfa.ir/en/newsview/619102/Joint-Communiqu%C3%A9-on-UCMs-and-their-Impacts.

US dollars. EU officials thus express concerns that it will close off any possibility for Iran to use 'foreign currency for humanitarian imports,' in particular medicine and grains.[118] The most urgent problems involve the impossibility to buy European medicines, including insulin necessary for the survival and well-being of millions of diabetics in the country.[119] Humanitarian organizations working in the targeted countries unanimously refer to the impossibility to make bank transfers to and from these states for the supply and delivery of essential goods.[120] Private companies and individuals from Venezuela, Syria, Cuba and other countries under sanctions refer to the impossibility to open or keep bank accounts or to do transactions because of their nationality also when they are not included in the lists.[121]

It is often maintained that the problem of blocking accounts is exacerbated by the extraterritorial application of sanctions[122] and over-compliance. Due to the high risks of applying criminal and civil penalties even for transactions taking place outside the US or the European Union, banks are reluctant to permit bank transfers or significantly extend transfer terms, and other companies are unwilling to be involved in transactions because of the fear of secondary sanctions, even when companies in targeted countries are not included in sanctions lists.[123] In particular, private and public sector banks in Switzerland have suspended money transfers to Cuba, preventing some Swiss humanitarian organizations from collaborating

118 John Hudson, 'Trump administration imposes crushing sanctions on Iran in defiance of European humanitarian concerns,' The Washington Post (2020), available at: https://www.washingtonpost.com/national-security/trump-administration-to-impose-crushing-sanctions-on-iran-in-defiance-of-european-humanitarian-concerns/2020/10/07/f29c052c-08f4-11eb-991c-be6ead8c4018_story.html.

119 Rohollah Faghihi, 'Millions of Iranians at risk as US sanctions choke insulin supplies,' Middle East Eye (2020), available at: https://www.middleeasteye.net/news/iran-insulin-medicine-us-sanctions-millions-risk.

120 Speech of the representative of the Syria Red Crescent at the Virtual Arria Meeting 25 November 2020 (2020), available at: http://webtv.un.org/live/watch/part-12-virtual-arria-meeting-on-%E2%80%9Cend-unilateral-coercive-measures-now%E2%80%9D/6212373519001/?term=.

121 See Preliminary findings of the visit to the Bolivarian Republic of Venezuela by the Special Rapporteur on the negative impact of unilateral coercive measures on the enjoyment of human rights, available at: https://www.ohchr.org/en/NewsEvents/Pages/DisplayNews.aspx?NewsID=26747&LangID=E.

122 Tzanakopoulos (n. 101), 139. The same opinion has been expressed by humanitarian NGOs at the Expert concultations on 21–22 October 2020.

123 Alan Boyle, 'Extra-territoriality and U.S. economic sanctions,' International Enforcement Law Reporter 36 (2020), 101–103.

with Cuban medical entities.[124] The illegality of this approach is cited *inter alia* in the study prepared upon the request of the INTA Committee, demonstrating its danger even for huge economies like that of the European Union.[125]

It has been repeatedly reported by states and humanitarian organizations that delays and the increasing costs of bank transfers and deliveries result in rising prices for medical equipment, food and other essential goods, notably in the Bolivarian Republic of Venezuela, Sudan, Syria, Iran and other countries.[126] Venezuela, in particular, refers to the fact that the duration of bank transfers from or to the country increased from 2 to 45 days, as bank fees rose from 0.5 per cent to 10 per cent.[127]

The complexity, comprehensiveness and extraterritoriality of legislation have resulted in the establishment of workarounds. One such workaround welcomed by the UN Special Rapporteur on the negative impact of unilateral coercive measures on the enjoyment of human rights is the Instrument in Support of Trade Exchanges (INSTEX), which was created in 2019 by France, Germany and the United Kingdom to foster trade between Eu-

124 CETIM, 'Economic sanctions and COVID-19 pandemic,' (2020) Europe -Third World Centre.

125 Stoll (n. 113), 18–19, 26–27.

126 Submission by the Coalition of Sudanese Doctors Abroad for SR UCM-Study on the impact of unilateral sanctions on human rights during the state of emergency in the context of COVID-19 pandemic of 15 June 2020 (2020), available at: https://www.ohchr.org/Documents/Issues/UCM/submissions/privates/SudaneseDoctorsAbroad.docx; Joint Submission by Center for Economic and Policy Research, Charity and Security Network, and American Friends Service Committee of 15 June 2020 (2020), available at: https://charityandsecurity.org/wp-content/uploads/2020/07/Joint-Comments-UNSR-Coercive-Measures.pdf; Note 100/20 of the Permanent mission of Syrian Arab Republic to the United Nations Office and Other Organizations in Geneva of 15 June 2020 (2020), available at: https://www.ohchr.org/Documents/Issues/UCM/submissions/states/Syria.doc; Note 252/2020 of the Permanent Mission of Cuba to the United Nations Office in Geneva and the International Organizations in Switzerland of 04 May 2020 (2020), available at: https://www.ohchr.org/Documents/Issues/UCM/submissions/states/CUBA.docx; Syria Red Crescent statements, 'End Unilateral Coercive Measures Now,' Virtual Arria meeting of 25 November 2020 (2020), available at: https://www.securitycouncilreport.org/whatsinblue/2020/11/arria-formula-meeting-on-unilateral-coercive-measures.php.

127 Note Verbale 0116 of 29 May 2020, 'Input of the Bolivarian Republic of Venezuela for the study regarding the impact of unilateral sanctions on human rights during the state of emergency in the context of COVID-19 pandemic' (2020), available at: https://www.ohchr.org/Documents/Issues/UCM/submissions/states/Venezuelapart1.docx.

rope and the Islamic Republic of Iran and to protect European businesses by circumventing United States sanctions against that country. The initial transactions involved humanitarian goods used by the Islamic Republic of Iran to fight COVID-19.[128]

Cyber-technologies are also influencing the scope of private entities involved in the implementation of sanctions regimes. In particular, the United States Cyber-Related Sanctions Regulations impose special obligations on US persons facilitating or engaging in online commerce.[129] The EU regulations request that 'natural and legal persons, entities and bodies supply immediately any information which would facilitate compliance with this Regulation...'[130] Humanitarian organizations repeatedly refer both to the impossibility to make money transfers or to buy essential goods to be delivered to targeted states and to their fear of being subjected to secondary sanctions because of their humanitarian activity.

Nothing in international law can be interpreted to permit any impediment of bank transfers without authorization of the UN Security Council or outside of criminal procedures under national legislation. Even in situations when countermeasures can be taken in response to violations of international law, they are to be taken in accordance with the principles of proportionality and necessity and in compliance with human rights and humanitarian obligations. The fear of secondary sanctions by banks and private companies results in over-compliance and non-selectivity in the sphere of online commerce, making it impossible for nationals of listed countries to enjoy their rights and limiting their access to humanitarian aid.

V. *Sanctions on Trade in and Access to Software*

1. *Overview*

The software can also be qualified as a commodity today. As a result, trade in software can also be limited as part of a sanctions regime. In

128 'EU sells medical goods via INSTEX,' Financial Tribune, (2020), available at: https://financialtribune.com/articles/business-and-markets/102669/eu-sells-medical-goods-via-instex; Stoll (n. 113), 75.

129 Executive Order 13694, section 1a; Executive Order 13757.

130 Art. 8, Council Regulation (EU) 2019/796 of 17 May 2019 concerning restrictive measures against cyber-attacks threatening the Union or its Member States.

particular, already by 2010 the EU had imposed restrictions on the transfer of software, notably those with dual – military and civilian – use.[131]

It shall also be noted that the EU regulations provide for substantial lists of exemptions. In particular, restrictions are not expanded to software that is in the public domain, 'designed for installation by the user without further substantial support by the supplier and which is generally available to the public by being sold from stock at retail selling points.'[132]

The US approach differs substantially. Today the United States has expanded the list of restrictions on the trade of software to 'technology, and software relating to materials processing, electronics, telecommunications, information security, sensors and lasers, and propulsion, including traditional encryption and geospatial software.'[133] It thus causes the companies developing software under US jurisdiction to be concerned about complying with sanctions regimes regarding trade in software provided through public offer, used for private purposes and sometimes even at no cost,[134] to a number of countries, including (as of 2017) the Balkan countries, Belarus, Burma, Cote d'Ivoire (Ivory Coast), Cuba, the Democratic Republic of the Congo, Iran, Iraq, Lebanon, Libya, North Korea, Somalia, Sudan, Syria, and Zimbabwe;[135] and also to become extremely concerned about the growing level of software piracy.[136] As a result, because of the imposed

131 Common Military List of the European Union, ST/5470/2020/INIT of 17 February 2020, OJ C 85, 2020, 1–37, ML 21; Council Regulation 428/2009 of 5 May 2009 setting up a Community regime for the control of exports, transfer, brokering and transit of dual-use items OJ L 134, 2009, p. 1–269, Art. 1(2); Council Regulation 267/2012 of 23 March 2012 concerning restrictive measures against Iran and repealing Regulation 961/2010 *OJ L 88, 2012, 1–112, Art. 2(2);* Council Regulation 2016/44 of 18 January 2016 concerning restrictive measures in view of the situation in Libya and repealing Regulation 204/2011 OJ L 12, 2016, 1–26, Annex I, para. 6; Council Regulation 401/2013 of 2 May 2013 concerning restrictive measures in respect of Myanmar/Burma and repealing Regulation 194/2008 OJ L 121, 2013, 1, Art. 3b, c.

132 Council Regulation (EC) No 428/2009 of 5 May 2009, Annex I; Council Regulation (EU) No 401/2013 of 2 May 2013, Annex III.

133 Gibsonn Dunn, 'Mid-year sanctions and export controls update' (2020), available at: https://www.gibsondunn.com/wp-content/uploads/2020/08/2020-mid-year-sanctions-and-export-controls-update.pdf.

134 Tyler Fuller, 'Global software collaboration in the face of sanctions,' The GitHub Blog (2019), available at: https://github.blog/2019-09-12-global-software-collaboration-in-the-face-of-sanctions/.

135 Ted Miracco, 'The Importance of Export Compliance for Software Companies,' Cylynt Blog (2017), available at: https://www.cylynt.com/blog/the-importance-of-export-compliance-for-software-companies.

136 Ibid.

prohibition on the export of technology, Syria appears to have been unable to buy software for CT scanners and ventilators that is produced only by US companies[137] and is vital in the course of the COVID-19 pandemic.

Because of the fear of secondary sanctions, companies under US jurisdiction have to comply with limitations concerning the software traditionally used for regular administration, public and private purposes, in particular for commercial Internet services or connectivity[138] and even for non-commercial activity. This has become especially dangerous in the course of COVID-19. In particular, the terms of service for Zoom as of 20 August 2020 precluded the use of the platform by those living in the DRPK, Iran, Syria and Crimea, or through legislation of the United States,[139] even for contacts and coordination among doctors to exchange their experiences on symptoms, diagnostics and means of treatment.

Limitations on the use of Zoom for official purposes appeared to be even greater. Because of the above reasons, it was not possible to use Zoom for UN communications as initially planned. Cuba, in particular, was unable to participate in a virtual summit meeting on Zoom of leaders of the Organization of African, Caribbean and the Pacific States on 3 June 2020 to discuss the COVID-19 pandemic.[140] Some countries (in particular, Belarus) have negotiated access permission on a bilateral basis. As a result, the UN Secretariat has had to invest in the development of a special UN platform.[141] It has been reported that Iranian citizens cannot get access to information on COVID-19 and its symptoms, even from the Iranian government, due to Google's censoring of AC19, an Iran-developed App.[142]

---

137 Note 100/20 of the Permanent mission of Syrian Arab Republic (n. 126).

138 Executive Order 13685 of 19 December 2014 blocking property of certain persons and prohibiting certain transactions with respect to the Crimea region of Ukraine: General License No. 9 – exportation of certain services and software incident to Internet-based communications authorized, available at: https://www.federalregister.gov/documents/2014/12/24/2014-30323/blocking-property-of-certain-persons-and-prohibiting-certain-transactions-with-respect-to-the-crimea, para. (d).

139 Zoom terms of service (2020), available at: https://zoom.us/terms.

140 Bloqueo de EE.UU. impide a Cuba participar en foro multilateral; Capturados en Venezuela 57 mercenarios; Protestas por racismo en EE. UU.; Bolsonaro bloquea fondos para lucha contra la COVID-19,' Granma (2020), available at: http://www.granma.cu/hilo-directo/2020-06-05/hilo-05-06-2020-00-06-14.

141 Note of the Permanent Mission of the Republic of Belarus to the United Nations Office and Other Organizations in Geneva 02–16/721 of 17 June 2020.

142 Responses and Comments from the Islamic Republic of Iran of 15 June 2020 (2020), available at: https://www.ohchr.org/Documents/Issues/UCM/submissions/states/Iran.docx.

Iranian doctors cannot get access to medical databases (Pub Med) after its server had been transferred to Google.[143]

2. Human Rights Impact

Therefore, impediments to accessing publicly offered platforms result in the violation of the rights of access to information and freedom of communication and the right to health. Violations of the right to education have also been cited in Iran, Sudan and Venezuela because of the impossibility of using online platforms for educational purposes. In the longer term, with a view to the deteriorating economic situation, OHCHR Sudan reported that unilateral sanctions in the course of COVID-19 are very probably affecting school enrolment and increasing the school dropout rate.[144]

The same problems remain no less relevant outside of the COVID-19 context. Access to Internet technologies and Internet resources have been referred to as a necessary element not only of the struggle against the pandemic but also of the right to development by the participants of the 'Global-local interlinkages I: Obstacles to realizing the right to development and to addressing poverty and inequality' panel of the UN Social Forum 2020.[145] The same approach is taken by the UN Human Rights Council[146] and by the Special Rapporteur on the freedom of opinion.[147]

143 Ibid.

144 Submission by the Coalition of Sudanese Doctors Abroad for SR UCM-Study on the impact of unilateral sanctions on human rights during the state of emergency in the context of COVID-19 pandemic of 15 June 2020, available at: https://www.ohchr.org/Documents/Issues/UCM/submissions/privates/SudaneseDoctorsAbroad.docx.

145 UN Social Forum on 8 October 2020 (2020), available at: http://webtv.un.org/watch/2nd-meeting-social-forum-2020-/6199054565001/?lan=russian#player.

146 HRC Res 32/13, 'The promotion, protection and enjoyment of human rights on the Internet,' A/HRC/32/L.20 of 27 June 2016, available at: https://documents-dds-ny.un.org/doc/UNDOC/LTD/G16/131/89/PDF/G1613189.pdf?OpenElement, preamble.

147 UNGA, 'Promotion and protection of the right to freedom of opinion and expression,' Report of the Special Rapporteur on the promotion and protection of the right to freedom of opinion and expression, 66/290 of 10 August 2011, available at: https://www.ohchr.org/documents/issues/opinion/a.66.290.pdf, paras 45–75.

The OSCE Declaration on Freedom of Communication on the Internet of 28 May 2003 thus called upon Member States to 'foster and encourage access for all to Internet communication and information services on a non-discriminatory basis at an affordable price' (principle 4).[148]

The Declaration of Principles 'Building the Information Society: a global challenge in the new Millennium' of 12 December 2003 calls for states to ensure for all access to information and communication infrastructure and technologies, information and knowledge (paras. 19–28)[149] and considers information and communication technology as the means to promote the Millennium Development Goals (paras. 1, 2). The report of the ILO Global Commission 'Work for a Brighter Future' of January 2019 speaks about using technology as the means of advancing education and decent work.[150]

The UN Special Rapporteur on contemporary forms of racism, racial discrimination, xenophobia and related intolerance correctly noted in her report to the Human Rights Council in June 2020 that people from the least developed countries have only one-fourth of the opportunity to access the Internet compared to people in other countries because of poverty and the underdevelopment of the cyberinfrastructure that results in the limitation of access to 'public health information online and to make use of digital schooling, working and shopping platforms' which are especially important in the time of COVID-19 (Report A/HRC/44/57 of 18 June 2020, para. 20[151]).

It is thus believed here that one should not speak about the possibility to choose trade partners when one speaks about publicly offered paid or non-paid cyber software or services. Preventing people in targeted countries to have access to these services violates a number of human rights, including access to information, freedom of communication, the right to

148 OSCE Declaration of 28 May 2003, 'Declaration on freedom of communication on the Internet,' OSCE (2003), available at: https://www.osce.org/fom/31507?download=true. Principle 4.

149 Declaration of Principles. Building the Information Society: a global challenge in the new Millennium of 12 December 2003, WSIS-03/GENEVA/DOC/4-E (2003), available at: https://www.itu.int/net/wsis/docs/Geneva/official/dop.html.

150 ILO, 'Work for a Brighter Future,' ILO Global Commission of January 2019, available at: https://www.ilo.org/wcmsp5/groups/public/---dgreports/---cabinet/documents/publication/wcms_662410.pdf, paras 43–44.

151 UNGA, 'Racial discrimination and emerging digital technologies: a human rights analysis,' Report of the Special Rapporteur on contemporary forms of racism, racial discrimination, xenophobia and related intolerance, A/HRC/44/57 of 18 June 2020, available at: https://undocs.org/en/A/HRC/44/57, para. 20.

education, the right to decent work and other economic rights, the right to health, the right to development and even the right to life; and it also constitutes *de facto* discrimination against targeted societies constituting around 20 per cent of the world population.

VI. Other Aspects of Application of Sanctions in the Digital Sphere

A number of other aspects of international law are affected by the development of sanctions in the digital age. One of them is the expanding practice of blocking social media accounts as part of sanctions regimes, as is done in particular by US-registered companies as part of the Magnitsky sanctions regime.[152] It has been repeatedly reported that cyber censorship takes place overall to prevent the distribution of information that may be considered harmful for the government for one or another purpose.[153] While recognizing that states are obliged to control the content of *inter alia* social media to prevent the commission of cybercrimes, involvement in terrorist activity as requested by the UN Security Council (see above) and other illegal activity, it shall be done only if international and national human rights standards are fully observed.

Access to the Internet and access to information can also be prevented by sanctions indirectly. In particular, Venezuela refers to the impediment to the access to information via television due to the cessation of operation of DirecTV Venezuela, which represented 43 per cent of the market, because of the US sanctions, in May 2020.[154] Shortages of fuel in the country also result in electricity shutdowns that make access to the Internet quite often impossible.

The availability of information via online news and press releases of state organs increases reputational risks affecting *inter alia* the right to reputation. The UN Human Rights Committee, in General Comment No. 16, refers to the obligation of states not only not to infringe the honour and reputation of individuals but also to provide adequate legisla-

152 Donie O'Sullivan and Artemis Moshtaghian, 'Instagram says it's removing posts supporting Soleimani to comply with US sanctions,' CNN Business (2020), available at: https://edition.cnn.com/2020/01/10/tech/instagram-iran-soleimani-posts/index.html; Jonny Tickle, 'Chechen leader Kadyrov banned from Instagram again, loses account with 1.4 million followers,' RT (2020), available at: https://www.rt.com/russia/488533-kadyrov-banned-instagram-again/.

153 See Avila Pinto (n. 110), 19.

154 Note Verbale 0116 (n. 127).

tion to guarantee their protection.[155] Moreover, General Comment No. 32 expressly notes that 'no guilt can be presumed until the charge has been proved beyond a reasonable doubt, ensures that the accused has the benefit of doubt' and requests governments to abstain from making public statements affirming the guilt of the accused.[156] As a result, the expansive distribution of negative information about individuals and companies while bypassing the presumption of innocence and due process guarantees reduces *inter alia* their attractiveness for investors and counter-parts, resulting in over-compliance with sanctions regimes. The problem becomes especially sensitive when one speaks about individuals and companies designated by one or several countries when there is no possibility for either judicial protection or redress.

The situation is exacerbated by the fact that quite often, targeted individuals and entities usually are not informed in an official and direct manner about their listing, the nature and cause of the accusation giving rise to the sanctions, the scope of limitations, the possibility to defend oneself and to have adequate time to prepare one's defense, and to have an effective remedy. Electronic databases of sanctioning states and international organizations are usually rather complicated and confusing, making the fact of sanctioning rather non-transparent. Unfortunately, the scope of individuals and legal entities targeted by such sanctions is expanding without any attempt to fill these gaps.

Promising rewards for locating individuals allegedly involved in terrorist activity without any case being started against them, and quite often without information being properly verified, on the Rewards for Justice official webpage or its Twitter account[157] is not only ruining their reputation but may endanger their life.

Some other authors refer to the use of online resources and to the element of so-called 'shaming campaign' in the course of the use of unilateral sanctions as a means, which increase reputational risks of states.[158] Social media are often used as an element of sanctions' advocacy tool by various

155 Human Rights Committee, General Comment No. 16 of 8 April 1988, 'Article 17 (Right to Privacy), The Right to Respect of Privacy, Family, Home and Correspondence, and Protection of Honour and Reputation,' CCPR/C/GC/16, para. 11.

156 HRC General Comment No. 32 (n. 91), para. 30.

157 UA USA 9/2021 of 2 February 2021, available at: https://spcommreports.ohchr.org/TMResultsBase/DownLoadPublicCommunicationFile?gId=25985.

158 Odoeme and Chijioke (n. 22), 106–107.

interlocutors.[159] Ph.M. Lutscher seeks to assess the use of DoS attacks by targeted states as a retaliation to the sanctions imposed.[160] All the above situations have not been assessed from the point of international law quite often because of the insufficiency or unavailability of data.

Quite often, countries facing serious economic sanctions, including freezing assets and blocking online commerce, start to develop their own crypto-currency (e.g. attempts done by Venezuela and North Korea). The world is currently facing the recent practice of imposing US sanctions for transactions with the use of these crypto-currencies regardless of the agents or banks in these transactions.[161]

Using cyber means and equipment as a part of sanctions policy and national sanctions acts have also been discussed in the legal scholarship. It is possible to cite here, in particular, cyber-espionage and cyber-surveillance.[162] The UN Special Rapporteur on terrorism and human rights, in his Report 34/61 of 21 February 2017, criticizes the emerging practice of using drones for targeted killings (lethal attacks) of terrorist leaders.[163] I align myself here with his opinion that this activity constitutes a clear violation of the right to life of the targeted person as well as people who may happen to be nearby; no procedural guarantees are observed (Article 14 ICCPR), and the presumption of innocence (Article 14(2) ICCPR) is also violated.[164] In practice, the use of drones for targeted killings in the considered situation could be qualified as the death penalty exercised without any guarantees, which is a clear violation of international legal standards even as regards international crimes, including war crimes (com-

159 Preliminary findings of the visit to the Republic of Zimbabwe by the Special Rapporteur on the negative impact of unilateral coercive measures on the enjoyment of human rights of 28 October 2021, available at: https://www.ohchr.org/Documents/Issues/UCM/Statements/Zimbabwe-country-visit_preliminary-observations-conclusions-Oct2021.docx.

160 Lutscher (n. 17).

161 U.S. Sanctions Venezuela's 'Petro' Cryptocurrency Amid Broader Trend of Sanctioned and Rogue Regimes Experimenting with Digital Assets, Cleary Gottlieb (2018), available at: https://www.clearytradewatch.com/2018/04/u-s-sanctions-venezuelas-petro-cryptocurrency-amid-broader-trend-sanctioned-rogue-regimes-experimenting-digital-assets/.

162 Romano (n. 67), 113.

163 HRC, 'Report of the Special Rapporteur on the promotion and protection of human rights and fundamental freedoms while countering terrorism,' A/HRC/34/61 of 21 February 2017, available at: https://www.ohchr.org/documents/issues/terrorism/a-hrc-34-61.pdf.

164 See also HRC Res 27/37 of 30 June 2014, A/RES/27/37, para. 14.

mon Article 3 of all Geneva Conventions 1949; Article 75(4) Additional protocol I).

VII. Conclusions

The development of digital technologies has changed and is still changing all aspects of human life and international law, including the scope, subjects, means and methods of international and unilateral sanctions. The following list provides some examples but is not exhaustive: response to armed attacks and threats to international peace and security; use of cyber means for terrorism financing; malicious cyber activity, including attacks on critical infrastructure not reaching the level of an armed attack; blocking online commerce of targeted states, companies and individuals as well as other nationals; preventing access to public online platforms; blocking trade with software or information-communication equipment; blocking social media accounts; listing of crypto-currencies; and many others.

The activity of natural and legal persons in cyberspace may endanger the existence of states and constitute a threat to international peace and security. The Charter of the United Nations does not prevent the UN Security Council from deciding to take enforcement measures in such conditions, in accordance with Chapter VII of the Charter. Until now, however, the Security Council has not taken any action in response to malicious cyber activity.

The implementation of Security Council decisions and FATF recommendations today involves measures taken by states in the cybersphere, including data surveillance and the blocking of terrorist and extremist sites, online schemes of transboundary crimes, terrorist recruiting, financing and money laundering. At the same time, no measures to enforce resolutions of the UN Security Council in the cybersphere can be taken without clear additional authorization of the Security Council. National mechanisms shall, in the first place, involve organizational, legislative and judicial means taken in accordance with international law, FATF and OSCE standards.

Unilateral measures can be taken by states and regional organizations in response to malicious cyber activity or with the use of cyber means only in full conformity with international law, and if they also do not violate any obligation of the corresponding states in the sphere of human rights or humanitarian law or in the course of countermeasures. The latter measures shall fully correspond to requirements of the law of international responsibility: proportionality, necessity, observance of peremptory norms of international law, fundamental rights and humanitarian standards, and prohibition of reprisals.

Criminal responsibility for the malicious cyber activity shall in no way be substituted by the application of unilateral sanctions. The application of targeted sanctions in such cases violates economic rights, freedom of movement, the presumption of innocence, due process standards, the right to judicial protection and the right to reputation. Public online announcements of lists of targeted individuals affect their reputations while not providing for access to justice, appeal procedures, protection or redress. Therefore, issues arising from the traditional application of targeted sanctions are equally relevant to the cyber area.

The increasing number of unilateral sanctions, with sanctions regimes that are not always transparent or for which information is not easily available results in growing over-compliance on the part of banks and trading companies; this impedes online banking, results in blocked accounts, and expands the length and costs of transactions to cover banking and entrepreneurial risks because of the threat of secondary sanctions. Consequently, not only directly listed entities but also people of the targeted countries, their businesses and other partners, humanitarian NGOs and their beneficiaries in targeted and other countries are affected. The easy access to cyber means to distribute negative information makes the reputation risk and the amount of over-compliance even greater.

The existence of a single or a few providers of online banking services (SWIFT), technology and software makes other countries and their national and legal entities more vulnerable. It appears that countries have started to develop alternative processes that, in the long term, undermine cooperation and integration schemes. Impediments to online bank transfers and e-commerce have very strong extraterritorial effects that go counter to the traditional standards of states' jurisdiction. They also undermine the economies of targeted states, impede the ability of these states to develop their economies further and guarantee the well-being of their populations, and violate the expanding number of human rights that appear to be especially clear in the course of the COVID-19 pandemic.

In accordance with the general rules of international trade, the right of final consumers to have access to publicly offered paid or non-paid cyber software or services shall not be limited. Preventing access to specific Internet resources goes counter to the whole scope of so-called 'human rights in the Internet': access to information, freedom of expression, the right to privacy, the right to education and the right to reputation, and also the right to decent work and other economic rights. It also violates the right to development and may result in the violation of the right to health and even the right to life in emergency situations; it constitutes *de facto* discrimination against targeted societies constituting around 20 per cent of the world population. It also goes counter to repeated calls of the United Nations and other organizations for solidarity, cooperation and multilateralism.

The development of digital technologies affects today all aspects of the introduction and implementation of sanctions, which mostly take the form of unilateral ones, the legality of which is rather dubious from the perspective of international law. Any measures shall be taken by states in the first place within generally recognized standards of international law with due account for their possible humanitarian impact and for the human rights of every individual concerned.

Part III
Rights

Digitalisation and International Human Rights Law: Opportunities and Critical Challenges

Stefanie Schmahl

Abstract At the time when the various universal and regional human rights treaties came into being, the digitalization of societies was still largely in its infancy. Only a very few human rights treaties dealt with the influence of the media and the Internet on situations relevant to the protection of human rights. Nowadays, the parameters have changed fundamentally. Numerous UN human rights committees are increasingly confronted with questions of digitalization and its effects on the legal position of the individual. The same applies to international courts at the regional level, in particular to the European Court of Human Rights. However, their decisions still focus mainly on substantive human rights issues, for instance, by resorting to an evolutive interpretation to outline the freedom of communication and the right to private life in the digital environment. The overall effects of the Internet and the growing digitalization of societies on the general dogmatic aspects of human rights treaties have not yet been thoroughly investigated. The aim of the chapter is, therefore, to shed a first light on the main challenges that typically arise when determining the structural relationship between international human rights norms on the one hand and behaviours of individuals in the digital environment on the other. These challenges relate to specific structural features such as the existence or non-existence of a right to access the Internet, the contouring of new digital spheres of human rights and the dangers resulting from the use of algorithms and increasing anonymization. It is also questionable whether the scope of the extraterritorial application of human rights treaties needs to be redesigned in the digital age. Finally, more general human rights aspects such as the determination and possible extension of both duty-bearers and rights-holders require closer analysis. The chapter examines to what extent a dynamic interpretation of human rights treaties appears possible in the age of digitalization and under what conditions this approach reaches its limits.

I. Introduction

At the time when the various universal and regional human rights treaties came into being, the digitalisation of societies was still largely in its infancy. The 1989 Convention on the Rights of the Child (CRC)[1] was the first, and so far, is the only international human rights convention that explicitly addresses a question touching upon digitisation, namely the influence of the (digital) media on situations relevant to the protection of human rights. From the initial draft proposal to include a protective regulatory clause against potential negative effects of media on children in the

1 Convention on the Rights of the Child of 20 November 1989, 1577 UNTS 3.

Convention[2] arose finally an extensive and rich text, which also recognises and promotes the positive opportunities that the mass media have on the evolvement and education of children.[3] In view of its elaboration in the 1980s, it is, however, obvious that 'media' within the meaning of Article 17 CRC were mainly understood to include those of the analogue world, such as books, magazines, radio and cinema films.[4]

In order to sound out the scope of Article 17 CRC in the digital age, at the initiative of the CRC Committee, numerous representatives of States, international organisations and non-governmental organisations held a joint 'Day of General Discussion' in 2014 on the media behaviour of children in general. Another 'Day of General Discussion' in the same year dealt specifically with the use of digital media by children. The results of both discussion days are reflected in two legally non-binding recommendations of the CRC Committee.[5] Both documents stress and further specify the importance of Article 17 CRC and its close relationship with other Convention guarantees, such as the right to private life, freedom of expression and information, and the protection of children against economic and sexual exploitation.[6] The CRC Committee repeatedly emphasises that the content of those guarantees does not only refer to selected types of media. Rather, the scope of the standard extends equally to analogue and digital media by way of a dynamic interpretation.[7] Thus, it is not astonishing

---

2 See UN Commission on Human Rights, Revised Draft Convention on the Rights of the Child of 30 July 1980, E/CN.4/1349, p. 4.

3 For more detail see Sharon Detrick, *A Commentary on the United Nations Convention on the Rights of the Child* (Leiden: Martinus Nijhoff 1999), 285–287.

4 See Kai Hanke, Luise Meergans and Isabell Rausch-Jarolimek, 'Kinderrechte im Medienzeitalter. Ausführungen zum Recht des Kindes auf Medienzugang gemäß Art. 17 UN-Kinderrechtskonvention,' RdJB 65 (2017), 330–350 (335).

5 CRC Committee, 'Day of General Discussion on the child and the media,' 12 September 2014, CRC/C/15/Add.65, and 'Day of General Discussion on digital media and children's rights,' 12 September 2014.

6 For more detail see Stefanie Schmahl, 'Kinderrechte und Medien – Herausforderungen eines modernen Risiko- und Befähigungsmanagements' in: Ingo Richter, Lothar Krappmann and Friederike Wapler (eds), *Kinderrechte. Handbuch des deutschen und internationalen Kinder- und Jugendrechts* (Baden-Baden: Nomos 2020), 375–403 (378–380).

7 See, e.g., CRC Committee, 'Day of General Discussion on the child and the media,' 12 September 2014, CRC/C/15/Add.65, para. 256, point 5 and 'General Comment No. 16,' 17 April 2013, CRC/C/GC/16, para. 60. For more detail see John Tobin and Elizabeth Handsley, 'Article 17' in: John Tobin (ed.), *The UN Convention on the Rights of the Child. A Commentary* (Oxford: Oxford University Press 2019), 600 (605–606).

that the CRC Committee recently, on 2 March 2021, released a new General Comment No. 25 on children's rights in relation to the digital environment and gives guidance on how to respect, protect and fulfil children's rights in the digital environment.[8] Even if General Comment No. 25 merely summarises the Committee's previous considerations on the matter, it is the first General Comment of a UN human rights treaty body that explicitly addresses the digital environment and its impacts on human rights by highlighting both the empowering character and the risks of the digital environment for children's rights. In that regard, the CRC Committee functions as a human rights seismograph, being the first UN human rights treaty body to deal with rising fundamental questions in modern human rights law.[9]

In addition to the CRC Committee, also other treaty-based expert committees and human rights courts are increasingly confronted with questions of digitalisation and its effects on the legal position of the individual. The UN human rights monitoring bodies unanimously underscore that the Internet and social media can be valuable tools for providing information and opportunities for debate.[10] In particular, it is undisputed that the right to freedom of expression and information clearly extends to cyberspace. As early as 2012, the UN Human Rights Council stated that 'the same rights that people have offline must also be protected online, in particular, freedom of expression, which is applicable regardless of frontiers and through any media of one's choice.'[11] This statement has been endorsed by the UN Human Rights Committee in several instances.[12] On the regional level, the African Commission on Human and Peoples'

---

8 CRC Committee, 'General Comment No. 25,' 2 March 2021, CRC/C/GC/25, paras 22 ff.

9 See Stephan Gerbig, 'Leaving the Pre-Digital Era, Finally!: Thoughts on the New UN CRC General Comment on Children's Rights in the Digital Environment,' Völkerrechtsblog, 4 May 2021, DOI: 10.17176/20210504–111252–0.

10 See, e.g., Human Rights Committee, 'General Comment No. 34,' 12 September 2011, CCPR/C/GC/34, para. 12; CESCR Committee, 'General Comment No. 25,' 30 April 2020, E/C.12/GC/25, paras 42, 45; CEDAW Committee/CRC Committee, 'Joint General Recommendation No. 31/General Comment No. 18,' 14 November 2014, CEDAW/C/GC/31-CRC/C/GC/18, para. 79.

11 Human Rights Council, 'The promotion, protection and enjoyment of human rights on the Internet,' 16 July of 2012, HRC/RES/20/8, para. 1.

12 See, e.g., Human Rights Committee, 'General Comment No. 34,' 12 September 2011, CCPR/C/GC/34, paras 12 ff. and 'General Comment No. 37,' 27 July 2020, CCPR/C/GC/37, para. 34.

Rights (ACHPR),[13] the Inter-American Commission of Human Rights (IACHR) and, the Inter-American Court of Human Rights (IACtHR)[14] as well as the European Court of Human Rights (ECtHR)[15] have also made it clear that freedom of expression and information applies to Internet communication.

Furthermore, almost all human rights conventions guarantee the right to a private life, which generally includes the integrity of personal data.[16] The UN Human Rights Council,[17] the UN Special Rapporteurs on freedom of expression and the right to privacy,[18] the UN General Assembly,[19] the Office of the High Commissioner for Human Rights (OHCHR),[20] the UN Human Rights Committee,[21] the European Union Agency for Fundamental Rights (FRA),[22] the Court of Justice of the European Union

---

13 See ACHPR, 'Resolution on the Right to Freedom of Information and Expression on the Internet in Africa, 4 November 2016, ACHPR/Res. 362(LIX)' and 'Declaration of Principles on Freedom of Expression and Access to Information in Africa,' 10 November 2019, Principle 17.

14 See IACHR, 'Standards for a Free, Open, and Inclusive Internet,' 15 March 2017, OEA/Ser.L/V/II and CIDH/RELE/INF.17/17; IACtHR, *Herrera-Ulloa v. Costa Rica*, judgment of 2 July 2004, paras 108 ff.

15 See, e.g., ECtHR, *MTE v. Hungary*, judgment of 2 February 2016, no. 22947/13, para. 56 and *Kharitonov v. Russia*, judgment of 23 June 2020, no. 10795/14, paras 33 ff.; *Văcean v. Romania*, judgment of 16 November 2021, no. 47695/14, paras 30 ff. For an early overview, see Robert Uerpmann-Wittzack and Magdalena Jankowska-Gilberg, 'Die Europäische Menschenrechtskonvention als Ordnungsrahmen für das Internet,' Multimedia und Recht 2008, 83–89, with further references.

16 See ECtHR, *Rotaru v. Romania*, judgment of 4 May 2000, no. 28341/95, paras 40 ff. The EU Charter of Fundamental Rights, however, guarantees these two rights separately in Articles 7 and 8.

17 See Human Rights Council, A/HRC/17/26, 16 May 2011, A/HRC/20/L.13, 29 June 2012 and A/HRC/28/L.27, 24 March 2015.

18 See the Reports of the Special Rapporteur on the promotion and protection of the right to freedom of opinion and expression, A/HRC/17/27, 16 May 2011, para. 55, A/HRC/23/40, 17 April 2013, para. 24, and the Report of the Special Rapporteur on the right to privacy, A/HRC/31/64, 14 November 2016, para. 8.

19 UNGA Res 68/167 of 18 December 2013, A/RES/68/167, para. 3; UNGA Res 69/166 of 18 December 2014, A/RES/69/166, paras 3 ff.

20 OHCHR, A/HRC/27/37, 30 June 2014, paras 12 ff.

21 Human Rights Committee, 'General Comment No. 16,' 8 April 1988, HRI/GEN/1/Rev.9 (Vol. I), para. 10 and 'General Comment No. 34,' 12 September 2011, CCPR/C/GC/34, paras 12, 15, 39, 43.

22 FRA, 'Report on surveillance by intelligence services: fundamental rights safeguards and remedies in the European Union' (Luxembourg: Publications Office of the European Union, 2015), *passim*. Yet, it has to be underlined that the

(CJEU)[23] and the ECtHR[24] – to name but a few – have all consistently and repeatedly emphasised the right to privacy in the online communication. In general, it can be said that both communication rights and the right to enjoy a private life apply to the same extent in the online as in the offline world.[25] However, this fact is not a surprising innovation to the international human rights regime, but rather a usual dynamic interpretation of existing human rights guarantees in the sense of Article 31(3) of the 1969 Vienna Convention on the Law of Treaties.[26]

Yet, the effects of the internet and the growing digitalisation of societies on the general dogmatic aspects of human rights treaties have not yet been thoroughly investigated. Most of the scholarly contributions that deal with the matter focus on selected human rights perspectives only, e.g., on those of children and adolescents, or on selected human rights topics such as, e.g., data protection without going into the overarching challenges of digitalisation for the dogmatic structures of the human rights

---

Agency's mandate only extends to carrying out studies on fundamental rights issues in so far as they fall into the scope of EU law.

23 See, e.g., CJEU, *Volker und Markus Schecke GbR and Hartmut Eifert v. Land Hessen*, judgment of 9 November 2010, cases no. C-92/09 and C-93/09, ECLI:EU:C:2010:662, paras 49, 52; *Digital Rights Ireland Ltd v. Minister for Communications, Marine and Natural Resources and Others*, judgment of 8 April 2014, cases no. C-293/12 and C-594/12, ECLI:EU:C:2014:238, para. 29; *EU-Canada PNR Agreement*, opinion 1/15 of 26 July 2017, ECLI:EU:C:2017:592, paras 122–123; *Data Protection Commissioner v. Facebook Ireland and Maximilian Schrems (Schrems No. 2)*, case C-311/18, judgment of 16 July 2020, ECLI:EU:C:2020:559, para. 170; *La Quadrature du Net and Others v. Premier Ministre and Others*, cases C-511/18 et al., judgment of 6 October 2020, ECLI:EU:C:2020:791, paras 117, 130.

24 See, e.g., ECtHR, *Weber and Saravia v. Germany*, judgment of 29 June 2006, no. 54934/00, para. 77; *S. and Marper v. The United Kingdom*, judgment of 4 December 2008, nos. 30562/04 and 30566/04, paras 66–7; *Iordachi and Others v. Moldova*, judgment of 10 February 2009, no. 25198/02, para. 29; *Kennedy v. The United Kingdom*, judgment of 18 May 2010, no. 26839/05, para. 118; *Ben Faiza v. France*, judgment of 8 February 2018, no. 31446/12, paras 53 ff.; *Breyer v. Germany*, judgment of 30 January 2020, no. 50001/12, paras 74 ff.; *Văcean* (n. 15), paras 43 ff.

25 See Matthias C. Kettemann, 'Das Internet als internationales Schutzgut: Entwicklungsperspektiven des Internetvölkerrechts anlässlich des Arabischen Frühlings,' HJIL 72 (2012), 469–482 (472–475); David P. Fidler, 'Cyberspace and Human Rights' in: Nicholas Tsagourias and Russell Buchan (eds), *Research Handbook on International Law and Cyberspace* (Cheltenham: Edward Elgar Publishing 2015), 94–117 (99–103).

26 Stefanie Schmahl, 'Intelligence and Human Rights' in: Jan-Hendrik Dietrich and Satish Sule (eds), *Intelligence Law and Policies in Europe* (München: Beck/Nomos/Hart 2019), 291–334 (para. 31).

system as a whole. Therefore, an attempt will be made to shed a first light on the main challenges that typically arise when trying to determine the structural relationship between international human rights law on the one hand and behaviours of individuals in the digital environment and of intelligent, human-like machines on the other. These main challenges, outlined in section II., include specific structural features such as the existence or non-existence of a right to access the Internet (1.) and of new digital spheres of human rights (2.), as well as more general human rights aspects such as the determination and possible extension of both duty-bearers and rights-holders (3., 4. and 7.), the extraterritorial application of human rights (5.) and the fight against new discrimination problems due to the growing use of algorithms (6.).

Of course, this contribution cannot conclusively determine the systematic relationship between digitalisation and international human rights either. Too many aspects are technologically, ethically and legally in flux. Moreover, the relevant constellations are so varied that it is impossible to give a 'one-size-fits-all' answer. Nevertheless, initial sketches of ideas shall be presented to what extent the digital environment offers opportunities for the realisation of human rights on the one hand and to what extent it critically challenges the functioning of the international human rights regime on the other.

II. Effects of the Digitalisation of Societies on the General Requirements of Human Rights Treaties

1. Right to Access the Internet

The first fundamental question that needs to be answered is whether there is a human right to access the Internet. This right may be understood in twofold ways, in that it entails not only access to the Internet in terms of infrastructure, availability of devices and Internet connection but also in terms of acquiring digital skills. As regards the former, there is no doubt that without infrastructural and unhindered access to the Internet and its content, people will not be able to take part in the potential of the digitalisation of societies.[27] In Africa, for instance, less than 20 % of the populati-

27 Matthias C. Kettemann, 'Menschenrechte im Multistakeholder-Zeitalter: Mehr Demokratie für das Internet?,' Zeitschrift für Menschenrechte 10 (2016), 24–36 (24).

on has access to the Internet and digital devices. In particular, women and people living in rural areas in the African continent are excluded from Internet access and thus from the knowledge and understanding that is conveyed online.[28] Also, in European countries, the digital infrastructure and the quality of the Internet connection is unevenly distributed. In rural areas in Germany, for instance, Internet access, if available at all, is often cumbersome, slow and unstable. Especially in times of the Covid19 pandemic, in which digital home schooling was deemed necessary to keep the interpersonal distance for medical reasons, the lack of expansion of the digital infrastructure in rural areas has had disadvantageous effects on the rights of the child to education. It widened the knowledge gap and existing inequalities for children living in rural areas and in vulnerable situations.

In addition to providing the necessary digital infrastructure, learning digital skills is also indispensable for effective participation in the digitalised society. The Committee on Economic, Social and Cultural Rights (CESCR Committee) has pointed out that predominantly older persons and persons with low levels of education and income do not have access to the Internet for financial reasons or have limited digital skills. They are therefore hindered from fully enjoying their human rights to information and education.[29] In particular, access to the Internet is of crucial importance for marginalised and minority groups in order to manifest and elaborate their personal and cultural identity.[30] Therefore, the Committee on the Elimination of Discrimination against Women (CEDAW Committee) rightly stresses that States parties are obliged to ensure access to and knowledge of the Internet and other information and communications technologies in order to improve women's education and access to justice systems at all levels.[31] The recommendations of the CRC Committee and

---

28 See African Union, 'Déclaration de l'Union Africaine sur la gouvernance de l'internet et le développement de l'économie numérique en Afrique,' Assembly/AU/Decl. 3(XXX), 29 January 2018, Recital no. 5.

29 CESCR Committee, 'Concluding Observations: Estonia,' 27 March 2019, E/C.12/EST/CO/3, para. 52.

30 CESCR Committee, 'General Comment No. 21,' 21 December 2009, E/C.12/GC/21, para. 32. Similarly, with particular regard to the rights of persons with disabilities, Dörte Busch 'Digitale Teilhabe für Menschen mit Behinderungen nach der UN-Behindertenrechtskonvention', Zeitschrift für europäisches Sozial- und Arbeitsrecht 20 (2021), 484-492 (485 ff.).

31 See CEDAW Committee, 'General Recommendation No. 33,' 3 August 2015, CEDAW/C/GC/33, para. 17d. Similarly, IACtHR, *Escher et al. v. Brazil*, judgment of 6 July 2009, paras 43–46.

the CESCR Committee point to a similar direction.[32] In fact, Internet access and digital skills are not only a prerequisite for exercising freedom of communication but also an essential starting point for exercising other rights. Access to the Internet is today a 'core utility' and can be regarded as an 'essential infrastructure for communities.'[33] Against this background, the UN Human Rights Council and various human rights monitoring bodies repeatedly call on States to promote and facilitate (infrastructural and learned) access to the Internet for everyone.[34]

However, a State's obligation to provide access to the Internet that can be enforced directly under human rights law is not existent.[35] The human rights monitoring bodies focus solely on an obligation of conduct, not of result. From a doctrinal perspective, an obligation of result could be justified, for example, as a derivative right of the States' obligation to guarantee everyone a decent subsistence level which, today, might include the access to digital infrastructure. An obligation of result could also be construed as being a legal precondition for exercising other rights.[36] The Community Court of Justice of the Economic Community of the West African States (CCJ ECOWAS) emphasises that access to the Internet is a derivative right within the context of the right to freedom of expression and should be treated as an integral part of the right.[37] However, the Court itself considers that restrictions, even a complete shutdown of the Internet, are permissible under certain conditions.[38]

Similarly, the CESCR Committee only recommends that States parties ensure that digital assistance is easily available for those who have neither access to the Internet nor the digital skills to access information and

32 See, e.g., CRC Committee, 'General Comment No. 13,' 18 April 2011, CRC/C/GC/13, para. 8; CESCR Committee, 'Concluding Observations: Estonia,' 27 March 2019, E/C.12/EST/CO/3, para. 53 and 'General Comment No. 25,' 30 April 2020, E/C.12/GC/25, para. 16.

33 Kettemann (n. 27), 27.

34 See, e.g., Human Rights Council, 16 July 2012, HRC/RES/20/8, para. 3; ACHPR, 'Resolution on the Right to Freedom of Information and Expression on the Internet in Africa,' 4 November 2016, ACHPR/Res. 362(LIX), para. 1; Human Rights Committee, 'General Comment No. 34,' 12 September 2011, CCPR/C/GC/34, para. 15.

35 See Fidler (n. 25), 106–107.

36 Similarly, Kettemann (n. 27), 25–26.

37 CCJ ECOWAS, *Amnesty International Togo et al. v. The Togolese Republic*, judgment of 25 June 2020, no. ECW/CCJ/JUD/09/20, para. 38.

38 CCJ ECOWAS, *Amnesty International Togo et al* (n. 37), para. 45.

communications technology based public services.[39] It further mentions the importance of Internet access for all those who seek assistance, employment and opportunities to develop their skills and calls upon States to facilitate access to the Internet, particularly for marginalised and disadvantaged groups.[40] But the CESCR Committee makes all these requirements dependent on available resources. Also, the legally non-binding 2030 Agenda for Sustainable Development focuses solely on an obligation of conduct by stating that universal and affordable access to information and communications technology, including the Internet, should significantly increase.[41] In sum, the States are called upon to adopt laws, policies and other measures in cooperation with all relevant stakeholders and make the best possible use of their resources to provide universal, equitable, affordable and meaningful access to the Internet without discrimination.

Conversely, however, it does not follow from the fundamental obligation of States to ensure access to the Internet on the basis of available resources that the individual is obliged to use the Internet or digital technologies in all circumstances. In this respect, negative freedom gives the individual, in principle, the right to abstain from any form of participation in a digital society. This means that there must generally be no legal, soft law or *de facto* obligations for the use of digital tools.[42] The right to self-determination and autonomy presupposes that every individual must have the possibility not to participate in the virtual world and to lead their lives exclusively in an analogous way. Thus, analogous options for, e.g., purchasing tickets or political elections, must continue to be available alongside online alternatives such as blockchain technology.[43] The provision and the use of analogue devices remains even possible in exceptional situations, like the Covid19 pandemic, which demands distance between people for medical reasons. For example, political elections can be organised as postal votes; and tickets can be ordered by phone and sent by conventional mail. At least at present, when not all people, in particular

39 CESCR Committee, 'Concluding Observations: Estonia,' 27 March 2019, E/C.12/EST/CO/3, para. 53.

40 CESCR Committee, 'Concluding Observations: Djibouti,' 30 December 2013, E/C.12/DJI/CO/1–2, para. 38.

41 UNGA Res 70/1 of 25 September 2015, A/RES/70/1, 21 October 2015, Goal 9c.

42 In regards to this aspect, see Wenguang Yu, 'Verlagerung von Normsetzungskompetenzen im Internet unter besonderer Berücksichtigung der Cybersecurity Standards,' DÖV 73 (2020), 161–172 (162).

43 As regards the use of the blockchain technology for political elections, see Tobias Mast, 'Schöne neue Wahl – Zu den Versprechen der Blockchain-Technologie für demokratische Wahlen,' JZ 76 (2021), 237–246.

older persons or persons with disabilities, are yet able or willing to use digital devices, any mandatory use of online tools would contradict the basic human rights of equality and freedom. Only in the case of distance learning for children and adolescents in times of pandemics may different parameters apply due to the compulsory character of schooling. But here, too, ventilation systems could be installed in classrooms and based on this, intelligent forms of face-to-face teaching could be organised in small groups or in alternating lessons in order to alleviate the hardships of purely digital lessons for children and parents.

2. *New Digital Spheres of Human Rights*

If individuals make use of their freedoms in a virtual form, a second challenge that must be resolved consists in whether all or only some human rights have a specific digital sphere of protection. With regard to freedom of expression and information and the protection of private life, the digital sphere has already been developed dynamically on several occasions by both international courts and human rights expert committees.[44] However, it is less clear whether this finding extends to other or even all human rights. This becomes relevant, for instance, when addressing freedom of assembly, which is primarily tailored to the physical presence of the participants.

It is debatable whether freedom of assembly can be transferred to political actions on online platforms, video conferences, or Internet fora that call for discussion, e.g., under a certain hashtag. Some scholars deny the relevance of the freedom of assembly for virtual gatherings with a view to the lack of physical danger emanating from such assemblies.[45] Another argument often put forward in this context is that there is no protection gap if freedom of assembly does not cover virtual assemblies since all

44 See the references in notes 8–24. Further see Udo Di Fabio, *Grundrechtsgeltung in digitalen Systemen* (München: Beck 2016), 83 ff.

45 See, e.g., Michael Kniesel, 'Versammlungs- und Demonstrationsfreiheit – Entwicklung des Versammlungsrechts seit 1996,' NJW 53 (2000), 2857–2866 (2860); Sebastian Hoffmanns, 'Die 'Lufthansa-Blockade' 2001 – eine (strafbare) Online-Demonstration?,' Zeitschrift für Internationale Strafrechtsdogmatik 7 (2012), 409–414 (412–413).

relevant actions may be sufficiently secured by freedom of expression and information.[46] However, this line of reasoning overlooks three aspects.

Firstly, online assemblies go beyond expressing one's opinions; they rather resemble a collective engagement in building and sharing views and opinions. Therefore, the UN Special Rapporteur on freedom of assembly and association rightly appeals to the States to recognise that 'the rights to freedom of peaceful assembly and of association can be exercised through new technologies, including through the Internet.'[47] Recently, the UN Human Rights Committee has explicitly concurred with this view.[48]

Secondly, there is a relatively high risk of interference by State authorities or third private parties in this virtual engagement. The UN Human Rights Committee stresses that States parties must not block or hinder Internet connectivity in relation to peaceful assemblies.[49] The same applies to geo-targeted or technology-specific interference with connectivity or access to content. States should ensure that the activities of Internet service providers do not unduly restrict online assemblies.[50]

Thirdly, virtual gatherings harbour considerable dangers if the inherent group dynamic leads to an anonymous 'shit storm' that violates the personal rights of others.[51] If the participants in a virtual meeting slow down or block the services of an external server through distributed denial of service attacks, they can threaten the property of third parties.[52] The UN Human Rights Committee has therefore made clear that virtual gatherings

46 See, e.g., Jürgen Bröhmer, 'Versammlungs- und Vereinigungsfreiheit' in: Oliver Dörr, Rainer Grote and Thilo Marauhn (eds), *EMRK/GG, Konkordanzkommentar* (Tübingen: Mohr Siebeck, 2nd. edn 2013), 1161–1232 (para. 25).

47 Report of the Special Rapporteur on the rights to freedom of peaceful assembly and of association, A/HRC/20/27, 21 May 2011, para. 84k. Similarly, Christian Möhlen, 'Das Recht auf Versammlungsfreiheit im Internet – Anwendbarkeit eines klassischen Menschenrechts auf neue digitale Kommunikations- und Protestformen,' Multimedia und Recht 2013, 227–230.

48 Human Rights Committee, 'General Comment No. 37,' 27 July 2020, CCPR/C/GC/37, para. 34.

49 Human Rights Committee, 'Concluding Observations: Cameroon,' 30 November 2017, CCPR/C/CMR/CO/5, paras 41–42.

50 Human Rights Committee, 'General Comment No. 34,' 12 September 2011, CCPR/C/GC/34, para. 34 and 'General Comment No. 37,' 27 July 2020, CCPR/C/GC/37, para. 34.

51 See Stephan Pötters and Christoph Werkmeister, 'Grundrechtsschutz im Internetzeitalter,' JURA 35 (2013), 5–12 (9); Corinna Nitsch and Michael Frey, 'Grundrechte im Zeitalter der Digitalisierung – Die digitale Sphäre der Versammlungsfreiheit,' DVBl. 135 (2020), 1054–1056 (1055).

52 See Nitsch and Frey (n. 51), 1056.

must be subject to the same restrictions as analogue assemblies. In the case of serious threat potential, Internet observations and isolated geo-targeted blocking by State authorities can be considered permissible under certain circumstances.[53]

These thoughts on the digital sphere of protection of the freedom of peaceful assembly can be transferred to other human rights, which typically required a physical presence in the 'pre-digital era.' As a rule, the interpretation and application of human rights can be adapted to the digital challenges by means of a dynamic interpretation. This is, in particular, made clear by General Comment No. 25 of the CRC Committee, which covers not only the non-physical human rights such as access to information and freedom of expression but also rights that, as a rule, presuppose a physical presence such as freedom of association, access to health services and to culture, leisure and play. The CRC Committee gives these rights a plausible interpretation in the light of the digital environment.[54] In a similar way, business freedom and property rights also claim validity on the Internet and in a digital environment.[55]

However, these human rights are coming under strong pressure from the opensource movement, which considers the assertion of property rights in intellectual services as an attack on the freedom of the Internet. Also, search engines and social networks growingly take advantage of the works and achievements of others. Consequently, the authors concerned see themselves deprived of the income from their intellectual work, on which they make a living.[56] The discussion about the EU Copyright Directive[57] has shown how heated the debate is and what negative consequences an all-encompassing 'free mentality' can have for the liberal human rights system.[58]

---

53 Human Rights Committee, 'General Comment No. 34,' 12 September 2011, CCPR/C/GC/34, para. 34.

54 See CRC Committee, 'General Comment No. 25,' 2 March 2021, CRC/C/GC/25, paras 50 ff.

55 See Christine Langenfeld, 'Der Schutz freier Kommunikationsräume in der digitalen Welt – Eine Gedankenskizze,' ZEuS 24 (2021), 33–42 (37).

56 Ibid., 37.

57 Directive (EU) 2019/790 of the European Parliament and of the Council of 17 April 2019 on copyright and related rights in the Digital Single Market and amending Directives 96/9/EC and 2001/29/EC, OJ 2019 L 130/92.

58 Di Fabio (n. 44), 79.

3. *Extension of Duty-Bearers of Human Rights*

It is well-known that threats to individual privacy no longer emanate exclusively from State authorities, but increasingly also from private third parties, above all from globally operating technology companies and the digital industry.[59] The right to privacy is probably the one where most cases of indirect third-party effects occur today, for example, when employers or companies resort to clandestine video surveillance and Internet tracking,[60] when Facebook and Cambridge Analytica siphon off vast amounts of data from their users without informed consent and prior authorisation,[61] or where a search engine operator includes an automatised reference and information system contained in a list of results displayed following a search conducted on the basis of an individual's name.[62] Also, the employment of big data and new technologies by State and third party agencies and the emergence of 'smart cities,' that include surveillance technologies in public spaces and further artificial intelligence tools to combat crime and terrorism, pose significant risks to human rights.[63]

---

59 See Hans-Jürgen Papier, 'Rechtsstaatlichkeit und Grundrechtsschutz in der digitalen Gesellschaft,' NJW 70 (2017), 3025–3031 (3026).

60 See, e.g., Klaus Herrmann and Michael Soiné, 'Durchsuchung persönlicher Datenspeicher und Grundrechtsschutz,' NJW 64 (2011), 2922–2928 (2927); Jobst-Hubertus Bauer and Mareike Schansker, '(Heimliche) Videoüberwachung durch den Arbeitgeber,' NJW 65 (2012), 3537 (3538 ff.); Viktoria Robertson, 'Excessive Data Collection: Privacy Considerations and Abuse of Dominance in the Era of Big Data,' CML Rev 57 (2020), 161–190 (171 ff.).

61 An illustrative case in that regard is CJEU, *Schrems No. 2* (n. 23), paras 2 ff. See further Walter Frenz, 'Anmerkung zu EuGH C-311/18: Schrems II,' DVBl. 135 (2020), 1270–1272 (1270); Alexander Golland, 'Datenschutzrechtliche Anforderungen an internationale Datentransfers,' NJW 73 (2020), 2593–2596; Thorsten Schröder, 'Wie Facebook über sich selbst stolperte,' ZEIT Online, 20 March 2018, available at: http://www.zeit.de/wirtschaft/2018-03/facebook-datenmissbrauch-cambridge-analytica-mark-zuckerberg-politik.

62 See CJEU, *Google Spain SL and Google Inc. v. AEPD and Mario Costeja González*, judgment of 13 May 2014, case C-131/12, ECLI:EU:C:2014:317, paras 80 ff.; *Bolagsupplysningen OU and Ingrid Ilsjan v. Svensk Handel AB*, judgment of 17 October 2017, case C-194/16, ECLI:EU:C:2017:766, para. 48; *Google LLC v. CNIL*, judgment of 24 September 2019, case C-507/17, ECLI:EU:C:2019:772, para. 56. See also John W. Kropf, 'Google Spain SL v. Agencia Española de Protección de Datos (AEPD),' AJIL 108 (2014), 502–509; Monika Zalnieriute, 'Google LLC v. Commission nationale de l'informatique et des libertés (CNIL),' AJIL 114 (2020), 261–267.

63 Lorna McGregor, 'Looking to the Future: The Scope, Value and Operationalization of International Human Rights Law,' Vand J Transnat'l L. 52 (2019), 1281–

Yet, it is still the State which remains the duty-bearer within international human rights law. The duty to ensure compliance with human rights treaties primarily establishes a direct obligation incumbent on the Contracting States, since it is the States' consents that underpin international law's content.[64] However, this duty contains a further obligation upon States parties to ensure that non-governmental or private service providers, such as multinational technology corporations, act in accordance with the provisions of the conventions. This means that States are required to put in place a framework that prevents human rights violations from occurring, establish monitoring mechanisms as safeguards and hold those responsible to account.[65] These obligations apply directly to State actions or omissions and, through the duty to protect human rights on the one hand and the due diligence principle on the other, the States must also protect individuals from harm by private third parties, including business enterprises.[66] In other words, human rights treaties create indirect obligations, or indirect horizontal effects, for non-State actors, by establishing (direct) positive duties on States parties.[67] The transfer of powers to private service providers or private institutions must not lead to a reduction of protection below the level required by the conventions. For instance, the CEDAW Committee recurrently underlines that States parties have to take measures, including the adoption of legislation and national action plans, to protect women from Internet crimes and other misdemeanours

---

1314 (1303); Alexander Kriebitz and Christoph Lütge, 'Artificial Intelligence and Human Rights: A Business Ethical Assessment,' Business and Human Rights Journal 5 (2020), 84–104 (85).

64 Jay Butler, 'The Corporate Keepers of International Law,' AJIL 114 (2020), 189–218 (194).

65 See Carlos Manuel Vázquez, 'Direct vs. Indirect Obligations of Corporations Under International Law,' Colum J Transnat'l L. 54 (2005), 927–959 (930).

66 See Lorna McGregor, Daragh Murray and Vivian Ng, 'International Human Rights Law as a Framework for Algorithmic Accountability,' ICLQ 68 (2019), 309–343 (311–312).

67 See, e.g., CRC Committee, 'General Comment No. 5,' 27 November 2003, CRC/GC/2003/5, paras 43, 56, 'General Comment No. 15,' 17 April 2013, CRC/GC/C/16, para. 8 and General Comment No. 21, 21 June 2017, CRC/C/GC/21, para. 15. See also CESCR Committee, 'General Comment No. 14,' 11 August 2000, E/C.12/2000/4, para. 42. As regards the regional level, see, e.g., Matthias Klatt, 'Positive Obligations under the European Convention of Human Rights,' HRLJ 71 (2011), 691–718; Laurens Lavrysen, 'Positive Obligations in the Jurisprudence of the Inter-American Court of Human Rights,' Inter-American and European Human Rights Journal 7 (2014), 94–115.

that women experience online.[68] Both the Committee on the Elimination of Racial Discrimination (CERD Committee) and the CRC Committee point out that States parties should take resolute action to combat hate speech, cyberbullying, and racial as well as sexual violence on the Internet and other electronic communications networks.[69] The CRC Committee further stresses that all human rights provisions must be respected in legislation and policy development, including the private and business sector.[70] While the implementation is primarily the responsibility of States parties, the duty to respect, to protect and to fulfil human rights extends indirectly beyond the State and State-controlled services. States parties are demanded to enact laws and policies directed to private institutions and other non-State services in order to ensure that their activities and operations do not have adverse human rights implications.[71]

As important as these requirements are, they also have shortcomings in the Internet context. The transnational, instantaneous nature of Internet communications makes it difficult for governments to directly influence the information entering or leaving a country, while at the same time, the power of the private Internet providers and search engine operators, which control this flow of information, is increasing.[72] This form of governance over digital platforms is problematic for a human rights system that treats human rights solely as a government responsibility. As demonstrated, most international human rights law is concerned with the obligations of States to provide remedies for the abuse of human rights by businesses and other non-State actors. However, such frameworks do not easily apply

68 See CEDAW Committee, 'General Recommendation No. 33,' 3 August 2015, CEDAW/C/GC/33, para. 51e, 'General Recommendation No. 35,' 26 July 2017, CEDAW/C/GC/35, para. 30, and 'Concluding Observations: Venezuela,' 11 January 2018, CEDAW/C/VEN/CO/7–8/Add.1, para. 7.

69 See CERD Committee, 'General Recommendation No. 35,' 26 September 2013, CERD/C/GC/35, paras 7, 15, 39 and 42, and 'Concluding Observations: Iceland,' 18 September 2019, CERD/C/ISL/CO/21–23, paras 13–14; CRC Committee, 'General Comment No. 13,' 18 April 2011, CRC/C/GC/13, paras 21, 31.

70 CRC Committee, 'General Comment No. 16,' 17 April 2013 CRC/C/GC/16, para. 8.

71 CRC Committee, 'General Comment No. 16,' 17 April 2013, CRC/C/GC/16, para. 5; Julia Sloth-Nielsen, 'Monitoring and Implementation of Children's Rights' in: Ursula Kilkelly and Ton Liefaard (eds), *International Human Rights of Children* (Cham: Springer 2019), 31–64 (52).

72 See Emily B. Laidlaw, *Regulating Speech in Cyberspace. Gatekeepers, Human Rights and Corporate Responsibility* (Cambridge: Cambridge University Press 2015), 83. Similarly, Josef Drexl, 'Bedrohung der Meinungsvielfalt durch Algorithmen,' Zeitschrift für Urheber- und Medienrecht 61 (2017), 529–543 (536).

to international digital enterprises and technology companies, which are often not the culprits themselves but enable or gatekeep the wrongdoing of others. Furthermore, States have to ensure that there is no risk for the maintenance of the principle of non-discrimination by the increasing use of algorithms. They have to secure that policies and practice are in place to identify and assess any actual or potential dangers to human rights.[73]

In this grey area of governance of Internet gatekeepers, search engine operators and technology companies, the work of the former Special Representative of the UN Secretary-General on the issue of human rights and businesses, John Ruggie, emerges as important, because it seeks to bridge the governance gap between the human rights impact of businesses and the historical focus of human rights law on States.[74] Ruggie's attempt to apply State-like human rights obligations to companies in his 2011 Report on Guiding Principles on Business and Human Rights[75] was strongly endorsed by the UN Human Rights Council, entrenching them as the authoritative global reference point for business and human rights.[76] The extension of the scope of human rights standards to a digital sphere with enlarged responsibilities of digital companies would therefore have to entail a corresponding extension of the duty to protect, in particular the possibility of horizontal interventions by market-dominant companies and the recognition of a direct third-party effect of human rights.[77] It is not a coincidence that, under Principles 11 and 13 of the UN Guiding Principles on Business and Human Rights, corporations, including technology com-

73 McGregor, Murray and Ng (n. 66), 329. But see also the rather reserved assessment regarding German constitutional law by Jürgen Kühling, 'Die Verantwortung der Medienintermediäre für die demokratische Diskursvielfalt', JZ 76 (2021), 529-538 (534).

74 Rightly so, Laidlaw (n. 72), 90. See also Kriebitz and Lütge (n. 63), 88.

75 Special Representative of the Secretary-General on the Issue of Human Rights and Transnational Corporations and Other Business Enterprises John Ruggie, 'Guiding Principles on Business and Human Rights: Implementing the United Nations 'Protect, Respect and Remedy' Framework,' A/HRC/17/31, 21 March 2011, paras 1–16.

76 Human Rights Council, 'Human rights and transnational corporations and other business enterprises,' A/HRC/RES/17/4, 16 June 2011, para. 1. See also Laidlaw (n. 72), 91.

77 Christian Hoffmann, Sönke Schulz and Kim Corinna Borchers, 'Grundrechtliche Wirkungsdimensionen im digitalen Raum,' Multimedia und Recht 2014, 89–95 (92); Butler (n. 64), 201. See also, in a more general way, Lottie Lane, 'The Horizontal Effect of International Human Rights Law in Practice,' European Journal of Comparative Law and Governance 5 (2018), 5–88 (16 ff.).

panies, must not only refrain from human rights violations, but also avoid adverse human rights impacts through their business activities.

As a result of their outstanding market position *vis-à-vis* citizens, private companies often act in the digital sector as powerfully as the State and can considerably restrict, lead or manipulate citizen's behaviour.[78] In the famous *Bosman* ruling regarding the free movement of workers, the CJEU recognised this role of certain private actors such as sports associations.[79] The Court has recently transferred this argument *mutatis mutandis* to the role of technology companies regarding the individual's 'right to be forgotten' and the ensuing obligation of the search engine operators, such as Google, to carry out de-referencing requests on versions of their search engine, provided that the data subject's right to privacy is adequately balanced against the right to freedom of information.[80] This view of the CJEU takes into account the limited ability of States to transfer the standards of international human rights law to transnationally operating digital corporations, by establishing direct horizontal effects of European fundamental rights.[81]

Another possibility is, of course, that States simply close the regulatory gaps that exist for technology companies by treating private governance as a modality of governance that must be strictly embedded in a framework of the rule of law.[82] This is the path taken by the 2017 German Network Enforcement Act, last modified in June 2021,[83] which forms part and is the

78 McGregor (n. 63), 1305; Utz Schliesky, 'Digitalisierung – Herausforderung für den demokratischen Verfassungsstaat,' NVwZ 38 (2019), 693–701 (694). For this reason, the (German) Federal Court of Justice has subjected the social media platforms active in Germany to an increased indirect third-party effect of fundamental rights, see Federal Court of Justice, judgment of 29 July 2021, III ZR 179/20.

79 CJEU, *Union royale belge des sociétés de football association ASBL and Others v. Jean-Marc Bosman*, judgment of 15 December 1995, case C-269/92, ECLI:EU:C:1995:463, paras 82–87.

80 CJEU, *Google Spain* (n. 62), paras 96–99; *Google LLC v. CNIL* (n. 62), para. 72. Similar arguments can be found in CJEU, *Schrems No. 2* (n. 23), paras 85–86.

81 Butler (n. 64), 208–209.

82 Nicholas Tsagourias, 'The Rule of Law in Cyberspace: A Hybrid and Networked Concept?,' HJIL 80 (2020), 433–451 (447).

83 Gesetz zur Verbesserung der Rechtsdurchsetzung in sozialen Netzwerken (Netzwerkdurchsetzungsgesetz – NetzDG) of 1 September 2017, Bundesgesetzblatt 2017 I, 3352, last modified on 3 June 2021 in: Bundesgesetzblatt 2021 I, 1436. For more detail, see Matthias Cornils, 'Präzisierung, Vervollständigung und Erweiterung: Die Änderungen des Netzwerkdurchsetzungsgesetzes 2021', NJW 74 (2021), 2465-2471. The UK's Online Safety Bill, published by the UK Government on 12

result of the State's duty to protect human rights. The German Network Enforcement Act aims to ensure that Internet platforms delete or block illegal or manifestly unlawful content – in particular in cases where the private invader remains anonymous vis-à-vis the victim. In a similar way, the Digital Services Act proposed by the European Commission on 15 December 2020[84] aims at encompassing a set of new rules applicable to online intermediaries and platforms across the whole European Union to create a safe digital space. The rules specified in the proposal primarily establish due diligence obligations for online intermediaries and online platforms to, *inter alia*, take measures against abusive notices and counter-notices and to report of suspicious criminal offences. These paths are preferable to establishing a direct human rights obligation on the part of technology companies, as they do not call into question the dogmatics and the liberal character of international human rights protection. In this respect, it is important to note that the operation of an online platform by a technology company is also protected by the freedom of expression, since it is the online platform that enables the exchange of opinions between people who do not know each other.[85]

4. *Modes of Protecting and Counteracting Anonymity in the Digital Sphere*

This fact leads to the next challenge for international human rights protection in the age of digitalisation, which is anonymity, i.e., the concealment of the identity of actors and their actions. It is true that anonymity has

---

May 2021, points to a similar direction. For more detail see Edina Harbinja, 'The UK's Online Safety Bill: Safe, Harmful, Unworkable?,' Verfassungsblog, 18 May 2021, DOI: https://dx.doi.org/10.17176/20210518-170138-0" \t

84 Proposal for a Regulation of the European Parliament and of the Council on a Single Market For Digital Services (Digital Services Act) and amending Directive 2000/31/EC, COM (2020) 825 final. For more detail, see, e.g., Michael Denga, 'Plattformregulierung durch europäische Werte: Zur Bindung von Meinungsplattformen an EU-Grundrechte,' EuR 56 (2021), 569-595 (579 ff.); Wolfgang Beck, 'Der Entwurf des Digital Services Act,' DVBl. 136 (2021), 1000-1005 (1000 ff.); Nico Gielen and Steffen Uphues, 'Digital Markets Act und Digital Services Act,' EuZW 32 (2021), 627-637 (632 ff.); Martin Eifert, Axel Metzger, Heike Schweitzer and Gerhard Wagner, 'Taming the Giants: The DMA/DSA Package,' CMLRev. 58 (2021), 987-1028 (1008 ff.).

85 Clearly so, (German) Federal Court of Justice, judgment of 27 January 2022, III ZR 3/21, para. 37; further see Stephanie Schiedermair/Johannes Weil, 'Online-Intermediäre als Träger der Meinungsfreiheit,' DÖV 75 (2022), 305-314.

always existed in the offline world. It was and is mostly used in order to avoid responsibility for an action, to reduce the risk of sanctions or to eliminate them altogether.[86]

The digitalisation of the living environment has not fundamentally modified traditional anonymous actions, but it has noticeably dynamized them. This is mainly due to the fact that the Internet is changing the time barriers, physical and spatial distances and financial costs of all activities, adding ubiquitous, simultaneous and immediately noticeable effects.[87] Internet users often make a conscious choice to communicate or use online activities anonymously, by not using full or real names, suppressing their IP addresses or even using subtle obfuscation techniques.[88] It is no coincidence that the Internet phenomenon 'Anonymous' – known from the Guy Fawkes mask – has become a political icon of a network-based activism that campaigns for Wikileaks and against racism and child pornography.[89] In his work '*L'art de la révolte*,' the French philosopher and sociologist Geoffroy de Lagasnerie transfigured this development towards a culture of anonymity into a political world citizenship that constructs a new legal order at the grassroots level.[90] This postulate must be clearly rejected. A democratic State based on the rule of law cannot be constituted by a collection of people who, due to their anonymity, evade any individual or democratic responsibility.[91] Furthermore, there is a high risk that information will be manipulated by artificial intelligence's filtering, which

---

86 See Jens Kersten, 'Anonymität in der liberalen Demokratie,' JuS 57 (2017), 193–203 (193).

87 See Volker Boehme-Neßler, 'Die Macht der Algorithmen und die Ohnmacht des Rechts,' NJW 70 (2017), 3031–3037 (3032); Thorsten Thiel, 'Anonymität und der digitale Strukturwandel der Öffentlichkeit,' Zeitschrift für Menschenrechte 10 (2016), 7–22 (13 ff.); Johannes Unterreitmeier, 'Das Internet als Herausforderung der inneren Sicherheit,' BayVBl. 2021, 689-696 (691 ff.).

88 Instructive analysis by Duncan B. Hollis, 'An e-SOS for Cyberspace,' Harv. Int'l. L. J. 52 (2011), 373–432 (397 ff.); Martha Finnemore and Duncan B. Hollis, 'Constructing Norms for Global Cybersecurity,' AJIL 110 (2016), 425–479 (435, 458–459).

89 See, e.g., Frédéric Bardeau and Nicolas Danet (translation by Bernard Schmidt), *Anonymous: Von der Spaßbewegung zur Medienguerilla* (Münster: Unrast 2012); Jacques de Saint Victor, *Die Antipolitischen* (Hamburg: Hamburger Edition 2015).

90 Geoffroy de Lagasnerie, *L'art de la révolte: Snowden, Assange, Manning* (Paris: Fayard 2015), 80 ff.

91 See Kersten (n. 86), 194; Schliesky (n. 78), 697 ff.; Gabriele Buchholtz, 'Demokratie und Teilhabe in der digitalen Zeit,' DÖV 70 (2017), 1009–1016 (1009).

could change the political discourse's direction and suppress parts of the opinion.[92]

However, different requirements are likely to apply to the protection of human rights. The right to private life gives everyone a subjective right to anonymity.[93] Every individual is generally free to decide on the reason, the mode and the duration of his or her identifiability.[94] For example, real names, private photos and personal data may, as a rule, only be published with the consent of the rights-holder.[95] States are therefore required to respect and guarantee the privacy and security of communication on the Internet and to protect the personal rights of every individual against unlawful interference by State authorities and non-State actors effectively, which may also be reflected in the promotion of encryption technologies.[96] Anonymity in expressing opinions serves to prevent feared State reprisals and other negative effects by non-State third parties (e.g., a private employer) that could arise if the person making the statement is identified.[97] Furthermore, anonymity in the expression of opinion is intended to protect politically active citizens from the negative consequences such as self-censoring, which could produce chilling effects in the democratic debate.[98]

Yet, the right to privacy against arbitrary or unlawful State interference is not guaranteed without restriction; the main limits are the public order and national security. Only the core area of private life, which relates to human dignity, is a legal asset that is absolutely protected against State intervention. In the social sphere, in contrast, the State may identify people

---

92 Kriebitz and Lütge (n. 63), 100.

93 Kersten (n. 86), 195. As to the following section, see also Stefanie Schmahl, 'Anonymität im Recht: Freiheitsverbürgung oder Freiheitsgefährdung?,' JZ 73 (2018), 581–590 (583).

94 For more detail see Ansgar Ohly, 'Verändert das Internet unsere Vorstellung von Persönlichkeit und Persönlichkeitsrecht?,' AfP 42 (2011), 428–438 (431–434).

95 Ohly (n. 94), 430–431.

96 Kettemann (n. 25), 475 ff.

97 See Mirko A. Wieczorek, *Persönlichkeitsrecht und Meinungsfreiheit im Internet* (Frankfurt am Main: Peter Lang 2013), 71 ff.; Jürgen Kühling, 'Im Dauerlicht der Öffentlichkeit – Freifahrt für personenbezogene Bewertungsportale!?,' NJW 68 (2015), 447–450 (448). Most recently, see also (German) Federal Court of Justice, judgment of 27 January 2022, III ZR 3/21 (n. 85), para. 51.

98 Kersten (n. 86), 196. As regards potential chilling effects under Article 10 ECHR, see Eckart Klein, 'Einwirkungen des europäischen Menschenrechtsschutzes auf Meinungsäußerungsfreiheit und Pressefreiheit,' AfP 25 (1994), 9–18 (17).

under certain circumstances.[99] On several occasions, however, European courts have repeatedly pointed out that interference by State authorities in the right to privacy and personal data protection is subject to high standards of justification and must be strictly necessary.[100] Especially in the case of secret mass surveillance, the States have to rule out the risk of abuse by issuing general, clear and precise rules governing the scope, application, purpose and objective of a measure and the timing and duration of the intervention.[101]

In multidimensional human rights situations, Internet anonymity and encryption technologies create further problems, for instance, in cases where one person's freedom of expression comes into conflict with general laws and the rights of others. It has become a commonplace that posting hateful comments or fake news on social networks under the guise of anonymity, including by Internet trolls and bots, is steadily increasing.[102] Or in other words: The rise in hate speech and bullying on the Internet clearly demonstrates the dangers (in particular for minorities) associated

---

99 See, e.g., ECtHR, *Rotaru v. Romania* (n. 16), para. 44; *Bărbulescu v. Romania*, judgment of 12 January 2016, no. 61496/08, paras 35 ff.; CJEU, *La Quadrature du Net* (n.), para. 135; *Privacy International*, judgment of 6 October 2020, case C-623/17, ECLI:EU:C:2020:790, paras 74 ff.; *H.K./Prokuratuur*, judgment of 2 March 2021, case C-746/18, ECLI:EU:C:2021:152, paras 29 ff.

100 See, e.g., ECtHR, *Klass v. Germany*, judgment of 6 September 1978, no. 5029/71, para. 41; *Copland v. The United Kingdom*, judgment of 3 April 2007, no. 62617/00, para. 39; *Breyer v. Germany* (n. 24), paras 83 ff.; CJEU, *Digital Rights Ireland* (n. 23), paras 50 ff.; *A./Staatsanwaltschaft Offenburg*, judgment of 21 June 2017, case C-9/16, ECLI:EU:C:2017:483, para. 63; *La Quadrature du Net* (n. 23), para. 141; *H.K./Prokuratuur* (n. 99), paras 32 ff.

101 See ECtHR *Weber and Saravia* (n. 24), paras 93–95; *Zakharov v. Russia*, judgment of 4 December 2015, no. 47143/06, para. 229; *Szabó and Vissy v. Hungary*, judgment of 12 January 2016, no. 37138/14, paras 77 and 80; *Big Brother Watch and Others v. The United Kingdom* (GC), judgment of 25 May 2021, nos. 58170/13, 62322/14 and 24960/15, paras 348 ff., para. 361; CJEU, *Digital Rights Ireland* (n. 23), paras 54 -55; *Schrems*, judgment of 6 October 2015, case C-362/14, ECLI:EU:C:2015:650, paras 91–98; *Tele2 Sverige*, judgment of 21 December 2016, cases C-203/15 and C-698/15, ECLI:EU:C:2016:970, paras 109–112, 119–125; *La Quadrature du Net* (n. 23), paras 132, 165.

102 See Dirk Heckmann, 'Persönlichkeitsschutz im Internet,' NJW 65 (2012), 2631–2635 (2632); Armin Steinbach, 'Meinungsfreiheit im postfaktischen Umfeld,' JZ 72 (2017), 653–661 (661). On the individual and societal dangers that arise from digital hatred, see Elisa Hoven and Alexandra Witting, 'Das Beleidigungsunrecht im digitalen Zeitalter,' NJW 74 (2021), 2397-2401 (2398 ff.).

with obfuscating identity in the digital world.[103] Under human rights law, States must therefore ensure that the right to anonymous expression of opinion does not apply without reservation on the Internet. It is true that freedom of expression includes both open and clandestine, even anonymous expressions of opinion.[104] In the latter cases, however, new evaluation criteria must be found for the balancing process at the level of justification.[105] It must be remembered that the individual affected by an anonymous attack cannot take effective countermeasures due to the lack of accountability of the anonymous attacker. Thus, the usual competition for the better argument, which is indispensable for free and democratic States, is led *ad absurdum*.[106] Even the guarantee of a legal remedy would be ineffective due to the concealment of the attacker's identity.[107]

Precisely for these reasons, national laws, such as the German Network Enforcement Act,[108] which oblige digital companies and social network platforms to set up complaint systems with the consequence of removing illegal online comments, are valuable measures to counter the increase in anonymous defamation on the Internet.[109] In order to uncover the identity of the commentator and to delete hate speech, the cooperation

---

103 See Hoffmann, Schulz and Borchers (n. 77), 89; Eva Maria Bredler and Nora Markard, 'Grundrechtsdogmatik der Beleidigungsdelikte im digitalen Raum,' JZ 76 (2021), 864-872 (865 ff.).

104 See Heckmann (n. 102), 2632; Ohly (n. 94), 436; Kersten (n. 86), 196–197.

105 Schmahl (n. 93), 584.

106 Similar assessment by Günther Wiese, 'Bewertungsportale und allgemeines Persönlichkeitsrecht,' JZ 66 (2011), 608–617 (612, 615).

107 Andreas Glaser, 'Grundrechtlicher Schutz der Ehre im Internetzeitalter,' NVwZ 31 (2012), 1432–1438 (1436).

108 Gesetz zur Verbesserung der Rechtsdurchsetzung in sozialen Netzwerken (Netzwerkdurchsetzungsgesetz – NetzDG) of 1 September 2017, Bundesgesetzblatt 2017 I, 3352, last modified on 3 June 2021 in: Bundesgesetzblatt 2021 I, 1436.

109 Schmahl (n. 93), 585. Similarly, Georg Nolte, 'Hate-Speech, Fake-News, das 'Netzwerkdurchsetzungsgesetz" und Vielfaltsicherung durch Suchmaschinen,' Zeitschrift für Urheber- und Medienrecht 61 (2017), 552–565 (553 ff.); Langenfeld (n. 55), 39–40; Benjamin Raue, 'Plattformnutzungsverträge im Lichte der gesteigerten Grundrechtsbindung marktstarker sozialer Netze,' NJW 75 (2022), 209-215 (213 ff.). – The human rights conformity of the German Network Enforcement Act is very controversial, see the critical assessments by, e.g., Eike M. Frenzel, 'Aktuelles Gesetzgebungsvorhaben: Verbesserung der Rechtsdurchsetzung in sozialen Netzwerken (NetzDG),' JuS 2017, 414–416; Nikolaus Guggenberger, 'Das Netzwerkdurchsetzungsgesetz – schön gedacht, schlecht gemacht,' ZRP 50 (2017), 98–101; Hubertus Gersdorf, 'Hate Speech in sozialen Netzwerken,' Multimedia und Recht 2017, 439–447.

of the operators of social networks with State authorities is pivotal.[110] The communication intermediaries are easier to localise than the anonymously acting private person and thus a valid alternative strategy for the protection of human dignity and the right to privacy in cyberspace.[111] It is no coincidence that provider liability has advanced to become an essential sanctioning instrument for Internet matters in tort law, which is not only backed by the ECtHR,[112] but also by the case-law of the CJEU.[113] Here too, of course, the principle of proportionality must be strictly taken into account when partially outsourcing control mechanisms to private third parties.[114] Hate speech restrictions should never be based solely on a private company's assessment, but on legal orders from States, which also have to provide effective legal remedies against a private third party's intervention.[115]

5. *Extraterritorial Application of Human Rights in the Digital Sphere*

Not only domestic authorities but also intelligence agencies of foreign States and non-State actors based abroad either increasingly intercept the

110 See Christoph M. Giebel, 'Zivilrechtlicher Rechtsschutz gegen Cybermobbing in sozialen Netzwerken,' NJW 70 (2017), 977–983 (978 ff.). See also CERD Committee, 'General Recommendation No. 35,' 26 September 2013, CERD/C/GC/35, paras 39 and 42; 'Concluding Observations: Iceland,' 18 September 2019, CERD/C/ISL/CO/21–23, para. 14.

111 See Matthias Cornils, 'Entterritorialisierung im Kommunikationsrecht,' VVDStRL 76 (2017), 391–442 (423, 425); Martin Eifert, 'Rechenschaftspflichten für soziale Netzwerke und Suchmaschinen,' NJW 70 (2017), 1450–1454 (1450–1451); Drexl (n. 72), 539 ff.

112 ECtHR, *Delfi AS v. Estonia*, judgment of 16 June 2015, no. 64569/09, paras 125 ff. and 159; *Magyar Tartalomszolgáltatók Egyesülete v. Hungary*, judgment of 2 February 2016, no. 22947/13, paras 62 and 69.

113 See CJEU, *Google Spain* (n. 62), paras 48 ff.

114 See the French Conseil Constitutionnel, decision of 18 June 2020, no. 2020–801 DC, ECLI: FR: CC: 2020: 2020.801.DC, paras 8 ff., which declares the French hate speech law 'Avia' partly unconstitutional for reasons of over-blocking.

115 See UNGA, 'Report of the Special Rapporteur on the promotion and protection of the right to freedom of opinion and expression' of 9 October 2019, A/74/486, para. 47b. See also (German) Federal Court of Justice, judgment of 29 July 2021, III ZR 179/20, paras 83 ff., as regards the social media users' fundamental rights protection through procedures. Procedural rights are now being given more emphasis in the Network Enforcement Act as modified in 2021 (n. 108) and in the Commission's proposal for the Digital Services Act (n. 84), too.

communication, collect data from individuals on foreign territory, or disrupt other individual rights and legitimate interests by, for instance, posting hateful comments.[116] Against this background, the question of whether and to what extent human rights treaties can be applied extraterritorially is the fifth crucial difficulty that needs to be resolved with regard to digitalisation.

a) Extraterritorial Applicability of Human Rights Treaties to Digital Interventions by State Authorities

In principle, human rights develop their protection only in relation to encroachments that are attributable to the public authorities of the States parties. However, the attribution of such interventions to the Contracting States is not excluded if and to the extent that interventions made by a third party are carried out with the approval or tolerance of the authorities of the territorial State. Therefore, the use of communication information that is collected by foreign intelligence but passed onto domestic authorities for use must be measured against the human rights guarantees entered into by the territorial State.[117] Correspondingly, State authorities, including the intelligence services, remain in principle bound by the guarantees of the human rights treaties even if they monitor cross-border telecommunications.[118]

A more delicate question in this context is whether State authorities have to respect human rights if they only intercept foreign telecommunications abroad. Although it has not yet been conclusively clarified to what extent international human rights apply extraterritorially, there is broad agreement that they generally claim extraterritorial applicability. Both the International Court of Justice (ICJ) and the UN Human Rights Committee underline that the obligations of the International Covenant on Civil and Political Rights (ICCPR) also apply beyond the national territory of the

116 See Marko Milanović, 'Human Rights Treaties and Foreign Surveillance: Privacy in the Digital Age,' HarvIntlLJ 56 (2015), 81–146 (101); Edzard Schmidt-Jortzig, 'IT-Revolution und Datenschutz,' DÖV 71 (2018), 10–15 (13).

117 Papier (n. 59), 3029.

118 See, e.g., Stefanie Schmahl, 'Nachrichtendienste in der Völkerrechtsordnung' in: Jan-Hendrik Dietrich et al. (eds), *Nachrichtendienste im demokratischen Rechtsstaat* (Tübingen: Mohr Siebeck 2018), 21–41 (34 ff.); Milanović (n. 116), 97–98. Different view by Klaus F. Gärditz, 'Die Rechtsbindung des Bundesnachrichtendienstes bei Auslandstätigkeiten,' Die Verwaltung 48 (2015), 463–497 (472–474).

Contracting States, provided that the State concerned has an effective control over the situation abroad.[119] Contrary to Israel and the United States of America, which take the long-standing positions that the Covenant does not apply extraterritorially,[120] the human rights monitoring bodies have adopted the view that anybody directly affected by a State party's action will be regarded, for the purpose of the ICCPR, as subject to that State party's jurisdiction, regardless of the circumstances in which the power or the sufficient factual control was obtained.

The views expressed by the ICJ and the Human Rights Committee are correct. They are consistent with the principles of universality and indivisibility of human rights.[121] From the human rights perspective, an individual is entitled to protection simply because he or she is a human being, irrespective of where he or she is located and what nationality he or she is. Decisive for the applicability of the ICCPR is not the place of the violation but the relationship between the individual and the intervening State.[122] Human rights treaties never intended to grant States unchecked power to do as they pleased with individuals living outside of the country and having a different citizenship. Jurisdiction clauses were rather meant

---

119 See ICJ, *Legal Consequences of the Construction of a Wall in the Occupied Palestinian Territory*, advisory opinion of 9 July 2004, ICJ Reports 2004, 136 (paras 106–111); *Armed Activities on the Territory of the Congo (Democratic Republic of Congo v. Uganda)*, judgment of 19 December 2005, ICJ Reports 2005, 168 (para. 216); Human Rights Committee, *López Burgos v. Uruguay*, views of 29 July 1981, no. 52/1979, CCPR/C/13/D/52/1979, para. 12.3; 'General Comment No. 31,' 26 May 2004, CCPR/C/21/Rev.1/Add.13, para. 10.

120 See Human Rights Committee, 'Concluding Observations on the Third Report of Israel,' 29 July 2010, CCPR/C/ISR/CO/3, para. 5; 'Concluding Observations on the (First) Report of the United States of America,' 3 October 1995, CCPR/C/79/Add. 50, para. 19; 'Concluding Observations on the Fourth Report of the United States of America, 28 March 2014,' CCPR/C/USA/CO/4, para. 4. See also US Department of State, Office of the Legal Advisor (Harald Koh), 'Memorandum Opinion on the Geographic Scope of the ICCPR,' 19 October 2010, 12–13.

121 See ICJ, *Construction of a Wall* (n. 119), para. 109. For a fuller account see Theodor Meron, 'Extraterritoriality of Human Rights Treaties,' AJIL 89 (1995), 78–82.

122 See Rick Lawson, 'Life after Bankovic: On the Extraterritorial Application of the European Convention on Human Rights' in: Fons Coomans and Menno T Kamminga (eds), *Extraterritorial Application of Human Rights Treaties* (Antwerp: Intersentia 2004), 83–123 (86); Sarah Joseph and Adam Fletcher, 'Scope of Application' in: Daniel Moeckli, Sangeeta Shah and Sandesh Sivakumaran (eds), *International Human Rights Law* (Oxford: Oxford University Press, 3rd edn 2017), part II, chapter 6.

to prevent the responsibility of States when they are actually unable to uphold rights abroad.[123]

However, when they are in the factual position to ensure the enjoyments of rights on foreign territory, the jurisdiction clause of Article 2(1) ICCPR was not drafted to allow States to escape from their responsibilities simply on the basis of the geographical location of the affected individual.[124] The majority in legal scholarship, too, argues for the assumption that the Covenants' human rights obligations are applicable in cases where State actions are exercised extraterritorially.[125] Other UN human rights expert bodies are also unanimously in favour of the extraterritorial application of human rights treaties.[126] Finally, this line largely conforms to the case-law of the ECtHR. After a long hesitation beginning with the restrictive ruling in the *Banković Case* (2001),[127] the Court today recognises the extraterritorial applicability of the Convention rights on the basis of the principle of effective control over territory or persons[128] in order to

---

123 See the individual opinion of Christian Tomuschat in: Human Rights Committee, *López Burgos v. Uruguay* (n. 119), Appendix.

124 Rightly so, Tomuschat (n. 123). See also Noam Lubell, *Extraterritorial Use of Force Against Non-State Actors* (Oxford: Oxford University Press 2010), 205.

125 See, e.g., Thomas Buergenthal, 'To Respect and Ensure: State Obligations and Permissible Derogations' in: Louis Henkin (ed.), *The International Bill of Rights: the Covenant on Civil and Political Rights* (New York: Columbia University Press 1981), 72–91 (74–75); Meron (n. 121), 81; Tomuschat, *Human Rights: Between Idealism and Realism* (3rd edn, Oxford: Oxford University Press 2014), 100 ff.; Martin Weiler, 'The Right to Privacy in the Digital Age: The Commitment to Human Rights Online,' GYIL 58 (2014), 651–665 (658); Thilo Marauhn, 'Sicherung grund- und menschenrechtlicher Standards gegenüber neuen Gefährdungen durch private und ausländische Akteure,' VVDStRL 74 (2015), 373–403 (380); Timo Schwander, *Extraterritoriale Wirkung von Grundrechten im Mehrebenensystem* (Berlin: Duncker & Humblot 2019), 117–129.

126 See, e.g., CEDAW Committee, *Y.W. v. Denmark*, decision of 2 March 2015, CEDAW/C/60/D/51/2013, paras 8.7; 'General Recommendation No. 35,' 26 July 2017, CEDAW/C/GC/35, para. 20; CERD Committee, 'Concluding Observations: Israel,' 27 January 2020, CERD/C/ISR/CO/17–19, paras 9, 22; CMW Committee and CRC Committee, 'Joint General Comment No. 3 and No. 20,' 16 November 2017, CMW/C/GC/3-CRC/C/GC/22, para. 12.

127 See ECtHR, *Banković and Others. v. Belgium and 16 Other Contracting States*, decision of 12 December 2001, no. 52207/99, paras 59, 61. Critical assessment by, e.g., Alexander Orakhelashvili, 'Restrictive Interpretation of Human Rights Treaties in the Recent Jurisprudence of the European Court of Human Rights,' EJIL 14 (2003), 529–568.

128 See ECtHR (Grand Chamber), *Al-Skeini v. The United Kingdom*, judgment of 7 July 2011, no. 55721/07, paras 132 ff.; *Hirsi Jamaa and Others v. Italy*, judgment of 23 February 2012, no. 27765/09, para. 172; *Mozer v. Moldavia and Russia*, judg-

prevent a vacuum in the protection of human rights.[129] In two recent decisions on surveillance measures by the secret service, in which the foreign persons concerned were not situated in the Convention State, the ECtHR has even unreservedly taken the European Convention on Human Rights as the relevant standard.[130]

Against this backdrop, the applicability of human rights treaties to digital interferences by State authorities, even if they take place extraterritorially, is now beyond question. At the national level, the (German) Federal Constitutional Court has recently recognised that the rights of the telecommunications under Articles 10(1) and 5(1) of the Basic Law, in their dimension as rights against State interference, also protect foreigners in other countries.[131] Due to technological developments, the strict concept of physical or territorial control on which the jurisdiction under Article 2(1) ICCPR and Article 1 ECHR is based, is also clearly outdated with regard to online communication.[132] Communication data typically encompass more than one person and often more than one jurisdiction. In addition, new technology on data portability frequently leads to a separation between the whereabouts of the person and the place where the privacy of the individual is invaded.[133] The choice of the virtual method must not result in the lowering of standards and the non-applicability of human rights treaties to the State that carries out extraterritorial mass surveillance. On the contrary, the focus of the assessment must shift to

---

ment of 23 February 2016, no. 11138/10, paras 110–111; *M.N. et al. v. Belgium*, judgment of 5 March 2020, no. 3599/18, paras 101–109. Similarly, with regard to digital mass surveillance, ECtHR, *Liberty and Others v. The United Kingdom*, judgment of 1 July 2008, no. 58243/00, paras 64–70.

129 Clearly so, ECtHR, *Al-Skeini* (no. 128), para. 142. See also Tomuschat (n. 125), 100 ff.

130 ECtHR, *Big Brother Watch and Others v. The United Kingdom*, judgment of 13 September 2018, nos 58170/13, 62322/14 and 24960/15, para. 271; *Centrum för Rättvisa v. Sweden*, judgment of 19 June 2018, no. 35252/08, para. 111. In that regard, both chamber judgments were fully confirmed by the Grand Chamber's judgments of 25 May 2021, see ECtHR, *Big Brother Watch and Others v. The United Kingdom* (GC), paras 272, 344, 358; *Centrum för Rättvisa v. Sweden* (GC), para. 258, 272.

131 Federal Constitutional Court, judgment of 19 May 2020, 1 BvR 2835/17, paras 87 ff. – BND.

132 Weiler (n. 125), 659.

133 See Milanović (n. 116), 124; Jürgen Kühling and Mario Martini, 'Die Datenschutz-Grundverordnung. Revolution oder Evolution im europäischen und deutschen Datenschutzrecht?,' EuZW 27 (2016), 448–454 (450).

the effects of the surveillance.[134] If virtual surveillance produces the same or similar infringements as physical surveillance, both approaches should not be treated differently.[135] The lack of direct physical impairment of the person whose data are intercepted is irrelevant.[136] It is sufficient that an effective accessibility to and control of the online data can be ascertained. No physical influence on the data owner is required.[137] In contrast to those human rights, which aim to protect the physical integrity of a person, such as the right to life and limb, the right to privacy aims to safeguard personal identity, autonomy and self-determination.[138] Finally, the finding that foreigners abroad fall within the object and purpose of human rights law does not produce asymmetries or collisions with the principle of non-intervention. Human rights treaties are grounded in the idea that all human beings possess inherent dignity that deserves protection. Moreover, since only the State authority itself is obliged to respect human rights when taking action beyond its territory, the allegation of an unlawful human rights *octroi* on a foreign State is erroneous.[139] There is simply no interference with the action and the legislative power of any foreign State authority.[140]

---

134 Peter Margulies, '*The NSA in Global Perspective: Surveillance, Human Rights, and International Counterterrorism,*' Fordham L. Rev. 82 (2014), 2137–2167 (2152).

135 Correctly so, Weiler (n. 125), 660.

136 See Ulrich Fastenrath, 'Article 1 ECHR' in: Katharina Pabel and Stefanie Schmahl (eds), *Internationaler Kommentar zur EMRK* (Köln: Wolters Kluwer 2022), Art. 1 para. 106; see also Wolfgang Hoffmann-Riem, 'Freiheitsschutz in den globalen Informationsinfrastrukturen,' JZ 69 (2014), 52–63 (56). Different assessment by Gärditz (n. 118), 476 ff.

137 See Wolfgang Ewer and Tobias Thienel, 'Völker-, unions- und verfassungsrechtliche Aspekte des NSA-Datenskandals,' NJW 67 (2014), 30–35 (32); Helmut P. Aust, 'Spionage im Zeitalter von Big Data – Globale Überwachung und der Schutz der Privatsphäre im Völkerrecht,' AVR 52 (2014), 375–406 (392). Different view by Stefan Talmon, 'Der Begriff der 'Hoheitsgewalt'' in Zeiten der Überwachung des Internet- und Telekommunikationsverkehrs durch ausländische Nachrichtendienste,' JZ 69 (2014), 783–787 (784).

138 Andreas Fischer-Lescano, 'Der Kampf um die Internetverfassung: Rechtsfragen des Schutzes globaler Kommunikationsstrukturen vor Überwachungsmaßnahmen,' JZ 69 (2014), 965–974 (970). Even metadata do provide detailed information about the intimate life of an individual, see Laura K. Donohue, *The Future of Foreign Intelligence. Privacy and Surveillance in a Digital Age* (Oxford: Oxford University Press 2016), 39 ff.

139 See Gärditz (n. 118), 472; Andreas von Arnauld, 'Freiheit und Regulierung in der Cyberwelt: Transnationaler Schutz der Privatsphäre aus Sicht des Völkerrechts,' Berichte der Deutschen Gesellschaft für Internationales Recht 47 (2016), 1–34 (12–13); Marko Milanović, *Extraterritorial Application of Human Rights Treaties* (Oxford: Oxford University Press 2011), 118 ff. Different assessment by Sa-

b) Extraterritorial Applicability of Human Rights Treaties to Digital Interferences by Private Third Parties and Non-State Actors

When it comes to cross-border and extraterritorial interventions by private third parties and non-State actors, other considerations must be made. Not every cyber activity by a non-State actor is attributable to a State. On the contrary, private third parties and non-State actors also collect or access data from others for their own (economic) motivation or even unlawful intent, without any State authority being responsible for these actions. For instance, the posting of hateful comments that exceed the threshold of tort law or criminal offenses are in principle excluded from the direct possibility of regulation under international law. Rather, hate speech by private individuals is subject to national tort or penal laws, which must, of course, be compatible with human rights.[141] The same applies to search engine operators, which are growingly confronted with de-referencing requests by individuals that relate to their 'right to be forgotten' enshrined in EU law, even in transnational settings.[142]

In these regards, cross-border situations between private third parties and non-State actors in cyberspace create difficulties. While no State (and, consequently, no international organisation) may claim sovereignty over cyberspace as such, States are empowered to exercise sovereign prerogatives and jurisdiction over any cyber infrastructure on their territory and over activities associated with that cyber infrastructure.[143]

In cross-border situations, however, the exercise of extraterritorial jurisdiction under customary law requires a legitimising genuine link.[144] This link can be based on the principles of subjective or objective terri-

---

mantha Besson, 'The Extraterritoriality of the European Convention on Human Rights: Why Human Rights Depend on Jurisdiction and What Jurisdiction Amounts to,' LJIL 25 (2012), 857–884 (864 ff.).

140 See Stefanie Schmahl, 'Grundrechtsbindung der deutschen Staatsgewalt im Ausland,' NJW 73 (2020), 2221–2224 (2223).

141 See Stefanie Schmahl, 'Herausforderungen der Regulierung im Cyberspace: Systematisierungsansätze aus der Perspektive des Völkerrechts,' ZÖR 73 (2018), 3–37 (19–20).

142 See, e.g., CJEU, *Google Spain* (n. 62), *Google LLC v. CNIL* (n. 62).

143 Kriangsak Kittichaisaree, *Public International Law of Cyberspace* (Cham: Springer 2017), 23; Victoria Ibold, 'Transnational Jurisdiction for Cybercrimes de lege lata and de lege ferenda,' Eu Const. L. Rev. 10 (2020), 255–271 (257), both with further references.

144 Cedric Ryngaert, *Jurisdiction in International Law* (2nd edn, Oxford: Oxford University Press 2015), 34 ff. and 79–80.

toriality, which concern the location of where an action is initiated or consummated, as well as on passive or active personality, depending on the nationality of the acting or the affected persons.[145] The courts called for in connection with cross-border online activities usually focus their attention primarily on the author of the unlawful Internet content or the illegal actions as well as on the nexus established by the effects principle, which focuses on the ramifications of an act within a State.[146] This approach to exercising extraterritorial jurisdiction to prescribe and adjudicate Internet disputes is legitimate. If States were unable to regulate extraterritorial actions by private individuals or private corporations, this would amount to surrendering their sovereignty in cyberspace.[147] This is exactly why Article 3 of the EU's General Data Protection Regulation[148] codifies an extensive type of 'territorial scope' built on an effect-based jurisdictional nexus. It aims at protecting the digital privacy of persons in the European Union against the backdrop of the global networked digital era, regardless of the geographical location of a data controller or data processor.[149]

While the States' extraterritorial jurisdiction to prescribe and adjudicate is determined by international law, the jurisdiction to enforce these rules beyond their territorial borders is severely limited.[150] Unless there is an agreement between the States in question, which is largely the case

---

145 See Uta Kohl, 'Jurisdiction in Cyberspace' in: Tsagourias and Buchan (n. 25), 30–54 (33); Kittichaisaree (n. 143), 24, 27–29. Skeptical assessment by Daniel Bethlehem, 'The End of Geography: The Changing Nature of the International System and the Challenge to International Law,' EJIL 25 (2014), 9–24 (22).

146 See, e.g., ECtHR, *Perrin v. The United Kingdom*, decision of 18 October 2005, no. 5446/03, The Law, B. & C., CJEU, *Weltimmo s.r.o. v. Nemzeti Adatvédelmi és Információszabadság Hatóság*, judgment of 1 October 2015, case C-230/14, ECLI:EU:C:2015:639, paras 19 ff.; *Google Spain* (n. 62), para. 80; *Google LLC v. CNIL* (n. 62), paras 56–58; *Bolagsupplysningen* (n. 62), paras 42 ff.; *Mittelbayerischer Verlag KG v. SM*, judgment of 17 June 2021, case C-800/19, ECLI:EU:C:2021:489, paras 34 ff. With regard to the case-law of German criminal courts, see Ibold (n. 143), 263–264.

147 Stefanie Schmahl, 'Zwischenstaatliche Kompetenzabgrenzung im Cyberspace,' AVR 47 (2009), 284–327 (305–306). Similar assessment by Ryngaert (n. 144), 81.

148 Regulation (EU) 2016/679 of the European Parliament and of the Council of 27 April 2016 on the protection of natural persons with regard to the processing of personal data and on the free movement of such data, and repealing Directive 95/46/EC, OJ 2016 L 119/1–88.

149 Stephan Koloßa, 'The GDPR's Extra-Territorial Scope. Data Protection in the Context of International Law and Human Rights Law,' HJIL 80 (2020), 701–818 (794–795, 807).

150 Kittichaisaree (n. 143), 26; Kohl (n. 145), 51 ff.; Schmahl (n. 147), 314 ff.

under EU and Council of Europe law,[151] there is no obligation under general international law for States to recognise, tolerate or enforce foreign sovereign acts on their own territory.[152] Enforcement jurisdiction remains almost exclusively territorial.[153] This again shows the particular difficulty of regulatory efforts in cyberspace. Deficits in identification, ambiguities in territorial localisation and areas, in which national tort or criminal law, as well as EU law, cannot be effectively enforced abroad, represent high hurdles in the fight against online crimes or unlawful online interferences. To counter this situation, both the ECtHR[154] and the CJEU[155] have established the principle of provider liability for cross-border online interferences by non-State actors. The liability of the online service provider reacts to the problem of de-territorialisation in cyberspace.[156] Internet platforms are easier to localise and therefore represent a valuable alternative strategy for protecting human rights in the digital sphere.[157] The already mentioned German Network Enforcement Act[158] addresses precisely this point and aims to establish the accountability of these intermediaries.

Similar parameters apply in relation to the automatised reference and information systems by search engine operators and the individual's request of transborder de-referencing based on the 'right to be forgotten' under EU law. It is true that an obligation of the search engine operators to worldwide de-referencing could initiate 'a race to the bottom, to the detriment of freedom of expression, on a European and worldwide scale,'[159]

---

151 For more detail see Ibold (n. 143), 259 ff.

152 See the fundamental essay by Michael Akehurst, 'Jurisdiction in International Law,' BYIL 46 (1972/73), 145–275. More recently, see Alex Mills, 'Rethinking Jurisdiction in International Law,' BYIL 84 (2014), 187–239.

153 Mills (n. 152), 195. See also Schmahl (n. 141), 24–26.

154 ECtHR, *Delfi AS* (n. 112), paras 125 ff., 159; *Magyar Tartalomszolgáltatók Egyesülete* (n. 112), paras 62 and 69.

155 CJEU, *Google Spain* (n. 62), paras 28 ff., 48 ff.; *Tobias McFadden v. Sony Music Entertainment Germany GmbH*, judgment of 15 September 2016, C-484/14, ECLI:EU:C:2016:689, paras 80 ff. Critical assessment by Reto Mantz, 'Rechtssicherheit für WLAN? Die Haftung des WLAN-Betreibers und das McFadden-Urteil des EuGH,' EuZW 27 (2016), 817–820 (819).

156 Cornils (n. 111), 425.

157 See Cornils (n. 111), 423. See also Kersten (n. 86), 202; Eifert (n. 111), 1450–1451.

158 Gesetz zur Verbesserung der Rechtsdurchsetzung in sozialen Netzwerken (Netzwerkdurchsetzungsgesetz – NetzDG) of 1 September 2017, Bundesgesetzblatt 2017 I, p. 3352, last modified on 3 June 2021 in: Bundesgesetzblatt 2021 I, 1436.

159 Advocate General Maciej Szunpar, *Google LLC v. CNIL*, opinion of 10 January 2019, case C-507/17, ECLI:EU:C:2019:15, para. 61.

since in particular non-European countries impacted by worldwide de-referencing could, in response, also implement worldwide de-referencing under their domestic laws.[160] Therefore, the CJEU is right in founding that the 'right to be forgotten' as recognised under EU law does not indispensably require search engine operators to comply with de-referencing requests on all the versions of their search engines that exist worldwide.[161] Or in other words, there is currently no obligation to introduce an extraterritorial scope on the operation of the 'right to be forgotten.' However, at the same time, the Court emphasises that EU law does not prohibit such a practice, by drawing attention to the EU Parliament's and the EU Member States' ability to extend the rights to privacy and the protection of personal data extraterritorially.[162] This approach is also reinforced by the CJEU's *GC, AF, BH, ED v. CNIL* decision, where the Court extended the grounds upon which EU citizens can request search engine operators to de-reference search results, specifically where such results contain sensitive personal information relating to, *inter alia*, ethnic origin, political opinions, religious beliefs, and sexual orientation.[163]

6. *Discrimination Issues in the Virtual World Through Algorithms*

Algorithms, predictive analytics and data-based differentiation decisions represent a sixth challenge for the implementation of international human rights. Algorithms are not only used in Internet search portals, but increasingly also in the business world, in legal technology, in social security systems, in administrative procedures and in the area of predictive policing.[164] The distinctions made by algorithms are based on programmed

---

160 Zalnieriute (n. 62), 263.

161 CJEU, *Google LLC v. CNIL* (n. 62), paras 66–71.

162 CJEU, *Google LLC v. CNIL* (n. 62), paras 73–75. See also Zalnieriute (n. 62), 266.

163 CJEU, *GC, AF, BH, ED v. CNIL*, judgment of 24 September 2019, case C-136/17, ECLI:EU:C:2019:773, paras 17 and 68–69.

164 For an overview of the various constellations, see, e.g., Mario Martini and David Nink, 'Wenn Maschinen entscheiden... vollautomatisierte Verwaltungsverfahren und der Persönlichkeitsschutz,' NVwZ 36 (2017), 681–682; Thomas Söbbing, *Fundamentale Rechtsfragen Künstlicher Intelligenz* (Frankfurt am Main: Deutscher Fachverlag 2019), 6 ff.; Carsten Orwat, *Diskriminierungsrisiken durch Verwendung von Algorithmen* (Baden-Baden: Nomos 2019), 17 ff.; Carmen Freyler, 'Robot-Recruiting, Künstliche Intelligenz und das Antidiskriminierungsrecht,' NZA 37 (2020), 284–290 (285); Ines Härtel, 'Digitalisierung im Lichte des Verfassungsrechts – Algorithmen, Predictive Policing, autonomes Fahren,' LKV 29 (2019),

and aggregated parameters and metrics, which in turn result from analyses of personal data from various groups of people.[165] The result of the parameters obtained resembles the application of stereotypes and increases the risk that people are no longer perceived as individuals and in their subject quality, but are only treated in a standardised manner as part of a group. Such a phenomenon affects not only the individual, but also the principles of equality and non-discrimination.[166] It is undisputed that the use of algorithms can reinforce structural inequality and power asymmetries.[167] Moreover, recent developments in some countries give cause for concern that the combination of artificial intelligence with big data might strengthen the surveillance mechanisms of States and non-State actors.[168] One example is the expanded surveillance by the Chinese Government, which uses artificial intelligence and algorithms to access biodata and DNA databases, particularly to monitor ethnic minorities.[169]

Against this background, the question must be answered how it can be ensured that the use of algorithms does not become a new form of discrimination that the prohibitions on discrimination enshrined in human rights treaties can no longer adequately cope with. Although a dynamic interpretation of the human rights prohibitions on discrimination remains fundamentally possible, the formation of individual comparison parameters, which are essential for handling prohibitions of discrimination, is challenging with artificially programmed algorithms. These are typically geared towards mathematical, leeway-free group fairness, and

---

49–50 (54 ff.); Renate Schaub, 'Verantwortlichkeit für Algorithmen im Internet,' Zeitschrift für Innovations- und Technikrecht 2019, 2–7; Raphael Koch and Christine Biggen, 'Der Einsatz Künstlicher Intelligenz zur Organisation and proaktiven Überprüfung von Onlinebewertungen,' NJW 73 (2020), 2921–2925.

165 For more detail see Orwat (n. 164), 3 ff. See also Thomas Wischmeyer, 'Regulierung intelligenter Systeme,' AöR 143 (2018), 1–66 (14).

166 See, e.g., Christian Ernst, 'Algorithmische Entscheidungsfindung und personenbezogene Daten,' JZ 72 (2017), 1026–1036 (1032 ff.); Mario Martini, 'Algorithmen als Herausforderung für die Rechtsordnung,' JZ 72 (2017), 1017–1025 (1018); Orwat (n. 164), 24 ff.; Philipp Hacker, 'Teaching Fairness to Artificial Intelligence,' CMLRev. 55 (2018), 1143-1186 (1145 ff.).

167 See Wischmeyer (n. 165), 26; Freyler (n. 164), 285; Hans Steege, 'Algorithmenbasierte Diskriminierung durch Einsatz von Künstlicher Intelligenz,' Multimedia und Recht 2019, 715–721 (716 ff.).

168 Kriebitz and Lütge (n. 63), 102.

169 See Uyghur Human Rights Project, 'China's Repression and Internment of Uyghurs: U.S. Policy Responses,' House Committee on Foreign Affairs: Subcommittee on Asia and the Pacific (26 September 2018).

not on individual justice.[170] This difficulty is particularly evident when a fully automated computer programme makes the decision, and neither the programmer nor the user can explain or reliably predict the result of the decision-making process. In these cases, machine algorithms function as black boxes.[171]

One of the most important regulations to protect against algorithmic discrimination risks is the prohibition of automated decisions in data protection law. According to Article 22 (1) of the EU's General Data Protection Regulation,[172] the individual concerned has the right not to be subject to a decision based solely on automated processing that has a legal effect on him or her or significantly affects him or her in a similar way. The General Data Protection Regulation does not fully specify what types of automated decisions are meant. However, it is certain that no content-related assessment can be made solely on the basis of algorithm-created decisions without a natural person having the final decision-making authority.[173] Simultaneously, it must also be taken into account that it will be difficult for the human decision-maker to completely free him- or herself from the automated preliminary decision by the algorithms. It is much more likely that the human decision-maker will only perform a plausibility check based on the result found by the algorithms.

Modern behavioural sciences have revealed that algorithms, as a rule, work as nudges and have a strong manipulation potential.[174] Thus, there remains the risk that even the prescribed control of the result based on al-

---

170 Jon Kleinberg et al., 'Discrimination in the Age of Algorithms,' Journal of Legal Analysis 10 (2018), 113–174 (161 ff.).

171 For a fuller account see Frank Pasquale, *The Black Box Society. The Secrect Algorithms that Control Money and Information* (Cambridge, MA: Harvard University Press 2015). *Cf.* also David Roth-Isigkeit, 'Staatshaftungsrechtliche Aspekte des Einsatzes automatisierter Entscheidungssysteme in der öffentlichen Verwaltung,' AöR 145 (2020), 321–351 (335). Different assessment by Yoan Hermstrüwer, 'Fairnessprinzipien in der algorithmischen Verwaltung,' AöR 145 (2020), 479–521 (492 ff.).

172 Regulation (EU) 2016/679 of the European Parliament and of the Council of 27 April 2016 and repealing Directive 95/46/EC, OJ 2016 L 119/1–88.

173 See Mario Martini, 'Article 22' in: Boris P. Paal and Daniel A. Pauly (eds), *Datenschutz-Grundverordnung/Bundesdatenschutzgesetz* (2nd edn, München: C.H. Beck 2018), para. 29.

174 See Laurence O'Hara, 'Grundrechtsschutz vor psychisch vermittelter Steuerung,' AöR 145 (2020), 133–187 (162–165); Sophie V. Knebel, *Die Drittwirkung der Grundrechte und -freiheiten gegenüber Privaten. Regulierungsmöglichkeiten sozialer Netzwerke* (Baden-Baden: Nomos 2018), 106 ff.

gorithms by a natural person will prove to be practically ineffective.[175] The States, in particular the Member States of the European Union, are therefore obliged to put in place a legal system that addresses these problems of bounded autonomy under a human rights perspective.[176] On the one hand, the programming of algorithms and self-learning intelligent systems must be carried out transparently, in accordance with the principle of non-discrimination.[177] The technological and socio-technical design of each automated decision-making system must further be performed in a way that corresponds to the rights, freedoms and legitimate interests of the data subjects. This requires a full assessment and balancing of the positive and negative impacts of automated decision-making.[178] On the other hand, it must be ensured that legal remedies are at hand that can effectively repeal any alleged unlawful discrimination by artificial intelligence systems.[179]

7. *Cyborgs and Humanoid Robots as New Rights-Holders or New Duty-Bearers?*

Finally, it is to be expected that the further development of technology can bring about fundamental changes in human rights protection in the medium or long term. To put it briefly: Will digitalisation, especially the development of artificial intelligence, lead to a new or additional form of rights-holders or duty-bearers? The creation of cyborgs and human-like machines seems to be within reach due to the evolvement of robotics. The 'artificial human being' does not necessarily have to be a physical artifact but can also be disembodied, for example, by simulating his or her

175 Wolfgang Hoffmann-Riem, 'Verhaltenssteuerung durch Algorithmen – Eine Herausforderung für das Recht,' AöR 142 (2017), 1–42 (36).

176 See Orwat (n. 164), 105 ff.; McGregor, Murray and Ng (n. 66), 337. See also Wibke Werner, 'Schutz durch das Grundgesetz im Zeitalter der Digitalisierung,' Neue Juristische Online-Zeitschrift 2019, 1041–1046 (1043).

177 Unanimous view, see, e.g., Martini (n. 166), 1022; Schaub (n. 164), 7; Freyler (n. 164), 290; McGregor, Murray and Ng (n. 66), 335 ff.; Kriebitz and Lütge (n. 63), 99; Kühling (n. 73), 535 ff.

178 For more detail, see Christian Djeffal, 'The Normative Potential of the European Rule on Automated Decisions: A New Reading for Art. 22 GDPR,' HJIL 80 (2020), 847–879 (857 ff.).

179 Werner (n. 176), 1043; Susanne Beck, 'Diskriminierung durch Künstliche Intelligenz?,' ZRP 52 (2019), 185 (185). For more detail, see Ljupcho Grozdanovski, 'In Search of Effectiveness and Fairness in Proving Algorithmic Discrimination in EU Law,' CMLRev. 58 (2021), 99-136 (120 ff.).

behaviour through a digital representation.[180] Is such a virtual person or humanoid robot suitable as a holder or as a duty-bearer of human rights? What are the limits of the dynamic interpretation of human rights treaties when human life (also) takes place virtually? In trying to answer these questions, it is important to make clear distinctions from the outset.

Firstly, it is to be noted that the recognition of the legal personality of new virtual or humanoid entities does not automatically entail that these entities enjoy human rights or that they are committed to respect or protect the human rights of others.[181] But experience shows that the ascription of legal personality and autonomy has often been linked to the ability to act which is secured with certain substantial human rights (such as freedoms of communication, business and property) and procedural rights. For instance, under Article 19(3) of the German Basic Law, the fundamental rights of the Basic Law shall also apply to domestic legal persons to the extent that the nature of such rights permits. The Federal Constitutional Court recognises the entitlement to enjoy basic rights not only for domestic legal persons but also for mixed-business companies,[182] legal persons based in an EU Member State,[183] and legal persons governed by private law, which are operated domestically for profit and entirely owned by a Member State of the EU.[184] In view of globalisation and digitalisation, legal scholars are even campaigning for a dynamic extension of the scope of Article 19(3) of the Basic Law to include companies that are based outside of Europe but are active in Germany.[185] This idea applies above all to global digital platforms, but it could also be transferred to artificial intelligence and humanoid robots.

Secondly, a distinction must be made between the types of artificial intelligence. So far, there has been no need to qualify cyborgs as a separate category of human rights-holders. The name 'cyborg' is an acronym

---

180 Christian L. Geminn, 'Menschenwürde und menschenähnliche Maschinen und Systeme,' DÖV 73 (2020), 172–181 (173).

181 As to the concepts of rights, laws, human rights, and critiques of rights see, e.g., Anne Peters, 'The Importance of Having Rights,' HJIL 81 (2021), 7–22, with further references.

182 Federal Constitutional Court, judgment of 22 February 2011, 1 BvR 699/06, BVerfGE 128, 226 – Fraport.

183 Federal Constitutional Court, decision of 19 July 2011, 1 BvR 1916/09, BVerfGE 129, 78 – Cassina.

184 Federal Constitutional Court, judgment of 6 December 2016, 1 BvR 2821/11, BVerfGE 143, 246 – Vattenfall.

185 See Ralf Müller-Terpitz, 'Die Grundrechtsberechtigung juristischer Personen im Zeitalter der Globalisierung und Digitalisierung,' JZ 75 (2020), 1080–1087.

derived from 'cybernetic organism.'[186] In medicine, the use of complex internal technology is no longer uncommon. According to a narrow interpretation, cyborgs are humans with technical implants such as cardiac pacemakers, complex prostheses and cochlea or retina implants.[187] There is no doubt that human beings with such in-body technology will continue to enjoy human rights to the same extent as individuals without such implants.[188]

However, the legal situation is more difficult when a person's brain is controlled by implants, for example, through brain stimulation. With the help of a stereotactic operation, electrodes are placed minimally invasively on the patient at a certain point in the brain, which is previously determined by a magnetic resonance and computer tomographic image of the brain.[189] For the time being, the devices have been used in particular for motoric problems suffered by Parkinson's patients.[190] Nevertheless, there are first insights into the possibility of influencing states of mind (which so far have mainly occurred as side effects) to increase memory performance and other cognitive abilities.[191] At this point, besides major ethical issues, the question arises as to whether a person with a brain implant, i.e. a cyborg in a wider sense, could be regarded as a new category of a holder of fundamental rights. In any case, such cyborgs constitute a tense combination of human and artificial intelligence.[192] If the artificial intelligence can be controlled from the outside, which is usually the case via computers with deep learning mechanisms, this entails considerable

---

186 Ronald Kline, 'Where are the Cyborgs in Cybernetics?,' Social Studies of Science 39 (2009), 331–362 (331).

187 Katherine Hayles, 'The Life Cycle of Cyborgs: Writing the Posthuman' in: Chris Hables Gray (ed.), *The Cyborg Handbook* (London: Routledge 1995), 321–340 (322–335).

188 See Karin Harasser, *Körper 2.0: Über die technische Erweiterbarkeit des Menschen* (Bielefeld: Transcript Verlag 2013), 9 ff.; Jens Kersten, 'Mensch und Maschinen,' JZ 70 (2015), 1–8 (4–5).

189 Söbbing (n. 164), 55–56.

190 See Schliesky (n. 78), 699.

191 See Dominik Groß, 'Neuro-Enhancement unter besonderer Berücksichtigung neurobionischer Maßnahmen' in: Albrecht Wienke et al. (eds), *Die Verbesserung des Menschen: Tatsächliche und rechtliche Aspekte der wunscherfüllenden Medizin* (Berlin/Heidelberg: Springer 2009), 85–118 (90 ff.); Christoph Kehl and Christopher Coenen, *Technologien und Visionen der Mensch-Maschine-Entgrenzung, Büro für Technikfolgen-Abschätzung beim Deutschen Bundestag (TAB)*, Arbeitsbericht Nr. 167 (Berlin, 2016), 82; Schliesky (n. 78), 699.

192 Söbbing (n. 164), 56–57.

risks for the human being concerned and others.[193] Such cyborgs are not entirely free in the legal sense and can therefore hardly be regarded as autonomous acting persons and be held responsible for their actions without taking into account the work of the manufacturer or the implanter of the artificial components.[194]

Similar considerations already apply to other preliminary stages of the 'virtual human being,' for example, to systems that can receive voice commands and conduct conversations, such as the Twitter bot named 'Tay.'[195] Such voice-controlled systems are in a sense human-like and influence or even replace the decision-making power of real people, similar to self-driving cars and unmanned aircraft systems.[196] In such situations, it is no longer clear who actually could be regarded as the holder of human rights – the human cyborg, the computerised brain stimulator, the programmer, or all together? The established human rights system reaches its limits when the attribution criteria become blurred. In any case, the question of when human existence begins and when it ends will have to be posed much more sharply in this context than ever before.

Last but not least, it is particularly challenging for the human rights system when one looks at the humanoid robots, i.e. machines which are built on deep self-learning in order to mimic human cognitive functions.[197] In 2017, Saudi Arabia granted 'citizenship' to a humanoid robot named Sophia.[198] This symbolic action has been described in the media as a cynical act for a country that denies girls and women equal rights.[199] Nonetheless, the episode is significant because it was the first time that a State purported to give a kind of legal personality to a robot or artificial

193 See Eric Hilgendorf, 'Menschenwürde und Neuromodulation' in: Jan C. Joerden, Eric Hilgendorf and Felix Thiele (eds), *Menschenwürde und Medizin* (Berlin: Duncker & Humblot 2013), 865–874 (867 ff.).

194 Söbbing (n. 164), 63 ff. See also Jochen Hanisch, 'Zivilrechtliche Haftungskonzepte für Robotik' in: Eric Hilgendorf (ed.), *Robotik im Kontext zwischen Recht und Moral* (Baden-Baden: Nomos 2014), 27–63 (38).

195 Wischmeyer (n. 165), 10 ff. See also Kriebitz and Lütge (n. 63), 98.

196 See, e.g., Söbbing (n. 164), 49–50, 67 ff.; Kersten (n. 188), 2.

197 For more detail see Themis Tzimas, 'Artificial Intelligence and Human Rights: Their Role in the Evolution of AI,' HJIL 80 (2020), 533–557 (544 ff.).

198 See the website of Hanson Robotics, Sophia (available at: https://www.hansonrobotics.com/sophia/).

199 See Cleve R. Wootson Jr., 'Saudi Arabia Which Denies Women Equal Rights, Makes Robot a Citizen,' Washington Post (29 October 2017).

intelligence entity.[200] A related possibility is that a human's personality or consciousness might be uploaded and stored on a computer or a network. Some scientists are already working on this idea.[201] Although these are isolated cases and the worldwide existence of human-like robots is part of science fiction (albeit probably not too far away), human rights doctrine is called upon to deal with this phenomenon at an early stage. Can or should humanoid robots enjoy legal personality and human rights? Or should they, in reverse, be considered as duty-bearers of human rights?

The first (human) reaction to the question of the enjoyment of human rights by humanoid robots is certainly negative, since the theoretical foundation for human rights is to be seen in the dignity of the human being, which includes personal autonomy and vulnerability.[202] On the other hand, it should be borne in mind that States and private companies are also artificial legal products, i.e., collective fictions of legal personhood.[203] In particular, private companies are endowed with a wide range of basic (human) rights, such as the right to a fair trial or the right to property.[204] A comparison with the legal status of animals also shows that animal rights have varied considerably over time.[205] In recent times, legal debate even growingly focuses on the judicial recognition of nature as a subject of rights.[206] Legal subjectivity has always been and still is relative. Legal systems are free to recognise non-human legal subjects and to define their

---

200 Jacob Turner, *Robot Rules. Regulating Artificial Intelligence* (London: Palgrave Macmillan 2019), 173.

201 See Geminn (n. 180), 173.

202 Similarly, Peters (n. 181), 10–11.

203 See Jan-Erik Schirmer, 'Rechtsfähige Roboter?,' JZ 71 (2016), 660–666 (662). See also Visa A J Kurki, 'Why Things Can Hold Rights: 'Reconceptualizing the Legal Person'' in: Visa A J Kurki and Tomasz Pietrzykowski (eds), *Legal Personhood: Animals, Artificial Intelligence and the Unborn* (Cham: Springer 2017), 69–89 (82 ff.).

204 See the Federal Constitutional Court judgments of 22 February 2011, 19 July 2011, and 6 December 2016, cited in n. 182–184.

205 For a fuller account see Rafal Michalczak, 'Animals' Race Against the Machines' in: Kurki and Pietrzykowski (n. 203), 91–101 (94 ff.); Ryan Abbott, *The Reasonable Robot. Artificial Intelligence and the Law* (Cambridge: Cambridge University Press 2020), 23; Jens Kersten, *Das Anthropozän-Konzept* (Baden-Baden: Nomos 2014), 88 ff.

206 See, e.g., Marjorie Andrea González Ramírez, 'The Judicial Recognition of Nature as a Subject of Rights: An Answer to Tackle Environmental Problems in Colombia and to Broaden the Community that is Granted Justice,' Die Friedens-Warte 93 (2020), 148–172 (149 ff.), with further references.

legal status and their rights.[207] This does not mean that animals, private companies, legal persons or artificial intelligence should have the same rights as human beings. For example, human-centric rights that are anchored in social relationships such as dignity or privacy will not be suitable for artificial intelligence.[208] However, tiered ownership of fundamental rights does not seem to be excluded from the outset.[209] Some scholars call for the development of a new category of the legal subject, halfway between person and object.[210]

Legal personality, rights and duties for artificial intelligence and humanoid robots are no longer just a matter for a purely academic debate.[211] In 2017, the European Parliament passed a resolution containing recommendations on Civil Law Rules on Robotics.[212] The European Parliament suggested, *inter alia*, to create a specific legal status for robots in the long run, so that at least the most sophisticated autonomous robots could be established as having the status of electronic persons responsible for compensating any damage they may cause, and possibly applying electronic personality to cases where robots make autonomous decisions or otherwise interact independently with third parties. Thereby, the European Parliament left open the question of whether artificial intelligence could be housed within

207 See Jens Kersten, 'Relative Rechtssubjektivität. Über autonome Automaten und emergente Schwärme,' Zeitschrift für Rechtssoziologie 37 (2017), 8–25 (9–10). Similarly, with regard to animals' rights: Anne Peters, 'Liberté, Égalité, Animalité: Human-Animal Comparisons in Law,' Transnational Environmental Law 5 (2016), 25–53 (46 ff.).

208 Geminn (n. 180), 175.

209 As far as can be seen, this is a uniform view, see Kersten (n. 188), 7–8; Schirmer (n. 203), 662 ff.; Susanne Beck, 'Sinn und Unsinn von Statusfragen' in: Eric Hilgendorf and Jan-Philipp Günther (eds), *Robotik und Gesetzgebung* (Baden-Baden: Nomos 2013), 239–260 (255 ff.); Andreas Fischer-Lescano, 'Natur als Rechtsperson,' Zeitschrift für Umweltrecht 29 (2018), 205–216 (213–214); Gerhard Wagner, 'Roboter als Haftungssubjekte? Konturen eines Haftungsrechts für autonome Systeme' in: Florian Faust and Hans-Bernd Schäfer (eds), *Zivilrechtliche und rechtsökonomische Probleme des Internet und der künstlichen Intelligenz* (Tübingen: Mohr Siebeck 2019), 1–39 (29).

210 See, Ryan Calo, 'Robotics and the Lessons of Cyberlaw,' Cal. L. Rev. 103 (2015), 513–563 (549); Jack B. Balkin, 'The Path of Robotics Law,' Cal. L. Rev. Circuit 6 (2015), 45–60 (57).

211 Rightly so, Turner (n. 200), 174.

212 European Parliament Resolution of 16 February 2017 with recommendations to the Commission on Civil Law Rules on Robotics, 2005/2103(INL), para. 59.

recognised legal categories of personality or whether new ones, with their own specific features and implications, would be needed.[213]

In any case, granting a humanoid robot legal personality could be a valuable firewall between existing humans and legal persons and the harm and injuries which artificial intelligence could cause.[214] The rights, duties and liabilities of a company are usually separate from those of its owners or controllers. A company's creditors can only recourse to that company's own assets, a feature known as 'limited liability.' The limited liability of companies is a powerful tool in protecting human beings from risk and thereby encouraging innovation.[215] Arguably, the justifications for providing such legal personality to artificial intelligence are even stronger than for protecting human owners from the liability of companies. Humanoid robots can do something that existing companies cannot do: make autonomous decisions without human input.[216] Whereas a company is merely a collective fiction for human volitions, artificial intelligence by its nature has its own independent 'consciousness' or 'will,' which functionally determines for itself in an autonomous manner how a given task is to be performed.[217]

Yet, as important as these concepts are, they all go beyond the anthropocentric character of human rights treaties.[218] Existing legal systems, both

---

213 See Melinda F. Lohmann, 'Ein europäisches Roboterrecht – überfällig oder überflüssig?,' ZRP 51 (2018), 168–171; Horst Eidenmüller, 'The Rise of Robots and the Law of Humans,' Zeitschrift für Europäisches Privatrecht 25 (2017), 765–777; Renate Schaub, 'Interaktion von Mensch und Maschine,' JZ 72 (2017), 342–349 (346).

214 Turner (n. 200), 187. See also Gunther Teubner, 'Elektronische Agenten und große Menschenaffen: Zur Ausweitung des Akteursstatus in Recht und Politik,' Zeitschrift für Rechtssoziologie 27 (2006), 5–30 (30); *id.*, 'Digitale Rechtssubjekte? Zum privatrechtlichen Status autonomer Softwareagenten,' AcP 218 (2018), 155–205 (162).

215 Rightly so, Turner (n. 200), 187.

216 Tzimas (n. 197), 546 ff.; Turner (n. 200), 187.

217 See Gunther Teubner, 'Rights of Non-humans? Electronic Agents and Animals as New Actors in Politics and Law,' Max Weber Lecture Series No. 2007/04 (available at: http://hdl.handle.net/1814/6960), 1–21 (10 ff.). See also Turner (n. 200), 187; Abbott (n. 205), 34.

218 Similarly, Claus Müller-Hengstenberg and Stefan Kirn, 'Intelligente (Software-)Agenten: Eine neue Herausforderung unseres Rechtssystems?,' Multimedia und Recht 2014, 307–313 (308); Jan-Erik Schirmer, 'Von Mäusen, Menschen und Maschinen – Autonome Systeme in der Architektur der Rechtsfähigkeit,' JZ 74 (2019), 711–718 (716). Different assessment by Fischer-Lescano (n. 209), 214–216; Kersten (n. 207), 22.

international and national, are fundamentally human-centred in the sense that they take for granted that humans are the most developed form of being and that the welfare of humans constitutes the ultimate goal of morals and laws.[219] Even a dynamic interpretation of human rights treaties in order to include humanoid robots at least partially as autonomous actors, responsible entities, duty-bearers, and rights-holders will be impossible. The Expert Group on Liability and New Technologies, set up by the European Commission in response to the European Parliament's 2017 proposal, explicitly stresses that it is neither necessary nor sensible to give legal personality to autonomous systems. Rather, the harm these systems may cause should be attributable to existing persons or bodies.[220] The digital agenda of the European Union of 19 February 2020, which consists of a European strategy for data, a report on the safety and liability implications of artificial intelligence, the Internet of things and robotics, and a white paper on artificial intelligence, fully supports this assessment.[221] The same holds true for the Commission's legislative initiative of 21 April 2021 to harmonise rules on artificial intelligence.[222] These views are also largely consistent with international artificial intelligence ethics codes that aim at active cooperation between States to progress responsible stewardship of trustworthy artificial intelligence.[223]

A similar observation can be found in the ECtHR's case-law on animal rights. In 2008, Austrian animal activists invoked the existence of an animal right to free movement in order to enforce judicially the release of

---

219 Tzimas (n. 197), 553.

220 See Expert Group on Liability and New Technologies, *Liability for Artificial Intelligence and Other Emerging Digital Technologies* (European Union, 2019), 37 ff.

221 European Commission, COM (2020) 66 final; COM (2020) 64 final; COM (2020) 65 final. For more detail, see Philipp Hacker, 'Europäische und nationale Regulierung von Künstlicher Intelligenz,' NJW 73 (2020), 2142–2147 (2142 ff.); Stefan Heiss, 'Europäische Haftungsregeln für Künstliche Intelligenz,' EuZW 32 (2021), 932-938.

222 European Commission, 'Proposal for a Regulation of the European Parliament and of the Council Laying Down Harmonised Rules on Artificial Intelligence (Artificial Intelligence Act) and Amending Certain Union Legislative Acts,' COM (2021) 206 final. Further see Andreas Ebert and Indra Spiecker gen. Döhmann, 'Der Kommissionsentwurf für eine KI-Verordnung der EU,' NVwZ 40 (2021), 1188-1193; Hannah van Kolfschooten, 'EU Regulation of Artificial Intelligence: Challenge for Patients' Rights,' CMLRev. 59 (2022), 81-112 (91 ff.).

223 See, e.g., the Recommendation of the OECD Council on Artificial Intelligence of 22 May 2019, reprinted in ILM 59 (2020), 30 ff. For more detail see Karen Yeung, 'Introductory Note to Recommendation of the Council on Artificial Intelligence (OECD),' ILM 59 (2020), 27–29; Kriebitz and Lütge (n. 63), 85–86.

great apes from confinement and zoos before the ECtHR. However, their complaints were rightly rejected on the grounds of incompatibility *ratione materiae*.[224] This decision shows that no existing human rights treaty can be interpreted so extensively and dynamically in relation to the holders of rights without at the same time contradicting its underlying assumptions and objectives. For this reason, humanoid robots cannot be included as (partial) rights-holders in the international human rights system.[225] It is true that the animal rights discourse aims at recognizing animals as sentient beings in law and as possible bearers of rights, while the current debate about humanoid robots focuses more on liability and obligations, and less on rights. The rationale for granting legal personhood is thus a different one. However, parallels exist in that both animals and humanoid robots do not fit within the human rights scheme; they cannot be considered either as holders or as duty-bearers of human rights.

If one wants to change this legal situation, new treaties would have to be concluded specifically dealing with the legal personhood of artificial intelligence and its ability to exercise rights and duties. But fortunately, this is still part of science fiction, as the influence of humanity is unlikely to be significant in that regard, once artificial, autonomous entities have emerged that surpass human intelligence in many or all aspects. Such an artificial intelligence is rather expected to choose and implement its own goals in a post-human legal or otherwise construed system.[226] In any case, one (dystopian) assumption seems irrefutable: the human focus of the existing legal systems can hardly be preserved after the emergence of artificial entities with an intelligence that is equal or superior to that of humans.[227]

III. Outlook

As always, modern technology is both a blessing and a curse. In general, digitalisation does not require a fundamental paradigm shift but a change of perspective in the normative interpretation of human rights treaties. Many questions can be solved by way of a dynamic interpretation.

---

224 See ECtHR, *Balluch v. Austria*, decision of 25 September 2012, no. 4471/06, paras 23 ff. See also *Stibbe v. Austria*, appl. no. 26188/08, lodged 6 May 2008.

225 Similarly, Tzimas (n. 197), 554; Wagner (n. 209), 30. Differently, Fischer-Lescano (n. 209), 215–216.

226 Geminn (n. 180), 174. Similarly, Teubner, AcP (n. 214), 200.

227 Rightly so, Tzimas (n. 197), 554–555.

However, despite the changed social and technological context due to digitalisation, the decisive factor in any dynamic interpretation of human rights must remain that freedom and responsibility remain two sides of the same coin, both in the analogue and the digital world. The organs of the Council of Europe have rightly expressed this demand in several resolutions.[228] In order to ensure that the negative symptoms of digitalisation do not evoke irreversible social upheaval, ultimately, the State has to prove itself as a guarantor for the protection of the right to privacy and self-determination against anonymous or veiled online attacks and autonomously operating software systems.[229]

In that regard, not everything that appears economically and technologically attractive and enforceable is compatible with the human-centred character of human rights treaties. At least, human-like robots, should they come to 'life' one day, will transform the social and human-centred character of the existing legal systems, both internationally and nationally. Even the current discussion-oriented project for a 'Charter of Digital Fundamental Rights of the European Union,'[230] which in principle deserves support, will not be able to stop such ground-breaking changes.[231] In a post-human era under the aegis of humanoid robots, the protection of human rights will necessarily have to enter a fundamentally new phase. Even more: The challenges which come along with humanoid robots cannot be coped with or solved in a human rights language. This would simply be an overload, which would put the very concept of human rights at fundamental risk.

---

228 See, e.g., Council of Europe, Report on Technological Convergence, Artificial Intelligence and Human Rights, Doc. 14288 (Recommendation 2102), 10 April 2017, with further references.

229 See Schmidt-Jortzig (n. 116), 13.

230 See https://digitalcharta.eu/.

231 For more detail see Albert Ingold, 'Der Entwurf für eine "Charta der Digitalen Grundrechte der Europäischen Union": Vorhaben, Vorstellungen, Vorbehalte,' Zeitschrift für Gesetzgebung 2018, 193–209; Friedrich Graf von Westphalen, 'Digitale Charta – Erweiterung der europäischen Grundrechte für das digitale Zeitalter,' BB 2018, 899–907. Overly critical assessment by Sebastian J. Golla, 'In Würde vor Ampel und Algorithmus,' DÖV 72 (2019), 673–681 (677 ff.).

The Impact of the Internet on International Criminal Law

Rossella Pulvirenti

Abstract This chapter discusses how international criminal tribunals and courts (ICTCs) collect, receive and share information through the internet and, thus, how the internet has changed International Criminal Law (ICL). More specifically, it focuses on the flow of information from society to ICTCs and, vice versa, on the data released via the internet by the ICTCs to local communities. Thus, this chapter covers two different aspects of the work of ICTCs. First, this chapter demonstrates that the internet enhances the quality of international criminal prosecutions because of the new low-cost and increasingly accessible technologies available via the internet, social networks such as Facebook and Twitter, crowdsourcing, as well as satellite imagery and other forms of surveillance technologies that might bring about better, cheaper, and safer prosecutions. Indeed, these technologies used to pursue individuals' retribution and deterrence might, for instance, help to preserve destroyed or threatened cultural heritage for future generations. Also, it gives individuals the power to gain control over the information and evidence that are then forwarded to the ICTCs. However, these positive trends are also characterized by some setbacks. For instance, considering the scarce international practice, some doubts on the admissibility and verifiability of this type of evidence exist. Also, the relationship with third parties that store the video footages still remains unchartered territory. Second, the internet has also strengthened the outreach programs of the ICTCs enhancing quality and the quantity of data released via the internet by the ICTCs to local communities. This chapter demonstrates that the failure to engage with the local population had a negative impact on the legitimacy and legacy of the ICTCs. Thus, outreach could benefit from developments in new forms of technology to design innovative and meaningful outreach strategies.

I. Introduction

This chapter demonstrates that the development of the internet has a positive influence on International Criminal Law (ICL) under two different perspectives. First, it enhances the quality of the international criminal prosecutions because it gives individuals the power to gain control over the information and evidence that are then forwarded to the international criminal courts and tribunals (ICTCs). Second, the internet has also strengthened the outreach programmes enhancing the quality and the quantity of data released via the internet by the ICTCs to local communities.

The *revolutionary force*[1] of the internet in the early 1990s changed almost every aspect of the society, both in the private and public sphere, from the way people work to the way people interact and socialise every day. For instance, the advent of the internet modified the way we gather, collect and share information about landmarks events.[2] The Indian Ocean Tsunami on the 26th December 2004, the Saffron revolution in Myanmar in 2009, the destruction of Rohingya villages in Myanmar in 2017 and 2018 and Arab Spring demonstrations in Tunisia, Libya, Egypt and Syria, to name a few, are some examples of this phenomenon.

New low-cost and increasingly accessible technologies available via the internet, social networks such as Facebook and Twitter, crowdsourcing, as well as satellite imagery and other forms of surveillance technologies changed the way in which we document human rights abuses. For instance, although it was difficult for NGOs to enter Syria following the 2011 uprising, several videos captured by Syrian citizens through their phones and uploaded on social media showed the level of atrocities in the country.[3] Alston considers the emerging role of digital open-sources information as a third-generation fact-finding approach to human rights.[4] During the first generation, lawyers, diplomats, or experts undertook a systematic review of available information and presented them to a political body, while the second-generation approach was largely influenced by the major international human rights NGOs, such as Amnesty International and Human Rights Watch.[5]

No similar considerations exist within the field of ICL. On the one hand, the internet has changed the character of armed conflict[6] and proved itself to be an efficient, non-traditional and unofficial recruitment channel

1 Raphael Cohen-Almagor, *Confronting the Internet's Dark Side* (Cambridge: Cambridge University Press 2015), 1.

2 Aryeh Neier, 'Foreword,' Sam Dubberley, Alexa Koening and Daragh Murray, *Digital Witness* (Oxford: Oxford University Press 2020), ix.

3 Ella McPherson, 'Advocacy Organizations' Evaluation of Social Media Information for NGO Journalism: The Evidence and Engagement Models,' Am. Behav. Sci. 59 (2015), 124 (124, 125).

4 Philip Alston, 'Introduction: Third Generation Human Rights Fact-Finding,' Proceedings of the ASIL Annual Meeting 107 (2003), 61–62 (62).

5 Ibid.

6 Lindsay Freeman, 'Law in Conflict: The Technological Transformation of War and Its Consequences for the International Criminal Court,' N. Y. U. J. Int'l L. & Pol. 51 (2018–2019), 807–869.

for crimes both at the international[7] and domestic level.[8] On the other hand, the internet has been an invaluable tool in the fight against those crimes, because not only does it plays a central role in determining individual and collective accountability but also because it helps challenge the official narratives, and it is able to reach communities across the globe, as it will be demonstrated in this chapter.

In light of the above, this chapter analyses how international criminal tribunals and courts (ICTCs) collect, receive and share information through the internet. It focuses on the flow of information from the society to the ICTCs and, vice versa, on the data released via the internet by the ICTCs to local communities. Thus, this chapter covers two different aspects of the work of ICTCs. In Section III, it discusses the newly implemented use of user-generated digital evidence (intended as 'data [...] that is created, manipulated, stored or communicated by any device, computer or computer system or transmitted over a communication system, that is relevant to the proceedings').[9] This may come in the form of photographs, video and audio recordings, e-mails, blogs, and social media. While the information derived from online open sources is starting to become critical in creating an evidentiary basis for international crimes, the existing literature has explored various aspects of digital investigation frameworks, focussing primarily on the challenges that the ICTCs are facing in using digital evidence.[10] Furthermore, special attention has been given to the

---

7 Michail Vagias, 'The Territorial Jurisdiction of the ICC for Core Crimes, Committed through the Internet,' Journal of Conflict and Security Law 21 (2016), 523–540; Ezekiel Rediker, 'The Incitement of Terrorism on the Internet: Legal Standards, Enforcement and the role of the European Union,' MJIL 36 (2015), 321–351 (342–43).

8 Natalia Krapiva, 'The United Nations Mechanism on Syria: Will the Syrian Crimes Evidence Be Admissible in European Courts?,' Calif. L. Rev. 107 (2019), 1101–1118.

9 Stephen Mason (ed.), *International Electronic Evidence* (London: British Institute of International and Comparative Law 2008), xxxv.

10 Keith Hiatt, 'Open-Source Evidence on Trial,' Yale L.J. 125 (2016), 323; Lindsay Freeman, 'Digital Evidence and War Crimes Prosecutions: The Impact of Digital Technologies on International Criminal Investigations and Trials,' Fordham Int'l L. J. 41 (2018), 283–336; Aida Ashouri, Caleb Bowers and Cherrie Warden, 'An Overview of the Use of Digital Evidence in International Criminal Courts,' Digital Evidence And Elec. Signature L. Rev. 11 (2014), 115–126 (118); Nikita Mehandru and Alexa Koenig, 'ICTS, Social Media, & the Future of Human Rights,' Duke Law & Technology Review 17 (2019), 129–145; Danielle K. Citron and Robert Chesney, 'Deep Fakes: A Looming Challenge for Privacy, Democracy, and National Security,' Calif. L. Re. 107 (2019), 1753–1819.

new expanded role and responsibilities of third parties, such as NGOs and private actors, in locating, preserving, verifying, and analysing online visual imagery.[11] Section IV discusses the under-researched use of the internet in the outreach programmes, which aim to build awareness and understanding of the ICTCs role and activities among the affected communities.

Against this background and in line with the scope of this book, this chapter explores the direction in which ICL and its goals have been evolving since the development of the internet. Using those principles as a theoretical framework, as set in Section II, the second part of this chapter analyses the benefits and the challenges that the internet brings to ICL and, more specifically, to the ICTCs and their aim to deliver justice.

II. ICL and Its Goals: Setting the Theoretical Framework

ICL revolves around two main aims: the principle of retribution and the principle of deterrence.[12] The first is based on the idea that perpetrators deserve punishment for the crimes they have committed. In this context, punishment does not aim to obtain vengeance,[13] but it is an expression of condemnation and outrage of the international community as these crimes cannot go unpunished.[14] The second, as equally important, the objective is the principle of deterrence, which is linked to the idea that punishment

11 Alexa Koenig, "Half the Truth Is Often a Great Lie': Deep Fakes, Open Source Information, and International Criminal Law,' AJIL 113 (2019), 250–255; Róisín Á Costello, 'International Criminal Law and the Role of Non-State Actors in Preserving Open Source Evidence,' Cambridge Int'l L. J. 7 (2018), 268–283; Jay D. Aronson, 'Preserving Human Rights Media for Justice, Accountability, and Historical Clarification,' Genocide Studies and Prevention: An International Journal 11 (2017), 82–99.

12 Herbert L. A. Hart, *Punishment and Responsibility* (Oxford: Oxford University Press 1968), pp. 1–27; Mark A. Drumbl, *Atrocity, Punishment and International Law* (Cambridge: Cambridge University Press 2007), 60.

13 Desmond Tutu, *No Future without Forgiveness* (London: Rider Books 1999).

14 ICTY, *Prosecutor v. Alekšovski*, Appeals Chamber, Judgement of 24 March 2000, IT-95–14/1, para. 185; ICTY, *Prosecutor v. Momir Nicolić*, Trial Chamber, Judgement of 2 December 2003, IT-02–60/1, paras 86–87; ICTY, *Prosecutor v. Erdemović*, Trial Chamber, Sentencing Judgment of 29 November 1996, IT-96–22-T, para. 65; ICTY, *Prosecutor v. Tadić*, Sentencing Judgement, IT-94–1-S, 11 November 1997, paras 7–9; ICTR, ***Prosecutor v. Serushago*, Trial Chamber I,**, Sentence of 5 February 1999, **ICTR 98–39-S,** para. 20.

should prevent both the offender and the society from reiterating the commission of a prohibited conduct.[15]

In addition to these, there is a Babel of further goals, which envisage a more long-term and utilitarian view for post-conflict societies. These are, for instance, the vindication of victims' rights because it has been demonstrated that prosecutions are beneficial for victims having a cathartic effect on both the individuals and the affected communities.[16] Furthermore, international prosecutions serve as a tool to permanently record history,[17] to demonstrate the existence of certain crimes[18] and to interpret the contextual elements of international offences.[19] Finally, ICL serves the purpose to achieve restorative justice and post-conflict reconciliation in order to help the society to move forward and guarantee a period of durable peace.[20]

---

15 Preamble 15 of the Rome Statute of the International Criminal Law, UN Doc. A/CONF.183/9. For case-law, see ICTY, *Prosecutor v. Delatić,* Trial Chamber, Sentencing Judgment of 29 November 1996, IT 96–21-T; ICTY *Nicolić* (n. 13), 89–90; ICTY, *Prosecutor v. Delatić,* Trial Chamber I, Sentencing Judgment of 29 November 1996, IT 96–21-T. For a different point of view see ICTY, *Prosecutor v. Češić*, Trial Chamber I, Sentencing Judgment of 11 March 2004, IT-95–10-S, paras 25–26; ICC, *Situation in the DRC in the Case of Prosecutor v Thomas Lubanga Dyilo*, Pre-Trial Chamber I, Warrant of Arrest of 10 February 2006, ICC-01/04–01/06–2-tEN, para. 48. See also Hector Olasolo, *The International Criminal Court in Preventing Atrocities through Timely Intervention* (The Hague: Eleven International Publishing 2011).

16 Ernesto Kiza, Corene Rathgeber and Holger-Christoph Rohne, *Victims of War: An Empirical Study on War-Victimization and Victims' Attitudes towards Addressing Atrocities* (Hamburg: Hamburger Edition online 2006); Elisa Hoven, Mareike Feiler and Saskia Scheibel, *Victims in Trials of Mass Crimes: A Multi-Perspective Study of Civil Party Participation at the Extraordinary Chambers in the Courts of Cambodia* (Köln: Institute for International Peace and Security Law, Universität zu Köln 2013), 25–30.

17 Antonio Cassese, 'Reflections on International Criminal Justice,' JICJ 9 (2011), 271–275. For the opposite view, see ICTY (Trial Chamber), *Prosecutor v. Karadžić*, Decision On The Accused's Holbrooke Agreement Motion of 8 July 2009, case no. IT-9S-SI18-PT, para. 46; see also Jose E. Alvarez, 'Rush to Closure: Lessons of the Tadić Judgment,' Mich. L. Rev. 96 (1998), 2031–2112; Jose E. Alvarez, 'Lessons from the Akayesu Judgment,' ILSA J. Int'l & Comp. L. 5 (1999), 359–370; Martha Minow, *Between Vengeange and Forgiveness: Facing History after Genocide and Mass Violence* (Boston: Beacon Press 1998), 46–47.

18 Robert Cryer et al., *An Introduction to International Criminal Law and Procedure* (3rd edn online, Cambridge: Cambridge University Press 2018), 40.

19 Jose E. Alvarez, 'Crimes of States/Crimes of Hate: Lessons from Rwanda,' Yale J. Int'l L. 24 (1999), 365–483 (375).

20 Mark Osiel, *Mass Atrocity, Collective Memory and the Law* (New Brunswick, N.J.: Transaction Publishers 1997).

With this framework in mind, this chapter analyses how the internet has changed the ICTCs' evidentiary system.

III. From Old Evidence to Digital Evidence

During the Nuremberg trial, the prosecution team led by Justice Robert Jackson relied almost exclusively on documents and films as evidence limiting as much as possible the use of witness testimony. His intent was to demonstrate 'incredible events by credible evidence.'[21] Indeed, cases should have been decided according to the rule of law as opposed to the emotions that survivor-witnesses would inevitably display in the courtroom.[22]

Fifty years after these happenings, the most recently established ICTCs have been making use of visual documentation or open sources, including books, documentaries, reports and photographs.[23] They grounded the admission of evidence on the principles of reliability and probative value.[24] The ICC used a similar approach, which relies on the probative value of this evidence. This principle became evident when the Office of the Prosecutor (OTP) increasingly relied on NGOs' reports. In confirming the charges in the case against Mbarushimana, the ICC disregarded all the facts that were solely based on UN and NGOs' reports arguing that it 'has not provided any other evidence in order for the Chamber to ascertain the truthfulness and/or authenticity of those allegations. The sources of the information contained in both the UN and Human Rights Watch Report are anonymous.'[25] Similarly, in *Gbagbo*, Pre-Trial Chamber I compared NGOs reports to anonymous hearsays, stating their limited probative value

21 Justice Robert Jackson, quoted in Lawrence Douglas, 'Film as Witness: Screening Nazi Concentration Before the Nuremberg Tribunal,' Yale L. J. 105 (1995), 449, 452.

22 Michael Salter, *Nazi War Crimes, US Intelligence And Selective Prosecution at Nuremberg* (London: Routledge-Cavendish 2007), 404; Alexa Koenig, Keith Hiatt and Khaled Alrabe, 'Access Denied? The International Criminal Court, Transnational Discovery, and The American Service members Protection Act,' Berkeley J. Int´L. 36 (2018), 404–409.

23 Jennifer L Mnookin, 'The Image of Truth: Photographic Evidence and the Power of Analogy,' Yale Journal of Law and Human 10 (1998), 1, 8–14.

24 Human Rights Law Centre, UC Berkeley School of Law, *The New Forensics: Using Open Source Information to Investigate Grave Crimes* (2020) 5.

25 ICC, *Prosecutor v. Callixte Mbarushimana*, judgement of 16 December 2011, no. ICC-01/04–01/10–465-Red 16–12–2011, paras 117, 194, 232 and 238.

for two reasons: first, it limited the right of the Defence to investigate and challenge the trustworthiness of the source of information and, second, the judges were unable to assess the trustworthiness of the source, making it impossible to determine what probative value to attribute to the information.[26]

Despite this timid use of open sources as evidence, contemporary international criminal investigations have been heavily dependent on witnesses' testimony.[27] However, it was soon clear that a system based on witness testimony was fragile and 'unsustainable due to a number of challenges,'[28] especially when some ICTCs conduct the investigations *in loco* while the crimes are still ongoing. This led to security issues of both the investigators in the field and of witnesses, who are vulnerable to be threatened, bribed, injured or even killed due to their participation in the proceedings. This was evident in Kenya's post-election violence in 2007–2008, which led to dropping charges against Kenyatta due to insufficient evidence and alleged intimidation of several witnesses.

While the ICTCs developed and strengthened programmes of witness protection,[29] the need for a change in the evidentiary strategy was waiting.[30] The OTP had begun introducing more digital evidence, such as some video portraying Lubanga inspecting troops with boys and girls in military fatigues.[31] Also, satellite imaging, including Google Earth, were used to track the destruction of some villages, killing of population and troop movements in *Banda Jerbo and Abu Garda*,[32] although the OTP Strategic Plan 2012–2015 underestimated the potentiality of the internet

26 ICC, *Prosecutor v. Laurence Gbagbo*, judgement of 3 June 2013, no. ICC-02/11-01/11–432, paras 28–29.

27 Stephen Cody, Alexa Koenig, Robin Mejia, and Eric Stover, *Bearing Witness At The International Criminal Court: An Interview Survey Of 109 Witnesses* (Berkeley: Human Rights Centre, UC Berkeley School of Law 2014); Keith Hiatt, 'Open Source Evidence on Trial,' Yale L.J. 125 (2016) 323–330.

28 International Bar Association, *Witnesses before the International Criminal Court* (London: International Bar Association 2013), 20.

29 Articles 68(2) and 69(2) of the Rome Statute, Rule 87 of the ICC RPE, Regulation 21(2) of Regulation of the Court and Regulation 94 of the Registry Regulation.

30 Alison Cole, 'Technology for Truth: The Next Generation of Evidence,' 18 March 2015, available at: https://www.ijmonitor.org/2015/03/technology-for-truth-the-next-generation-of-evidence/.

31 ICC, *Prosecutor v Lubanga*, judgment of 14 March 2012, no. ICC-01/04–01/06, para. 1244.

32 ICC, *Prosecutor v Abdallah Banda Saleh Jerbo Jamus*, judgment of 28 August 2013, no. ICC-02/05–03/09; ICC, *Prosecutor v Bahr Idriss Abu Garda*, judgement of 7 March 2011, no. ICC-02/05–02/09.

as a source of evidence.[33] It was necessary to wait until the OTP Strategic Plan 2016–2018 to see the first signs of the impact of the internet on the ICC's trials.[34] In stressing the importance of using computers, the internet, mobile phones, and social media as a 'coming storm,'[35] it recommended to increasingly incorporate online open source content into their investigations to corroborate witness testimony and fill evidentiary gaps.[36]

The importance of the internet for the investigation can be seen in some milestone cases, where the ICC largely relied on digital evidence. In 2016 the *Al-Mahdi Case*, the accused pleaded guilty to having destroyed some cultural heritage sites in Timbuktu in Mali.[37] In order to corroborate this, the OTP used satellite images to show the situation of the mausoleums before, during and after the destruction. Some videos were taken from YouTube or social networks to prove the participation of the accused in war crimes.[38] Also, in the trial against Bemba and his affiliates for witness tampering and corruption under Article 70 of the Rome Statute, the OTP used screenshots of Facebook to clarify the relationship between the parties of the alleged bribery.[39]

Similarly, in 2017, the ICC issued two arrest warrants against Mustafa Busyl Al-Wefalli, commander of an elite force unit of the Libyan National Army, the Al-Saiqa Brigade, in Benghazi, allegedly responsible for having committed war crime under Article 8(2)(c)(i) of the Rome Statute.[40] The first arrest warrant was based on evidence (seven videos and transcripts of those videos) collected through the internet and, more specifically, posted by the Media Centre of the Al-Saiqa Brigade on Facebook and social

33 Alexa Koening, 'Open Source Evidence and Human Rights Cases: A Modern Social History' in: Sam Dubberley, Alexa Koening and Daragh Murray (eds), *Digital Witness* (Oxford: Oxford University Press 2020), 32–47 (34).

34 See Office of the Prosecutor, 'Strategic Plan (2016–2020),' 8 July 2015, available at: https://www.icc-cpi.int/Pages/item.aspx?name=otp-rep-150708, para. 58.

35 Peggy O'Donnell et al., *Beyond Reasonable Doubt: Using Scientific Evidence to Advance Prosecutions at the ICC* (Human Rights Centre School of Law University of California Berkeley, Workshop Report 7, 23 October 2012).

36 See Office of the Prosecutor, 'Strategic Plan (2016–2020)' (n. 34), para. 58.

37 ICC, *Prosecutor v. Al Mahdi*, judgement of 27 September 2016, no. ICC-01/12–01/15–171.

38 ICC, *Prosecutor v. Al Mahdi*, Transcript of 22 August 2016, no. ICC-01/12–01/15-T-4-Red-ENG, p. 41 ll. 4–10.

39 ICC, *Prosecutor v. Bemba*, judgement of 27 June 2013, no. ICC-01/05–01/08–2721.

40 ICC, *Prosecutor v. Al-Werfalli*, judgement of 15 August 2017, no. ICC-01–11–01/17–2.

media.[41] Those videos showed Al-Werfalli, wearing camouflage trousers and a black t-shirt with the logo of the Al-Saiqa Brigade, and carrying a weapon, while shooting three men in the head. Other videos displayed him speaking into the camera, ordering two men to proceed with an execution. Then, the two men shoot the persons kneeling, who fall to the ground. Following that, a group of volunteers and full-time investigators, known under the name of Bellingcat, geolocated the incidents in Benghazi and established the date of those videos.[42]

As suggested by Freeman, the use of digital evidence in the above-mentioned cases does not constitute an 'anomal[y] or temporary deviation [...], but rather the first in a growing trend.'[43] In agreeing with this view, this chapter aims to assess how this growing trend is influencing ICL goals. More specifically, Section V will deal with it, while the following section focuses on how the communication of the ICTCs toward the local communities changed with the advent of the internet.

IV. Outreach Programmes

Outreach programmes were an unknown concept at the time when the two *ad hoc* tribunals were created.[44] It is not until 1999, five years after the investigations had begun that the ICTY President Gabrielle Kirk McDonald reported to the UN that the ICTY's work was 'frequently politicised and used for propaganda purposes by its opponents, who portray[ed] the Tribunal as persecuting one or other ethnic groups and mistreating persons detained under its authority.'[45] Thus, given that ICTY was seen as disconnected from the population, the importance of having an effective

---

41 Emma Irving, 'And so it Begins... Social Media Evidence on an ICC Arrest Warrant,' 17 August 2017, available at: http://opiniojuris.org/2017/08/17/and-so-it-begins-social-media-evidence-in-an-icc-arrest-warrant/.

42 See at: https://www.bellingcat.com/news/mena/2017/10/03/how-an-execution-site-was-geolocated/. See also at: https://www.bellingcat.com/news/mena/2017/09/04/geolocating-libyas-social-media-executioner/.

43 Lindsay Freeman, 'Digital Evidence and War Crimes Prosecutions: The Impact of Digital Technologies on International Criminal Investigations and Trials,' Fordham Int'l L. J. 41 (2018), 283–335 (333).

44 Sara Darehshori, 'Lessons for Outreach from the Ad Hoc Tribunals, The Special Court for Sierra Leone, and the International Criminal Court,' New England Journal of International and Comparative Law 14 (2008), 299–307 (300).

45 Sixth Annual Report of the International Tribunal for the Prosecution of Persons Responsible for Serious Violations of International Humanitarian Law Commit-

communication with the affected communities was recognised of paramount importance. Similarly, the majority of the population in Rwanda was not aware of the work of the ICTR.[46] Despite these concerns, the budget of these two institutions did not include any funding for outreach. A small group of States, NGOs and other institutions funded the ICTY outreach activities on a voluntary basis.[47]

Against this background, the internet has been an invaluable tool to promote access to and understanding of judicial proceedings and foster realistic expectations about the ICTCs' work.[48] For this reason, the International Residual Mechanism for Criminal Tribunals has a web page, from which it broadcasts its hearings.[49] Similarly, the ICC made outreach one of its priorities.[50] The latter, for instance, streams hearings with 30 minutes of delays to allow the redaction of the audio or visual display for confidentiality reasons.[51] In January 2009, at the opening of its first trial, Lubanga's trial, the ICC organised a public screening of the proceedings in a community hall in Bunia and, then, suspended them over security concerns.[52] After that, the ICC regularly streamed the hearings against Lubanga in the DRC.[53] Similarly, in the *Bemba* case, the ICC broadcasted some screenings of public hearings to an estimated 800,000 people nationwide.[54] More

---

ted in the Territory of the Former Yugoslavia since 1991, UN Doc. A/54/187-S/1999/846 (25 August 1999).

46 Eric Stover and Harvey M. Weinstein, *My Neighbor, My Enemy: Justice and Community in the Aftermath of Mass Atrocity* (Cambridge: Cambridge University Press 2004).

47 See for a list of the contributors, ICTY, Support and Donations, available at: https://www.icty.org/en/content/support-and-donations.

48 ICC, Outreach Report 2010,https://www.icc-cpi.int/iccdocs/PIDS/publications/OUR2010Eng.pdf; ICC, Interacting with communities affected by crimes, https://www.icc-cpi.int/about/interacting-with-communities.

49 UNIRMCT, The Hague Branch Courtroom Broadcast, available at: https://www.irmct.org/en/cases/mict-courtroom-broadcast.

50 Hans-Peter Kaul, 'Victims' rights and peace' in: Thorsten Bonacker and Christoph Johannes Maria Safferling (eds), *Victims of International Crimes: An Interdisciplinary Discourse* (The Hague: Asser Press 2013), 223–229.

51 ICC, 'Regulations of the Court,' (2004), ICC-BD/01–05–16, Reg. 21(1) and 21(7).

52 Coalition for the International Criminal Court, 'Ntaganda's ICC trial in DRC?,' 26 March 2015, available at: https://www.coalitionfortheicc.org/.

53 M. Cherif Bassiouni, *Introduction to International Criminal Law* (Leiden: Martinus Nijhoff Publishers 2013), 361.

54 ICC, Outreach Report (n. 48), 60.

recently, the *Ongwen* case was live streaming in the affected community.[55] In addition to those, the ICC created a web page dedicated to its suspects at large[56] and has a YouTube channel, where it uploads different types of videos, with summaries narrated by the Court's judges or with simple explanations of complex decisions to facilitate the understanding of its proceedings to the public.[57]

Against this background, the second part of this chapter aims at analysing how the internet is influencing ICL goals, starting from the goals of retribution and deterrence.

V. Retribution and Deterrence: New Positive Trends and Areas of Concern

Retribution and deterrence are strictly linked to the impact of the internet on the ICTCs evidentiary system.[58] Section III of this chapter showed that ICTCs, and more specifically the ICC, are increasingly using digital evidence. Although this practice is recent, it has produced encouraging results. For instance, it reduces the overreliance on eyewitnesses, and it reduces the risk of witness tampering since witnesses are not going to be considered the primary evidentiary sources anymore, as clarified in Section III of this chapter. However, it is worth to be asked whether the approach to open source evidence will change depending on the facts that be proved and the stage of proceedings. For instance, according to Article 58(1) of the Rome Statute, the standard of proof for the issuance of an arrest warrant is 'reasonable grounds to believe.' Seven videos and the transcripts of those videos posted on social media were considered enough to meet this threshold in the *Al-Werfalli* case since Trial Chamber VIII issued two arrest warrants, as clarified in Section III of this chapter. Irving questions the use of digital open sources evidence when the required standards of proof becomes higher, for instance, when initiating an investigation ('reasonable basis to believe,' Article 53(1)(a)) or, later in

55 Coalition for the International Criminal Court, ''Only justice could make us feel alive again' – Week one of the Ongwen ICC trial,' 16 December 2016, https://www.coalitionfortheicc.org/.

56 Annual Report of the International Criminal Court to the United Nations on its activities in 2019/20, 24 August 2020, A/75/324, 17.

57 The YouTube Channel of the ICC is available at: https://www.youtube.com/channel/UC183T5VoMh5wISSdKPaMgRw.

58 ICC, 'Integrated Strategy for External Relations, Public Information and Outreach,' 18 April 2007, 2.

the proceedings, when 'substantial grounds to believe' (confirmation of charges, Article 61(5)) and 'beyond reasonable doubt' (conviction, Article 66(3)) are necessary.[59] In accordance with Rule 63(2), ICC judges determine the probative value and the 'appropriate weight' of admitted evidence at the end of a case, when they are considering the evidence as a whole.[60] While the golden standard rule suggests triangulating physical, testimonial and documentary evidence, the ICC developed some guidelines on how to interpret open-sources.[61]

The latter were applied to the new digital era evidence in the *Al-Mahdi*, *Bemba* and *Al-Werfalli* cases, but all of them are quite peculiar cases. Al-Madhi had already pleaded guilty, acknowledging that he had destroyed certain religious buildings in the area of Timbuktu, when the OTP decided to use some videos from YouTube against him. Also, the type of crime lends itself well to the use of digital evidence and satellite imagery. Conversely, digital technologies were used to prosecute Bemba and his associates of witness tampering under Article 70 of the Rome Statute. However, the accused was within the ICC's detention facilities, and a certain type of evidence was readily available to the investigation team. Furthermore, this case was closer to a case of national public corruption case rather than an investigation into war crimes. In addition to this, it has to be noted that both Al-Werfalli and Al-Mahdi were the direct perpetrators of the alleged crimes. Conversely, it remains to be asserted whether digital evidence can be used to demonstrate, for instance, the existence of a chain of command.

Against this background, using digital evidence also presents some challenges. These are, for instance, authentication of the evidence and its verifiability,[62] which might undermine the defendant's right to a fair trial

---

59 Emma Irving, 'And So It Begins… Social Media Evidence in an ICC Arrest Warrant,' 17 August 2017, available at: http://opiniojuris.org/.

60 ICC Unified Technical protocol ('e-Court Protocol') for the provision of evidence, witness and victims information in electronic form, ICC-01/04–01/10–87-Anx 30–03–2011, para. 1 [online] Available at: https://www.icccpi.int/RelatedRecords/CR2011_03065.PDF.

61 Lindsay Freeman, 'Prosecuting Atrocity Crimes with Open Source Evidence: Lessons from the International Criminal Court' in: Sam Dubberley, Alexa Koening and Daragh Murray (eds), *Digital Witness* (Oxford: Oxford University Press 2020), 48–67.

62 Lawrence Douglas, 'Film as Witness: Screening Nazi Concentration Camps before the Nuremberg Tribunal,' Yale L.J. 105 (1995), 449–481; Susan Schuppli, 'Entering Evidence: Cross-Examining the Court Records of the ICTY' in: Forensic Architecture (ed.), *Forensic: The Architecture of Public Truth* (Berlin: Stenberg Press 2014).

and, indirectly, the efficacy of the principles of retribution and deterrence. Although authentic, it might be difficult to verify online videos uploaded on online platforms because they often lack valuable metadata on the date and time of the recording.[63] For instance, the footage on Syria was largely unusable because there was no way of verifying the authenticity of the material that had been uploaded on social media.[64] These verification problems led to the idea that it was necessary to develop some apps that are able to guarantee that the uploaded material has not been manipulated or tampered with.

EyeWitness to Atrocities,[65] Videre Est Credere[66] and CameraV[67] are some examples of how these new technologies, built around an internet connection, are equipping individuals and training them to safely capture visual evidence of human rights abuses and international crimes. Those apps are free, and they can be downloaded on personal mobile phones from Google Play. When the users launch the app, it automatically transforms metadata into recording and attaches to them some hash values, which aims to verify whether the original file has been manipulated.[68] Those metadata include GPS coordinates, light meter readings and cell towers signals with the time and the location of the footage. Once the users have finished filming, they can upload the material through a secure transmission system. Then, a team of lawyers is responsible for reviewing the uploaded material, which might be used by ICTCs at their request.[69]

In order to understand whether the internet had an impact on the way ICTCs deliver retribution and deterrence, it is necessary to analyse the approach of the ICTCs towards digital evidence against the general approach to the admission of evidence in trial proceedings. According to Rules 89(c)

63 EyeWitness, Verifying Eyewitness Video: How to Verify Footage of Human Rights Abuse.

64 Ella McPherson, 'Advocacy Organizations' Evaluation of Social Media Information for NGO Journalism: The Evidence and Engagement Models,' Am. Behav. Sci. 59 (2015), 124 (133–134).

65 See at: https://www.eyewitness.global/welcome. For a specific application see at: https://www.eyewitness.global/Combining-our-technology-with-satellite-imagery-to-uncover-environmental-crimes-in-The-Gambia.

66 See at: https://www.videreonline.org/.

67 See at: https://exposingtheinvisible.org/en/tools/camerav/.

68 Mark S Ellis, 'Shifting the Paradigm – Bringing to Justice those who Commit Human Rights Atrocities,' Case W. Res. J. Int'l L. 47 (2015), 265–282 (273).

69 Rule 104(2) ICC RPE. Assembly of States Parties to the Rome Statute of the International Criminal Court, Rules of Procedure and Evidence, First session, New York, 3–10 September 2002 (ICC-ASP/1/3 and Corr.1), part II.A.

of both the ICTY and ICTR Rules of Procedure and Evidence, judges must assess the probative value of the evidence.[70] First, in order to be admitted, the evidence must satisfy 'minimum standards of relevance and reliability.'[71] Then, judges must evaluate its weight separately.[72] Similarly, the ICC Rules of Procedure and Evidence clarifies that evidence must be admitted or rejected based on its relevance, probative value, and prejudicial impact.[73] Thus, the ICC does not require judges to rule separately on the authenticity of the evidence.[74]

With specific reference to digital evidence, the ICC adopted an 'e-court Protocol' designed to 'ensure authenticity, accuracy, confidentiality and preservation of the record of proceedings.'[75] The Protocol does not discuss the issue of probative value, which is still within the judges' discretion, but it establishes some criteria to use digital open-source evidence. For instance, it requires that metadata (including the chain of custody in chronological order, the identity of the source, the original author and recipient information, and the author and recipient's respective organizations) must be attached. A strong chain of custody, which shows '[t]he movement and location of real evidence, and the history of those persons who had it in their custody, from the time it is obtained to the time it is presented in court'[76] increases the weight judges give to the evidence.[77] For this reason, an unsolvable problem, which can undermine the principle of retribution or deterrence, can be the anonymity of the user when the footage is collected through an app, which guarantees the anonymity of its users. The ICC reiterated this flexible approach towards the authenticity

---

70 ICTY, *Prosecutor v. Popovic, and others*, decision of 7 December 2007, IT-05–88-T, para. 4, 22, 26, 33.

71 ICTY, *Prosecutor v Brdanin & Talic*, order of 15 February 2002, case no. IT-99–36-T, para. 13; ECCC, decision of 26 May 2008, case No. 001/18–07–2007/ECCC/TC, para. 7.

72 ICTY, *Prosecutor v Brdanin & Talic*, order of 15 February 2002, case no. IT-99–36-T, para. 18; ICTY, *Prosecutor v. Boškoski & Tarčulovski*, judgment of 10 July 2008, case No. IT-04–82, para. 10.

73 ICC, *Prosecutor v Jean- Pierre Bemba Gombo*, decision of 8 October 2012, case no. ICC-01/05–01/08–2299, para. 7.

74 ICC, *Prosecutor v Jean- Pierre Bemba Gombo*, decision of 8 October 2012, case no. ICC-01/05–01/08, para. 9.

75 International Criminal Court e-Court Protocol, para. 1, ICC01/04–01/10–87-Anx 30–03–2011.

76 Bryan S. Gardner (ed.), *Black's Law Dictionary* (9th edn, St. Paul: West 2009), 260.

77 ICTY, *Prosecutor v Brdanin and Talic*, IT-99–36-T, Order on the Standards Governing the Admission of Evidence, 15 February 2002, para. 18.

of digital evidence in the *Bemba* case.[78] There, the OTP used ten audio recordings of broadcasts that provided background information about the conflict in the Central African Republic and some accounts from eyewitnesses and victims.[79] However, the defence questioned the authenticity of the recordings, considering the defence also takes aim at the prosecution's method.[80] Indeed, it stressed that the OTP did not have access to metadata (such as a timestamp or the IP address of the uploader) to assist in authentication, and it mainly relied on screenshots of Facebook pages showing the photos.[81] However, the ICC judges used a circular argument, which did not resolve the doubts surrounding the authenticity of the evidence. Indeed, they argued that 'recordings that have not been authenticated in court can still be admitted, as in-court authentication is but one factor for the Chamber to consider when determining an item's authenticity and probative value.'[82] However, to determine the probative value of the evidence, the judges should 'take into account innumerable factors, including the indicia of reliability, trustworthiness, accuracy [...] as well as [...] the extent to which the item has been authenticated.'[83] Whether this affects negatively, the principles of retribution and deterrence will become clear over time.

Another aspect that might challenge retribution and deterrence is the impact of digital evidence on the principle of equality of arms, under which each party should have a reasonable opportunity to present its case.[84] On the one hand, the sheer amount of incriminating evidence might create a sort of disadvantage for the defendants, especially in high-profile cases. On the other hand, the ICTCs might lack time and resources to analyse all the relevant material. For this reason, the ICTCs have developed partnerships with third-party organisations, which employ trained data scientists with forensic knowledge to verify open-source evidence.

---

78 ICC, *Prosecutor v Jean-Pierre Bemba Gombo*, judgement of 8 October 2012, no. ICC-01/05–01/08, paras 80–122.

79 Ibid.

80 Ibid.

81 ICC, *Prosecutor v Jean-Pierre Bemba Gombo*, judgement of 8 October 2012, no. ICC-01/05- 01/08, para. 85.

82 ICC, *Prosecutor v Jean- Pierre Bemba Gombo*, judgement of 8 October 2012, no. ICC-01/05–01/08, para. 120.

83 Ibid.

84 ECHtR, *Bulut v. Austria*, judgment of 22nd February 1996, no. 17358/90; ECtHR, *Foucher v. France*, judgment of 18th March 1997, no. 10/1996/629/812; ECtHR, *Platakou v. Greece*, judgment of 11th January 2001, no. 38460/97; ECtHR, *Bobek v. Poland*, judgment of 17th July 2007, no. 68761/01.

However, this raises some further questions on how this data is examined. Indeed, there might be the risk that although some information might be relevant for the investigators, some recording will never be transferred to the ICTCs for a criminal investigation. Unfortunately, there is too little practice to understand how to overcome those setbacks.

Finally, international criminal law cases are complex endeavour as the type of evidence used are only parts of a bigger puzzle and must be incorporated into a larger strategy for justice. Indeed, the scope of the cases before the ICTCs is often narrower than the actual extent of the crimes. For instance, the former ICC Prosecutor, Louis Moreno-Ocampo, followed a 'sequenced' approach, which meant that the OTP selected a limited number of incidents, according to their gravity, in order to carry out short investigations and propose expeditious trials.[85] However, doubts exist on the efficacy of this strategy. For instance, Lubanga was only prosecuted for the war crimes of enlisting and conscripting children under the age of 15 years and using them to participate actively in hostilities (child soldiers),[86] although there were allegations of other crimes, such as rape against the civilian population in the DRC.[87] In this perspective, digital evidence might help in prioritising a line of investigation or corroborating evidence alongside witness testimony.

VI. Recording History

As clarified in Section II of this chapter, one of the ICL objectives of international prosecutions serves as a tool to permanently record history.[88] From this perspective, digital evidence has several advantages.

---

85 ICC, Report on Prosecutorial Strategy, https://www.icc-cpi.int/nr/rdonlyres/d673dd8c-d427-4547-bc69-2d363e07274b/143708/prosecutorialstrategy20060914_english.pdf, p. 5; Alex Whiting, 'Prosecution Strategy at the International Criminal Court in Search of a Theory' in: Florian Jeßberger and Julia Geneuss (eds), *Why Punish Perpetrators of Mass Atrocities? Purposes of Punishment in International Criminal* Law (Cambridge: Cambridge University Press 2020), 285–304.

86 ICC, *The Prosecutor v. Thomas Lubanga Dyilo*, judgement of 7 February 2007, no. I, ICC-01/04–01/06–803-tEN.

87 See Jim Freedman, 'A Conviction in Question – Lessons from the International Criminal Court's Inaugural Trial in Justice in Conflict,' 17 January 2018, available at https://justiceinconflict.org/2018/01/17/a-conviction-in-question-lessons-from-the-the-international-criminal-courts-inaugural-trial/.

88 Antonio Cassese, 'Reflections on International Criminal Justice,' JICJ 9 (2011), 271–275.

First, it is not subject to the lure of time. International investigations generally reach the sites of the investigations months after the crimes have been committed, given that certain zones might not be physically accessed for security, diplomatic, or logistical reasons. This might also have a negative impact on witnesses, who might forget details of their testimony. Conversely, with the use of phone cameras and an internet connection, evidence collection is quicker, can be secured in real-time and reduces the risk that evidence will be lost or destroyed. Indeed, local users can capture images and videos that could be used as evidence or to corroborate or discredit witness testimony and other evidence.[89]

Second, digital evidence can secure a more thorough approach to the case. For instance, a satellite or aerial image may capture elements that were outside a person's range of vision, such as an overview of a larger area or an inaccessible location, while eyewitnesses only provide an account based on their perception and recollection of a certain event. Similarly, computer and phone records may reveal communications and patterns of communications, which might be undisclosed otherwise. This will allow the investigators to put them in context with other evidence. For instance, the digital content is not only produced by the people witnessing atrocities but sometimes also by the perpetrators who film themselves for propaganda purposes.[90]

Furthermore, the use of digital evidence has the power to cover the knowledge and cultural gap of the ICC personnel that is often called to interpret conflict-related evidence from a different social and political context. For instance, digital sources are often used to understand the

---

89 Bellingcat Investigation Team, 'How a Werfalli Execution Site was Geolocated,' 3 October 2017, https://www.bellingcat.com/news/mena/2017/10/03/how-an-execution-site-wasgeolocated/; See, e.g., Anna Banchik et al., Chemical Strikes on Al Lataminah (Human Rights Center, UC Berkeley School of Law, 2018), https://humanrights.berkeley.edu/publications/chemical-strikes-al-lataminah; Conor Fortune, 'Digitally Dissecting Atrocities—Amnesty International's Open Source Investigations,' 26 September 2018,available at: https://www.amnesty.org/en/latest/news/2018/09/digitally-dissecting-atrocities-amnesty-internationals-open-source-investigations/; BBC NEWS, 'Cameroon Atrocity: Finding The Soldiers Who Killed This Woman,' 24 September 2018, available at: https://www.bbc.com/news/av/world-africa-45599973/cameroon-atrocityfinding-the-soldiers-who-killed-this-woman; Steven Stecklow, 'Why Facebook is Losing the War on Hate Speech in Myanmar,' 15 August 2018, available at: https://www.reuters.com/investigates/special-report/myanmar-facebook-hate/.

90 Jarret M Brachman, 'High-Tech Terror: Al-Qaeda's Use of New Technology,' Fletcher F. Wld. Aff. 30 (2006), 149–164.

broader context in which the crimes are committed, prove the contextual and specific element, as well as linkage evidence connecting the alleged perpetrator to the crime.[91] However, scholars accused the ICC of imposing foreign understanding when interpreting concepts engrained in the African context.[92]

Indeed, the way events are portrayed with a strictly hierarchical conception, and a linear chain of command suggests an interpretation linked to the way Nazis were perpetrating those crimes rather than an approach, which acknowledges the broader context of individual and societal causes.[93] A specific example is the case of the criminal gang called Mungiki in the Kenyan cases against Muthaura, Kenyatta, Ali. In his dissenting opinion, Judge Kaul clarified that he did not agree with the background description of the role of Mungiki provided by the OTP, according to which they possessed the necessary degree of 'state-like' organisation to target the civilian population on a large scale.[94] Scholars agree with this view. For instance, Kenneth Rodman conducted a study on the role of the National Congress Party and collective leadership/decision-making, agrees with him[95] and did not concur with the way President Al-Bashir was portrayed as 'the mastermind ... [with] absolute control [...] at the apex of [...] the state's hierarchical structure authority.'[96] Also, Megret made

---

91 Lindsay Freeman (n. 61), 59.

92 David M Anderson, 'Vigilantes, Violence and the Politics of Public Order in Kenya,' Afr. Aff. 101 (2002), 531–555; Peter M Kagwanja, 'Facing Mount Kenya or Facing Mecca? The Mungiki, Ethnic Violence and the Politics of the Moi Succession in Kenya, 1987–2002,' Afr. Aff. 102 (2003), 25–49.

93 Solomon A Dersso, 'The ICC's African Problem: A Spotlight on the Politics and Limits of International Criminal Justice' in: Kamari M. Clarke, Abel S. Knottnerus and Eefje de Volder (eds), *Africa and the ICC: Perceptions of Justice* (Cambridge: Cambridge University Press 2016), 61–77 (69); Severine Autesserre, 'Dangerous Tales: Dominant Narratives on the Congo and their Underintended Consequences,' Afr. Aff. 11 (2012), 202–22.

94 ICC, *The prosecutor v. Francis Kimiri Muthaura and Uhury Muigai Kenyatta and Mohammed Hussein Ali*, no. ICC-01/09–02/11; Dissenting Opinion by Judge Hans-Peter Kaul to Pre-Trial Chamber II's Decision on the Prosecutor's Application for Summonses to Appear for Francis Kimiri Muthaura, Uhuru Muigai Kenyatta and Mohammed Hussein Ali of15 March 2011.

95 Kenneth A Rodman, 'Justice as a Dialogue between Law and Politics: Embedding the International Criminal Court with Conflict Management and Peace Building,' JICJ 12 (2014), 437–469 (448).

96 ICC, *Prosecutor v. Omar Hassan Ahmad Al Bashir ('Omar Al Bashir')*, judgement of 17 April 2008, case no. ICC-02/05–01/09–3, para. 1.

a similar criticism[97] on the role of the former traditional doctor, Allieu Kondewa, considered by the SCLS the commander of the Civil Defence Forces and responsible for commanding war crimes.[98] These are a few examples, but the research on the field is quite extensive.[99]

Among the biggest challenges of recording history, the circumstances under which the data are stored must be mentioned. Human Rights Watch has published a report denouncing the widespread practice of social media platforms of permanently removing posts from their platforms, which contain terrorist and violent extremist content (TVEC), hate speech, organized hate, hateful conduct, and violent threats because they violate community standards.[100] Furthermore, some of them use algorithms, which identify and take down the content so quickly before any user can see it, or others have filters to prevent content identified as TVEC from being uploaded in the first place.[101]

Also, the purpose of permanently recording history is undermined by 'deep fakes,' i.e. digitally distorted content such as 'videos generated via algorithms that make it look like a person said or did something she did not.'[102] In this sense, the chain of custody plays an important role to guarantee that the evidence has not been manipulated or tampered with.[103]

Finally, it has to be noted that the use of the internet has the power to shape history not only at the macro-level but also at the micro-level. Indeed, Miguel argued that social media like FB, Instagram, Twitter and YouTube promote an 'intimate [form of] storytelling,'[104] which leads the

---

97 Frédéric Mégret, 'Cour Pénale Internationale et Néocolonialisme: au-delà des évidences,' Études Internationales 45 (2014), 27–50.

98 Special Court for Sierra Leone, *The Prosecutor v Moinima Fofana and Allieu Kondewa*, Judgment of 28 May 2008, no. SCSL-04–14-A, para. 69.

99 Philip Clark, *Distant Justice: The Impact of the International Criminal Court on African Politics* (Cambridge: Cambridge University Press 2018), 100–149.

100 Human Rights Watch, ''Video Unavailable': Social Media Platforms Remove Evidence of War Crimes,' 10 September 2020, available at: https://www.hrw.org/report/2020/09/10/video-unavailable/social-media-platforms-remove-evidence-war-crimes.

101 Ibid.

102 Koenig (n. 11), 252.

103 On this point see Section V.

104 Cristina Miguel, 'Visual Intimacy on Social Media: From Selfies to the Co-Construction of Intimacies Through Shared Pictures,' Social Media + Society 2 (2016), 1–10 (1).

individual towards a form of 'voluntary self-disclosure.'[105] This form of historic account pertains victims' rights.

VII. Victims' Rights

The widespread use of social networks, as well as the decreased cost of communication through mobile telephony and social media, opened up new opportunities for victims of crimes.[106] In this new context, the internet could be seen as a 'democratising' tool,[107] which shifts power to the powerless because it gives individuals across all levels of society control over the information.[108] In simple words, it gives a voice to the formerly powerless, who would have been otherwise silenced by the alleged perpetrators, the government or by those that traditionally retain information.[109] This means that people could use their phones to redirect the focus of an international criminal investigation.

Despite its many strengths, the development of the internet is also a source of some serious setbacks for victims or, more in general, for everyday citizens committed to documenting atrocities through video and photography. Indeed, this opportunity may result to be a double-edged sword given that evidence collection requires a certain degree of in-person contact. While on the one hand, it reduces the risks of retaliation against witnesses,[110] it shifts the risk from witnesses to the users who record footage through their smartphones.[111] Thus, digital evidence might expose the

105 Ibid.

106 Alston (n. 4), 62.

107 Rebecca J Hamilton, 'New Technologies in International Criminal Investigations,' Proceedings of the ASIL Annual Meeting 112 (2018), 131–133.

108 Christoph Koettl, Daragh Murray and Sam Dubberley, 'Open Source Investigation for Human Rights Reporting: A Brief History' in: Sam Dubberley, Alexa Koenig and Daragh Murray (eds), *Digital Witness* (Oxford: Oxford University Press 2020), 12–31 (18); Christine Chinkin and Mary Kaldor, *International Law And New Wars* (Cambridge: Cambridge University Press 2017), 58–68.

109 Molly Beutz Land, 'Peer Producing Human Rights,' Alberta L. Rev. 46 (2009), 1115–1139 (1116); David Patrikarakos, *War In 140 Characters: How Social Media Is Reshaping Conflict In The Twenty-First Century* (New York: Basic Books 2017), 92, 133.

110 David A Sonenshein and Robin Nilon, 'Eyewitness Errors and Wrongful Convictions: Let's Give Science a Chance,' Or. L. Rev. 89 (2010), 263–304, 263.

111 UC Berkeley First Responders: An International Workshop on Collecting and Analysing Evidence of International Crimes 4 (2014).

identity of some users, their families and endanger third parties.[112] For this reason, the user can dis-install the app or delete the original video without compromising the material uploaded once it has been transferred to the servers.[113] This guarantees a certain level of anonymity because the hash values identify the phone rather than the user. While Camera V asks for an e-mail address, it is not a compulsory requirement in the Eyewitness app.[114] However, the practical reality is that those apps are not as widely shared as some more familiar platforms like YouTube.[115] Thus, downloading the app and using it correctly might prove itself a significant obstacle for the same victims.[116]

Another equally challenging issue is represented by the involvement of third parties once the footage has been collected using an app. This material is uploaded and generally stored on the servers of NGOs. For instance, eyeWitness has a partnership with LexisNexis and secures the uploaded material on LexisNexis servers located in London.[117] Thus, it seems that individuals do not retain full control over the material they collect. Some authors, such as Caswell, believe that the preservation and availability of this evidence should be governed by the wishes of victims' families and survivors.[118] According to Caswell, this should be the primary ethical concern of documenting human rights violations to guarantee a full 'survivor-centred' approach.'[119] While this argument has some merit, it must be taken into account that ICTCs have always outsourced their investigations to third parties. This happened, for instance, in the *Lubanga* case, where the strategy to use local activists that knew better the community and attracted less attention than ICC investigative teams from The

---

112 On retaliation by the police arresting users for filming see N Steward Hanley, 'A Dangerous Trend: Arresting Citizens for Recording Law Enforcement,' 34 American Journal of Trial Advocacy (2010), 645- 668, 647–50.

113 EyeWitness User Safety FAQs, available at: https://eyewitness.tech/about-us/faqs/.

114 Ellis (n. 68), 273.

115 Roisin A Costello, 'International criminal law and the role of non-state actors in preserving open source evidence,' Cambridge International Law Journal 7 (2018), 268–283.

116 Kelly Matheson, Witness, *Video as Evidence Field Guide* (New York, Witness 2016), 1, 5.

117 Rebecca Lowe, 'Witnessing Atrocity' (International Bar Association), 11 June 2015, available at: https://www.ibanet.org/Article/NewDetail.aspx?ArticleUid=11e76b66-d949-4738-9347-e67fbfbb9441.

118 Michelle Caswell, 'Toward a Survivor-Centered Approach to Human Rights Archives: Lessons from Community-Based Archives,' Archival Science 14 (2014), 307–322 (309).

119 Ibid.

Hague backfired because in the first trial at the ICC, the first witness, a former child soldier, recanted his testimony because an intermediary manipulated him into testifying. Thus, the idea to avail of third-parties for the investigation is not new.[120] What is different is the '[l]ines of authority and responsibility [which] are 'obscur[ed], and fragment[ed]' as decision-making is distributed among the new mix of actors in the space.'[121] For instance, Hamilton identifies four groups of actors in this process: first, the NGOs that pushed for the creation of those apps; the technologists, who have the technical expertise to build the app; the users who record the data and, finally, the lawyers who catalogue and coordinate the user-generated evidence.

It must also be recognised that, in addition to engaging local users with a bottom-up approach through the collection of some evidence, the internet has changed the way ICTCs relate to individuals through a top-down approach. As already mentioned in Section IV, the internet has been an invaluable tool for outreach programmes. For instance, the ICC has been accused of having a neo-colonialist, and biased agenda since the majority of the defendants charged by the ICC are from the African continent.[122] Some authors even drew a parallelism between the Western investigators who fly from The Hague to Africa and back to 'extractive industry.'[123] Conversely, it has been demonstrated that outreach programmes promote victims' participation because, without a certain degree of understanding of what ICTCs do, it is unlikely that victims may come forward and participate in the proceedings.[124]

In conclusion, the use of the internet also helps in reshaping the society, incorporating diverse and less traditional canons and in challenging the narrative of official channels, as it will be clarified in the next section.[125]

---

120 Elena Baylis, 'Outsourcing Investigations,' UCLA Journal of International Law and Foreign Affairs 14 (2009), 121–148.

121 Rebecca J. Hamilton (n. 107).

122 Douglas Smith, The International Criminal Court: The Long Arm of Neo-colonialism?,' International Affairs Review (1 November 2009).

123 Dustin N Sharp, 'Human Rights Fact Finding and the Reproduction of Hierarchies' in: Philip Alston and Sarah Knuckley (eds), *The Transformation of Human Rights Fact-Finding* (Oxford, New York: Oxford University Press 2016), 69–88 (78).

124 Patrick Vinck and Phuong N Pham, 'Outreach Evaluation: The International Criminal Court in the Central African Republic,' International Journal of Transitional Justice 4 (2010), 421–442.

125 Molly K. Land and Jay D. Aronson, 'The Promise and Peril of Human Rights Technology' in: Molly K. Land and Jay D. Aronson (eds), *New Technologies for*

VIII. Restorative Justice

The internet and new technologies can empower the community to find pathways to redress and to close the gap between the ICTCs and the local communities.

On the one hand, in terms of open source investigations, the evidence gathered for accountability purposes might also be used to preserve or re-create the cultural heritage that has been destroyed. Indeed, it might not only help under an architectural perspective to restore or recreate the building that has been destroyed or damaged but this evidence could be employed to develop educational materials, which aim to keep alive cultural rites, traditions and performing arts. The *Al-Mahdi* case is a clear example of that. As clarified in Section 3, Al-Mahdi was convicted for war crimes for the destruction of several religious buildings in Timbuktu. With the use of old pictures and YouTube videos, local craftsmen have already reconstructed many of the destroyed religious buildings.[126] Similarly, some organisations have understood the incredible potential of the internet and technology in this field. For instance, CyArk, a non-profit organization founded in 2003 following the destruction of 5th century Bamiyan Buddhas in Afghanistan, aims to digitally record, archive and share the world's most significant cultural heritage threatened by climate change, urban development, natural disasters and armed conflict.[127] Also, CyArk have recreated destroyed landmarks using 3D printing and virtual reality. Thus, news articles, maps, and social media posts can assist in documenting, restoring and recreating those landmarks building.

On the other hand, Section II discusses the ICTC's engagement programmes. Outreach programmes might help to fight the narrative according to which ICTCs are the new expression of the Western neo-colonialism power.[128] For instance, the ICC has been accused of being biased against the African continent.[129] The charges against the former Sudanese

---

Human Rights Law and Practice (Cambridge: Cambridge University Press 2018), 1–20 (7).

126 See https://ilg2.org/2020/09/30/using-open-source-investigations-to-protect-and-preserve-cultural-heritage/.

127 See https://www.cyark.org/ourMission/.

128 Available at: https://theconversation.com/how-colonialisms-legacy-continues-to-plague-the-international-criminal-court-142063.

129 Mahmood Mamdani, 'Darfur, ICC and the New Humanitarian Order: How the ICC's 'Responsibility to Protect" is being turned into an Assertion of Neocolonial Domination,' Pambazuka News (396), 17 September 2008; Patrick Labu-

President Omar al-Bashir, Kenyan President Uhuru Kenyatta, Kenyan Deputy President William Ruto, former Ivorian President Laurent Gbagbo and former Congolese Vice-President Jean-Pierre Bemba are evidence of that.[130] Similarly, the little information about ICTCs' aims and plans foster misconceptions about their powers and activities.[131] Indeed, several studies have shown that the respect for the rule of law, accountability, and peace and reconciliation in the affected communities requires, at a minimum, some level of understanding of the work of the Court.[132]

In certain circumstances, however, logistical reasons suggested to hold some of the hearings in locations close to the locations where crimes were allegedly committed. For instance, the Trial Chambers suggested this approach in *Ruto and Sang*,[133] in *Ntaganda*[134] and in *Ongwen*.[135] However, the Presidency, the body responsible for holding hearings in a different location than The Hague, rejected those recommendations grounding its decision on costs and security risk.[136] Thus, the internet and new techno-

---

da, 'The International Criminal Court and Perceptions of Sovereignty, Colonialism and Pan-African Solidarity,' AYILO/AADIO 20 (2014), 289–321.

130 Makau W. Mutua, 'Africans and the ICC' in: Kamari M. Clarke, Abel S. Knottnerus and Eefje de Volder (eds), *Africa and the ICC: Perceptions of Justice* (Cambridge: Cambridge University Press 2016) 1–36; Jean-Baptiste J. Vilmer, 'The African Union and the International Criminal Court: Counteracting the Crisis,' International Affairs 92 (2016), 1319–1342.

131 Clark (n. 99), 125.

132 Pierre Hazan, 'Measuring the Impact of Punishment and Forgiveness: A Framework for Evaluating Transitional Justice,' International Review of the Red Cross 88 (2006), 19–47; Janine N. Clark, 'International War Crimes Tribunals and the Challenge of Outreach,' ICLR 9 (2009), 99–116; Varda Hussain, 'Sustaining Judicial Rescues: The Role of Outreach and Capacity-Building Efforts In War Crimes Tribunals,' Va. J. Int'l L. 45 (2005), 547–585; Kingsley C. Moghalu, 'Image and Reality of War Crimes Justice: External Perceptions of the International Criminal Tribunal for Rwanda,' Fletcher F. Wld. Aff. 26 (2002), 21–46; Victor Peskin, 'Courting Rwanda: The Promises and Pitfalls of the ICTR Outreach Programme' JICL 3 (2005), 950–961.

133 ICC, *Prosecutor v. Ruto and Sang*, Recommendation of 3 June 2013, no. ICC-01/09–01/11–763.

134 ICC, *Prosecutor v. Ntaganda*, Recommendation of 19 March 2015, no. ICC-01/04–02/06–526.

135 ICC, *Prosecutor v. Ongwen*, Recommendation of 10 September 2015, no. ICC-02/04–01/15–300.

136 ICC, *Prosecutor v. William Samoei Ruto and Joshua Arap Sang*, Decision of 36 August 2013, no. ICC-01/09–01/11–875-Anx; ICC, *Prosecutor v Ntaganda*, Decision of 15 June 2015, no. ICC-01/04–02/06–645-Red; ICC, *Prosecutor v. Ongwen*, Decision of 28 October 2015, no. ICC-02/04–01/15–330.

logies are often critical to establishing presence and enabling dialogue with the affected communities. However, since technology is unevenly distributed within and between countries, an initial assessment phase is of paramount importance. Thus, the ICTC should conduct a mapping exercise to determine the level of access and technology infrastructure within a given community.

In terms of technology tools, a useful solution would be to entrust this task to organisations active in mapping global communication infrastructure and to build partnerships with technology actors, such as the Engine Room, which is developing a project called TechScape to provide empirical data on technology use.[137] In addition to this, to fight the unequal distribution of the internet in remote and volatile realities, the ICTC could benefit from the use of innovative solutions, including a device known as 'BRCK,' which permits to access the internet without electricity.[138] However, the internet cannot help in terms of the substance of the engagement. Indeed, the ICTC must tailor their communication in multiple languages to reach different communities under investigation, as well as ensure that these messages are culturally sensitive, gender-balanced and empowering for those individuals whose voices might have been silenced within their own community.

IX. Conclusions

This chapter assessed the impact of the internet over ICL, focusing on two different aspects: evidentiary system and outreach programme. Section III discussed how the internet changed the type of evidence presented in the courtroom, while Section III demonstrated that the failure to engage with the local population had a negative impact on the legitimacy and legacy of the ICTCs. Thus, outreach could benefit from developments in new forms of technology to design innovative and meaningful outreach strategies.

With this background in mind, this chapter concluded that the internet had a positive influence on ICL goals. The internet might bring about better, cheaper, and safer prosecutions. Also, not only the use of social media is a tool to empower the individual to gain control over the information but the same technologies used to pursue individuals' retribution, and deterrence might, for instance, help to preserve destroyed or threatened

137 See at: https://www.theengineroom.org/.
138 See at: https://www.brck.com/.

cultural heritage for future generations. However, this chapter also showed these positive trends are also characterised by some setbacks. For instance, in light of the scarce international practice, some doubts on the admissibility and verifiability of this type of evidence exist. Further, the relationship with third parties that store the video footages was very concerning. For instance, YouTube recently removed many videos, accounts and channels documenting violence and human rights abuses, potentially jeopardising the future of war crimes prosecutions.

Online Communication and States' Positive Obligations: Towards Comprehensive European Human Rights Protection

Adam Krzywoń

Abstract This chapter analyses the impact of the Internet and the shift in communication processes on the States' obligations emerging from the European Convention on Human Rights (ECHR). It claims that the environment created by the Internet is different from the traditional one; that is, it substantially empowers a range of private actors such as social media and other Internet platforms. That is why in the light of the actual development of the ECHR's standards, both the strict distinction between positive and negative State's obligations, and an overall preference for the latter are anachronistic. This chapter claims that it is crucial to keep developing European minimal safeguards in horizontal online relations when human rights violation is a result of a State's non-compliance with the positive duty. Against this backdrop, this chapter centers around the influence of the Internet on the exercise and protection of selected human rights and the changing nature of communication processes, as well as the game-changing shift caused by the growing power of private actors. It also includes a detailed analysis of the scope and content of positive State's obligations emerging from the use of the Internet, focusing on substantive obligations (i.e., the legal framework and the allocation of responsibilities), as well as on the issue of the public guarantees for online pluralism and procedural obligations (the duty to provide responses to allegations concerning online ill-treatment inflicted by private individuals).

I. Introduction

The traditional and long-established interpretation of international human rights laws is based on the non-interference principle, which means that such instruments as the European Convention on Human Rights (ECHR or Convention) oblige public authorities primarily to abstain from interfering with the free exercise of the rights (negative obligations).[1] Moreover, human rights were primarily conceived to protect individuals against intrusive and arbitrary acts of the State. That is why it is claimed that private actors are generally not directly bound by international human rights law, which is effective predominantly in vertical relations.[2]

1 Cf. Janneke Gerards, *General Principles of the European Convention on Human Rights* (Cambridge: Cambridge University Press 2019), 108.

2 Cf. Christian Tomuschat, *Human Rights: Between Idealism and Realism* (3rd edn, Oxford: Oxford University Press 2014), 119–135.

Against this backdrop, the idea of this chapter is to demonstrate that due to the impact of the Internet and the shift in communication processes, both the strict distinction between positive and negative obligations, and an overall preference for the latter are anachronistic. The environment created by the Internet is different from the traditional one, i.e., it empowers a range of private actors such as social media and other Internet platforms. That is why – primarily where substantial inequalities between individuals appear – it is not enough for the States to comply only with the obligation to abstain from interfering. Accordingly, the main argument of this chapter is that it is crucial to keep developing European minimal standards of protection in horizontal online relations, when human rights violation is a result of a state's non-compliance with the positive obligation.

The key issue of this analysis is to define and develop the scope and content of these obligations, primarily referring to the online communication processes. As the existing body of literature provides a comprehensive theory of positive obligations under the Convention,[3] there is no need to keep asking if the state's positive obligations exist. Instead, we should focus on expanding them in different horizontal spheres in order to achieve more comprehensive European human rights protection. The Convention must undoubtedly be interpreted and applied in a manner that renders its safeguards practical and effective, not theoretical and illusory.[4]

With regard to the latter, this chapter sets out – in section II – to analyse the influence of the Internet on the exercise and protection of human rights and the changing nature of communication processes. Special attention will be drawn to the freedom of expression (Article 10 ECHR) and the right to respect for private and family life (Article 8 ECHR). In this analysis, some references are also made to the right to free elections (Article 3 of Protocol No. 1 to ECHR, P1–3). Section III seeks to present the game-changing shift caused by the growing power of private actors. Finally, section IV is dedicated to the issue of scope and content of positive

---

3 See e.g. Laurens Lavrysen, *Human Rights in a Positive State. Rethinking the Relationship between Positive and Negative Obligations under the European Convention on Human Rights* (Cambridge-Antwerp-Portland: Intersentia 2016) and Malu Beijer, *Limits of Fundamental Rights Protection by the EU: The Scope for the Development of Positive Obligations* (Cambridge-Antwerp-Portland: Intersentia 2017). Accordingly, the existence of the positive obligations under the Convention should be taken for granted, meaning that its detailed theoretical justification is not necessary.

4 ECtHR (Grand Chamber), *Mihalache v. Romania*, judgment of 8 July 2019, no. 54012/10, para. 91.

obligations emerging from the use of the Internet. It focuses on substantive obligations (i.e., the legal framework and the allocation of responsibilities), as well as on the issue of the public guarantees for online pluralism and procedural obligations (the duty to provide responses to allegations concerning online ill-treatment inflicted by private individuals).

II. Online Media and Changing Communication Processes

The new technologies, including online communication, can undermine the effectiveness of long-established public law instruments for human rights protection.[5] One of the reasons for their inadequacy is that exercising fundamental rights online is substantially different than in traditional social reality. In this regard, one of the most affected spheres is the communication process, where the constant creation of new online media and communication techniques is to be observed. They obviously have a positive impact on human rights (e.g., as far as political participation, access to information, debate on public issues, freedom of conducting business and education are concerned).[6] As noted by the European Court of Human Rights (ECtHR or Court), the Internet constitutes one of the essential foundations for a democratic society, and one of the basic conditions for its progress and for each individual's self-fulfilment.[7]

Before moving on to the detailed analysis, the definition of online media should be specified. As indicated in the legal scholarship, this concept encompasses diverse entities and a wide range of actors.[8] Primarily, it includes blogs, social media networks and video-sharing portals that

5 Cf. Jan van Dijk, *The Network Society. Social Aspects of New Media* (2nd edn, Thousand Oaks, CA: SAGE Publications 2006), 128; Molly Land, 'Toward an International Law of the Internet,' Harv. Int'l L.J. 54 (2013), 393–459 (456); Katharina Kaesling, 'Privatising Law Enforcement in Social Networks: A Comparative Model Analysis,' Erasmus Law Journal 11(3) (2018), 151–164 (153).

6 See e.g. ECtHR, *Kalda v. Estonia*, judgment of 19 January 2016, no. 17429/10; see also ECtHR, *Mehmet Reşit Arslan and Orhan Bingöl v. Turkey*, judgment of 18 June 2019, nos 47121/06, 13988/07 and 34750/07 and ECtHR, *Times Newspapers Ltd (nos. 1 and 2) v. the United Kingdom*, judgment of 10 March, nos 20093002/03 and 23676/03.

7 ECtHR (Grand Chamber), *Stoll v. Switzerland*, judgment of 10 December 2007, no. 69698/01, para. 101.

8 Cf. András Koltay, *New Media and Freedom of Expression: Rethinking the Constitutional Foundations of the Public Sphere* (Oxford-London-New York-New Delhi-Sydney: Hart Publishing 2019), 23 and 82; Emily B. Laidlaw, *Regulating Speech in*

provide platforms for their users to upload publicly available content and share it with others. It also concerns news portals which enable users to publicly comment on its content. All these actors are also called gatekeepers, traditionally understood as persons or entities whose activity is necessary for publishing the opinion of another person or entity. The latter, together with the notion of Internet platforms, is used interchangeably in this chapter.

It should be noted right at the outset that the very nature of online media enables their unlawful use.[9] A wide range of private actors may employ them for the purposes of societal fragmentation, polarization, discrimination and political disinformation.[10] Echo chambers and information cocoons are being created, causing like-minded people to speak only among themselves.[11] AI-driven systems are able to detect individual preferences, entailing that the user is no longer confronted with information of various types. It is thus not surprising that false stories easily enter the public domain and have the appearance of legitimacy. Similarly, online communication makes it easier to attack the integrity of the electoral process and the candidate's reputation and can undermine electoral equality. The phenomenon of online disinformation (sometimes denominated as 'fake news'[12]) with regard to elections seems to be one of the most important challenges for policy-makers, courts, and legal scholars.[13]

Modern communication processes have become more open and partially anonymous. Every day millions of Internet users post online comments, and many of them express themselves in ways that might be regarded as

---

Cyberspace: Gatekeepers, Human Rights and Corporate Responsibility (Cambridge: Cambridge University Press 2015).

9 The fact that the Internet can be used for illegal purposes does not mean that arbitrary and disproportionate public measures are possible. In the recent ECtHR's case-law an interesting comparison was made, when the Court stated that suppressing information about the technologies for accessing information online on the grounds they may incidentally facilitate access to extremist material is no different from seeking to restrict access to printers and photocopiers because they can be used for reproducing such material, ECtHR, *Engels v. Russia*, judgment of 23 June 2020, no. 61919/16, para. 30.

10 Siva Vaidhyanathan, *Antisocial Media: How Facebook Disconnects Us and Undermines Democracy* (New York: Oxford University Press 2018).

11 Cass R. Sunstein, *#Republic: Divided Democracy in the Age of Social Media* (Princeton: Princeton University Press 2017), 13–16.

12 ECtHR, *Brzeziński v. Poland*, judgment of 25 July 2019, no. 47542/07, paras 35 and 55.

13 Adam Krzywoń, 'Summary Judicial Proceedings as a Measure for Electoral Disinformation. Defining the European Standard,' 22(4) GLJ (2021), 673–688 (676).

offensive and malicious.[14] These factors affect the exercise and protection both of the right to privacy (reputation, Article 8 ECHR) and freedom of expression (Article 10 ECHR). Defamatory and other types of clearly unlawful speech can be disseminated as never before, worldwide, in a matter of seconds, and sometimes remain persistently available online.[15] Similarly, the issue of online anonymity is crucial as far as the mentioned rights are concerned, since it provides a certain sense of safety when expressing views and ideas. The opportunity to remain anonymous has inspired users to express opinions – on both public or private matters – who previously, perhaps being afraid of the consequences, had remained silent.[16] However, while being one of the fundamental values for the functioning of the Internet, anonymity, together with the lack of accountability and interpersonal social control, can foster online aggression.[17]

The ECtHR seems to be partially conscious that Internet-based communication involves structural differences not present in traditional media, and this has an important impact on the Convention rights. According to the Court, some aspects of the Internet as a platform for the exercise of freedom of expression – such as the potential for user-generated expressive activity – are unprecedented.[18] Posting a comment on a freely accessible popular Internet portal or blog has a very powerful effect nowadays.[19] In the Court's opinion, the same applies to the comments on somebody's Facebook profile.[20] The Court also emphasises also that an individual is confronted with vast quantities of information circulating via online

---

14 ECtHR, *Tamiz v. the United Kingdom*, decision of 19 September 2017, no. 3877/14, para. 80.

15 ECtHR (Grand Chamber), *Delfi AS v. Estonia*, judgment of 16 June 2015, 64569/09, para. 110.

16 Koltay (n. 8), 14.

17 András Sajó and Clare Ryan, 'Judicial reasoning and new technologies. Framing, newness, fundamental rights and the internet' in: Oreste Pollicino and Graziella Romeo (eds), *The Internet and Constitutional Law. The protection of fundamental rights and constitutional adjudication in Europe* (London-New York: Routledge 2016), 3–25 (20).

18 ECtHR, *Akdeniz v. Turkey*, decision of 11 March 2014, no. 20877/10, para. 24; ECtHR (Grand Chamber), *Ahmet Yildirim v. Turkey*, judgment of 18 March 2013, no. 3111/10, para. 54 and ECtHR, *Delfi AS* (n. 15), para. 110.

19 ECtHR, *Fatullayev v. Azerbaijan*, judgment of 22 April 2010, no. 40984/07, para. 95.

20 ECtHR, *Beizaras and Levickas v. Lithuania*, judgment of 14 January 2020, no. 41288/15, para. 127. The ECtHR has also analysed the weight of the 'like' button and its role in online communication, see ECtHR, *Melike v. Turkey*, judgment of 15 July 2021, no. 35786/19, para. 51.

media, which involves an ever-growing number of players.[21] Once connected, Internet users may no longer enjoy effective protection of their privacy in some spheres, as they expose themselves to unwanted messages, images and information.[22] Similarly, a person who runs a blog presenting his/her political views, willingly exposing himself/herself to public scrutiny, should be more tolerant towards criticism and interference with their private life.[23]

With regard to the latter, the Court emphasizes that the Convention principles governing traditional media cannot be automatically applied to online media due to the different kinds of risks they pose. As indicated in the case-law, 'the Internet is an information and communication tool particularly distinct from the printed media, especially as regards the capacity to store and transmit information. The electronic network […] is not and potentially will never be subject to the same regulations and control. The risk of harm posed by content and communications on the Internet to the […] human rights and freedoms […] is certainly higher than that posed by the press.'[24] That is why the scope of 'duties and responsibilities' concerning the individual exercise of the freedom of expression (Article 10(2) ECHR) depends – among other things – on the potential impact of the medium.[25]

Against this backdrop, the main argument following from this part is that the changing nature of the communication processes and the emergence of the online media require the adoption of a more proactive approach towards Convention guarantees of privacy, freedom of expression and the right to free elections. Such a conclusion corresponds well with the established understanding of the Convention as a living instrument, which must be interpreted in the light of present-day conditions, so as

21 ECtHR, *Stoll* (n. 7), para. 104.

22 ECtHR, *Muscio v. Italy*, decision of 13 November 2007, no. 31358/03.

23 ECtHR, *Balaskas v. Greece*, judgment of 5 November 2020, no. 73087/17, paras 48–50.

24 ECtHR, *Editorial Board of Pravoye Delo and Shtekel v. Ukraine*, judgment of 5 May 2011, no. 33014/05, para. 63. See also ECtHR, *Węgrzynowski and Smolczewski v. Poland*, judgment of 16 July 2013, no. 33846/07, para. 58 and *Arnarson v. Iceland*, judgment of 13 June 2017, no. 58781/13, para. 37.

25 ECtHR, *Magyar Tartalomszolgáltatók Egyesülete and Index.hu Zrt v. Hungary*, judgment of 2 February 2016, no. 22947/13, para. 56.

to reflect the increasingly high standard required in the sphere of human rights protection.[26]

III. Private Governance Systems and Fair Balance Between Private Actors on the Internet

Although the international human rights protection system was initially created to protect individuals from unlawful acts of public authorities (i.e. the State), the privatization of some public tasks and functions, and the problem of the horizontal application of human rights, are not new issues.[27] It is commonly argued that States may breach their international human rights obligations where they fail to take appropriate steps to prevent, investigate, punish and redress a private actor's abuse.[28] Also, the Court claims that genuine, effective exercise of human rights may require positive measures of protection, even in the sphere of relations between individuals.[29]

The Convention system provides the 'prohibition of abuse of rights' clause (Article 17 ECHR), which expressly lists States, groups and persons whose actions may jeopardize Convention rights or limit them beyond the permitted extent. This is clear evidence of the fact that already in 1950, there existed the conviction that human rights can be used by an individual to attack another person. It has therefore become a truism that States are not the only agents responsible for violations. Nonetheless, in the context of the Internet, this affirmation seems even more complex since the online environment creates a field for the variety of conflicts between private actors. Some of them (i.e., gatekeepers) are not only able

---

26 See e.g. ECtHR (Grand Chamber), *Demir and Baykara v. Turkey*, judgment of 12 November 2008, no. 34503/97, para. 146 and ECtHR (Grand Chamber), *Öcalan v. Turkey*, judgment of 12 May 2005, no. 46221/99, para. 163.

27 See e.g. Mark Tushnet, 'The issue of state action/horizontal effect in comparative constitutional law,' I.CON 1 (2003), 79–98 and John H. Knox, 'Horizontal Human Rights Law,' AJIL 102 (2008), 1–47.

28 See e.g. Rikke Frank Jørgensen, 'When private actors govern human rights' in: Ben Wagner, Matthias C. Kettemann and Kilian Vieth (eds), *Research Handbook on Human Rights and Digital Technology. Global Politics, Law and International Relations* (Cheltenham-Northampton: Edward Elgar Publishing 2019), 346–362 (349).

29 See e.g. ECtHR, *Özgür Gündem v. Turkey*, judgment of 16 March 2000, no. 23144/93, para. 43 and *Herbai v. Hungary*, judgment of 5 November 2019, no. 11608/15, para. 36–38.

to threaten other individual rights but are also accountable for solving conflicts between individual rights that occur online. Those private actors are likewise responsible for the enforcement of some online rights and freedoms.[30] As a consequence, public authorities are obliged to increasingly rely on Internet platforms and scrutinize their actions.[31]

Against this backdrop, the category of 'new governors' is emerging.[32] Online media are seen not only as companies that conduct their business based on the shift in communication but also as entities that exercise powers similar to public authorities. They cannot be treated as mere intermediaries and facilitators of the speech of others, since they have become active political actors and holders of considerable power for shaping opinion.[33] Important evidence of this privatization of governance, also reflecting an aspiration to interpret and apply fundamental rights, is the creation of a series of documents (e.g. terms of use, terms of service) which are characterized by their constitutional nature and attempt to function as bills of rights, coordinated with a progressive institutionalization of the platforms.[34] Private companies have therefore become arbiters and engineers of free speech, and one of the most important sources of news and information. They control the flow of information and set binding rules for the end-users. In this environment, the exercise of political and civil rights – such as freedom of expression, the right to respect for private life and the right to free elections – cannot be explained in terms of 'limited government.'[35]

---

30 E.g. the right to be forgotten, see Giovanni De Gregorio, 'From Constitutional Freedoms to the Power of the Platforms: Protecting Fundamental Rights Online in the Algorithmic Society,' European Journal of Legal Studies 11 (2019), 65–103 (69).

31 Oreste Pollicino, Giovanni De Gregorio and Laura Somaini, 'Europe at the Crossroad: The Regulatory Conundrum to Face the Raise and Amplification of False Content in Internet' in: Giuliana Ziccardi Capaldo (ed.), *The Global Community Yearbook of International Law and Jurisprudence 2019* (Oxford: Oxford University Press 2020), 319–356 (320).

32 Kate Klonick, 'The New Governors: The People, Rules, And Processes Governing Online Speech,' Harv. L. Rev. 131 (2018), 1598–1670.

33 Natali Helberger, 'The Political Powers of Platforms: How Current Attempts to Regulate Misinformation Amplify Opinion Power,' Digital Journalism 6 (2020), 842–854; David Kaye, *Speech Police: The Global Struggle to Govern the Internet* (New York: Columbia Global Reports 2019), 19.

34 Cf Rory Van Loo, 'Federal Rules on Platform Procedure,' U. Chi. L. Rev 88 (2021), 829–895 (866).

35 Kai Möller, *The Global Model of Constitutional Rights* (Oxford: Oxford University Press 2012), 31.

In this context, the necessity of broadening the scope of long-established legal concepts is being raised as an issue, since it seems doubtful that the traditional interpretation of certain human rights categories is fit-for-purpose in the modern digital world. This shift should respond to the mentioned emergence of online non-state intermediary social forces.[36] One of the most important tools that can be used to legitimize their power and balance horizontal relations is the language of human rights.[37] It provides the universal set of values that both the State and – especially if holding some kind of power – private entities should respect, protect and promote. These processes are already visible on the national (constitutional) level. The best example is the recent German case-law on the horizontal application of fundamental rights by the platforms. The latter have a legal obligation to consider users' fundamental rights and avoid any arbitrary acts.[38]

Obviously, as some scholars claim, almost every conflict in the private sphere can be described in terms of a clash between different fundamental rights, and it can potentially lead to the extension of constitutional (human rights) obligations to every private relationship.[39] Nonetheless, in order to avoid the latter state of affairs, some additional criteria could be adopted. First, public intervention in horizontal relations should primarily take place when these relations are characterized by a lack of balance between private entities, which is common as far as the Internet is concerned. Second, as the Convention does not create the possibility to present an application against private actors[40], it is precisely the concept of positive obligations that could be an effective remedy. One of the crucial responsibilities of the public authorities is, therefore, the establishment of a fair

---

36 Gunther Teubner, 'Horizontal Effects of Constitutional Rights in the Internet: A Legal Case on the Digital Constitution,' The Italian Law Journal 3 (2017), 193–205 (193).

37 Nicolas P. Suzor, *Lawless: The Secret Rules That Govern Our Digital Lives* (Cambridge: Cambridge University Press 2019), 169–170.

38 Federal Court of Justice, *III ZR 179/20*, judgment of 29 July 2021 and *III ZR 192/20*, judgment of 29 July 2021. See also Matthias C. Kettemann and Torben Klausa, 'Regulating Online Speech: Ze German Way' (Lawfare Blog, 20 September 2021, available at: https://www.lawfareblog.com/regulating-online-speech-ze-german-way).

39 De Gregorio (n. 30), 100.

40 The application to the ECtHR must be 'verticalized,' see Claire Loven, "Verticalized' cases before the European Court of Human Rights unravelled: An analysis of their characteristics and the Court's approach to them,' NQHR 38 (2020), 246–263.

balance (e.g., by creating a legal framework, ensuring political and social pluralism, and providing an adequate response to allegations) between the conflicting rights of private actors on the Internet. Thanks to the latter, an individual can insist on the State's international responsibility when he/she is able to prove that a violation inflicted by other individuals is a result of the State's non-compliance with a positive obligation.

IV. Horizontal Positive Obligations and the Internet

1. General Remarks

Horizontal positive obligations, as indicated in recent studies, govern relations between private persons.[41] They are typically triangular, since they are invoked by individuals against State to oblige its authorities to intervene in horizontal relations. The responsibility of the State exists because of the link between private ill-treatment and the failure to comply with the positive obligation. Horizontal positive obligations can be of a substantive or procedural nature, depending on whether they oblige public authorities to put in place a legislative and administrative framework to effectively protect human rights against threats inflicted by private individuals, or to provide adequate and effective responses to the allegations concerning violations committed by private parties.

In the case of online communication, the nature of the relations is even more complex, and the triangular model seems to be insufficient for describing them adequately. First of all, there can indeed be a conflict between an individual (Internet user) and a gatekeeper (i.e., online media, Internet platform). In this situation, the public authorities are legitimized and obliged to intervene in order to prevent the latter from abusing its position and infringing individual rights. Secondly, it is possible that one person attacks another (e.g., incitement to violence or comments undermining someone's reputation), using the services provided by a platform. In this scenario, in the light of the Convention, the State may also be obliged to intervene in those multi-actor relations. Moreover, making the situation even more complex, the Internet creates an environment where some violations can be attributed to automatic systems, such as bots and Artificial

41 Lavrysen (n. 3), 78–79.

Intelligence.[42] The impact of the individual infringement does not depend entirely on human actions; for example, Internet search engines are able to amplify the scope of the interference that results from the acts of third parties.[43]

The most common critique of the State's positive obligations is based on the argument that its further development would cause a considerable financial burden for the public authorities. For this reason, the ECtHR emphasises that under the Convention, positive obligations should be interpreted in such a way that they do not impose excessive (impossible or disproportionate) costs on the State.[44] Moreover, in determining the scope and nature of positive obligations, the factor of knowledge turns out to be crucial. The responsibility of the State for compliance with its positive obligations is based on the foreseeability on the part of the State of an actual or potential harm.[45]

With regard to the latter, two arguments should be highlighted. First of all, the positive obligation to provide a necessary balance between conflicting rights on the Internet does not necessarily entail high (excessive) costs. Unlike some other rights (e.g., social rights), these obligations usually do not impose direct financial transfers on behalf of the State. Public authorities do not have to create a new public system (i.e., infrastructure) or mechanism of redistribution of income and wealth. They can employ the instruments already created and being used by the private actors or oblige them to apply their own instruments according to certain rules (e.g., notice-and-take-down system).[46] In the case of online human rights conflicts, it is primarily a matter of organizing some processes and balan-

42 Natali Helberger, Sarah Eskens, Max van Drunen, Mariella Bastian and Judith Moeller, 'Implications of AI-driven tools in the media for freedom of expression,' Background Paper to the Ministerial Conference Artificial Intelligence – Intelligent Politics, Challenges and opportunities for media and democracy, Cyprus, 28–19 May 2020 (Council of Europe 2020), 11. See also: Ronald K.L. Collins and David M. Skover, *Robotica. Speech Rights and Artificial Intelligence* (Cambridge: Cambridge University Press 2018).

43 ECtHR, *M.L. and W.W. v. Germany*, judgment of 28 June 2018, nos 60798/10 and 65599/10, para. 97.

44 ECtHR (Grand Chamber), *O'Keefee v. Ireland*, judgment of 28 January 2014, no. 35810/09, para. 144 and ECtHR (Grand Chamber), *Verein gegen Tierfabriken Schweiz (VgT) v. Switzerland (No. 2)*, judgment of 30 June 2009, no. 32772/02, para. 81.

45 Lavrysen (n. 3), 131–137.

46 Cf. Giancarlo F. Frosio, 'The Death of 'No Monitoring Obligations': A Story of Untameable Monsters,' Journal of Intellectual Property, Information Technology and Electronic Commerce Law 8 (2017), 199–215 (208).

cing individual rights. Secondly, as far as the criterion of knowledge is concerned, there is absolutely no doubt that modern governments are fully conscious of the multiple possibilities of illegal use of the Internet and the harmful effects it can cause to freedom of expression, the right to respect for private life and the right to free elections.[47] Public authorities are also able to easily foresee which are the exact aspects of online communication processes that require intervention in the first place.

Apart from that, there is another type of limit of the State's positive obligations under the Convention. It cannot be expected that human rights are never affected, especially when online communication is so intense and complex. For this reason, in the light of the ECHR, public authorities do not have a duty to introduce absolute guarantees. In the majority of cases, there is no obligation with regard to results, but there are obligations with regard to the measures to be taken.[48] Similarly, States are allowed a margin of appreciation in complying with positive obligations. The reason – as in a negative obligation scenario – is that national authorities are sometimes in a better position to strike a fair balance between competing private interests.[49]

Finally, it has to be emphasized that the State's obligation to ensure the individual's freedom of expression (Article 10 ECHR) does not give private citizens or organisations an unfettered right of access to the media in order to put forward opinions.[50] Similarly, the Convention does not establish a freedom of forum.[51] The latter substantially limits the scope of the State's positive obligations concerning online communication, since an individual is not legitimized to claim the right to use a particular space – especially private – in order to express an opinion. However, when the ban on access to the property (other private space or forum) has the effect of preventing any effective exercise of freedom of expression or it can be said that the essence of the right has been destroyed, the Court would not exclude that a positive obligation could arise for the State to protect the enjoyment

---

47 The Court stated that already in 1999 public authorities should have been conscious of the fact that the anonymous character of the Internet can foster its use for criminal purposes, see ECtHR, *K.U. v. Finland*, judgment of 2 December 2008, no. 2872/02, para. 48.

48 ECtHR, *Frumkin v. Russia*, judgment of 5 January 2016, no. 74568/12, para. 36.

49 Lavrysen (n. 3), 194.

50 ECtHR, *Murphy v. Ireland*, judgment of 10 July 2003, no. 44179/98, para. 61 and *Saliyev v. Russia*, judgment of 21 October 2010, no. 35016/03, para. 52.

51 ECtHR, *Appleby and others v. the United Kingdom*, judgment of 6 March 2003, no. 44306/98, para. 47.

of the Convention rights by regulating property rights.[52] Applying these arguments to online platforms, it can be claimed that public authorities are legitimized to limit their discretion in order to provide a fair balance between rights and freedoms. It does not automatically imply that there is a possibility to introduce a law prohibiting the removal or moderation by social media of lawful content, which is at the same time contrary to their community standards (internal rules). From the Convention standpoint, public authorities do not have such a far-reaching positive obligation, and national law, which obliges the platforms to host the content they do not want to host, may amount to the violation of Article 10 ECHR.

2. *Substantive Obligations and Effective Allocation of Responsibility in Online Communication*

After having analysed the changing nature of communication and the emergence of powerful online media, we can now move on to the issue of the nature and content of the State's positive obligations. As mentioned before, there are two types of positive obligations concerning horizontal relations: substantive and procedural. In this section, attention will be drawn only to the substantive ones, while the procedural obligations constitute the subject of the following section. Nonetheless, since it is sometimes difficult to distinguish between the substance and procedure, some references to the latter will also be made in this part.

Substantive positive duties oblige public authorities to apply *ad hoc* measures or to create a legal framework.[53] The latter should be put in place when *ad hoc* responses are insufficient to provide effective human rights protection.[54] As far as online communication is concerned – as already explained – the complexity of horizontal relations and the lack of balance between multiple actors make *ad hoc* measures rather inadequate. Moreover, reducing substantive positive obligations to *ad hoc* responses may imply that dealing with human rights conflicts depends on the discre-

---

52 ECtHR, *Khurshid Mustafa and Tarzibachi v. Sweden*, judgment of 16 December 2008, no. 23883/06, *Berladir and others v. Russia*, judgment of 10 July 2012, no. 34202/06, para. 58 and *Remuszko v. Poland*, judgment of 17 July 2013, no. 1562/10, para. 79.

53 ECtHR, *Köpke v. Germany*, decision of 5 October 2010, no. 420/07.

54 Dimitris Xenos, *The Positive Obligations of the State under the European Convention of Human Rights* (London-New York: Routledge 2012), 107.

tionary powers of the State. It creates the risk of unequal treatment and discrimination and often the necessity of judicial intervention.

In the context of online communication, the obligation to adopt a regulatory framework turns out to be of fundamental importance under the Convention. The task of national law-makers is to reconcile various individual claims.[55] The most common horizontal conflicts appear between the freedom of expression (Article 10 ECHR) and the protection of privacy (Article 8 ECHR). As indicated, online media and communication techniques facilitate verbal attacks on reputation and other personal rights. Freedom of expression can also be (ab)used in order to disseminate false electoral information, infringing the guarantees of free elections (P1–1).

Against this backdrop, the most important challenge for the legislative framework is the effective allocation of responsibility in online communication.[56] In other words, under the Convention, national legislative bodies have a positive obligation to create a legal framework in order to decide who is responsible for the expressions that infringe individual (Article 8 ECHR) and/or collective rights (P1–1), and under which circumstances. First of all, the national authorities have at their disposal traditional enforcement instruments such as criminal responsibility.[57] Nonetheless, introducing domestic legal provisions criminalising online conduct which violates the Convention right of another person may be insufficient and ineffective, as evidenced by the penalization of dissemination of electoral disinformation. This common form of law enforcement exists in almost every European country,[58] but is no longer operative towards the massive spreading of false electoral information online.[59] The legal framework for the allocation of responsibility must therefore be more detailed and sophisticated, reflecting the complexity of online communication.

It is, however, possible to indicate certain situations when criminalization of acts of online expression is inevitable and in the light of the Convention constitutes a basic State's positive obligation. The Court has

55 ECtHR, *K.U.* (n. 47), para. 49.

56 For the notion of allocation of responsibility see Stefan Somers, *The European Convention on Human Rights as an Instrument of Tort Law* (Cambridge-Antwerp-Portland: Intersentia 2018), 29.

57 Alastair Mowbray, *The Development of Positive Obligations under the European Convention on Human Rights by the European Court of Human Rights* (Oxford-London-New York-New Delhi-Sydney: Hart Publishing 2004), 225.

58 OSCE, The Representative on Freedom of the Media, *International Standards and Comparative Approaches to Countering Disinformation in the Context of Freedom of the Media* (OSCE 2020), 27–42.

59 Krzywoń (n. 13), 685.

noted that a criminal law response is appropriate in cases concerning incitement to commit acts of violence against others (incitement to hatred and hate speech).[60] It has even gone further, pointing out that criminal law measures constitute a positive obligation and are required under the Convention with respect to direct verbal assaults and physical threats motivated by discriminatory attitudes.[61] Where acts that constitute serious offences are directed against a person's physical or mental integrity, only efficient criminal law mechanisms can ensure effective protection and serve as a deterrent.[62] All these arguments are obviously fully adequate as far as infringements inflicted by individuals who take place in online communication are concerned. The penalization of such acts is necessary, as online incitement to violence, hatred, and discrimination can be very harmful. Under the Convention, public authorities are therefore obliged to take positive actions when the volume and seriousness of online attacks on human rights (e.g., privacy or reputation) can cause individual harm.[63] Nonetheless, even a simple online comment and the lack of effective public prosecution can lead to the State's international responsibility. As the recent case-law shows, the posting of a single hateful comment on someone's Facebook account, suggesting that he/she should be 'killed,' was sufficient to be taken seriously.[64] In these circumstances, expecting that victims will exhaust other national remedies, including civil law measures, may turn out to be manifestly unreasonable, since public authorities should act proactively and apply criminal law provisions in order to protect Internet users against personal attacks.[65]

More recently, the ECtHR has also examined the issue of the responsibility for the statements published by third parties on the 'wall' of publicly accessible Facebook accounts. The Court accepted the criminal conviction of the account's owner (politician) for incitement to hatred or violence, following his failure to take prompt action in deleting hate speech con-

60 ECtHR, *Belkacem v. Belgium*, decision of 27 June 2017, no. 34367/14 and ECtHR, *Delfi AS* (n. 15), paras 153 and 159.

61 ECtHR, *R.B. v. Hungary*, judgment of 12 April 2016, no. 64602/12, paras. 80 and 84–85; ECtHR, *Király and Dömötör v. Hungary*, judgment of 17 January 2017, no. 10851/13, para. 76 and ECtHR, *Alković v. Montenegro*, judgment of 5 December 2017, no. 66895/10, paras 65 and 69.

62 ECtHR, *Identoba and Others v. Georgia*, judgment of 12 May 2015, no. 73235/12, para. 86 and ECtHR, *M.C. v. Bulgaria*, judgment of 4 December 2003, no. 39272/98, para. 150.

63 ECtHR, *Delfi AS* (n. 15), para. 137.

64 ECtHR, *Beizaras and Levickas* (n. 20), para. 127.

65 ECtHR, *Beizaras and Levickas* (n. 20), para. 128.

tent.[66] The lack of vigilance and responsiveness in relation to the comments posted by others may therefore justify such intrusive measures as criminal responsibility, especially if the unlawful speech is publicly accessible for a long time. This judgement demonstrates that national authorities may comply with a part of their positive obligations under the Convention by holding responsible the account's owner who seriously neglects to monitor the content of the 'wall.'

With regard to the latter, the challenge for public authorities consists of an inadequate configuration of the criminal responsibility, primarily its personal scope and nature of sanctions, as well as its appropriate application (procedural aspect). As one of the main challenges both for the law-makers and courts in this respect is the definition of the online hate speech, the Court recently tried to present its conceptual understanding. It indicated a variation of possible thresholds: from the gravest forms excluded from the protection to 'less grave' ones which do not fall entirely outside of Article 10 ECHR but are subject to important restrictions.[67] National authorities should therefore be aware of different ways that hatred can be incited online. They must adopt the view that hate speech does not necessarily entail a call for an act of violence or other criminal acts. On the one hand, online attacks on persons committed by insulting, holding up to ridicule, slandering, publicly mocking and denigrating specific groups of the population (e.g., on the basis of sexual orientation) can be sufficient to allege non-compliance with positive obligations.[68]

On the other hand, the Court seems to be conscious of the vulgarization of online communication. A lot of statements which in common traditional discourse are undoubtedly considered as offensive, when expressed online, constitute little more than 'vulgar abuse.' For the ECtHR, this reflects the character of the communication on many Internet portals.[69] In other cases, the Court noted that the clearly offensive and shocking language used in a blog post (e.g., calling for police officers to be killed)

66 ECtHR, *Sanchez v. France*, judgment of 2 September 2021, no. 45581/15, paras 90 and 100.

67 ECtHR, *Vejdeland and Others v. Sweden*, judgment of 9 February 2012, no. 1813/07, para. 55 and ECtHR, *Beizaras and Levickas* (n. 20), para. 125. There is also some margin of appreciation related to the national historical experience. The latter can be a weighty factor to be taken into account when determining the online use of some symbols, see ECtHR, *Nix V. Germany*, decision of 13 March 2018, no. 35285/16.

68 ECtHR, *Carl Jóhann Lilliendahl v. Iceland*, decision of 12 May 2020, no. 29297/18.

69 ECtHR, *Magyar Tartalomszolgáltatók Egyesülete and Index.hu Zrt* (n. 25), para. 77 and ECtHR, *Tamiz* (n. 14), para. 81.

does not justify interference with the freedom of expression, since the national courts never looked at how many people had actually read the blog.[70]

As has already been mentioned, the simple criminalization of some sorts of online behaviors is not sufficient to comply with the positive obligations under Article 8 and Article 10 ECHR. The current Convention standard entails not only the obligation to criminalize and prosecute certain online behaviors, but a duty to elaborate a system that deals with two specific aspects of liability of the Internet platforms: liability for their own acts of delegated power, and liability for user-generated content. It has to be borne in mind that in both cases, the complexity of online communication requires detailed consideration of the roles, capacities, knowledge and incentives of the different stakeholders (online media, users and public institutions). In other words, it seems that in a digital world, allocating the responsibility to a single central actor would not lead to the necessary balance between all the parties.[71]

The first aspect concerns the issue of delegating power to gatekeepers and holding them liable. In order to effectively protect human rights in horizontal online relations, public authorities often transfer some tasks and obligations to private actors. The crucial element of this model is the accountability of the latter for their governance. This doctrine has been presented in the ECtHR's case-law concerning the organization of the labour market, but it perfectly matches the online communication environment. The Court noted that delegating the power to legislate, or regulate, important issues to independent organisations acting on that market, requires, in the light of the Convention, that these organisations are held accountable for their activities.[72]

As a consequence, public authorities, who – in the first instance – are not obliged to solve individual conflicts, should actively monitor how these private actors (Internet platforms) deal with horizontal infringements caused by users' activity. From the Convention standpoint, when some

70 ECtHR, *Savva Terentyev v. Russia*, judgment of 28 August 2018, no. 10692/09, para. 79.

71 Natali Helberger, Jo Pierson and Thomas Poell, 'Governing Online Platforms: From Contested to Cooperative Responsibility,' The Information Society 34 (2018), 1–14.

72 ECtHR, *Evaldsson and Others v. Sweden*, judgment of 13 February 2007, no. 75252/01, para. 63. See also ECtHR, *Muscio* (n. 22), where the Court indicated that an Internet provider operates under the terms of agreement with the State and under its supervision and can be held liable for damages.

irregularities are detected, there should be a public response. The latter is a common pattern in the 'notice-and-take-down' systems, as evidenced, for example, by the German law.[73] When a user alleges a horizontal violation, the gatekeeper should immediately and effectively deal with it. At the same time, through a system of financial responsibility, the State supervises how the platform resolves this horizontal conflict.

The second aspect consists in deciding when and under which conditions Internet platforms can be held liable for user-generated content that threatens the rights and freedoms of third-parties. This positive obligation to establish a legal framework requires balancing different rights and interests and considering various circumstances and threats. As indicated in the legal scholarship, when the State holds one private party, A, liable for the speech of another private party, B, and A has the power to block, censor, or otherwise control B's access to free speech, the phenomenon of 'collateral censorship' can occur.[74]

Important principles ruling the liability of Internet platforms for the user-generated content have been presented in the Court's case-law. The ECtHR has confirmed that imposing a liability on the news portals for some categories of offensive (anonymous) comments posted by its users can be an adequate way of protecting the human rights of others, especially in cases concerning incitement to violence and hate speech.[75] Public authorities should therefore oblige the platforms to monitor and remove clearly unlawful comments without delay, even without notice from the alleged victim or third parties. However, the imposition of this liability is justified and proportionate only when users post 'extreme comments' in reaction to an article published on a professionally managed and commercial portal. As the Court sees it, this doctrine does not automatically concern 'other

73 Gesetz zur Verbesserung der Rechtsdurchsetzung in sozialen Netzwerken (Netzwerkdurchsetzungsgesetz -NetzDG); the Network Enforcement Act of 1 September 2017), available at: https://www.bmjv.de/SharedDocs/Gesetzgebungsverfahren/Dokumente/BGBl_NetzDG.pdf; see Thomas Wischmeyer, 'What is illegal offline is also illegal online – The German Network Enforcement Act 2017' in: Bilyana Petkova and Tuomas Ojanen (eds), *Fundamental Rights Protection Online. The Future Regulation of Intermediaries* (Cheltenham-Northampton: Edward Elgar Publishing 2020), 28–55.

74 Jack M. Balkin, 'Free Speech is a Triangle,' Colum. L. Rev. 118 (2018), 2011–2056 (2019).

75 ECtHR, *Delfi AS* (n. 15), para. 162. See also János Tamás Papp, 'Liability for Third-Party Comments before the European Court of Human Rights – Comparing the Estonian Delfi and the Hungarian Index-MTE Decisions,' Hungarian Yearbook of International Law and European Law 4 (2016), 315–326.

fora on the Internet' (e.g., a discussion forum, a social media platform, a private person running a blog).

While developing this model in further cases, the Court in principle confirmed the possibility of holding Internet platforms liable, but also established some limits. It indicated that objective liability for allowing unfiltered comments – that might be illegal – may sometimes imply 'excessive and impracticable forethought capable of undermining freedom of the right to impart information on the Internet' (Article 10 ECHR).[76] Moreover, the Court took into consideration the fact that this particular case concerned offensive comments that did not constitute hate speech or direct threats against individuals, and that the gatekeeper had taken important preventive measures.[77] Similarly, the Court excluded the Internet platform's liability in the case of hyperlinking the defamatory content.[78] In further cases, examined from the perspective of the victim of the alleged horizontal violation, the Court emphasized that the limited liability of the gatekeepers (Internet platforms and blog operators) does not violate Article 8 ECHR when the impugned comments do not amount to hate speech or incitement to violence.[79] The size of the platform and time factor (how long the comments remain accessible online) are also important.[80]

The lack of a specific legal framework for dealing with the issue of the liability of gatekeepers for the third-party acts (comments) necessitates the use of traditional civil law instruments. It entails an unnecessary burden for the aggravated party, can lead to the negative phenomenon of libel tourism,[81] and in some cases, to the deprivation of any judicial protection. As evidenced by one of the cases, the ECtHR accepts that refusing to pursue a civil claim against the owner of the platform (Google Inc., which provided a blog-publishing service where some defamatory comments concerning the applicant were published) falls within the national margin of apprecia-

---

76 ECtHR, *Magyar Tartalomszolgáltatók Egyesülete & Index.hu Zrt* (n. 25), para. 82.

77 ECtHR, *Magyar Tartalomszolgáltatók Egyesülete & Index.hu Zrt* (n. 25), para. 64, see also ECtHR, *Jezior v. Poland*, judgment of 4 June 2020, no. 31955/11, para. 56.

78 ECtHR, *Magyar Jeti Zrt v. Hungary*, judgment of 4 December 2018, no. 11257/16.

79 ECtHR, *Høiness v. Norway*, judgment of 19 March 2019, no. 43624/14, para. 69.

80 ECtHR, *Rolf Anders Daniel Pihl v. Sweden*, decision of 7 February 2017, no. 74742/14, paras 25 and 31–35; a comment did not amount to hate speech or an incitement to violence; it had been posted on a small blog run by a non-profit association; it was taken down the day after the applicant made a complaint; and it had only been on the blog for around nine days.

81 See e.g., Trevor C. Hartley, 'Libel Tourism and Conflict of Laws,' ICLQ 59 (2010), 25–38.

tion.[82] Due to the transnational nature of the claims, the Court agreed with the argument of the national authorities, namely that the damage and any eventual vindication would be minimal, and that the costs of the exercise would be out of all proportion to what would be achieved.

Concluding this section, it is necessary to emphasize that the system that provides a simple exemption from liability, even when the Internet platforms play a passive role, is not sustainable from the Convention standpoint. National authorities, therefore, have a positive obligation to create a legal framework and properly enforce it (the procedural aspect, discussed below). It is necessary to decide when these gatekeepers are liable for third-party acts (comments) and what the limits of such liability are.[83] The lack of balance in these horizontal relations (between multinational private entities and individual users) and the anonymity of the online communication entail that it is insufficient for the aggravated party to have access only to traditional civil law instruments. The crucial issues are defining the personal scope of the liability[84] and identifying the preventive measures that platforms could adopt to detect potentially illegal content. With regard to the latter, the national authorities should ensure that all the procedures are not designed in a manner that incentivises the takedown of legal content (e.g., due to inappropriately short timeframes). Moreover, the legal framework should satisfy the quality requirement, since one of the positive obligations under the Convention is to create foreseeable law.[85] Due to the constant development of online communication techniques, States are also obliged to provide a periodical assessment of the adequacy of such laws and address any gaps.

82 ECtHR, *Tamiz* (n. 14), para. 90.

83 The existence or non-existence of moderation, and its prior or ex post nature can have important implications for the establishment of the liability, see Koltay (n. 8), 204.

84 As indicated by the ECtHR, *Delfi AS* (n. 15), para. 115, the liability concerns 'professionally managed and commercial' portals, although a question is being raised if this doctrine may be also applied to other types of hybrid intermediaries that host user comments, including professionally managed career sites or widely read blogs that are affiliated with commercial institutions, see Lisl Brunner, 'The Liability of an Online Intermediary for Third Party Content. The Watchdog Becomes the Monitor: Intermediary Liability after Delfi v Estonia,' HRLR 16 (2016), 163–174.

85 ECtHR, *Centro Europa 7 S.R.L. and Di Stefano v. Italy*, judgment of 7 June 2012, no. 38433/09, para. 156.

3. *The State as a Guarantor of Online Pluralism*

A specific sphere of positive substantive obligations concerning online communication is related to the role of the State as a guarantor of pluralism. The essence of democracy – the only political model contemplated by the Convention[86] – is to allow diverse political programs to be proposed, disseminated and debated, even those that call into question the way a State is currently organized. The democratic order can be threatened if a single voice within the media, with the power to propagate a single political viewpoint, becomes too dominant. As a consequence, public authorities have, in addition to their negative duty of non-interference, a positive obligation to put in place an appropriate legislative and administrative framework to guarantee effective pluralism.[87] This refers to both political pluralism and the pluralistic society; in these spheres – rather than relying on the mere absence of State regulation – policy intervention should ensure that a plausible framework exists.[88]

The responsibility of the public authorities as to the ultimate 'guarantor of pluralism' is recognized both under Article 10 ECHR and P1–3. With regard to the latter, the adoption of positive measures, which ensure a favourable environment for participation in public debates, is of fundamental importance.[89] It concerns allowing all persons to express their opinions, ideas and political viewpoints without fear.[90] Moreover, as indicated in recent studies, there is no doubt that substantive political equality can be a basis for positive free speech rights, with an ideal of equal distribution to communicative resources.[91] Public intervention should take place, especially in order to open up the media to different viewpoints.[92] Under

86 ECtHR, *Refah Partisi (the Welfare Party) and Others v. Turkey*, judgment of 13 February 2003, nos 41340/98, 41342/98, 41343/98 and 41344/98, para. 86.

87 ECtHR, *Centro Europa 7 S.R.L. and Di Stefano* (n. 85), para. 134.

88 Thomas Gibbons, 'Providing a Platform for Speech: Possible Duties and Responsibilities' in: Andrew T. Kenyon and Andrew Scott (eds), *Positive Free Speech: Rationales, Methods and Implications* (Oxford-London-New York-New Delhi-Sydney: Hart Publishing 2020), 11–23 (19).

89 ECtHR, *Dink v. Turkey*, judgment of 14 September 2010, nos 2668/07, 6102/08, 30079/08, 7072/09 and 7124/09, para. 137.

90 ECtHR, *Khadija Ismayilova v. Azerbaijan*, judgment of 10 January 2019, no. 65286/13 and 57270/14, para. 158.

91 Jacob Rowbottom, 'Positive Protection for Speech and Substantive Political Equality' in: Kenyon and Scott (eds) (n. 88), 25–41 (26).

92 ECtHR, *Communist Party of Russia and Others v. Russia*, judgment of 19 June 2012, no. 29400/05, paras 125–128.

Article 10 ECHR, not only the freedom of the press to inform the public is guaranteed, but also the right of the public to be properly informed. National authorities are therefore obliged to create a pluralistic public service that transmits impartial, independent and balanced news, information and comment.[93] This duty concerns both establishing favourable conditions for the audience to be exposed to a variety of content and removing obstacles to this exposure to diversity and pluralism. As already mentioned, this positive obligation concerning the variety of views that should reach the public does not imply, however, the possibility of compelling platforms to host speech they do not want to host. Positive duties in the sphere of pluralism are not so far-reaching to oblige private entities to publish any lawful opinion or statement.

Positive obligations are also crucial for organizing democratic elections under conditions that will ensure the free expression of the opinions of the people in the choice of the legislature. In the light of Convention provisions (primarily P1–1, but also Article 10 ECHR), there must be an adequate legal response towards certain phenomena (primarily electoral disinformation), especially those which could lead to serious consequences, resulting in a loss of public confidence in democratic procedures, and the violation of individual rights (i.e., lower public esteem and depriving a person of the necessary public trust, and damaging the candidate's reputation).[94]

Against this backdrop, it is possible to indicate three detailed positive measures that – in the light of the Convention – are necessary for providing political and social pluralism in online communication.

First of all, anti-discrimination rules must be established. In the context of the Internet, particular importance should be given to the protection of minorities, because online communication processes and their anonymity expose them to significant risk. As indicated in the ECtHR's case-law, the State's positive obligations are of particular importance for persons holding unpopular views or belonging to minorities, since they are more vulnerable to victimisation.[95] This obviously concerns not only the existence

93 ECtHR, *Manole and Others v. Moldova*, judgment of 17 September 2009, no. 13936/02, para. 101.

94 ECtHR, *Brzeziński* (n. 12), paras 35 and 55; according to the Court, public authorities have a duty to rectify electoral disinformation as soon as possible to preserve the quality of public debate.

95 ECtHR, *Bączkowski and Others v. Poland*, judgment of 3 May 2007, no. 1543/06, para. 64.

of the legal framework, but also its appropriate enforcement (procedural aspect), as evidenced by some of the ECtHR's recent case-law.[96]

Secondly, in order to ensure the political and social pluralism of online communication, transparency is of fundamental importance. As already indicated in the previous parts of this study, gatekeepers are able to create complex systems of governance and bureaucracy that can rule end users' behavior arbitrarily and without transparency. They use algorithms and automated systems, which could lead to the exclusion of certain groups of people or users with particular characteristics from accessing diverse and pluralistic information. Under the Convention, this automation of editorial processes and AI-driven tools, therefore, requires that the public authorities identify potentially vulnerable groups and oblige Internet platforms to ensure the transparency of their governance.[97] The public should at least understand the basis on which algorithmic decisions are made and have the minimal knowledge to verify them. The policies of the gatekeepers, including the use of algorithms, should be under public surveillance, and Internet platforms must be made accountable for violating them. An example of complying with this positive obligation is already available since, in France, the legislation introducing transparency requirements for political advertising on social media was adopted in December 2018.[98]

Finally, States must comply with the obligation to provide measures combating online disinformation. If the public authorities allow false (e.g., electoral) information to be produced and massively disseminated in online media, without offering legitimate actors (e.g., candidates) any effective measures, the pluralism protected by Article 10 ECHR and P1–3 is directly affected. Remaining passive towards disinformation and adopting only a policy of non-interference may also have an impact on the electoral equality and the fairness of the electoral process. Against this backdrop, one of the positive measures adopted in some countries (e.g., France and Poland) are summary judicial proceedings, which are able to halt a part of electoral disinformation.[99] The Court has already confirmed that the

---

96 ECtHR, *Beizaras and Levickas* (n. 20), paras 125–128.

97 Helberger, Eskens, van Drunen, Bastian and Moeller (n. 42), 20–25.

98 Loi n° 2018–1202 du 22 décembre 2018 relative à la lutte contre la manipulation de l'information, available at : https://www.legifrance.gouv.fr/affichTexte.do?cidTexte=JORFTEXT000037847559&categorieLien=id.

99 Rachael Craufurd Smith, 'Fake news, French Law and democratic legitimacy: Lessons for the United Kingdom?' Journal of Media Law 11 (2019), 52–81 and Amélie Heldt, 'Let's Meet Halfway: Sharing New Responsibilities in a Digital Age,' Journal of Information Policy 9 (2019), 336–369 (346).

provision of such a summary remedy serves the Convention's legitimate aim of ensuring the fairness of the electoral process.[100] They provide a partial solution to the problem of false information; nonetheless, they have to be adequately designed and applied (procedural aspect), as there is a choice between different models of such proceedings.[101]

4. Procedural Obligations and Investigation into Horizontal Online Violations

In the light of the Convention, States also have to comply with a number of procedural obligations. They have been extended from the majority of its provisions, including freedom of expression (Article 10) and the right to respect for private life (Article 8).[102] There is no doubt that an adequate official response to allegations contributes to the effective protection of substantive human rights.[103] Importantly, the current Convention standard obliges the public authorities to hold an investigation both when the alleged infringement involves violence and in a non-violent context.[104] Several of these procedural aspects have already been mentioned in this study, but since both types of obligations are often conflated, the separation of substance and procedure is not easily done, and in these situations, the Court effectuates a single global examination.[105]

Against this backdrop, in the case of online communication – due to its complexity – there are various aspects of the procedural positive obligations concerning horizontal violations of human rights (primarily freedom of expression and protection of private life). They are obviously of a different nature than with regard to other rights violations, such as, for example, the right to life or the prohibition of inhuman treatment (Article 2 and Article 3 ECHR). As already said, individuals can allege that the violations were committed directly by gatekeepers or committed by other

100 ECtHR, *Kwiecień v. Poland*, judgment of 9 January 2007, no. 51744/99, para. 55; ECtHR, *Kita v. Poland*, judgment of 8 July 2008, no. 57659/00, para. 50 and ECtHR, *Brzeziński* (n. 12), para. 55.

101 Krzywoń (n. 13), 682–687.

102 Lavrysen (n. 3), 16–17 and 51–52.

103 E.g. ECtHR, *Tysiąc v. Poland*, judgment of 20 March 2007, no. 5410/03, para. 113.

104 Eva Brems, 'Procedural protection – An examination of procedural safeguards read into substantive Convention Rights' in: Eva Brems and Janneke Gerards (eds), *Shaping Rights in the ECHR* (Cambridge: Cambridge University Press 2013) 137–161, (144).

105 Lavrysen (n. 3), 49–50.

individual users. Nonetheless, the latter can entail the liability of the user or the liability of the platform, since we have identified situations where the Internet platform can be held liable for third-party content. This entails important differences as far as the entity obliged under the Convention to launch the investigation is concerned. In certain situations, it would be the positive obligation of national authorities (to conduct an official investigation into online threats inflicted by private individuals, e.g., hate speech or the lack of adequate reaction of the platform with regard to the threats of other users) and in other circumstances, the State would have surveillance duties over the investigation initiated by the gatekeeper. The majority of these procedural positive obligations would have a remedial function, since they regulate an adequate response once a human right is horizontally affected in online communication.

In all these situations, the Convention standards require an effective investigation to be held, which – in principle – should be capable of leading to the establishment of the facts of the case and to the identification and punishment of those responsible. The lack of any appropriate procedures to deal with alleged horizontal infringements is incompatible with the Convention standards.[106] As far as the qualitative aspect of the investigation is concerned, due to the nature of online communication and the impact of the violations, this duty has to comply with the following general requirements. Firstly, the procedural framework should avoid excessive formalism. Every act of a horizontal violation must be easy for the Internet user to notify. Secondly, the time frame plays an important role since, in online communication, the flow of information is faster than in traditional media. In order to avoid the viral effect of an illegal act (i.e., an online comment), the investigation should be prompt, whether conducted by the state authorities or the gatekeeper. Nonetheless, when the gatekeeper is obliged to deal with a notification from an individual user concerning alleged illegal content, the time frame should not be inappropriately short in order to avoid 'private censorship.'

The national authorities usually delegate some procedural responsibilities to Internet platforms and enable them to deal with the allegations in the first instance. This subsidiary model is compatible with the Convention standards, and the allocation of tasks and avoiding one central actor – as claimed in the previous parts of this study – guarantees a better balance between different rights and freedoms. Nonetheless, the delegation of these procedural competences, as mentioned before, requires public

106 ECtHR, *K.U.* (n. 47), paras 43 and 46.

surveillance and implies that gatekeepers are held liable for how they investigate each case and react towards illegal third-party content.

Moreover, due to the anonymity of online communication, Internet platforms are sometimes in a better position to identify a person who threatens another individual's rights. Generally speaking, anonymity can constitute one of the limits of the procedural positive obligations under the Convention. As evidenced by one of the cases before the ECtHR, objective technical difficulties in identifying the person who threatens third-party rights can constitute a legitimate reason to refuse to institute legal proceedings. According to the Court, due to the fact that the sender of unwanted and offensive communications concealed his/her email address, any official investigation never had a chance of success. In these circumstances, the State's inaction did not amount to a violation of the Convention.[107]

Another limit of the procedural obligations is the volume and seriousness of the infringement. This issue overlaps with the problem of the criminalization of certain online conduct, discussed in the previous part of this study. Some extreme online acts require prompt official reaction and for a prosecution to be launched.[108] In other cases, both the gatekeeper and public authorities are obliged to determine if the ill-treatment inflicted by the private individuals exceeded the 'real and substantial tort' threshold.[109] On the one hand, they should be conscious of the scale and vulgarization of online communication, and, on the other, be aware that illegal acts can become viral and that minorities are especially vulnerable to victimisation. It is also necessary to mention that, in the context of online communication, the issue of extraterritoriality can constitute a challenge as far as procedural obligations are concerned.[110]

There is, therefore, a certain margin of appreciation as far as procedural positive obligations are concerned. This is associated with the difficulties of identification, the massive scale of online communication, and the fact

---

107 ECtHR, *Muscio* (n. 22).

108 E.g., ECtHR, *Beizaras and Levickas* (n. 20), paras 127–128.

109 ECtHR, *Tamiz* (n. 14), paras 50–53 and 82.

110 See e.g., *Perrin v. the United Kingdom*, decision of 18 October 2005, no. 5446/03, where the Court accepted the reasoning of the national courts that if the courts only were able to examine publication related cases if the place of the publication fell within the court jurisdiction, it would encourage publishers to publish in countries where prosecution was unlikely. See also Catherine Van de Heyning, 'The boundaries of jurisdiction in cybercrime and constitutional protection. The European perspective' in: Pollicino and Romeo (eds) (n. 17), 26–47 (37–38).

that in some online fora, the abusive tone is frequent. As indicated in the recent scholarship, this leads to the conclusion that, due to the difficulties of enforcement being sometimes disproportionately large, no legal recourse is needed for minor infringements of personality rights committed anonymously.[111]

V. Concluding Remarks

This analysis has shown that the State's obligations emerging from Article 8 and Article 10 ECHR, and P1–1, are not exclusively positive or negative. Insisting on a strict distinction between them and privileging the State's negative duties with regard to online communication is anachronistic. The negative understanding of the freedom of expression and protection of privacy does not provide the conceptual apparatus to deal with many current problems. The changing role of private entities – gatekeepers – implies that both these categories are mutually dependent, and the doctrine of the Convention as a living instrument does not permit one to be considered in isolation from another.

In this study, we have identified a number of substantive and procedural positive obligations concerning horizontal relations, primarily online communication. Developing its content usually does not entail high and excessive costs for the public authorities, since such positive obligations do not imply direct financial transfers and wealth redistribution. Moreover, public authorities have sufficient knowledge and are fully aware of the multiple possibilities of online ill-treatment inflicted by private individuals.

This study has shown that the regulatory framework is of fundamental importance. It should be able to deal with the issue of allocating responsibility for the content posted online. Under the Convention, public authorities should monitor the acts of power delegated to Internet platforms and decide who is liable for user-generated content, and under which circumstances. This legal framework must be detailed and sophisticated but cannot be reduced to criminal law enforcement. Minimal Convention standards also oblige the public authorities to adopt measures that ensure pluralism and a favourable environment for public debates (anti-discrimination rules, transparency mechanisms, measures against electoral disinfor-

111 Koltay (n. 8), 203–204.

mation). The Convention also creates a complex system of procedural obligations concerning horizontal violations of human rights.

All these positive duties, in the context of international law, form part of the broader concept of the normative order of the Internet, which integrates norms materially and normatively connected to the use and development of the Internet.[112] Nonetheless, the discussed examples of the State's duties are not comprehensive, since in both cases – the positive and negative dimension – it is hard to indicate an exhaustive collection. Similarly, as the positive aspect of human rights does not concern the legal review of restrictions, there are choices to be made with regard to the positive dimension of freedom, and they necessarily involve a certain degree of discretion on the national level.

112 Matthias C. Kettemann, *The Normative Order of the Internet. A Theory of Rule and Regulation Online* (Oxford: Oxford University Press 2020), 46.

Part IV
Participation

#WhoseLawIsItAnyway – How Social Media Augments Civil Society Participation in International Law-Making

Katharina Luckner

Abstract Social movements are an important part of a functioning society – also on a global scale. I argue that the internet and social media enable the formation of informal civil society movements and provide the means for such movements to participate in the shaping of international law to an unprecedented extent. In addition to being key to collective action and thus the formation of informal civil society movements in the first place, communication technology enables such movements to (1) bypass nation-state politics, (2) develop normative claims, and (3) change the setting in which international law is made. I outline these mechanisms of engagement theoretically and show them in a case study of the current anti-climate change movement, spearheaded by Fridays for Future, which serves as a case study. The paper closes with suggestions for the empirical study of the mechanisms of engagement.

I. Introduction

The internet has fundamentally and permanently altered the way in which people engage with each other. At the time of the women's suffrage movement 'America was a mere two weeks away,' making cooperation across the Atlantic possible, albeit tedious from today's perspective.[1] Now, most inhabited places in the world are a mere click away.[2] The internet and the subsequent development of social media platforms determine how most people engage with the world, both with information and with each other. Shared grievances can be known and communicated much more easily, and coordination becomes easier through faster and more widely available communication technology. This aids collective action across countries, leading to social movements that gain relevance beyond their immediate,

1 Margaret E. Keck and Kathryn Sikkink, *Activists beyond Borders: Advocacy Networks in International Politics* (Ithaca N.Y.: Cornell University Press 1998), 57.

2 World Bank data indicate that almost half of the world's population uses the internet. See at: https://data.worldbank.org/indicator/IT.NET.USER.ZS?view=chart. For visual representations of internet and social media usage, see Max Roser, Hannah Ritchie and Esteban Ortiz-Ospina, 'Internet,' 2015, available at: https://ourworldindata.org.

local context. I posit that it leads to a new type of civil society actor, namely *informal civil society movements*.[3]

Understanding how such informal civil society movements engage with international actors, organisations, and international law is important as the relationship between those who govern and the governed strongly affects the legitimacy and effectiveness of governance.[4] Nevertheless, informal civil society movements, representing the demands of the governed vis-a-vis the governing, have largely been overlooked as a constitutive force in the scholarship on international law. As Balakrischnan Rajagopal details,[5] international legal scholars have simply not taken note of or engaged with the copious literature on civil society movements and their relationships to states that exist in other disciplines.[6] This is a missed opportunity for theoretically and empirically examining how the rich variety of actors that shape international law and the environment in which it is made exert their influence.

This gap has become even more relevant with the emergence of informal civil society movements as important actors on the international scene through the advent of widespread internet and social media usage. As a contribution to bridging this gap, I draw on legal research, political science and media studies to outline the mechanisms by which social media and the internet act as a medium for civil society at large to access the international community and collectively demand to be heard on the international stage. This chapter thus sheds light on an undertheorised phenomenon – informal civil society movements' role in shaping interna-

---

3 'Informal' as opposed to formally organised civil society organisations, such as non-governmental organisations, for example.

4 Martha Finnemore, 'Dynamics of Global Governance: Building on What We Know,' International Studies Quarterly 58 (2014), 221–224 (224).

5 First in a paper, see Balakrishnan Rajagopal, 'International Law and Social Movements: Challenges of Theorizing Resistance,' Colum. J. Transnat'l L. 41 (2003), 397-433, and later in his seminal work on the topic: Balakrishnan Rajagopal, *International Law from Below: Development, Social Movements, and Third World Resistance* (Cambridge: Cambridge University Press 2003).

6 For an analysis of the reasons for the exclusion of social movements in (constitutional) legal theory and some implications of their inclusion, see Gavin W. Anderson, 'Societal Constitutionalism, Social Movements, and Constitutionalism from Below,' Ind. J. Global Legal Stud. 20 (2013), 881-906. For an analysis of civil society engagement and social movement impact on European Union constitutionalism, see Paul Blokker, 'Constitutional Mobilization and Contestation in the Transnational Sphere,' J. L. & Soc. 45 (2018), 52-72.

tional law – enabled by communication technology, specifically social media platforms.

While more inclusive international law-making might be a positive development and could aid in bridging the democratic deficit,[7] no systematic analysis or commentary on the normativity of civil society involvement, i.e., whether global decision making 'should' be impacted by informal civil society movements, is presented here. The chapter rather aims to describe this undertheorised phenomenon and outline some strategies to test it empirically.

To do so, I first review the concepts of civil society, social movements and introduce informal civil society movements in section I. In section II, I draw on the New Haven School of International Law, as well as concepts and case studies from different disciplines to show how civil society has been incorporated into scholarship. Subsequently, in section III, I develop the mechanisms by which informal civil society movements impact international law-making, namely *bypassing locality*, *creating normativity* and *changing conditions* in which international law is made. In section IV, the current anti-climate change movement, spearheaded by Fridays for Future, will serve as a case study. Section V gives an outlook on possible strategies to empirically test the three mechanisms.

II. Informal Civil Society Movements

Social movements have always shaped local and national policy-making.[8] Their role in an active civil society is a much studied phenomenon, which has taken on as many meanings and functions as there are disciplines interested in civil society structures.[9] I will use civil society as 'a marketplace of *interests, ideas and ideologies*'[10] driven by citizens of different political leaning and socio-economic standing, who can coordinate via this market-

---

7 Janet K. Levit, 'Bottom-up International Lawmaking: Reflections on the New Haven School of International Law,' Yale J. Int'l L. 32 (2007), 393-420; Jutta Brunnée and Stephen J. Toope, 'International Law and Constructivism: Elements of an Interactional Theory of International Law,' Colum. J. Transnat'l L. 39 (2000), 19-74.

8 Margaret E. Keck and Kathryn Sikkink, 'Transnational Advocacy Networks in International and Regional Politics,' International Social Science Journal 68 (2018), 65-76.

9 Michael Edwards, *Civil society* (3rd edn, Cambridge: Polity Press 2014), 1-17.

10 John D. Clarke, 'The Globalization of Civil Society' in: James W. St.G. Walker and Andrew S. Thompson (eds), *The Emergence of Global Civil Society* (Waterloo,

place to find common ground and joint interest. Outcomes of this coordination may range from the founding of a sports club, a neighbourhood food drive, to a social movement, which gathers more widespread support and may transcend its original community.

Non-governmental organisations (NGOs) and non-state actors (NSAs) can develop out of civil society groups and social movements. Some of these actors are formally recognised in international law-making processes,[11] and their influence on national and international law-making is well documented, for example, through the coordinated actions of transnational advocacy networks.[12] This need not be the case, though. Civil society movements can stay decentralised, distributed, identity-driven and leaderless, attributes which characterised the so-called New Social Movements of the 1970s,[13] which formed as the power of the nation-state decreased. Since then, institutional power has shifted from the national upwards to the supranational level and downwards to the regional level, with social movements shifting correspondingly.[14]

Ont.: The Centre for International Governance Innovation and Wilfrid Laurier University Press 2008), 3-23 (10), original italics.

11 See for example the status of NGOs and special interest lobby groups that have observer status according to the United Nations Framework for Climate Change, available at: https://unfccc.int/process-and-meetings/parties-non-party-stakeholders/non-party-stakeholders/information-by-category-of-observer/admitted-ngos.

12 Keck and Sikkink, *Activists beyond Borders* (n. 1); Naghmeh Nasiritousi, Mattias Hjerpe and Björn-Ola Linnér, 'The Roles of Non-State Actors in Climate Change Governance: Understanding Agency through Governance Profiles,' International Environmental Agreements: Politics, Law and Economics 16 (2016), 109-126.

13 Alberto Melucci, *Nomads of the Present: Social Movements and Individual Needs in Contemporary Society* (Philadelphia: Temple University Press 1989), 58-80; Claus Offe, 'New Social Movements: Challenging the Boundaries of Institutional Politics,' Social Movements 52 (1985), 817-868 (830 ff.).

14 Della Porta and Tarrow coin this 'Transnational Social Activism,' which co-developed with the shift towards multilevel governance and supranational institutional power. See Donatella Della Porta and Sydney Tarrow, 'Transnational Processes and Social Activism: An Introduction' in: Donatella Della Porta and Sydney Tarrow (eds), *Transnational Processes and Social Activism* (New York: Rowman and Littlefield Publishers, Inc. 2005), 1-17. This development already accounts for quick and simplified communication through the internet and increasingly cheap travel across continents. It does not account for the more readily available character of social media communication which not only changes how people can communicate with each other but also how they can interact with international law and global actors.

With the advent of widespread internet and social media usage,[15] *informal civil society movements* are likewise characterised by a lack of hierarchical structure and a decentralised organisational structure; they mobilise people in different countries or even around the globe; they address international problems, which need not affect participants directly; they go beyond localised grievances, demanding global solutions.[16]

Social media and messaging platforms give large numbers of people the means to mitigate the costs of collective action, and thus enable the formation of informal civil society movements in the first place.[17] Before the inception of these platforms, formal representation and organisation of civil society were especially important because they provided the necessary logistics for coordination, i.e., successful collective action, as well as information exchange and publicity creation. Today that strategy is still very effective, but it is no longer a necessary condition for civil society's

15 Social movements characterised by internet use perhaps started with the widespread action against the WTO summit in Seattle in 1999, where internet-based listservs and websites were used to spread information and mobilise people. See Jeffrey S. Juris, 'Reflections on #Occupy Everywhere: Social Media, Public Space, and Emerging Logics of Aggregation,' American Ethnologist 39 (2012), 259-279. Today, the relevant technology ranges from traditional social media platforms like Facebook and Twitter, to messenger apps like WhatsApp and Telegram, to newer platforms such as Instagram and TikTok. Different movements organise via different platforms. The #MeToo movement largely took to Twitter, while in the Tunisian Revolution in 2010/11, Facebook played a significant role. It is crucial to point out that these platforms are not designed for such purposes and that they are not neutral. They follow their own business models and interests, which can be antithetical to a movement's interest and purpose. Additionally, they are not immune to governmental oversight and censorship. For an overview of the complex relationship of social media platforms and social activism, see William L. Youmans and Jillian C. York, 'Social Media and the Activist Toolkit: User Agreements, Corporate Interests, and the Information Infrastructure of Modern Social Movements,' Journal of Communication 62 (2012), 315-329. For the strategies of the #MeToo movement as an example for so called hashtag activism, see Ying Xiong, Moonhee Cho and Brandon Boatwright, 'Hashtag Activism and Message Frames among Social Movement Organizations: Semantic Network Analysis and Thematic Analysis of Twitter during the #MeToo Movement,' Public Relations Review 45 (2019), 10-23.

16 I do not claim that all informal civil society movements are necessarily forces of 'good,' representative of 'progressive' agendas, nor do I claim that their interaction with international actors and potential influence on global governance is necessarily beneficial.

17 For a classical text on the analysis of collective action, see Mancur Olson, *The Logic of Collective Action: Public Goods and the Theory of Groups* (Cambridge, Mass.: Harvard University Press 2012).

influence on international law and global governance, as the internet and especially social media have changed the way in which social movements facilitate communication, organise, and raise awareness.[18]

Social media also change the way in which a group's identity is developed and how it is experienced by the individual. Group identity, the production of symbols and cultural claims, are central characteristics of identity-based, networked social movements, as they were first topologised by Alberto Melucci in 1989.[19] Today, such identities are increasingly constructed with social media facilitating the process.[20] Social media, therefore, not only make it cheaper and easier to mobilise people, but they also change the potential dynamics of identity building. By giving all participants of a social movement a voice and opportunity, social media bridges the gap between personal stories and collective narrative and thus facilitates the reproduction of the movement's social capital.[21]

Evidently, social movements in general, and informal civil society movements, in particular, are not synonymous with the corporate actors or even non-governmental organisations that are traditionally objects of scholarly interest. While the former hold agency in the strict sense, the latter do not.[22] Informal civil society movements cannot bring cases before courts as of now, and they cannot enter into strategic partnerships. NGOs might serve as a connector between different local civil society movements, but they need not lead these movements, nor do they constitute them. Hence, their impact on international law and global governance will be different. This makes scholarship on the impact of informal civil society movements on international law and global governance even more important.

---

18 Rodrigo Sandoval-Almazan and J. Ramon Gil-Garcia, 'Towards Cyberactivism 2.0? Understanding the Use of Social Media and Other Information Technologies for Political Activism and Social Movements,' Government Information Quarterly 31 (2014), 365-378; Youmans and York (n. 15).

19 Melucci (n. 13).

20 Stefania Milan, 'From Social Movements to Cloud Protesting: The Evolution of Collective Identity,' Information, Communication & Society 18 (2015), 887-900 (893).

21 For an analysis of the weaknesses of 'networked protests,' especially due to the disconnect between their temporary public signaling power and actual, long term capacities, see Zeynep Tufekci, *Twitter and Tear Gas: The Power and Fragility of Networked Protest* (New Haven, London: Yale University Press 2017). This analysis serves as a reminder that every new wave of social movements faces the same uphill battle, regardless of its technological advancement. Without pluralist forms of organisational structure, the inherent weaknesses in social media-based mass protest overpowers its strengths.

22 Nasiritousi, Hjerpe and Linnér (n. 12).

III. Research on Civil Society in International Law and Global Governance

Conventionally, international law scholarship has only rarely considered the interaction of social movements and international law for a number of reasons. First, movements have traditionally been formed locally or on a national level, while international law is, by definition, international in nature. Second, the solutions to problems in international law are generally seen as coming from the top rather than from below, and third, the actors of international law-making are sovereign states.[23] Lastly, neither international legal texts nor its methods lend themselves to the inclusion of civil society. The sources of legal texts are almost exclusively texts emerging from public institutions; methodologically, international legal scholarship is often focused on the internal logical structure of the law above all else. This leaves no room for political and social contexts and does not contribute to the law's dynamicity.[24]

Nevertheless, social movements that explicitly engage with and utilise international ideals, have 'often foreshadowed and helped bring about major shifts in international [legal] norms,'[25] and there are a number of examples in legal scholarship and concepts that can be drawn on from other disciplines, which can help us think about international law and civil society in general and informal civil society movements in particular.

1. Law-Making as a Participatory Process

I adopt an understanding of law-making as means for people to ensure communication with one another, a means to ensure knowledge acquisition and transmission, as well as conscious and deliberate coordination amongst people.[26] This understanding of law-making relies on a constructivist notion of international law and global governance, where – alongside states – non-state actors, ideas and informal norms, organised and disseminated in networks, matter for the process of developing law, implementing it, and determining its consequences.[27] It takes international

23 Frédéric Mégret, 'Civil Disobedience and International Law: Sketch for a Theoretical Argument,' Can. Yb. Int'l L. 46 (2012), 143–192.
24 Rajagopal, *International Law from Below* (n. 5).
25 Mégret (n. 23), 161.
26 Brunnée and Toope (n. 7), 60.
27 For the concept of network of international law applied to the European Union as a case of supranational authority, see Karl-Heinz Ladeur, 'Towards a Legal

law-making as a participatory process of decision or policy-making that requires the 'incorporation of plural cultural influences into the evolution of legal norms,'[28] because norms, behaviors and practices create it.[29]

Crucially, this does not diminish the importance of the traditional sources of international law as they are defined by Article 38 ICJ Statute.[30] One of the ways that non-state actors, ideas, and informal norms matter is by influencing states' interests and thereby influencing their explicit declarations of will, i.e., treaty law and indirect displays of custom, i.e., customary law. A constructivist understanding of law-making, therefore, allows the conception of states as complex actors who are subject to norms and whose interests are based on a complex set of considerations and determined by a variety of actors.[31]

It does add another dimension, however, as it gives non-state actors agency in the development and interpretation of both formal and informal international norms, assigning them an active part in the continued creation and maintenance of the international legal system.[32] The mechanisms that are developed in section III speak to both, the influence on state

---

Theory of Supranationality – The Viability of the Network Concept,' ELJ 3 (1997), 33–54; Kal Raustiala, 'The Architecture of International Cooperation: Transgovernmental Networks and the Future of International Law,' Va. J. Int'l L. 43 (2002), 1-92.; For a comprehensive overview of a network understanding of international relations, see Anne-Marie Slaughter, *The Chessboard and the Web: Strategies of Connection in a Networked World* (New Haven, London: Yale University Press 2017).

28 Brunnée and Toope (n. 7), 65; Melissa A. Waters, 'Normativity in the New Schools: Assessing the Legitimacy of International Legal Norms Created by Domestic Courts,' Yale J. Int'l L. 32 (2007), 455–484.

29 Levit (n. 7), 409.

30 As McDougal and Reisman criticised in 1980: 'In light of the developments of recent decades, the most striking omission from the itemization in Article 38 is, of course, that of reference to the role of international governmental organizations in the creation of both explicitly formulated law and customary expectations, it is increasingly recognized that these organizations, and especially the United Nations, contribute to the creation of international law in many different ways and that any realistic description of transnational prescribing processes must take this contribution into account,' see Myres S. McDougal and W. Michael Reisman, 'The Prescribing Function in World Constitutive Process: How International Law is Made,' Yale Studies in World Public Order 6 (1980), 249-284 (266). Today, the factor left out of theorising on international law making are civil society movements.

31 Jeffrey T. Checkel, 'The Constructivist Turn in International Relations Theory,' Wld. Pol. 50 (1998), 324-248.

32 McDougal and Reisman (n. 30).

actors' interests as well as the active co-creation of international law as the medium of conscious and deliberate coordination between people(s).[33]

Formally, the UN recognises a changing role and general importance of civil society in international and global governance, as evident in the establishment of a panel of eminent persons to review the relationship between the United Nations and civil society.[34] Assessing this role requires an understanding of law-making, where social practice plays a central role. Law-making becomes 'prescription,' namely a 'process of communication which creates, in a target audience, a complex set of expectations.'[35] Through this process, international law at least partially derives from 'the peoples of the world communicate to each other expectations about policy, authority and control, not merely through state or intergovernmental organs, but through reciprocal claims and mutual tolerances in all their interactions.'[36] With the internet and social media, these interactions and communication happen more than ever, so that the process comes to include 'the power of public opinion and civil society.'[37]

2. *Civil Society in International Law Scholarship*

Notable examples in legal scholarship on the influence of non-governmental actors, though not necessarily social movements, are the ban on land mines and the development of the international human rights regime.[38]

In the early 1990s, in a concerted effort of six international NGOs, the use of antipersonnel mines was re-coined as the 'Coward's War' and a campaign was launched to attain a total ban on landmines: the Internatio-

33 Brunnée and Toope (n. 7), 60.

34 Panel of Eminent Persons on United Nations & Civil Society Relations, 'We the peoples: civil society, the United Nations and global governance,' (Geneva, Switzerland: 11 June 2004), 3. Available at: https://digitallibrary.un.org/record/523950.

35 McDougal and Reisman (n. 30), 250.

36 Ibid. (n. 30), 269.

37 Clarke (n. 10), 5.

38 Other prominent examples include the case of international norms of corruption and the establishment of the International Criminal Court. See Kenneth W. Abbott and Duncan Snidal, 'Values and Interests: International Legalization in the Fight against Corruption,' JLS 21 (2002), 141-177, on corruption and Marlies Glasius, *The International Criminal Court* (London: Routledge 2006) on the establishment of the Court. In the interest of space, the two examples are used to illustrate how a variety of civil society actors are conceptualised in international law studies.

nal Campaign to Ban Landmines (ICBL). In 1993, its first international conference was held with 50 representatives of 40 NGOs. By 1995, efforts were distributed between national governments, with Belgium being the first to institute a national law banning landmines, international institutions, which held awareness raising events at the annual Convention on Certain Conventional Weapons in Geneva, as well as the general public through an international media campaign. In 1996, the Ottawa process was launched, and the Mine Ban Treaty was adopted and opened for signature by 1997, becoming law in 1999.[39] The campaign, which was initiated and implemented by NGOs, is an example of formal civil society groups being a central factor in the successful articulation and expansion of international norms. Through a combination of education and public shaming campaigns against producing companies and exporting countries, they were able to re-frame supposed security issues in terms of previously abstract and neglected humanitarian norms, expand the audience beyond state actors, fast-track the codification of a novel international law into international law.[40]

The other central example is the scholarship on the development of international human rights law (IHRL). Tsusui et al.[41] detail how social movements were key to understanding the widespread uptake of international human rights law – by using both established as well as extra-institutional routes. At the UN Conference on International Organisation in San Francisco in 1945, for example, some 1,200 NGOs were present to urge nation-state delegations to include human rights as a central tenet of the United Nations.[42] The impact of civil society groups in the Universal Declaration of Human Rights has been documented in legal scholarship. One example is the successful lobbying of women's NGOs for the inclusion of gender-neutral language in the text of the declaration.[43] The relationship also works in reverse. Once these universal human rights principles were established, they were – and are – successfully used by local and national

39 See at: icbl.org, especially at: http://www.icbl.org/en-gb/news-and-events/news/2012/20-years-in-the-life-of-a-nobel-peace-prizewinning.aspx.

40 Lesley Wexler, 'The International Deployment of Shame, Second-Best Responses, and Norm Entrepreneurship: The Campaign to Ban Landmines and the Landmine Ban Treaty,' Ariz. J. Int'l & Comp. L. 20 (2003), 561-606.

41 Kiyoteru Tsutsui, Claire Whitlinger and Alwyn Lim, 'International Human Rights Law and Social Movements: State's Resistance and Civil Society's Insistence,' Annual Review of Law and Social Science 8 (2012), 367-396.

42 Ibid., 370.

43 Arvonne S. Fraser, 'Becoming Human: The Origins and Developments of Women's Human Rights,' HRQ 21 (1999), 853-906.

civil society actors to put pressure on national governments by exposing their human rights violations and thus improving people's living conditions.[44]

3. *Civil Society in Global Governance Scholarship*

Sociology, political science, and international relations research provide a number of frameworks to understand the involvement of civil society in international law. Institutional sociology has provided comprehensive insights into the development and spread of norms about individual rights, for example.[45] Global governance and international relations scholars further show how the access to norm contestation[46] on a formal international rule or institution is a key feature of a legitimate and just international system. The continued interaction between norm interpretation through different social groups and formal international institutions shapes normative meaning and evolution, especially in circumstances where norm contestation would be enhanced, because fundamental rights are moved outside of the normative framework of the nation-state.[47] Such groups can also act as norm entrepreneurs, actively shaping a normative understanding of behaviors that they find appropriate or desirable.[48]

Oftentimes, such norm contestation and/or creation is most effective if it happens as part of a concerted effort of different actors. In their 1998 seminal work, Keck and Sikkink show how collective actors, which they call transnational advocacy networks, were key to the success of the international human rights regime, international environmental law, and

---

44 Beth A. Simmons, *Mobilizing for Rights: International Law in Domestic Politics* (Cambridge, New York: Cambridge University Press 2009).

45 Martha Finnemore, 'Norms, Culture, and World Politics: Insights from Sociology's Institutionalism,' IO 50 (1996), 325-347.

46 The concept of norm contestation is central to the study of democratic governance beyond the nation state, where normative meaning is often ambiguous – by design or due to the imprecisions inherent in language. In situations of conflicting or changing meanings of norms, social practices and activities of norm contestation, i.e., who interprets a norm how and in what context, adds to the understanding of norm compliance and normative change. See Antje Wiener, 'Contested Compliance: Interventions on the Normative Structure of World Politics,' European Journal of International Relations 10 (2004), 189-234.

47 Antje Wiener, *A Theory of Contestation* (Berlin, Heidelberg: Springer 2014).

48 Martha Finnemore and Kathryn Sikkink, 'International Norm Dynamics and Political Change,' IO 52 (1998), 887-917 (896 ff).

women's rights.[49] Generally, the networks' strategies are not merely targeted at influencing policy outcomes, but rather at changing the very terms and nature of the debate. They might take ideas that seem unimaginable at the time of their conception and introduce them into the international debate in ways that make them palpable and imaginable to more classic international actors. At some point, the solutions they suggest to international problems will seem inevitable. A prominent example of a precursor to transnational advocacy networks that used a *strategy of symbolism* is the International Movement for Woman Suffrage.[50] Subsequent women's rights movements have also made use of transnational advocacy networks' ability to leverage *information politics*, i.e., the ability to 'quickly and credibly generate politically usable information and move it to where it will have the most impact,'[51] and to demand *accountability*, holding states to their previously stated principles. Finally, advocacy networks also have the unique ability to employ the 'Boomerang Pattern' that is prevalent in human rights campaigns; for example, transnational advocacy networks bypass a state unwilling or unable to provide rights to its citizens and *leverage* connections to international actors to pressure their state into providing these rights.[52] Alternatively, these connections can be used to mobilise international resources that can be used at the national level in an attempt at what Della Porta and Tarrow call 'externalization.'[53] This research shows that international law and international legal concepts are not made in a vacuum: for example, transnational advocacy networks have successfully managed to reframe the concept of national sovereignty – one of the key tenants of international law – in such a way that allows for their work to fruitfully influence the making of international law.[54]

Thus, global governance and international relations concepts provide the means to study the influence of organised civil society on international law-making. However, the key concepts of the scholarship were developed in the wake of the worldwide onset of internet access and before the development of social media platforms. I argue that the internet and especially social media provide an additional means of civil society engagement with and influence on international law that can be, but need not be, accompanied by transnational advocacy networks.

49 Keck and Sikkink, *Activists beyond Borders* (n. 1), 10.
50 Ibid. (n. 1), 63.
51 Ibid. (n. 1), 24.
52 Ibid. (n. 1), 20.
53 Della Porta and Tarrow (n. 14).
54 Keck and Sikkink, *Activists beyond Borders* (n. 1), 42 ff.

IV. Mechanisms of Engagement

In this section, I develop three mechanisms of engagement, enabled by the internet and social media, through which informal civil society movements influence the making of international law and thereby might shape its content: the bypassing of nation-state boundaries, the development of normative claims and the alteration of the setting in which international law is made.

1. Bypassing Locality

Prior to the internet, communication was often tedious, slow, and most importantly, expensive. Today, most of the world is mere clicks and a bit of bandwidth away. While this brings with it a whole array of problems, such as filter bubbles, crowding out effects and information fatigue,[55] it also means that local grievances can be communicated much more quickly to a much larger audience. A global problem might have global effects, but what is felt much more are the local changes. Without modern, widely accessible communication technology, it would be difficult to properly assess the global dynamics of the problem and the need for global solutions. Realising the commonality of problems across the world has been simplified significantly through the internet and social media – think hashtags[56] – and has given non-elites the chance to voice, compare and aggregate grievances. In the terminology of transnational advocacy networks, civil society now holds the key to information politics at large.[57]

---

55 Eli Pariser, *The Filter Bubble: How the New Personalized Web Is Changing What We Read and How We Think* (New York, N.Y.: Penguin Books 2011); Monika Djerf-Pierre, 'The Crowding-Out Effect,' Journalism Studies 13 (2012), 499-516; Stephen Hilgartner and Charles L. Bosk, 'The Rise and Fall of Social Problems: A Public Arenas Model,' American Journal of Sociology 94 (1988), 53-78.

56 The pound key '#' is used to mark words or word strings as searchable on social media platforms, especially and originally Twitter. Rallying around a cause is facilitated by creating a unique hashtag that accompanies all contributions and comments on that cause. One prominent example is the #MeToo movement. Though first initiated before the use of hashtags, the movement against sexual abuse and harassment gained momentum when the widespread use of the hashtag revealed the magnitude of women's abuse stories and their prevalence across borders, industries, and generations.

57 This appears as the inevitable development when transnational collective action, as outlined by Della Porta and Tarrow in 2005, met the subsequent development

This increased freedom from locality has further effects. It frees people from the boundaries of nation-state politics, and it gives national politicians common ground. While traditional forms of participation within (democratic) nation-states depend very much on where someone is located, i.e., registered and therefore able to vote or demonstrate, the internet, social media and messaging platforms provide a global reach. This reach can bypass the boundaries and constraints of the nation-state and connect civil society directly with international actors, thus lowering the threshold for the participation of civil society movements and the making of international law. In a sense, informal civil society movements are 'forging *participatory* democracy, by entering directly into the debates that most interest them.'[58] This opens the door for a new addressee of civil society movements: while social movements in the past primarily addressed nation-state politics to right the wrongs they are lamenting, informal civil society movements call on the global community as well; the protests thus become relevant for international organisations and international law. They are reacting to a world where 'the substance of politics has been globalised [...], the process of politics has not,'[59] being keenly aware that international law and policy have a significant impact on public well-being in all nation-states around the world.[60] In a way, informal civil society movements have the potential to 'skip' the state level and directly address the international community, engaging in the co-creation of international law.

The second effect of bypassing locality, on the other hand, changes the interests of states as the formal actors in international law: by bridging nation-states and demonstrating cross-country support for a certain issue, this freedom from locality also gives nation-state representatives common ground on the international stage. It makes it easier for them to navigate and 'win' the two-level game[61] of reaching agreements among states that are acceptable to their respective domestic interest groups. As they all

---

of social media and mass access to this new technology. For their analysis of transnational collective action, see Della Porta and Tarrow (n. 14).

58 Clarke (n. 10), 4, original italics.

59 Ibid. (n. 10), 3.

60 Rafael Leal-Arcas, 'Power to the People: From Top-Down to Bottom-Up Approaches' in: Daniel C. Esty and Susan Biniaz (eds), *Cool Heads in a Warming World: How Trade Policy Can Help Fight Climate Change* (Yale: Yale Center for Environmental Law & Policy 2020), 257-280.

61 Robert D. Putnam, 'Diplomacy and Domestic Politics: The Logic of Two-Level Games,' IO 42 (1988), 427-460.

face the same pressure from their constituents and have to validate their decisions against similar claims, it is easier to reach satisfying agreements and thus overcome their own collective action problem.

2. *Creating Normativity*

Compliance with international legal norms in the absence of coercion is a central question within international law scholarship.[62] Studies in international relations argue that international norms[63] have similar effects within the international legal system as have been ascribed to domestic norms within nation-states, giving international law avenues of success in the absence of central enforcement mechanisms.[64] Social movements and civil society actors often serve as 'value actors'[65] and agenda setters,[66] advancing normative claims rather than following interest-driven agendas.[67]

Social media serves as the vehicle for developing and transporting the movement's normative messages in that it allows a diverse body of 'global civil society'[68] to jointly move from a (local) grievance-based approach to an issue to the development of a global normative claim. More specifically, informal civil society movements become integral in what Finnemore and Sikkink call the 'norm emergence'[69] stage of an international norm, i.e., the stage when an international norm – formal, or more likely informal

---

62 For a comprehensive overview, see for example Gentiana Imeri, *The Expressive Function of Law: Experimental Studies on the Behavioral Effect of Non-Coercive Law in Social Dilemma Settings* (St. Gallen: University of St. Gallen 2019).

63 Standards of appropriate behavior for an actor with a given identity. These can be informal or codified into law as legal norms, but – crucially – need not be. When such behavioral rules are structured together and interrelated, they might be referred to as 'institutions' in the sociological sense; see Finnemore and Sikkink (n. 48), 891.

64 For a discussion of state 'acculturation' in the absence of coercive means, see Ryan Goodman and Derek Jinks, 'How to Influence States: Socialization and International Human Rights Law,' Duke Law Journal 54 (2004), 621-704. For an international relations perspective, see Finnemore and Sikkink (n. 48), 893.

65 Abbott and Snidal (n. 38).

66 Anne Peters, Till Förster and Lucy Koechlin, 'Towards Non-State Actors as Effective, Legitimate, and Accountable Standard Setters' in: Anne Peters et al. (eds), *Non-State Actors as Standard Setters* (Cambridge: Cambridge University Press 2009), 492-562.

67 Blokker (n. 6).

68 Clarke (n. 10).

69 Finnemore and Sikkink (n. 48), 893.

– is first formulated. Informal civil society movements thus participate or even drive the symbolism politics of other civil society actors.

Informal civil society movements are also key in the subsequent stage of 'norm cascading,'[70] where the norm is widely taken up and imitated. In their original framework, a successful norm's life cycle presupposes specific organisational platforms for the norm emergence stage and states or networks for the subsequent stage of norm cascading. I argue that the widespread use of messaging and social media platforms muddles the delineation between the two stages and eliminates the necessity of concrete organisational platforms and formal networks. This is not to say that formal types of actors and mechanisms no longer exist; I merely claim that they are no longer necessary for a new international norm to form and establish itself, rather they can be (co-)created by informal civil society movements. This broadens the scope of who can act as so-called norm entrepreneurs, i.e., entities which 'call attention to issues or even 'create' issues by using language that names, interprets, and dramatizes them.'[71] The onset of the internet and social media has increased access to information and decentralised information transmission, so that anybody might become a norm entrepreneur, opening up space for informal civil society movements to influence the international agenda directly.

Once a norm is created, there are two ways that these norms can spread. Both impact the interests of state actors: Finnemore and Sikkink[72] show how norm entrepreneurs can persuade states that are more sympathetic to the issue to join the cause, leading to a so-called norm cascade. Studies on the impact of transnational advocacy networks show that many issues are first only slowly adopted by a number of states until a tipping point is reached. Afterwards, the issue is adopted in quick succession by the majority of nations.[73]

Besides active persuasion, norms can also spread by a process which Goodman and Jinks call acculturation, 'the general process of adopting the beliefs and behavioral patterns of the surrounding culture.'[74] In the process of acculturation, it is not (only) actors' incentives or convictions that are changed, but their social environment. Accordingly, while 'persuasion requires acceptance of the validity or legitimacy of a belief, practice, norm-acculturation requires only that an actor perceives that an important

70 Ibid. (n. 48), 895.
71 Ibid. (n. 48), 897.
72 Ibid. (n. 48), 901.
73 Keck and Sikkink, *Activists beyond Borders* (n. 1), 68.
74 Goodman and Jinks (n. 64), 638.

reference group harbours the belief, engages in the practice, or subscribes to the norm.'[75] Such a change in the environment also changes actors' incentive structures, as they now have a certain (self-)identity to take into account when making decisions.[76]

With evidence mounting that states do respond to cultural forces,[77] civil society movements, in creating new normative claims in the contested sphere of norms, can impact international law-making. The mechanism operates both by creating the space for informal civil society movements to directly engage with and co-create (informal) international norms, as well as allowing them to pressure states into considering these norms, which in turn alters their interests.

3. *Changing Conditions*

Third and finally, informal civil society movements have an important signalling function. Based on the premise that people have a certain perception of themselves and choose actions such that they correspond to that identity,[78] we can assume that campaigning for a certain set of values will also inform many other aspects of people's life and behavioral choices. In the aggregation of informal civil society movements, this changes the interests of states and non-state actors. Informal civil society movements make their claims known loudly, so that local governments, NGOs and domestic as well as international corporations and also courts can hear.

We know that governments respond to the public regarding policy,[79] and even unelected bodies do respond to public attitudes.[80] Supra- and international courts might co-develop new regimes that determine natio-

---

75 Ibid. (n. 64), 642 ff.

76 George A. Akerlof and Rachel E. Kranton, 'Economics and Identity,' Quarterly Journal of Economics 115 (2000), 715-753.

77 For an overview, see Goodman and Jinks (n. 64), 654.

78 Akerlof and Kranton (n. 76).

79 Christopher J. Williams and Shaun Bevan, 'The Effect of Public Attitudes Toward the European Union on European Commission Policy Activity,' European Union Politics 20 (2019), 608-628 (613).

80 Ibid., 616.

nal policy-making,[81] and they might make decisions against governmental interests given a supportive public opinion in leading member states.[82]

Similarly, businesses have incentives to adjust their production practices to appeal to popular demand. The effect here is two-fold, however. More significant than the adjustment of their own business practices, which can easily result in base-less virtue signalling, they also have incentives to lobby for stricter standards to make their changes in business practices more believable and to level the international playing field. We know that 'pressure on multinational corporations, much of it is originating in civil society groups, can reshape business practices.'[83] Thus, as consumers pay more attention due to information available via social media and because of informal civil society movements, this can trigger a business-led move towards stricter business practices.

People who find themselves part of an informal civil society movement proclaiming certain values might also be more likely to also support formal organisations that work towards goals that coincide with those values. If so, then NGOs working on the same topic, perhaps while being part of a strategically equipped transnational advocacy network, will experience an increase in funding and membership. The tacit endorsement from a larger audience might also propel them into new alliances, for example, with local governments and decision-makers, which can scale up their actions.

To summarize, I propose that the internet and especially social media facilitate the formation of informal civil society movements, which go beyond localised grievances, demanding global solutions from international actors beyond nation-states. I posit three channels through which these informal civil society movements impact international law-making: bypassing locality, creating normativity, and changing conditions in which international law is made. In the following section, I will use Fridays for Future as a case study to illustrate the shape of an informal civil society movement and the three mechanisms of influence.

---

81 Rachel A. Cichowski, *The European Court and Civil Society: Litigation, Mobilization and Governance* (Cambridge: Cambridge University Press 2007).

82 Michael F. Harsch and Vladislav Maksimov, 'International Courts and Public Opinion: Explaining the CJEU's Role in Protecting Terror Suspects' Rights,' J. Common Mkt. Stud. 57 (2019), 1091-1110.

83 Finnemore, 'Dynamics' (n. 4), 224.

V. *Fridays for Future and Climate Change*

I offer the case study of Fridays for Future, a global anti-climate change movement, to illustrate the mechanisms that I have outlined above.[84] Fridays for Future, by its own account, began in 2015 when Greta Thunberg, then a 15-year old high school student, and other young activists, sat in front of the Swedish parliament every school day for three weeks, to protest against the lack of action on the climate crisis. They posted what they were doing on Instagram and Twitter; posts that quickly went viral.[85] At the time of writing, there are initiatives in 7,500 cities with more than 13 million participants spread across all continents. Their demands, very succinctly phrased in the Declaration of Lausanne, call for the curbing of global warming to under 1.5 degrees Celsius compared to pre-industrial levels, ensuring climate justice and equity, and listening to the best united climate science available.[86] The first comprehensive study on the demographics and motivations of participants characterises the movement as a new generation of activists with unique tactics and a global scope that appeals to high school students but also marks a historical turn in climate activism. The movement is credited with a level of global attention that no previous youth movement has received thus far.[87]

In their means, such as protests, civil disobedience, strikes – high school students staying away from school on Fridays, employees from work – as well as local and creative interventions, Fridays for Future looks very similar to the social movements of the past. It sports a significant number of young people, for whom Fridays for Future is the first experience with protests, who profess 'limited commitment to established environmental organisations, with varying interpretations of the importance of lifestyle politics and a hopeful attitude towards the future.'[88] As a network of very locally organised initiatives, and inspiration for spin offs such as Scientists for Future, it might also be reminiscent of the transnational advocacy

84 Naturally, other case studies would have also been possible and might be looked at in the future. The #MeToo movement as a component of the larger movement for women's rights in one example, net-neutrality and the movement for internet rights is another.

85 See Fridays for Future, available at: https://fridaysforfuture.org.

86 See Fridays for Future, 'Our Demands,' available at: https://fridaysforfuture.org/what-we-do/our-demands/.

87 Matthias Wahlström et al., 'Protest for a future: Composition, mobilization and motives of the participants in Fridays For Future climate protests on 15 March, 2019 in 13 European cities,' available at: https://osf.io/xcnzh/.

88 Ibid, 5.

networks that Keck and Sikkink[89] established as a unit of analysis. It is, however, less strategically situated than transnational advocacy networks, and rather uses the brute force of the masses, capturing social and traditional media and thus widespread attention. It is also not a coherent, unified movement with clear structures, representation, and goals, as the case of FFF Germany shows.[90]

Whether intentionally or not, Fridays for Future is establishing a new normative claim and carving out the space for it internationally. Finnemore and Sikkink suggest that 'international norms will be more successful, if they are clear and specific, have been around for a while and make universalistic claims about what is good for all people in all places.'[91] Early stage research analysing the content of several hundred thousand tweets that were posted with a set of related hashtags around on the dates of the first Fridays for Future global school strike, shows the normative framing of climate change by the movement:[92] inaction of governments, as well as industries, who are failing to initiate change and stick to the 1.5-degree goal, are bad to the extent of being criminal. This normative frame does not only focus on the environmental depletion, but rather equates the failure of addressing climate change with the wilful risking of millions of lives.[93] By aligning any greenhouse gas emissions to mass killings and future 'social collapse,'[94] which is the quintessential stand in for 'bad,' inaction and continued greenhouse gas emissions are framed as 'bad.' Hence,

89 Keck and Sikkink, *Activists beyond Borders* (n. 1).

90 Jens Marquardt, 'Fridays for Future's Disruptive Potential: An Inconvenient Youth Between Moderate and Radical Ideas,' Frontiers in Communication 5 (2020), 1–18.

91 Finnemore and Sikkink (n. 48), 908.

92 Viktoria Spaiser, Nicole Nisbett, and Cristina Stefan, 'How dare you? – Normative Challenge posed by Fridays for Future,' SSRN (2021), available at: https://papers.ssrn.com/sol3/papers.cfm?abstract_id=3581404.

93 According to the World Health Organization, climate change is expected to cause about a quarter million additional deaths per year between 2030 and 2050, available at: https://www.who.int/news-room/fact-sheets/detail/climate-change-and-health. While it is difficult to assess the total number, the Intergovernmental Panel on Climate Change's fifth assessment report also holds it to be very likely that the number of displaced people will be increased both due to changing climate conditions and increased weather events, see Intergovernmental Panel on Climate Change, 'Climate Change 2014: Synthesis Report: Contribution of Working Groups I, II and III to the Fifth Assessment Report of the Intergovernmental Panel on Climate Change,' (Geneva, Switzerland: 2014), available at: https://www.ipcc.ch.

94 Spaiser, Nisbett, and Stefan (n. 92), 6.

there is a clear and specific ('stay below 1.5 degrees of warming'), widely shared (movement around the world), universalistic claim about what is good for all people in all places (inaction causes climate change, causes people to die; hence it is bad, and action is good).

This normative framing prescribes and prohibits certain behavior of states – inaction, inadequate action, or sabotage being chief among them. Its widespread acceptance could put Conferences of the Parties under the UNFCCC[95] under new normative strain, giving especially smaller and more adversely affected states with little economic bargaining power new moralistic/normative advantages.[96]

Besides the development of a normative framework, the movement also provides what Keck and Sikking call an 'intentionalist frame.'[97] In a speech to the UN plenary in Katowice in 2019, Greta Thunberg proclaimed: 'You only speak of green eternal economic growth because you are too scared of being unpopular. You only talk about moving forward with the same bad ideas that got us into this mess, even when the only sensible thing to do is pull the emergency brake.'[98] This was widely shortened to '[y]ou are stealing our future,' thus establishing a causal chain. Of course, for climate change itself, causal chains are often extremely complex, but proclamations like the one above give the listener an impression of a short causal chain for the ongoing inaction on climate change mitigation.

It might be in large parts too early to tell which concrete effects this normative development will have on international law and global governance. However, some anecdotal evidence will provide a good transition to looking at some strategies and necessary steps to investigate the claims of this essay empirically. One example is the European Commission and its president, Ursula von der Leyen, who, during the height of the Corona pandemic in Europe, continuously reminded mass media and its consumers that climate change mitigation was very much still of the European

---

95 United Nations Framework Convention on Climate Chang of 9 May 1992, 1771 UNTS 107.

96 See for example the Alliance of Small Island States (AOSIS), a coalition of 44 small islands and low-lying coastal developing states, available at: https://www.aosis.org.

97 Keck and Sikkink, *Activists beyond Borders* (n. 1), 34.

98 Democracy Now, 'You Are Stealing Our Future: Greta Thunberg, 15, Condemns the World's Inaction on Climate Change' (YouTube, 13.12.2018). Video available at: https://www.youtube.com/watch?v=HzeekxtyFOY&ab_channel=DemocracyNow%21; Transcript available at: https://www.democracynow.org/2018/12/13/you_are_stealing_our_future_greta.

Commission's mind.[99] She also invited Fridays for Future initiator and figurehead Greta Thunberg to participate in the weekly meetings of the European Commission, so that she could 'present her opinion on the new environmental law before the commission.'[100] Many of the speeches by Fridays for Future organisers have been directed at international bodies,[101] indicating that the movement prominently addresses its claims towards international actors, not just national governments.

One central tenet of the movement is its insistence on states adhering to the 2015 Paris Agreement,[102] advancing its claims in a rights-based frame. Recent decisions by the Dutch[103] and the Irish Supreme Court[104] show that frame at work and indicate the influence of civil society on the interpretation and implementation of international environmental law. The latter recognised that its ruling is of special importance not only for the NGO, who brought the case before the Court, but also to the general public, and with its ruling opened its doors for rights-based climate litigation.[105] The Dutch case had been advanced on the basis of the human rights to life and well-being of the Dutch people. Similar claims are made in the case of a group of Portuguese children and young adults, which has recently reached the European Court of Human Rights[106] and in the case of a group of young Colombian plaintiffs, in whose favour the Columbi-

99 See for example, at: https://twitter.com/eu_commission/status/1278947680908165120; or at: https://ec.europa.eu/commission/presscorner/detail/en/ac_20_1265.

100 Frankfurter Allgemeine Zeitung/AFP, 'Greta Thunberg als Meinungsgeberin' (Frankfurt am Main, 04.03.2020), available at: https://www.faz.net/aktuell/politik/klimagesetz-greta-thunberg-als-meinungsgeberin-16663125.html.

101 For a collection of speeches by different public Fridays for Future figures, see at: https://fridaysforfuture.org/what-we-do/activist-speeches/.

102 Marquardt (n. 90), 7.

103 Otto Spijkers, 'Pursuing Climate Justice through Public Interest Litigation: the Urgenda Case,' Völkerrechtsblog, available at: https://voelkerrechtsblog.org/de/pursuing-climate-justice-through-public-interest-litigation-the-urgenda-case/.

104 The Supreme Court of Ireland, *Friends of the Irish Environment CLG and The Government of Ireland*, judgement of 31 July 2020, appeal no. 205/19.

105 Orla Kelleher, 'The Supreme Court of Ireland's decision in Friends of the Irish Environment v. Government of Ireland ('Climate Case Ireland'),' EJIL Talk, available at: https://www.ejiltalk.org/the-supreme-court-of-irelands-decision-in-friends-of-the-irish-environment-v-government-of-ireland-climate-case-ireland/ .

106 Paul Clark, Gerry Liston and Ioannis Kalpouzos, 'Climate Change and the European Court of Human Rights: The Portuguese Youth Case,' EJIL Talk, available at: https://www.ejiltalk.org/climate-change-and-the-european-court-of-human-rights-the-portuguese-youth-case/.

an Supreme Court decided in 2018.[107] The Court not only considered the issue of human rights, intergenerational justice and environmental accountability, but even recognised the Colombian Amazon as a subject of rights.[108] Most recently, a group of young adolescents have opened a case with the 14th Federal Court of Sao Paulo accusing the Brazilian government of skirting its responsibilities under the Paris agreement.[109]

VI. Empirical Outlook

I suggest strategies for empirically examining the influence of global civil society on international law. These are by no means comprehensive, but they can serve as a departure point for future research.

While it is undoubtedly difficult to determine 'the empirical paternity of particular prescriptions'[110] in international law, it is an important step in understanding the making of the law. Process tracing[111] can be the method of choice for determining where specific legal provisions come from and what role (informal) civil society has played in their conception.

Besides this qualitative understanding, the text can also serve as a data source for quantitative insights: As Spaiser et al.[112] show, tweets can serve as a basis for extracting normative shifts in the claims that informal civil society movements make. Similarly, sentiment analysis around environmental claims and discourse analysis can show how conversations around certain topics change and are influenced by the social media activities of informal civil society movements. Despite the fact that the movement has quickly grown in support, it is still a relatively new phenomenon, so that not many fully formed studies have been conducted so far. However, works in progress can serve as a good indicator of what

---

107 For the court documents on Future Generations v. Ministry of the Environment and Others, see at: https://climate-laws.org/geographies/colombia/litigation_cases/future-generations-v-ministry-of-the-environment-and-others.

108 Joana Setzer and Lisa Benjamin, 'Climate Litigation in the Global South: Constraints and Innovations,' Transnational Environmental Law 9 (2020), 77-101.

109 For the complaint Six Youths v. Minister of Environment and Others, see at: https://climate-laws.org/geographies/brazil/litigation_cases/six-youths-v-minister-of-environment-and-others.

110 McDougal and Reisman (n. 30), 256.

111 David Collier, 'Understanding Process Tracing,' PS 44 (2011), 823-830.

112 Spaiser, Nisbett, and Stefan (n. 92).

can be done. Brückner et al.[113] have taken Instagram comments replying to Fridays for Future posts to better understand the constitutive factors of the movement. In a preliminary analysis, they find more evidence for group cohesion rather than indications of solidarity in those comments. Studies on movements that were predominantly conceived online and/or have a strong online component have investigated how information is distributed,[114] the co-creation of meanings and their establishment in a public (online) space,[115] which roles exist in social movements online, how those roles communicate,[116] and which roles individual social media platforms play.[117]

Supplementing that, it would also be valuable to understand how global informal civil society movements are perceived from the perspective of decision-makers at the different levels. Expert interviews can shed light on the direct and indirect influence that these movements have. Experimental studies, such as vignette studies[118] like those conducted on the international human rights regime,[119] could further supplement our understanding of how normative framings of climate change matter for people on the streets as well as within the international decision-making structure.

---

113 Felix Brünker, Fabian Deitelhoff and Milad Mirbabaie, 'Collective Identity Formation on Instagram – Investigating the Social Movement Fridays for Future,' Australasian Conference on Information Systems 2019 (Perth: 2019), available at: https://arxiv.org/pdf/1912.05123.

114 Yannis Theocharis, 'The Wealth of (Occupation) Networks? Communication Patterns and Information Distribution in a Twitter Protest Network,' Journal of Information Technology & Politics 10 (2013), 35-56.

115 Xiong, Cho and Boatwright (n. 15).

116 Felix Brünker, Magdalena Wischnewski, Milad Mirbabaie and Judith Meinert, 'The Role of Social Media during Social Movements – Observations from the #metoo Debate on Twitter' in: Tung Bui (eds), *Proceedings of the 53rd Hawaii International Conference on System Sciences* (Honolulu: University of Hawaii at Manoa 2020).

117 Lydia Manikonda, Ghazaleh Beigi, Huan Liu and Subbarao Kambhampati, 'Twitter for Sparking a Movement, Reddit for Sharing the Moment: #metoo through the Lens of Social Media,' *11th International Conference on Social, Cultural, and Behavioral Modeling, SBP-BRiMS* (Washington: 2018), available at: https://link.springer.com/chapter/10.1007/978-3-319-93372-6_13.

118 Vignette studies use scenarios in order to immerse study participants into certain situation or simulate circumstances, before asking them to make a decision. They often provide more external validity than laboratory studies, while keeping internal validity high.

119 Matthew Kim, 'Legalization and Norm Internalization: An Empirical Study of International Human Rights Commitments Eliciting Public Support for Compliance,' Penn State Journal of Law & International Affairs 7 (2019).

Finally, informal civil society movements exist in a complex system of international actors, prevalent (international) norms and their contestation. These actors have different sets of possible actions, interests, constraints and normative convictions. In such a setting with heterogeneous actors, which lobby for or against a given resolution in international law and negotiate the provision of a public good, computational methods such as agent-based modelling (ABM) can tease out the dynamics of the international community and how those dynamics determine the successes and failures of international (environmental) law.

Computational social science approaches create the opportunity to observe which parameters determine the emerging patterns as well as the intermediate steps and actions involved in their generation. They are especially useful in understanding interdependencies between the dynamics of different actors that have different behavioral options available to them and act within different spheres of influence. This leads to complex interdependencies in the design and implementation of international law and global governance processes. As Rajagopal summarizes, '[a] social movements approach, [by contrast,] focuses on the actual way political choices are shaped in collective settings, thereby allowing analyses to either 'scale up' from the level of individuals or 'scale down' from the level of states.'[120] Simulations of dynamics thus also provide the opportunity to test how local normative realities might be conceptualised in a co-constitutive relationship to global normative change.[121]

VII. Conclusion

I posit three mechanisms by which the internet and especially social media enable *informal civil society movements* to impact international law-making either by engaging directly with the international legal sphere or by changing the interest structures of nation-states: (1) *bypassing locality* – traditional forms of participation within the (democratic) nation-state very much depend on where someone is located, i.e., registered and therefore able to vote or demonstrate. Messaging and social media platforms provide a global reach that can bypass traditional boundaries and constraints of the nation-state. Civil society can directly connect to international actors; (2)

120 Rajagopal (n. 5), 417.

121 Antje Wiener, *Contestation and Constitution of Norms in Global International Relations* (Cambridge: Cambridge University Press 2018), 21.

creating normativity – it allows a diverse body of civil society to develop a global normative claim and to carve out the space for this normative claim on the global stage; and (3) *changing conditions* – in the dynamic and complex international law-setting, these movements change the interests of all international actors: businesses start taking into account different incentives to lobby for stricter standards because their consumers pay more attention; governments are more likely to be at the forefront of progressive treaties if that increases their chances of re-election; civil society organisations might see an increase in membership and funds. These mechanisms are illustrated through the global environmental movement, with Fridays for Future as the central initiative.

With its focus on state actors and international organisations, international law scholarship is missing the opportunity to theorise and empirically examine the influence of the rich variety of actors that shape international law and the environment in which it is made. New developments in text analysis, network analysis, as well as tried and tested methods of process tracing and interviews can help in bridging this gap and have been briefly outlined. Collaborations with researchers in political science, sociology or economics can fruitfully pair novel methods for the study of the law and in-depth understanding of the forces that shape international law.

Strategic Litigation and International Internet Law

Vera Strobel

Abstract The phenomenon of strategic litigation is becoming more global, inter-disciplinary and its prevalence is increasing in various areas of law. This chapter is based on the prima facie definition of strategic litigation as a method using legal means to achieve a change in the interpretation or implementation of the law beyond the scope of an individual case and to bring societal or political change. The internet has played a multidimensional role in strategic litigation activities and their influence on society, international legal scholarship and the development and interpretation of the law. Activities of legislators concerning the internet are under particular scrutiny of the digital internet community and have mobilized mass protests of the public. Internet law and digital rights have become important and ever-growing objects of strategic litigation by civil society as a resort from the political sphere to the judiciary. Based on this background, the chapter briefly analyses strategically litigating NGOs and strategic cases with transnational effects regarding international internet law and digital rights, in particular before European and US courts. NGOs and strategic litigation networks, as well as groups and individuals, have taken action against regulations and practices in the field of the internet; a well-known case is the action of Schrems against Facebook. Actors of strategic litigation are especially increasing their online public outreach activities and using the internet and its capacities for spreading information to raise public awareness. While there is much potential for strategic litigation regarding international internet law, there are also challenges and concerns requiring an examination. Nevertheless, strategic litigation enhances civil society's impact on law-making as well as the application, implementation and enforcement of international internet law. Moreover, it contributes to furthering an individual right's centred understanding of internet governance.

I. Introduction

Human rights issues today are becoming more transnational and international due to globalisation and today's interconnectedness, especially because of the internet. Simultaneously, the so-called phenomenon of strategic litigation is *prima facie* becoming more global, inter-disciplinary and professional, and it is increasingly common in the field of internet law and in the prevalence of its online public outreach activities. Strategic litigation is a method using legal means to make proclaimed injustices or rights' violations more visible and attempting to bring societal or political change as well as trying to achieve a change in the interpretation or implementation of the law beyond the scope of an individual case.[1] Although its exact definition and elements are not uniformly agreed upon, this explanation of the term serves as the basis of this chapter. The phenomenon is also known under the terms of public interest litigation, cause lawyering and impact litigation.[2]

What is remarkable and new about this form of strategic engagement is not primarily the specific usage of litigation, but its new actors and their approaches,[3] which have emerged in the last decades, and now influence how violations and individual rights are litigated. This chapter will not discuss strategic approaches in litigation by multinational corporations, like online service providers or digital communication platforms, but will rather focus on actors of civil society. It will analyse one important aspect of the professionalization of strategic litigation by civil society: Non-governmental organizations (NGOs) and strategic litigation networks. The latter can be defined as associations or alliances of civil society actors striving for contributing to a sustainable and effective implementation of human rights through legal means.[4]

The internet has also played a multidimensional role in strategic litigation activities and their influences on society, international legal scholarship and the development and interpretation of public international law itself. Regarding internet law, international, regional and national guarantees of human and fundamental rights like the right to privacy, the right to protection of personal data, and the sparsely guaranteed and still contested right to access to the internet[5] have served as an important basis to enable a strategic individual rights approach. As many individual rights guarantees were adopted decades ago, they only rarely contain explicit provisions regarding the internet or the digital sphere. Yet, courts have often developed extensive case-law regarding the internet and digital rights based on a dynamic interpretation of *de lege lata* provisions. Judicial development of individual rights has especially become necessary due to an increase in national, regional, and international law-making regarding the internet, in

---

1 Alexander Graser, 'Was es über Strategic Litigation zu schreiben gälte' in: Alexander Graser and Christian Helmrich (eds), *Strategic Litigation* (Baden-Baden: Nomos 2019), 9–19 (14).

2 Helen Duffy, *Strategic Human Rights Litigation* (Oxford: Hart Publishing 2018), 3.

3 Duffy (n. 2), 13–19.

4 Florian Jeßberger, 'Research Project 'Strategic Litigation',' available at: https://uni-hamburg.de/.

5 Paul Bernal, *Internet Privacy Rights: Rights to Protect Autonomy* (Cambridge: Cambridge University Press 2014), 4.

order to keep up with technological advances and regulate activities within cyberspace.[6]

The following contribution is not meant as a final compilation, but rather as an impulse for further research in this field. It will focus on three important aspects in this realm: Firstly, strategic litigation with the object of laws regulating the internet. Secondly, the internet as an instrument for strategic litigation. Thirdly, the interplay between these elements. In the first part of the chapter, the role of civil society in law-making regarding the internet is analysed (II.). Afterwards, strategic litigation activities in the field of (international) internet law will be examined based on cases brought forward by NGOs and individuals (III.). Thereafter a focus will be put on the strategic usage of the internet in the context of strategic litigation activities, and subsequently, the interplay between both will be explored (IV.). Finally, based on the research results so far, the potential and perils of strategic litigation in the realm of the internet will be investigated (V.), before concluding remarks are drawn (VI.).

II. Civil Society and Internet Law

In the following, developments in legislation, democratic participation by civil society and litigation with regard to internet rights are described in order to introduce the main topic of strategic litigation. The last decade saw a global surge in the number of laws governing the internet and the digital sphere. With the development and the rapid spread of the internet at the beginning of this century, legislators worldwide saw a necessity to regulate the cybersphere with specific national laws and regulations to combat a legal vacuum that could not be filled by legal regulations already in place. For example, recently, the Network Enforcement Act[7] in Germany and the law on fighting hate on the internet ('Loi Avia')[8] in France were passed, both codifying the controversial duty of online platforms to delete certain illegal content. At the same time, supranationally, the EU is working on a Digital Services Act after the General Data Protection Re-

6 Ben Wagner et al., 'Surveillance and Censorship: The Impact of Technologies on Human Rights,' 16 April 2015, available at: https://europarl.europa.eu/.

7 Netzwerkdurchsetzungsgesetz of 1 September 2017 (BGBl. I p. 3352), which was changed by Article 274 of the Decree of 19 June 2020 (BGBl. I p. 1328).

8 Assemblée nationale, proposition de loi visant à lutter contre les contenus haineux sur internet, loi n° 2020–766 de 24 juin 2020.

gulation (GDPR) was passed and has been implemented since 2018.[9] Yet, as the world wide web and access thereto is not confined or confineable within state borders, states have also agreed on and adopted international regulations for cyberspace in the context of international organizations and transnational frameworks.

Alongside with the passing of these laws, which are increasing in number and are becoming more detailed and comprehensive, parts of civil society and NGOs have scrutinized regulations of what they perceive to be their free and equal sphere. Due to more and more daily, social and political as well as economic and professional activities taking place digitally – especially having accelerated because of the COVID-19 pandemic – fundamental human rights like privacy rights and other digital rights essential for a liberal democracy are increasingly vulnerable and at risk of infringements. Cases of influence on politics and interference with democracy through the usage of social media platforms,[10] and increasing legislation for expansive government surveillance are only a few examples of the recent alarming developments regarding such vulnerabilities of individual rights and democracy.[11] Additionally, civil society has critically monitored the activities of transnational corporations active in cyberspace. Consequently, when perceiving activities of legislators or corporations concerning cyberspace as a violation of their rights or of other laws, the digital internet community has mobilized mass protests of the public. An example of such protest and their impact are the civil mobilization and protest against the Draft Article 13 (now Article 17) of the EU's Directive on Copyright in the Digital Single Market in 2019.[12] In the context of which civil society tried to have some of the substantive regulations chan-

---

9 European Commission, 'The Digital Services Act package,' available at: https://digital-strategy.ec.europa.eu/.

10 Regarding election interferences, see Michael Schmitt, 'Foreign Cyber Interference in Elections: An International Law Primer,' 16 October 2020, available at: https://ejiltalk.org.

11 Francesca Bignami, 'Schrems II: The Right to Privacy and the New Illiberalism,' 29 July 2020, available at: https://verfassungsblog.de/; Valsamis Mitsilegas, 'The Preventive Turn in European Security Policy: Towards a Rule of Law Crisis?' in: Francesca Bignami (ed.), *EU Law in Populist Times: Crises and Prospects* (Cambridge: Cambridge University Press 2020), 301–318 (301, 315–317).

12 'Gegen EU-Urheberrechtsreform: 4,7 Millionen Unterschriften gegen Upload-Filter,' 18 February 2019, available at: https://tagesschau.de/; Julia Reda, 'Walking from Luxembourg to Brussels in two hours: The European Court of Justice will rule on the legality of upload filters,' 16 November 2020, available at: https://verfassungsblog.de/.

ged, with the result of a few amendments to the original draft.[13] Another example are marches against the Anti-Counterfeiting Trade Agreement (ACTA), which was supposed to establish an international legal framework for targeting *inter alia* copyright infringement on the internet in 2012, but which has not entered into force due to a lack of ratification after mass protest and petitions.[14]

Moreover, in taking action against regulations through democratic participation, not only politically, e.g. in the form of protest and petitions regarding internet law, cracking down on laws has taken the form of legal action. Besides civil society, the affected multinational corporations also resort to speaking out and lobbying against planned law-making, and if that does not satisfy their demands, they sometimes utilize litigation in order to combat regulations of their activities.[15] When legal action goes beyond a single individual case, is supposed to have implications for a broader dimension, and litigation takes place in order to reach certain legal or socio-political aims, it can be classified as strategic litigation. The targeted resort to a specific forum with a particular selected case constellation and a predetermined approach is also a characteristic of strategic litigation. Recently, this method has become more common, especially in the field of internet law – as will be shown on the basis of the discussed cases below – simultaneously with the acceleration of law-making described above.

III. Strategic Litigation in Matters of Internet Law

Before analysing cases, NGOs and strategic litigation networks in the field of litigation regarding international internet law, it should be noted that the cases illustrated mainly focus on domestic and European regulations with an inherent transnational component. The reason behind this prevalence of cases is that there is no international court for individual rights claims regarding internet law or digital rights and only very fragmentary regulations awarding individual rights in transnational internet law. Ne-

13 Julia Reda, 'EU copyright reform: Our fight was not in vain,' 18 April 2019, available at: https://juliareda.eu/en/.

14 Quinn Norton, 'How the European Internet Rose Up Against ACTA,' 21 February 2012, available at: https://wired.com/.

15 See e.g., James Vincent, 'European Wikipedias have been turned off for the day to protest dangerous copyright laws,' 21 March 2019, available at: https://theverge.com/; ECJ, *Google LLC. v. Commission nationale de l'informatique et des libertés (CNIL)*, judgment of 24 September 2019, case no. 507/17, ECLI:EU:C:2019:772.

vertheless, most of the largest IT service providers are active on a pan-European and global level.[16] Even though, e.g., the EU's GDPR only applies to IT operators that act within the European single market,[17] many global providers have adapted their regulations, standards and practices to implement the EU's regulations.[18] The same worldwide effect is expected for the EU's new copyright directive when implemented in the Member States.[19] This phenomenon of establishing a *de facto* high global standard through unilateral legislation by the EU is called the 'Brussels effect,'[20] named after the comparable 'California effect.'[21] This process of externalizing the EU's standards outside its Member States through single market mechanisms is also driven by numerous global providers operating subsidiaries within the EU for non-EU markets.[22] Thus, strategic litigation within the EU directly or indirectly against its regulations as well as against EU frameworks with third states or national implementation thereof is able to produce transnational and global implications and can lead to a change of legislation and practice regarding the internet worldwide.

One of the oldest NGOs active, *inter alia*, in the field of litigating digital and internet rights is the American Civil Liberties Union (ACLU). It was founded in 1920 to defend and preserve rights and liberties in the US.[23] The ACLU has been active with targeted impact litigation in many cases, including, *inter alia*, freedom of speech and distribution via the internet

---

16 See NOYB, 'Making Privacy a Reality. Public Project Summary,' March 2020, available at: https://noyb.eu/, 3.

17 Ibid.; Council of the European Union, 'Proposal for a Regulation of the European Parliament and of the Council on the protection of individuals with regard to the processing of personal data and on the free movement of such data (General Data Protection Regulation),' 11 June 2015, 2012/0011 (COD).

18 E.g. Julie Brill, 'Microsoft's commitment to GDPR, privacy and putting customers in control of their own data,' 21 May 2018, available at: https://blogs.microsoft.com/; Facebook, 'Complying With New Privacy Laws and Offering New Privacy Protections to Everyone, No Matter Where You Live,' 17 April 2018, available at: https://about.facebook.com/.

19 Michelle Kaminsky, 'EU's Copyright Directive Passes Despite Widespread Protests – But It's Not Law Yet,' 26 March 2020, available at: https://forbes.com/.

20 Anu Bradford, 'The Brussels Effect,' Nw. U. L. Rev. 107 (2012), 1–67 (3–5); Mark Scott and Laurens Cerulus, 'Europe's new data protection rules export privacy standards worldwide,' 31 January 2018, available at: https://politico.eu/.

21 'Three Questions: Prof. David Bach on the Reach of European Privacy Regulations,' 25 May 2018, available at: https://insights.som.yale.edu/.

22 E.g., regarding Europe, Middle-East and Africa (EMEA) and all non-US markets, see NOYB (n. 16), 3.

23 ACLU, 'FAQs,' available at: https://aclu.org/faqs.

in *Reno v. American Civil Liberties Union*[24] in 1997 and internet services providers' obligation to reveal private internet access information to the government in *Doe v. Holder*.[25] Important cases have also emerged in the context of government surveillance of internet activity and communication in *American Civil Liberties Union v. National Security Agency*[26] and by the Center for Constitutional Rights (CCR), another US-based legal advocacy organization, in *Center for Constitutional Rights v. Obama*.[27]

In a pending case, the ACLU and the Electronic Frontier Foundation (EFF) are seeking access to a judicial ruling reportedly finding that the US Department of Justice cannot oblige Facebook to alter its Messenger to allow for the FBI to conduct investigative wiretaps.[28] The EFF is a leading NGO, active – according to their mission – in defending civil rights and liberties in the digital sphere, predominantly in the US.[29] Strategic cases of the EFF, which they conduct under the name of impact litigation, comprise issues in the field of privacy, security and free speech in the online world.[30] While the cases mentioned so far are national US cases, due to many of the digital service providers operating from the US and digital communication as well as government surveillance not halting at domestic borders, the consequences also have a far-reaching global dimension.

The strategic turn to the courts has also led to individuals taking action against regulation in the field of the internet, even though legal action is not always taken originally in order to achieve a landmark strategic case. A well-known case is *Schrems* in the context of Facebook and EU law. In

---

24 US Supreme Court, *Reno v. American Civil Liberties Union*, judgment of 26 June 1997, 521 U.S. 844; ACLU, 'Feature on Reno v. ACLU I – The battle over the CDA,' available at: https://www.aclu.org; for other internet free speech cases of the ACLU, see ACLU, 'Technology and Liberty: Internet Free Speech,' available at: https://aclu.org.

25 US District Court Southern District of New York, *Doe v. Ashcroft*, Decision of 28 October 2004, 04 Civ. 2614 (VM); the case led the court to strike down the National Security Letters provisions of the USA PATRIOT Act; ACLU, *Doe v. Holder*, judgment of 17 November 2009, available at: https://aclu.org.

26 US Court of Appeals for the Sixth Circuit, *ACLU v. NSA*, judgment of 6 July 2007, 493 F.3d 644; ACLU, 'ACLU v. NSA – Challenge to warrantless wiretapping,' September 10, 2014, available at: https://aclu.org.

27 CCR, Historic Cases, 'CCR v. Obama (formerly CCR v. Bush),' 21 October 2014, available at: https://ccrjustice.org/.

28 ACLU, 'ACLU v. US Department of Justice,' 23 January 2020, available at: https://aclu.org/.

29 EFF, 'About,' available at: https://eff.org/.

30 EFF, 'Legal Cases,' available at: https://eff.org/; EFF, 'Legal Victories,' available at: https://eff.org/.

the *Schrems I* case, the European Court of Justice (ECJ) invalidated the European Commission's Decision 2000/5205 ('the Safe Harbour Decision') in 2015 in light of Article 7, the right to the respect for private life, Article 8, the right to the protection of personal data, and Article 47, the right to an effective remedy and to a fair trial, of the EU Charter of Fundamental Rights.[31] The Commission's Decision allowed for data transfers between the US and the EU, declaring that the US provided for adequate safeguards for data protection. This decision was based on the Safe Harbour framework, which consisted of data protection principles for US companies.

In the following *Schrems II* case, the ECJ declared the Decision 2016/1250 on the adequacy of the protection provided by the EU-US Data Protection Shield as invalid in July 2020.[32] The ECJ examined the Decision in the light of the requirements by the GDPR and the EU Charter of Fundamental Rights guaranteeing respect for private and family life, personal data protection and the right to effective judicial protection. The court decided that the limitations on the protection of personal data in US law for transferred data from the EU are not confined in a way essentially equivalent to EU law. In the court's view, the surveillance programmes based on those provisions are not proportionally limited to what is strictly necessary.[33] Additionally, the ECJ ruled that the Ombudsperson mechanism referred to in Decision 2016/1250 does not provide data subjects with any cause of action before a body which offers guarantees substantially equivalent to those required by EU law. Yet, the court found the Commission Decision 2010/87 on standard contractual clauses for the transfer of personal data to processors established in third countries to be valid.[34] This case shows that national internet law, here US law, in combination with international frameworks or conventions as well as supranational or international organizations, is not only a domestic matter but has important European and international implications and consequences.[35]

Schrems was supported by the non-profit organization NOYB – European Center for Digital Rights, which was founded in 2017. NOYB uses

31 ECJ, *Maximillian Schrems v. Data Protection Commissioner*, judgment of 6 October 2015, case no. 362/14, ECLI:EU:C:2015:650.

32 ECJ, *Data Protection Commissioner v. Facebook Ireland and Maximillian Schrems*, judgment of 16 July 2020, case no. 311/18, ECLI:EU:C:2020:559.

33 Ibid.

34 Ibid.

35 See Christopher Kuner, 'Schrems II Re-Examined,' 25 August 2020, available at: https://verfassungsblog.de/.

targeted and strategic litigation to enforce the right to privacy and digital rights. It predominantly works on cases against multinational corporations active in the EU.[36] Another example of its cases is the filing of complaints against Google, Instagram, WhatsApp and Facebook due to an alleged violation of the GDPR,[37] thus, illustrating the potential power of individuals and civil society associations through litigation regarding international internet law.

Besides individual approaches, social movements can also seek collective legal solutions and therefore resort to strategically litigating NGOs. In the following, European actors within this field will be examined. Similar to NOYB, the non-profit Digital Rights Ireland has litigated a strategic case regarding EU law and achieved what they call a 'landmark success'[38] when the ECJ declared the EU's Data Retention Directive[39] as invalid in 2014.[40] The Directive was set out to harmonize the retention of certain data by providers of electronic communications services or communications networks. The ECJ had to decide on the validity of the directive after being asked to determine this question by, *inter alia*, the Irish High Court, where Digital Rights Ireland had sued the Irish authorities regarding the legality of their measures.[41] The ECJ found the directive to encompass a wide-ranging and particularly serious interference with the fundamental right to respect for private life and the right to protection of personal data of the EU Charter of Fundamental Rights.[42]

In Germany, one focus of the litigation organization Society for Civil Rights (Gesellschaft für Freiheitsrechte; GFF), initially operating primarily

---

36 NOYB, 'Making Privacy a Reality: Public Project Summary,' available at: https://noyb.eu/, 2–3; NOYB, 'FAQs,' available at: https://noyb.eu/en/faqs.

37 NOYB, 'noyb.eu filed four complaints over 'forced consent' against Google, Instagram, WhatsApp and Facebook,' 25 May 2018, available at: https://noyb.eu/.

38 Digital Rights Ireland, 'DRI welcomes landmark data privacy judgment,' 6 October 2015, available at: https://digitalrights.ie/.

39 Directive 2006/24/EC of the European Parliament and the Council of 15 March 2006 on the retention of data generated or processed in connection with the provision of publicly available electronic communications services or of public communications networks and amending, Directive 2002/58/EC (OJ 2006 L 105, 54).

40 ECJ, *Digital Rights Ireland and Seitlinger and Others*, judgment of 8 April 2014, case nos 293/12 and 594/12, ECLI:EU:C:2014:238.

41 ECJ, Press Release No 54/14, 8 April 2014, judgment in joined cases C-293/12 and C-594/12, *Digital Rights Ireland and Seitlinger and Others*, available at: https://curia.europa.eu/.

42 Ibid.

on a national level, is data security, informational freedom and privacy.[43] In 2019, the GFF declared copyright law and freedom of communication to be a focus of their work in the context of their project 'control ©,'[44] in which they want to have individual rights issues decided by courts and critically examine the drafting and implementation of internet law, especially regarding the EU's Copyright Directive.[45] In November 2020, the NGO published a study on Article 17 of the Copyright Directive in the form of a fundamental rights assessment.[46] In their study, they find that the regulation does not include a fair balance between intellectual property rights, the freedom of expression and information of platform users, their right to protection of personal data and the freedom of platform operators to conduct a business, thus violating fundamental rights of the EU's Charter.[47] Even though the GFF is a primarily national actor, it takes into account possible international dimensions of their cases.[48] In the context of national laws implementing EU law, especially regarding the EU's copyright directive, a European dimension of the GFF's work is clearly visible. One case which the NGO calls a big success is the action against parts of the law regarding the surveillance powers of the German Federal Intelligence Service.[49] With its decision of 19 May 2020, the German Federal Constitutional Court declared the constitutional complaint, initiated and coordinated by the GFF, as successful and pronounced the German law regulating the surveillance powers of the Federal Intelligence Service in their current form regarding foreign telecommunications as violating fundamental rights of the Basic Law. Even though the case is primarily centred in German constitutional law, the litigants, as well as the court,

43 Boris Burghardt and Christian Thönnes, 'Die Gesellschaft für Freiheitsrechte' in: Graser and Helmrich (n. 1), 65–71 (69).

44 Daniela Turß, 'control ©: Urheberrecht und Kommunikationsfreiheit,' 13 April 2019, available at: https://freiheitsrechte.org; Julia Reda, 'Introducing control © – Strategic Litigation for Free Communication,' Kluwer Copyright Blog, 13 April 2020, available at: http://copyrightblog.kluweriplaw.com/.

45 See e.g. Julia Reda, 'In copyright reform, Germany wants to avoid over-blocking, not rule out upload filters,' Kluwer Copyright Blog, 9 July 2020, available at: http://copyrightblog.kluweriplaw.com.

46 Julia Reda, Joschka Selinger and Michael Servatius, 'Article 17 of the Directive on Copyright in the Digital Single Market: a Fundamental Rights Assessment,' 16 November 2020, available at: https://freiheitsrechte.org.

47 Reda, Selinger and Servatius (n. 46), 52.

48 GFF, 'About GFF,' available at: https://freiheitsrechte.org/.

49 EDRi, 'German Constitutional Court stops mass surveillance abroad,' 27 May 2020, available at: https://edri.org/.

also considered international law arguments in regards to the surveillance of internet communication abroad on the basis of international human rights and human rights within the scope of the European Convention on Human Rights.[50]

The GFF works in close cooperation with the above-mentioned NGO EFF.[51] Other partners of the GFF and simultaneously NGOs active in the field of national and international internet law are, inter alia, European Digital Rights (EDRi), the Humboldt Law Clinic Internetrecht (HLCI), La Quadrature du Net, Netzpolitik.org and Privacy International. These NGOs are all non-profit organizations active in the field of digital rights and civil liberties in the cybersphere. Privacy International is an NGO based in the UK, which uses strategic litigation as one of the various methods to combat violations of privacy rights.[52] In their cases regarding internet law, they have litigated before British domestic courts, the ECJ and the ECtHR against, most prominently, surveillance of the government.[53] La Quadrature du Net is a French NGO which engages strategically against the legislation as well as activities by the government and by corporations which it perceives as infringing fundamental freedoms in cyberspace.[54] An example thereof are the critical observations before the Conseil Constitutionnel in the context of the above mentioned French Loi Avia,[55] that was then declared unconstitutional by the Conseil,[56] which the NGO perceives as a success.[57] Due to similar laws or legislative plans in Europe and planned EU legislation in digital services as well as human rights

50 Constitutional Complaint of the Legal Representative working in cooperation with the GFF, available at: https://freiheitsrechte.org/bnd-gesetz-2/, 46–48; Federal Constitutional Court of Germany, judgment of 19 May 2020, 1 BvR 2835/17, paras 96–103.

51 GFF, available at: https://freiheitsrechte.org.

52 Privacy International, Strategic Areas, 'Contesting Government Data and System Exploitation,' available at: https://privacyinternational.org.

53 E.g. Privacy International, 'Tele2/Watson,' available at: https://privacyinternational.org; ECJ, *Tele2 Sverige v. Post- och telestyrelsen*, judgment of 21 December 2016, C-203/15, available at: https://privacyinternational.org; the pending case of 10 Human Rights Organisations v. United Kingdom before the ECtHR, Application No. 24960/15, available at: https://privacyinternational.org.

54 La Quadratur du Net, 'Nous,' available at: https://laquadrature.net.

55 La Quadratur du Net, 'Loi Avia, Nos Observations devant le conseil constitutionnel,' 26 May 2020, available at: https://laquadrature.net.

56 Conseil Constitutionnel, *Loi visant à lutter contre les contenus haineux sur internet*, Décision n° 2020–801 DC du 18/06/2020.

57 La Quadratur du Net, 'Loi Haine: Le Conseil Constitutionnel refuse la censure sans juge,' 18 June 2020, available at: https://laquadrature.net.

guaranteed by the European Convention on Human Rights, these national cases have implications far beyond one state's borders. Thus, besides already pending or decided cases, the growing number of legal activities of legislators regarding the internet as well as transnational cooperation both show the possibilities and potential for strategic litigation in the future. As a dynamic between legislative processes and civil society can be observed in the form that if a certain aim cannot be achieved or a planned regulation cannot be prevented by actors of civil society, recourse from the political process to the judiciary is sought in order to reach the intended outcome for internet rights.

Over 30 privacy and digital rights non-profit organizations all over Europe involved in strategic litigation and other activities like lobbying and campaigns in the field of digital rights and internet law have joined forces in the non-profit organization European Digital Rights (EDRi) based in Brussels.[58] It is active in the fields of data protection and privacy, surveillance, copyrights and net neutrality and with campaigns, e.g., regarding the GDPR and its implementation in the EU's Member States. Therefore, it submits interventions, amicus curiae briefs and expert opinions in national, regional and international proceedings, and provides legal support to partners and clients.[59] Besides litigating non-profits, organizations working in the background with research and the gathering of information are also important aspects regarding strategic litigation of internet rights.[60]

Internet law and digital rights are also litigated in the Global South, where public interest litigation has long been established in countries like India, Pakistan and South Africa. Among others, in some states of South and Southeast Asia as well as Africa, strategic public interest litigation has been used especially in defence of the freedom of expression online and against internet bans.[61] A remarkable case that could also be classified as strategic is the one of *The Gambia v Facebook, Inc.* before the US District Court for the District of Columbia to get access to information in the

58 EDRi, 'About,' available at: https://edri.org.

59 Ibid.

60 E.g., Algorithm Watch, available at: https://algorithmwatch.org.

61 See e.g. Françoise Mukuku, 'Digital rights strategic litigation: Suing governments when online freedoms are violated,' Association for Progressive Communications, available at: https://apc.org, 13 October 2017; Software Freedom Law Center India, 'Our Statement on Delhi High Court's Dismissal of the Public Interest Litigation Challenging Internet Shutdown in Delhi,' 1 March 2020, available at: https://sflc.in; Internet Governance Forum 2016, 'Strategic Litigation: Freedom of Expression Online,' available at: https://intgovforum.org.

context of the ongoing case *Application of the Convention on the Prevention and Punishment of the Crime of Genocide (The Gambia v. Myanmar)* before the International Court of Justice.[62]

After the examination of these NGOs' and individuals' activities regarding internet law, a short insight will be given into how NGOs finance these activities in order to examine which actors enable strategic litigation financially and what motives might be behind certain activities. Besides donations and supporting memberships, grants are an important source of revenue for non-profit organizations.[63] The Digital Freedom Fund (DFF) is an NGO which also awards financial grants to strategic litigators for cases in all Council of Europe Member States and engages in skill building and networking.[64] The NGO is based in the Netherlands and sees its mission in supporting strategic litigation to advance digital rights in Europe. DFF works in the field of digital rights, which they define broadly as human rights applicable in the digital sphere and encompassing rights and freedoms concerning the internet.[65] NGOs the DFF has supported in their case work are, for example, the GFF and epicenter.works regarding a lawsuit against the EU's Passenger Name Records Directive 2016/681, which requires airlines to automatically transfer passengers' data to government centres.[66] The NGO epicenter.works is an Austrian non-profit advocating for fundamental rights in the digital age as well as equal rights regarding the internet and a self-determined usage thereof.[67] In this context, they also use strategic proceedings before national and European courts to achieve their goals.[68] Another case, which the DFF has financially supported, is litigation against the government's use of an automated surveillance system, named System Risk Indication (SyRI), in the Netherlands by, *inter alia*, the Dutch non-profits Public Interest Litigation Network and Privacy

62 Priya Pillai, 'The Republic of The Gambia v Facebook, Inc.: Domestic Proceedings, International Implications,' OpinioJuris, 8 August 2020, available at: https://opiniojuris.org.

63 Jason M. M. Wilson, 'Litigation Finance in the Public Interest,' Am. U.L. Rev. 64 (2014), 385–455 (390, 400–401).

64 Digital Freedom Fund, 'About,' available at: https://digitalfreedomfund.org.

65 Digital Freedom Fund, 'Grants,' available at: https://digitalfreedomfund.org.

66 Digital Freedom Fund, 'De Capitani and others v. Federal Republic of Germany and others, Criminal Police Office of Austria and others,' available at: https://digitalfreedomfund.org; No PNR, 'We are taking legal action against the mass processing of passenger data!,' available at: https://nopnr.eu.

67 Epicenter.works, 'Vision,' available at: https://en.epicenter.works.

68 Epicenter.works, 'History,' available at: https://en.epicenter.works.

First.[69] In this case, The Hague District Court found that the law enabling SyRI violates international human rights guarantees, namely Article 8 of the European Convention on Human Rights, which protects the right to respect for private life.[70] In the Netherlands, strategic litigation on the basis of international law is possible through domestic regulations.[71]

Thus, a certain independence of strategic litigation networks, as well as their activities and strategies, can be observed, while they at the same time have to rely on donations, supporting memberships and grants awarded for action in special areas with certain legal, political or social narratives and goals. Additionally, financial transparency is an important aspect of many strategic litigation networks.

To conclude, laws regulating the internet have globally become an important and ever-growing object of scrutiny through strategic litigation, especially when lobbying and protest by civil society and internet platforms during the process of law-making are unsuccessful. Strategic litigation has therefore led to a professional legal engagement of civil society monitoring the making, application, implementation and enforcement of national and international internet law. Transnational connectedness of actors leads to the forming of new cooperation and support in cases or campaigns, multiplier effects and an exchange of important learning experiences. Nevertheless, strategic cases do not only focus on internet law and digital rights, but on many different fields of the law, most often based on individual rights. In these cases, the internet plays an important role, not necessarily as an object for strategic litigation, but as an instrument in strategic litigation activities. The latter will be closely examined in the next chapter.

IV. Usage of the Internet for Strategic Litigation

Strategic litigation activities of individuals, NGOs or strategic litigation networks rely on the usage of different instruments. Besides legal and procedural means within proceedings before a court, lawsuits and other

69 Digital Freedom Fund, 'NCJM et al. vs. The State of The Netherlands – SyRI Verdict,' available at: https://digitalfreedomfund.org; The Public Interest Litigation Project, 'Profiling and SyRI,' available at: https://pilpnjcm.nl.

70 The Hague District Court, judgment of 5 February 2020, C/09/550982 / HA ZA 18–388.

71 Otto Spijkers, 'Public Interest Litigation Before Domestic Courts in The Netherlands on the Basis of International Law: Article 3:305a Dutch Civil Code,' EJIL:Talk! Blogpost, 6 March 2020, available at: https://ejiltalk.org.

complaints, an important instrument consists of public outreach activities via the internet. In this kind of public relations work, especially the internet and its capacities for spreading information are utilized to raise public awareness. In this context, individuals and NGOs use their web presence and engagement in social media to raise awareness of the cases at hand, their work, ongoing legal proceedings and their demands on how courts should rule, what the legislator needs to change about existing laws or what the authorities need to do differently in their application of legal regulations. Apart from awareness-raising and education, the strategy is built on the multiplier effect and public pressure through the conscious and targeted usage of the cybersphere. The internet is also essential in strategic litigation for communicating with clients, lawyers, legal representatives, partner organizations and building networks. Information technology has thus helped in overcoming a major communication barrier,[72] especially in international and transnational strategic litigation. Consequently, it is contributing to the growth and spread of strategic litigation.[73]

Simultaneously, democratic participation nowadays is becoming more and more digitalized, especially during the current COVID-19 pandemic. New technology has provided faster and more effective ways to communicate, seek like-minded individuals, express one's opinion, opposition or support and protest online. Even civil disobedience has taken up new forms in the digital world.[74] Thus, digitalization offers new platforms for strategic litigants to spread information and to point out perceived injustices. This form of changing public opinion through case-based activities and publications is one important aspect of strategic litigation. An example of the usage of the internet as an instrument in strategic litigation are the outreach activities of the European Center for Constitutional and Human Rights (ECCHR) during the trial against two suspected members of the Syrian regime. Besides a trial monitoring on its website, different online publications and participation in different virtual formats, it uses

72 Daniel Joyce, 'Internet Freedom and Human Rights,' EJIL 26 (2015), 493–514 (494–495).

73 See Christian Helmrich, 'Strategic Litigation rund um die Welt' in: Graser and Helmrich (n. 1), 115; Christian Boulanger and David Krebs, 'Strategische Prozessführung,' Zeitschrift für Rechtssoziologie 39 (2019), 1–4 (1).

74 See e.g., Vaclav Jirovsky, 'Anonymous, a new Civil Disobedience Phenomenon' in: Helmut Reimer, Norbert Pohlmann and Wolfgang Schneider (eds), *ISSE 2012 Securing Electronic Business Processes* (Wiesbaden: Springer 2012).

different social media platforms to promote its case work.[75] Another example are the internet activities by the NGO Earthjustice in the context of the complaint before the Committee on the Rights of the Child on climate change.[76] The German-based GFF also uses its website, social media and professional platforms to showcase its activities. The same applies to many other NGOs active in strategic litigation. Generally, public outreach campaigns and PR before, during and after strategic litigation have become an important element of case work. These activities are oftentimes not carried out by NGOs or litigating representatives themselves, but instead, professionals or professional NGOs specialized in press communication are hired. The impact of these PR activities, especially through the internet, can be remarkable.

Yet, it is to be noted that this kind of usage of the internet does not reach all areas of society, given that a reception of such information requires access to the internet and being a user or reader of the respective (social) media platforms. Thus, the recipients of this strategic engagement are especially the generations with a certain cyber literacy and an openness to social media. Internet and computer accessibility can also have many barriers, especially in cases of disability or impairment[77] and in cases of internet censorship. Besides that, a socio-financial aspect through the necessary infrastructure of an internet connection and the necessary devices is to be taken into account, which leads to some sectors of society being excluded from this information, especially in countries of the Global South or through surveillance and internet restrictions[78]. This phenomenon of unequal access and usage of internet communication technologies is called the digital divide.[79] It also has a gender aspect which has to be taken into

75 ECCHR, 'Trial Updates: First Trial Worldwide on Torture in Syria in the context of the criminal complaint in the criminal trial before the OLG Koblenz for crimes against humanity in Syria,' available at: https://ecchr.eu.

76 Earthjustice, '16 Young People File UN Human Rights Complaint on Climate Change,' 23 September 2019, available at: https://earthjustice.org.

77 Lainey Feingold, 'Digital Accessibility and the Quest for Online Equality,' Journal of Internet Law 21 (2017), 3–12 (3–4).

78 See e.g., Anita R. Gohdes, 'Repression Technology: Internet Accessibility and State Violence,' AJPS 64 (2020), 488–503.

79 Bridgette Wessels, 'The Reproduction and Reconfiguration of Inequality. Differentiation and Class, Status and Power in the Dynamics of Digital Divides' in: Massimo Ragnedda (ed.), *The Digital Divide: The Internet and Social Inequality in International Perspective* (Florence: Taylor and Francis 2013), 17–28 (17–19).

account.[80] Causes for such gender-based discrepancies are obstacles to access, socio-economic reasons, and lack of technological and digital literacy, gaps in education, inherent biases as well as socio-cultural norms.[81] Consequently, existing inequalities are reflected in a digital divide, transposing offline divides into the digital space.[82] In order to combat some of these issues, there are also projects in a place like 'Decolonising Digital Rights' by the DFF.[83] Another important barrier is the language and complexity of legal matters. Besides the digital divide, another key factor is knowledge about one's own rights in the sphere of the internet. Here (online) education campaigns set out by NGOs active in the field to inform internet users play an important role.[84]

Additionally, it is to be pointed out that strategic litigation is not only used in the public interest, but also in the context of strategic lawsuits *against* public participation (SLAPPs).[85] This phenomenon often recurs in the context of online activities by NGOs and so-called internet speech. These lawsuits took place, e.g., regarding activism in cases of Amnesty International and Greenpeace.[86] Thus, the usage of the internet for public interest litigation or political campaigns has itself become a target of strategic litigation. Recently, campaigns and litigation against these national and transnational SLAPPs by affected NGOs and allies have grown.[87] Legislative measures and judicial procedure reforms are being demanded for

80 Nani Jansen Reventlow, 'The Gender Divide in Digital Rights,' 3 March 2020, Digital Freedom Fund Blog, available at: https://digitalfreedomfund.org.

81 Report of the Organisation for Economic Co-operation and Development, 'Bridging the Digital Gender Divide Include, Upskill, Innovate,' 2018, available at: https://oecd.org, 22.

82 OHCHR, 'Ways to bridge the gender digital divide from a human rights perspective,' Submission by the Human Rights, Big Data and Technology Project of the University of Essex, available at: https://ohchr.org, 1.

83 DFF, 'Decolonising Digital Rights,' available at: https://digitalfreedomfund.org; Aurum Linh, 'What Decolonising Digital Rights Looks Like,' DFF Blog, 6 April 2020, available at: https://digitalfreedomfund.org.

84 See e.g., the campaign #SaveYourInternet by EDRi, available at: https://saveyourinternet.eu.

85 Penelope Canan and George W. Pring, 'Strategic Lawsuits against Public Participation,' Social Problems 35 (1988), 506–519 (506).

86 Annalisa Ciampi, UN Special Rapporteur on the Rights to Freedom of Peaceful Assembly and of Association, 'Info Note – SLAPPs and FoAA rights,' available at: https://ohchr.org; Business and Human Rights Resource Centre, 'Silencing the Critics – How big polluters try to paralyse environmental and human rights advocacy through the courts,' available at: https://business-humanrights.org.

87 See e.g., the NGO Protect the Protest, available at: https://protecttheprotest.org.

a containment of the increasing phenomenon in order to change this practice which supposedly endangers public interest in the name of economic interests.[88]

Besides civil society as a whole, it is to be examined more closely what influence the strategic engagement through the usage of the internet has on international legal scholarship. Particularly noteworthy in this context are the ways in which strategic litigants seek connection to international legal scholarship and what influence this can have or already has on legal positions within international legal scholarship. NGOs active in strategic litigation cite as an aspect of their activities the engagement in legal scholarship.[89] Such activities often consist of publications in relevant journals, books or blog contributions. The latter is an important instrument for giving impulse, raising awareness and stating one's opinions. In the long term, this engagement in international legal scholarship can lead to changing legal opinions and positions, e.g., in the interpretation of legal regulations in public international law or regarding accountability for human rights' violations which might then influence law-making and the judiciary. One example is the online symposium by Verfassungsblog.de on international supply chains as well as responsibility and liability therein, while the German government is working on a draft of a law regulating supply chains.[90] Additionally, members of NGOs often participate in real life or online discussions or give interviews to influential newspapers on the relevant topics, which can also influence international legal scholarship and bring attention to certain issues. Furthermore, strategic litigators are oftentimes legal scholars themselves participating in establishing chains of argument in cases, writing lawsuits and appearing in court.

Another new digital method for strategic litigation is legal enforcement through legal tech. A massive surge of lawsuits through digital automatization can also act as a strategy in trying to enforce certain rights and in attempting to accomplish a broader change in administrative or business behaviour or policy.[91] Access to legal tech instruments for (potential)

---

88 See e.g. the Open Letter 'Ending gag Lawsuits in Europe – Protecting Democracy and Fundamental rights,' available at: https://edri.org.

89 See Burghardt and Thönnes (n. 43), 67; Arite Keller and Karina Theurer, 'Menschenrechte mit rechtlichen Mitteln durchsetzen: Die Arbeit des ECCHR' in: Graser and Helmrich (n. 1), 62.

90 Verfassungsblog, 'Lieferkettengesetz Made in Germany,' available at: https://verfassungsblog.de.

91 Britta Rehder and Katharina van Elten, 'Legal Tech & Dieselgate. Digitale Rechtsdienstleister als Akteure der strategischen Prozessführung. Legal Tech & Dieselga-

clients often takes place through the internet by online forms enabling quick legal reviews of claims. Legal tech platforms additionally oftentimes inform digitally and publicly about the rights and legal possibilities one has in certain situations, mostly within the realm of the specialization of a legal tech business. Thereby, obstacles to access to justice are easier to overcome.[92] Digitalization has thus enabled the emergence and rapid growth of legal tech mechanisms. Yet, the economic motives and dynamics for achieving this form of legal mobilization need to be considered.

After having examined the internet as an instrument of strategic litigation networks' activities and the internet's legal regulation regime as an object of strategic litigation separately, a significant mobilization takes place in cases where an interaction of the two aspects occurs. Namely, in cases whose object of strategic litigation consists of (international) internet law and the method of mobilizing the public through intensive digital activities in cyberspace is applied. The cases of *Schrems* are a prominent example of this effect. Oftentimes NGOs attempt to make use of PR and media campaigns and activities to vocalize their demands or bring attention to issues of present internet regulations or lack of data protection before turning to the courts. If this is done to no avail, NGOs active in strategic litigation often use the internet during their court cases in order to spread further awareness and create pressure not only on the judges who seem less likely to be influenced by media attention due to their independent role, but more so on government, parliament and large corporations to change legislation or practice. The benefits of this kind of mobilization, as well as dangers arising thereof, will be discussed in the next chapter.

V. *Potential and Perils of Strategic Litigation regarding Internet Law*

When looking at the legal outcome and the impact of strategic litigation regarding internet law, the possible effects on affected individuals and their rights as well as on the law must be stressed. Strategic litigation can lead to legal mobilization whereby an unlawful or unconstitutional application, interpretation or implementation of legal regulations or laws regarding cybersphere can be changed or a change enforced.[93] Besides

te – How digital providers of legal services foster strategic litigation,' Zeitschrift für Rechtssoziologie 39 (2019), 64–86 (82–83).

92 Ibid., 67–71.

93 NOYB, 'Making Privacy a Reality, Public Project Summary,' available at: https://noyb.eu, 16–17; Duffy (n. 2), 59–60.

achieving that laws, governmental or corporate practices are declared (partly) unconstitutional, unlawful or in violation of European or international law, another advantage consists in the participation of individuals and NGOs in the development of the law.[94] Additionally, litigants can force the legislative to reform the law, the government to change policy and companies to change their practice.[95] Thus, as the above-mentioned cases and judgments illustrate, participation mechanisms and networking capacities – through the format of strategic litigation – enhance society's impact on law-making, application and implementation of internet law. In the case of internet law, strategic litigation is thus able to contribute to a liberal, individual right's centred understanding of internet governance.

Nevertheless, a success through the strategic engagement of the courts is not always guaranteed. While dismissals by lower courts are not as far-reaching and often act as an enabler of legal action before higher courts, dismissive decisions by higher or the highest competent courts can lead, in the worst case, to a deterioration of individual rights or at least prevent future legal action in similar cases. In many cases, national courts, European and other regional courts have rejected lawsuits regarding internet law and not found a violation of fundamental or human rights. For example, a lawsuit against the German Network Enforcement Act was found inadmissible for procedural reasons, thus upholding the alleged 'privatization of censorship.'[96] In the cases of the ACLU and the CCR against government surveillance, the courts also dismissed the lawsuits, yet they can be seen as part of a wider social and political transnational movement against executive surveillance of digital communication.

However, legal change can also be accomplished without success before court, as it might be brought about through the legislator or authorities. Moreover, losing in court does not always mean that no positive impact has been made by litigating.[97] Through a court case concerning internet regulations, awareness of the media and the public can be raised, especially if this litigation is accompanied by a campaign addressing the general public

94 Duffy (n. 2), 61–62.
95 Duffy (n. 2), 63–65.
96 VG Köln, 'Netzwerkdurchsetzungsgesetz: FDP-Bundestagsabgeordnete scheitern mit vorbeugender Feststellungsklage,' 14 February 2019, available at: https://vg-koeln.nrw.de.
97 See Jules Lobel, *Success Without Victory: Lost Legal Battle and the Long Road to Justice in America* (New York: New York University Press 2003), 264–269; Ben Depoorter, 'The Upside of Losing,' Columbia Law Review 113 (2013), 831–833.

or the affected internet community.[98] Additionally, the accountability of the government or of multinational digital corporations for their practices and policies, as well as the results thereof, can be enhanced. Thus, a loss can be an impetus for long-term change.[99] Besides this outcome, a certain influence on future law-making through public and political pressure is not to be underestimated. Additionally, court proceedings can also serve as an important step towards getting access to information, which has previously been confidential, as a learning experience for the involved litigating actors and as a necessary precondition to submitting the case before higher, supreme or regional courts as an exhaustion of (domestic) remedies.[100] Still, a major difficulty for strategic litigation regarding international internet law is the overwhelming lack of international courts or bodies with competences for individual complaints regarding regulations of international conventions as well as regarding international lawsuits against non-state actors like multinational companies.[101]

Beyond the direct legal and regulatory outcomes, strategic litigation can sometimes change policies and practices by holding those in charge accountable. Moreover, through campaigns before, during and after strategic litigation, public awareness is raised and influenced through public debate.[102] Besides the general public and oftentimes the respective affected internet community, a potential impact on international legal scholarship is to be acknowledged, especially regarding academic involvement with publications and cooperation with universities and law clinics. Digitalization in this regard has a certain influence as especially law blogs and social media activities of academic institutions, chairs, professors and legal scholars have increased, thus enabling a digital interaction and discourse on the regulation of the internet.

Nonetheless, strategic litigation is criticized for causing issues in regards to the democratic legitimacy of court decisions and the separation of powers due to the recourse to the judiciary in order to influence laws and policies originally in the constitutional competence of the legislative

---

98 See e.g., NOYB, 'Making Privacy a Reality, Public Project Summary,' available at: https://noyb.eu, 21.

99 Susan Hansen, 'Atlantic Insights. Strategic Litigation,' The Atlantic Philanthropies, 2018, 13–15, available at: https://atlanticphilanthropies.org.

100 Duffy (n. 2), 69–72.

101 Duffy (n. 2), 27.

102 Lobel (n. 97), 4.

as well as raising problems for national sovereignty.[103] However, seeking recourse to the courts through fundamental or human rights for review of laws and practices is also part of constitutional procedural rights and often guaranteed by regional human rights instruments.[104] Criticism is to be set aside in most cases where only an interpretation or clarification of laws is sought, which is the constitutional competence of courts. Attempts to overturn democratically passed laws or achieve law-making in certain areas for political reasons need to be further researched following the constitutional issues it raises. Nevertheless, it has to be examined carefully whether a claim or application is deemed to pose questions of democratic legitimacy and resulting court decisions are seen as overstepping the separation of powers.

Using legal instruments for strategic litigation can also perpetuate existing hegemonic structures[105] by its recourse to the law, which also might enshrine certain inequalities and uphold them through the usage of the internet and access thereto. In court proceedings, the procedural legal regulations must be respected, and the claimed rights and matters have to be proven with sufficient evidence. Furthermore, one must pay attention to NGO activities. Often NGOs primarily from the Global North represent claimants from the Global South, especially in cases with a high level of public attention in the online sphere.[106] In the following, these activities are examined in order to point out the socio-legal impacts this dynamic can have and already has. One element in the approach of strategic litigation consists of NGOs or other associations actively looking for or selecting possible plaintiffs they can then represent or for whom

---

103 See e.g. Bernhard W. Wegener, 'Urgenda – Weltrettung per Gerichtsbeschluss? Klimaklagen testen die Grenzen des Rechtsschutzes,' Zeitschrift für Umweltrecht 1 (2019), 3–13 (10–13).

104 See e.g. Alexander Graser, 'Vermeintliche Fesseln der Demokratie: Warum die Klimaklagen ein vielversprechender Weg sind,' Zeitschrift für Umweltrecht 1 (2019), 271–278.

105 See generally Alejandra Ancheita and Carolijn Terwindt, 'Auf dem Weg zu einer funktionierenden transnationalen Zusammenarbeit auf Augenhöhe,' Forschungsjournal Soziale Bewegungen 28 (2015), 56–65; and for a detailed analysis Karina Theurer and Wolfgang Kaleck, *Dekoloniale Rechtskritik und Rechtspraxis* (Baden-Baden: Nomos 2020).

106 E.g. US District Court Southern District of New York, *Shell v. Wiwa* and *Lliuya v. RWE*; Ken Wiwa against Royal Dutch Petroleum Co (Shell) and Brian Anderson, Case 1:96-cv-08386-KMW-HBP; CCR, Wiwa et al v. Royal Dutch Petroleum et al., available at: https://ccrjustice.org; OLG Hamm, *Lliuya against RWE AG*, Az. 5 U 15/17; Germanwatch, 'Saúl versus RWE – The Huaraz Case,' available at: https://germanwatch.org.

they can use their developed legal strategy and legal arguments in court or before authorities. Thus, the claimants and their rights have a certain predetermined role; they act as the enabler of strategic litigation. This can lead to issues like a collision of interests, especially regarding settlements, completely different starting positions, an instrumentalization of individuals and their rights for political or legal motives far beyond the respective case, a disproportionate psychological toll, excessive demands and disappointed hopes. Therefore, it is important to have a common understanding and mutual respect as well as a clearly defined mandate. Yet, it seems as if most NGOs have a proficient understanding of the power dynamics of the law and its institutions as well as social power structures of which they are a part of and in which they operate.[107] These power structures and power dynamics are also present in cyberspace and NGOs' activities operating therein. Additionally, NGOs display a careful operation in their field and behaviour, attentively listening to people's stories and seeking cooperation with NGOs' and activists on the ground, not acting like the 'saviours' from the Global North for 'victims' in the Global South. Yet, they cannot overcome the power dynamics and requirements national and international law set out.

Nevertheless, besides the dangers of strategic litigation, there is also potential which should not be neglected. Increasingly, funding strategic litigation by donors and foundations has not only become an altruistic and philanthropic investment joined by initiatives and non-profits awarding grants with large sums,[108] but it is also increasingly motivated by the will to achieve certain results according to a determined vision of the content of law and policy. This has also led to a demand for detailed evaluation and impact assessment of the recipient NGOs' activities. Non-profits like the DFF have made attempts in developing a framework to methodically monitor and measure the impact of strategic litigation in the field of digital rights.[109] Yet, independent socio-legal research is necessary for an extensive impact evaluation in this and other fields of strategic litigation in

107 See as one example ECCHR, 'New Perspectives on the Law: Decolonial Legal Critique and Practice,' available at: https://ecchr.eu.

108 See e.g. the Digital Freedom Fund, 'Grants,' available at: https://digitalfreedomfund.org; regarding digital rights and more generally the Open Society Foundations, available at: https://opensocietyfoundations.org and in the past the Atlantic Philanthropies, available at: https://atlanticphilanthropies.org.

109 DFF, 'Measuring the Impact of Strategic Litigation in Digital Rights. Developing a Tool for the Field,' 2019, available at: https://digitalfreedomfund.org.

order to enable the judging of consequences this form of engagement of civil society has on the law and beyond.

VI. Conclusion

This chapter has focused on strategic litigation regarding global dimensions of internet law and its implications. It has provided an overview of different strategic litigation networks, NGOs and individuals as well as their strategic cases, activities and outcomes. Strategic litigation has, in a few cases, been effective in the regard that it has pushed towards taking human rights aspects more holistically into account in areas of international and national internet law. Even in cases where litigation was not successful in the sense of an intended judicial outcome, public attention was drawn to digital rights aspects. However, this mobilization was not always enough to lead to a change in practice, policy or legal regulations. A broader and more detailed analysis of and research on the specific impacts of strategic litigation on public international law would be necessary, but would reach beyond the scope of this contribution. While strategic human rights litigation and public interest litigation in other fields have increasingly become a topic for in-depth research, strategic litigation regarding internet law and digital rights has been largely academically unexplored, leaving room for future research. An analysis in this sense could build on studies and research in the field of the internet and society. As the development of the internet and its capacities are ever-evolving, so is the dynamic field and potential for strategic litigation and research therein.

Contributors

Edoardo Celeste Assistant Professor in Law, Technology and Innovation, Dublin City University, Dublin, Ireland

Alena Douhan Professor of International Law, Belarusian State University, Minsk, Belarus; UN Special Rapporteur on the negative impact of the unilateral coercive measures on the enjoyment of human rights

Angelo Jr Golia Senior Research Fellow, Max Planck Institute for Comparative Public Law and International Law, Heidelberg, Germany

Pia Hüsch PhD Candidate in International Law & Cyber Security, University of Glasgow, UK

Matthias C. Kettemann Professor of Innovation, Theory and Philosophy of Law, Department of Theory and Future of Law, University of Innsbruck, Austria; Head of Research Programme, Leibniz Institute for Media Research | Hans-Bredow-Institut, Hamburg, Germany; Head of Research Group, Humboldt Institute for Internet and Society, Berlin, Germany

Adam Krzywoń Assistant Professor of Constitutional Law, University of Warsaw, Poland; Fellow at the German Research Institute for Public Administration (FÖV), Speyer, Germany

Raffaela Kunz Senior Research Fellow, Max Planck Institute for Comparative Public Law and International Law, Heidelberg, Germany

Katharina Luckner PhD Candidate, University of Hamburg, Germany

Uchenna Jerome Orji Assistant Professor of Law, American University of Nigeria, Yola, Nigeria

Fellow of the African Center for Cyber Law and Cybercrime Prevention (ACCP), UN African Institute for the Prevention of Crime, Kampala, Uganda

Rossella Pulvirenti Senior lecturer in Law, Manchester Metropolitan University, Manchester, UK

Stefanie Schmahl Professor of German and Foreign Public Law, Public International Law and European Law, Julius-Maximilians-Universität Würzburg, Germany

Vera Strobel PhD Candidate in Public Law and International Law, University of Gießen, Germany